HARRAP'S

English Usage

John O. E. Clark

HARRAP

London Paris

First published in Great Britain 1989
by HARRAP BOOKS Ltd
Chelsea House, 26 Market Square,
Bromley, Kent BR1 1NA

© *John O. E. Clark* 1989

All rights reserved. No part of this
publication may be reproduced in any
form or by any means without the prior
permission of Harrap Books Ltd.

ISBN 0 245 54830 0

Reprinted 1990

By the same author:

Word Perfect
Word for Word
Word Wise

Typeset by Action Typesetting Ltd., Gloucester
Printed in Great Britain by
Richard Clay Ltd.,
Bungay, Suffolk

Preface

This Dictionary is principally a guide to the usage of English words. It sets out to distinguish between words of similar spelling — often of very different meanings — and words of similar meaning, but usually of quite different spelling. It also deals with those particularly difficult pairs of words that are close both in meaning and spelling. Foreign words used in English, new words, old fashioned words and even classes of offensive words are included. There are various Dictionary entries dealing with the addition of prefixes and suffixes, which are designed to point out the resultant spelling changes.

Many other types of entries and articles are included; where appropriate examples of words used in context are offered to illustrate meaning or preferred usage. Shorter entries consist of little more than a single word, although each is included because it might present a difficulty such as spelling, hyphenation, italicization, use of accents or spelling of the plural. Some of the longer articles contain lists of words that exemplify the point under discussion.

J.O.E.C. — London, 1989.

A

a (indefinite article) *See* **a** or **an**.

-a For plurals of words ending in *-a*, *see* **plurals**.

a/an can be used to mean **per**, and is less formal. E.g.:

> three times *per* week   three times *a* month
> 80 kilometres *per* hour   30 miles *an* hour

With imprecise numbers, *a* is preferred (e.g. "several times a year").
For *a/an* as indefinite articles, *see* **a** or **an**.

a-/an- *See* **negative prefixes**.

a or **an** (indefinite article)

1. Before all normal vowels (and diphthongs), use *an*:

an animal	an aim	an authority
an easel	an 8-year-old	an entertainer
an illness	an opening	an unusual

2. Before a silent *h*, use *an*:

an heiress	an honorary	an hour

(which are pronounced as if spelled "airess", "onorary", "our").

3. Before an aspirated *h*, use *a*:

a habitual	a heraldic	a heroic
a historical	a hotel	a hypothesis

which, in older usage, would have taken *an* (because the first syllable of each is unaccented; old usage would have been "an history" and "an historical").

4. Before a syllable beginning with a vowel but with the sound of *w*- or *y*-, use *a*:

a eucalyptus	a ewe	a once-only
a one-off	a unity	a useful

5. Before all normal consonants, use *a*.

6. With letters or groups of letters, be guided by pronunciation:

a BBC broadcast	a D-shaped part	an FA Cup Winner
a KLM flight	a NATO conference	an OPEC country
an RAC rating	an S-bend	a U-turn

abacus (pl. abacuses).

abaft = to the rear of the middle of a ship; **abeam** = across the middle of a ship; **astern** = behind a ship. Anything in front of the middle of a ship is **forward** (pronounced *forrard* in nautical circles). E.g.:

"The steering gear is abaft of the ship's engines."
"The drive-shaft for the paddles lies abeam the ship."
"The pilot's cutter continued to follow us astern."
"The wheelhouse is forward of the funnel."

abate, abatable, abatement, abater.

abattoir (= slaughter-house, which is preferred to the French euphemism).

abbreviate, abbreviator.

abbreviations As a general rule, abbreviations should be avoided in narrative text. Despite the list of exceptions described later, the most important fact to note is the formal difference between an abbreviation and a contraction (*see* **contractions**). A contraction ends with the final letter of the word when it is spelled in full; an abbreviation does not, and thus requires a full point. E.g.:

a.m.	*d.*(died)	Ho.	Q.C.
b.(born)	e.g.	*ibid.*	R.I.P.
c.(circa)	etc.	i.e.	Sq.
Co.	fig.	p.m.	u.c.
c.v.	*fl.*(flourished)	Prof.	Ven.

Unfortunately, there are very many exceptions.

1. Names, titles, honours and acronyms for organizations; the preferred modern style is without full points:

AA	FOC	MA	SOGAT
BA	FRCO	MBE	UNESCO
BBC	GLC	MP	UNICEF
BSc	GPO	NATO	UK
CH	HMS	OBE	USA
DD	HMSO	OM	USSR
DDT	ILEA	RAC	VC
EFTA	ITV	RAF	WRAC
EEC	KLM	QE2	YMCA

(Some people prefer to retain full points in B.A., B.Sc., M.A., etc).

2. Measurements and units:

bhp	gm	lb (pound)	mm
cc	km	m (metre)	mph
cm	kg	mg	oz
ft	l (litre)	min	sec

Note that the abbreviations of these measurements are both singular and plural.

3. Miscellaneous:

    AD BC
    N S E W NNE SSW (*see also* **compass directions**)
    MS PS
    CAT-scan L-dopa Rh +

General notes:
The abbreviations e.g. and i.e. should be avoided in running narrative text (but are usually allowable in parentheses, tables, and so on).
Symbols of chemical elements have no full points (e.g. Al, Cu, Fe, etc.). Use uranium 235, carbon-14, etc. for first mention but U-235, C-14 thereafter (do not use an initial capital letter for spelled out names of chemical elements). Full points are, however, used in some molecular formulae, in which they have special meanings to a chemist.
In astronomical works, Messier numbers (M) are set with no space before the catalogue number (e.g. M32, M109).
New General Catalogue numbers (NGC), however, do have a space (e.g. NGC 54, NGC 7332).

Note mph (miles per hour) but km/h (kilometres per hour).
S. Giorgio (S. = San) but Sta Maria (Sta = Santa) and Ste Juliette

(Ste = Sainte) for names of Italian, Spanish, Portuguese or French saints. The abbreviation S for the English word Saint has the plural SS (= Saints).

Abbreviations of British county names should be avoided and used only as a last resort when pressed for space in captions. Similar advice applies to the names of American (USA) states (*see* **US states**). Avoid abbreviations of months and days of the week but, if necessary (e.g. in tabular matter), use:

Jan Feb March Apr May June July Aug Sept Oct Nov Dec
Sun Mon Tues Wed Thurs Fri Sat (all without full points).

Do not use ′ and ″ as abbreviations of foot (feet) and inch(es), although these symbols are correct for minutes and seconds of arc.

Plurals of abbreviations:

BAs MAs MPs O-Levels (not BA's etc.)
p. (page) pp. (pages)
f. (folio or following page) ff. (folios etc.)
v. (verse) vv. (verses)
w. (word) ww. (words)
MS (manuscript) MSS (manuscripts)
sp. (singular species) spp. (plural species)

See also **acronym; contractions; shortened words**.

abeam *See* **abaft.**

abet, abetting, abettor (preferred to abetter).

abide is archaic when it is used to mean *wait for*, and is colloquial for *live, remain, stay, endure* or *tolerate*, any of which is preferred. **Abide by** (= adhere to, conform) is acceptable usage; e.g. "A good sportsman abides by the rules of the game". The past tense and participle of the former is *abode*, of the latter is *abided by*.

ability = power to do or skill in doing something; **capability** = **capacity** (non-technical) = capability or the inborn power of a person to learn something, or of a thing to do something. E.g.:

"He has outstanding ability as an editor, but his capacity for biology is negligible."

-ability and **-ibility** are the endings of nouns formed from adjectives ending in *-able* or *-ible*. The usual spelling difficulty is *a* or *i*? For a list, *see* **-able and -ible**.

ab initio (italics) = from the beginning; this Latin form should be avoided.

abjure = to renounce an oath, repudiate, recant; **adjure** = to charge on oath, appeal in a solemn way. E.g.:

"He must abjure Roman Catholicism before joining the sect."
"I adjured him to think twice before joining the sect."

able, like **competent**, takes an infinitive (e.g. "She was able to go", "He was competent to do it"); **capable** takes *of* and a gerund (e.g. "It was capable of moving quickly").

-able and -ible One of the most vexatious problems in English spelling occurs when verbs (and some nouns) are converted into adjectives by adding the suffix *-able* or *-ible*. There are some general rules, but unfortunately there are also many exceptions (for this reason, many such adjectives are included in this Dictionary).

1. Words ending in a *y* preceded by a vowel retain the *y*; e.g. *buyable, deployable, layable, payable*.

2. Words ending in a *y* preceded by a consonant have an *i* for the *y*; e.g. *deniable, dutiable, justifiable, variable* (exception *flyable*).

3. Words ending in a silent *e* usually drop the *e*; e.g. *solvable, usable*.

4. Words ending in an *e* retain the *e* if it is necessary as an aid to pronunciation; e.g. *blameable, changeable, chargeable, dyeable, gaugeable, hireable, holeable, likeable, liveable, nameable, noticeable, pronounceable, rateable, replaceable, saleable, shareable, traceable, tuneable, unshakeable*.

5. Words ending in *-ee* usually retain both *es*; e.g. *agreeable*.

6. *-ible* is the suffix on certain words of Latin origin, and these have to be learned. Examples include:

accessible	avertible	comprehensible	convertible
adducible	coercible	compressible	corrigible
admissible	collapsible	contemptible	corrodible
apprehensible	combustible	contractible	corruptible
audible	compatible	controvertible	credible

deducible	extensible	miscible	reproductible
deductible	fallible	negligible	resistible
defensible	feasible	ostensible	responsible
destructible	fencible	perceptible	reversible
diffusible	flexible	perfectible	revertible
digestible	forcible	permissible	risible
dirigible	fusible	persuasible	seductible
discernible	gullible	plausible	sensible
dismissible	horrible	possible	suggestible
dispersible	immersible	prehensible	susceptible
distendible	impassible	producible	tangible
divisible	includible	reducible	terrible
edible	incredible	reflectible	transmissible
eligible	indelible	remissible	vendible
evincible	intelligible	rendible	vincible
exhaustible	irascible	reprehensible	visible
expressible	legible	repressible	

and their opposites (*inaccessible, illegible, immiscible, irresistible*, and so on).

ablution(s) = the act of washing oneself; it should be reserved for religious contexts and not used as a pompous way of describing a simple routine act.

abnormal = any difference from normal; **subnormal** = below normal; **supranormal** = above the normal. E.g.:
"We have had an abnormal amount of rain for this time of the year."
"The oil becomes very viscous at subnormal temperatures."
"The winning candidate demonstrated supranormal intelligence."

abode is precious for **house** or **home**, either of which is preferred. *See also* **abide**.

abolish, abolishable, abolishment, abolition, abolitionist. *Abolishment* and *abolition* (preferred) both = doing away with or ending something, usually of official or legal status. An *abolitionist* was someone who believed in the abolition of slavery.

aboriginal (adj. and noun, sing.; pl. aborigines) = an original inhabitant of a country, but Australian Aborigines (initial capital letters).

Aboriginal words *See* **Australia and New Zealand.**

about, applied to dates can be represented by *c.* (the abbreviation of *circa*). *See also* **around.**

above/below Do not write "... as described above (or below)"; write instead "... as described earlier (or later) in this article". But *above/below* is correct in captions. *Above* or *below* should not be used to mean *more than* or *less than* when referring to specific quantities (e.g. write "more than 20km" or "less than 3cm"); but "above/below zero, boiling point, etc." is correct. **Above** = *at/on a higher level* can be synonymous with *over* (e.g. "above the window", "over the window"), just as **below** (= *at/on a lower level*) can mean *under*.

abridge, abridgement (preferred to abridgment).

abrogate = abolish, annul; **arrogate** = make an unjust/unreasonable claim or assumption. E.g.:
"The first act of the new committee was to abrogate the rule about the non-admission of women to the club."
"The chairman of the new committee arrogated all important decisions to himself."

abscess (note spelling).

abseil, abseiled, abseiling.

absence = state of being not present, not existing, missing;
lack = shortage, deficiency, insufficiency. E.g.:
"We could not continue because of the absence of three members of staff."
"We could not finish because of lack of time."

absent, absentee, absence.

absinthe is the liqueur flavoured with the wormwood plant *absinth*.

absolutely = unconditionally, separately; it should not be used as an intensifier. E.g.:
in "The text is absolutely perfect" delete *absolutely*;

in "She was absolutely overcome" substitute *completely* for *absolutely*.
"His co-operation is guaranteed absolutely" is correct usage.

absolute words should not be qualified by *less*, *more*, *most*, *very*, and so on. Examples include *infinite*, *maximum*, *minimum*, *ultimate*, and *unique*. Combinations of the following kind should therefore not be used:

> most infinite extent
> very maximum effort
> at the very minimum
> more unique example

See also **qualifying adverbs**.

absorption = the taking up of one substance within the structure of another (like water into a sponge); **adsorption** = the taking up of a gas or vapour on the surface of a solid (as gases into charcoal). The corresponding verbs are *absorb* and *adsorb*, with *absorbent* and *adsorbent* as adjectives and nouns (not *absorbant*).

abstain = to go/do without, to refrain from doing something; **abstinent** describes someone who abstains (i.e. has none); **abstemious** describes someone who eats or drinks sparingly, who is not overindulgent (i.e. has some, but not too much). Thus *abstention* is having none, whereas *abstemiousness* (or in its strict meaning *temperance*) is having some but in moderation.

abstemious *See* **abstain**.

abstinent *See* **abstain**.

abuse (verb) = use wrongly (usually something that is abstract); **misuse** = use incorrectly (usually something that is visible or tangible). E.g.:
"He abused his authority by using his official car to go shopping."
"He so misused his car that it soon needed a new clutch."

abut, abutment, abutted, abutting, abuttal.

abyss = deep trench or cavity, deep ocean; **abyssal** = relating to the

ocean depths; **abysmal** = extremely low in merit, quality or interest.
E.g.:

"Most abyssal fish have extremely poor eyesight."
"He made an abysmal attempt at drawing a fish."

academic = to do with teaching or learning, but has come also to
have the derogatory (and vogue) meaning of not really relevant,
useless (e.g. "of only academic interest"). It should therefore be used
with care in case the second meaning is assumed when the first is
intended.

acanthus (pl. acanthuses).

accelerate, accelerator.

accent confers a different manner of pronunciation on language;
dialect confers a different vocabulary − accent is the way we speak,
dialect is what we say. *See also* **non-standard English; slang.**

accents and diacritical marks Common accents include acute (*é*),
cedilla (*ç*), circumflex (*ê*), grave (*è*), tilde (*ñ*) and umlaut (*ü*). In certain
languages there are means of avoiding accents. In French only, capital
letters do not (have to) have accents. In German only, vowels with an
umlaut ¨ can be spelled as vowel + *e*; e.g. *über = ueber, schön =
schoen.* In Danish and Norwegian only, *å* can be spelled *aa*; e.g.
Århus = Aarhus. These rules should not be transferred to other
languages. *See also* **foreign words and phrases.**

accentuate − make prominent, throw into relief, draw attention to; it
does not mean *worsen* or *increase.* E.g.:

"The continuing bad weather accentuated the sale of umbrellas" is
incorrect.

accept, acceptable, accepter (but acceptor in law/chemistry/
electronics), acceptance. **Accept** = to receive or take; **except** (verb) =
to exclude. E.g.:

"She accepted my present gratefully."
"Nobody is excepted from having to pay the extra charge."

access, accessory, accessary, accessible, accession. **Access** = means of entry, act of approach; **accession** = attaining office, power or status, an increase, an addition. E.g.:

"A gap in the hedge provided access to the next field."
"The holiday was to celebrate the anniversary of the king's accession."

Both *accessary* and *accessory* can be noun or adjective. The former was originally an accomplice or helper, the latter is usually an additional (but non-essential) feature, but *accessory* now usually serves for both.

accident, accidental, accidentally (not *accidently*). **Accident** = an unforeseen (usually unfortunate) event; it should not be used to describe the outcome. E.g.:

"She could not draw because of an accident to her hand" should be "... because of an injury to her hand" or "... because she had an accident involving her hand".

acclimatize, acclimatization.

accommodate (with two *c*s and two *m*s), accommodation (which should be avoided as a synonym for *flat, home, house* or *lodgings*). *See also* **home**.

accompany *by* another person or people; **accompany** *with* another thing or things. The noun (in music) is **accompanist**. E.g:

"He entered the room accompanied by a policeman in uniform."
"My favourite is grilled cod accompanied with cheese sauce."

accomplish *See* **attain**.

account, accountable, accountant. **Account** = description, bill (invoice) or way of keeping money in a bank; **accounts** = record of financial transactions. When *accountable* is used to mean *responsible*, it should be applied only to a person or persons (e.g. "The officer is accountable for his actions"; the actions are not accountable). Note "*on* one's own *account*" and "*of* one's own *accord*." *See also* **responsible**.

accredit *See* **credit**.

accrue = accumulate gradually, increase piece by piece, happen to one's advantage; the word should not be used of any, particularly sudden, increase. The corresponding noun is *accrual*.

accumulate, accumulator, accumulation.

acetic = to do with acetic (ethanoic) acid, found in vinegar; **ascetic** = spartan, deliberately lacking in comfort.

achieve = succeed in an attempt (to do something); it does not mean simply to *get*, *obtain* or *reach*. E.g.:

"She achieved her ambition to win the tournament." (correct)
"I shall be lucky to achieve enough points." (incorrect)

acknowledge, acknowledgeable, acknowledgement (preferred to acknowledgment).

acme = peak (of perfection); **acne** = pimply disorder of the face.

acoustics, the science, is singular (e.g. "Acoustics is the science of sound"); when used to describe the sound properties of, say, a concert hall, it is plural (e.g. "The acoustics of the Festival Hall are excellent").

acquaint with seldom means more than **tell** or **inform**. (Note the -*cqu*- in the spelling of this and the next two entries.)

acquiesce(nce) *in*, (not acquiesce(nce) *to*).

acquit, acquitted, acquitting, acquittance (let off a debt), acquittal (found not guilty).

acre, acreage.

acronym = pronounceable word from the initials or opening letters of a name or phrase − not merely any set of (unpronounceable) initials, which constitute an abbreviation. Acronyms consisting of capital letters should be printed without full points and typeset close up. Particularly in computer technology, phrases are sometimes selected so that they make memorable acronyms (such as ERNIE − *E*lectronic *R*andom *N*umber *I*ndicating *E*quipment). E.g.:

AIDS	(*a*cquired *i*mmune *d*eficiency *s*yndrome)
BASIC	(*B*eginners' *A*ll-purpose *S*ymbolic *I*nstruction *C*ode)

EFTA	(*E*uropean *F*ree *T*rade *A*ssociation)
EOKA	(*E*thnike *O*rganosis *K*yprion *A*goniston)
FORTRAN	(*for*mula *tran*slation)
NASA	(*N*ational *A*eronautical and *S*pace *A*dministration)
SALT	(*S*trategic *A*rms *L*imitation *T*reaty)

Acronyms that have passed wholly into the language are treated as ordinary words (usually without an initial capital letter). E.g.:

bren (gun)	(*Br*no and *En*field armouries)
laser	(*l*ight *a*mplification by *s*timulated *e*mission of *r*adiation)
qwerty	(standard keyboard, named after the first six letters on it)
radar	(*ra*dio *d*irection-finding *a*nd *r*anging)
sonar	(*so*und *n*avigation *a*nd *r*anging)

See also **abbreviations**.

acrophobia = neurotic fear of heights; **agoraphobia** = neurotic fear of open spaces. These are terms in psychology relating to specific mental disorders, and should not be used of mere dislike of heights/open spaces.

act (noun) = law as passed (enacted) by Parliament; **bill** = proposed law submitted to Parliament for debate/approval.

act as = stand in for, take the (specific) part of; it should not be used as a grand way of saying *is* or *are*. E.g.:

"A rubber band acted as a temporary spring." (correct)
"I act as manager of the department." (incorrect)

activate = bring about, cause to act, inspire; **actuate** = start or use a mechanism (i.e. cause to act), motivate. E.g.:

"He actuated the series of switches that activated the rocket's firing sequence."

active, activate, activation, activeness (to be avoided), activity (preferred).

actual, actually. These overworked and often superfluous words should be avoided. *See also* **really**.

acute = an accent, as in *café*. *See* **accents and diacritical marks**.

-acy or **-asy** These word endings are sometimes confused. Words ending in *-acy* include:

adequacy	intimacy
aristocracy	obstinacy
autocracy	privacy
bureaucracy	

whereas *ecstasy, fantasy,* and *idiosyncrasy* are the only common words ending in *-asy.* Note also *prophecy* (noun) and *prophesy* (verb).

AD (the abbreviation of *anno Domini*) usually comes before the relevant date.

adagio (pl. adagios).

adapt, adapter (general), adaptor (gadget), adaptation; *adaption* does not exist. **Adapt** = make suitable; **adept** = skilled, expert; **adopt** = take as one's own. E.g.:
"We could mend the machine if we could adapt an ordinary washer to fit the outlet valve."
"Barry is adept at modifying ordinary washers to make them fit this machine."
"It would pay us to adopt Barry as a full-time mechanic instead of as a temporary employee"

add, addable, additive.

addendum (pl. addenda).

adduce, adducible.

add up to usually = **mean** or **come to,** which are preferred. E.g.:
"It all adds up to a disaster" is better put as
"It means a disaster."

adept *See* adapt.

adequate = sufficient in quantity, enough (which is preferred); **adequate to** = sufficient in quality, suitable. E.g.:
"The quantity of material was adequate for the task".
"The quality of the workmanship was barely adequate to the task."

adequate enough is a tautology (omit either word).

adhere, adhesion, adhesive, adhesiveness, adherence (which takes *to* not *of*), adherent [noun, preferred to adherer] (which takes *of* not *to*), adherent [adj.] (which takes *to* not *of*). E.g. (correct use):

"He proclaimed his adherence to the faith."

"He was an adherent of the faith."

"The tar was adherent to his shoes."

ad hoc (italics) = for a special purpose, improvised.

ad infinitum (italics) = to infinity; the Latin form should be avoided.

adit = tunnel or sloping shaft at the entrance to a mine. The word is found mainly in crossword puzzles; mining engineers prefer the term *entrance* or *entrance shaft*.

adj. is the abbreviation of adjective. In this Dictionary, *adjective* or *adjectival* is used of any describing word. Thus in the expressions "small blue car", "in the pouring rain", "pour on melted butter" and "systems analyst", *small* and *blue* are adjectives whereas *pouring* and *melted* are verbs and *systems* is a noun, all three being used adjectivally.

adjacent = near, neighbouring; **contiguous** = bordering, touching.

adjective order It is unusual to find four or more adjectives before a noun, but when adjectives do accumulate there is a conventional order. Of the two phrases

　　　1. the old green Chinese jade perfume bottle

and 2. the green perfume jade Chinese old bottle,

(1) makes sense whereas (2) does not. The usual order is (using the same example):

the	old	green	Chinese	jade	perfume	bottle
article	(e)	(d)	(c)	(b)	(a)	noun
	age	colour	origin	material	purpose	
	shape	texture	ownership	composition	function	
	size					

adjectives and nouns with the same spelling are usually distinguished by different pronunciations, involving differences in stress. In the following examples, which give the adjectival use first, the stressed syllable is in italics:

"The flat had a small, com*pact* kitchen."
"She keeps a powder *com*pact in her handbag."

"Don't hurry — I'm quite con*tent* to wait until you have finished."
"I dislike the anti-Semitic *con*tent of the article."

"Fog consists of min*ute* droplets of water suspended in the air."
"My new kettle takes less than a *min*ute to boil a pint of water."

"She used to be an *up*stairs maid."
"We have to move some furniture up*stairs*."
See also **nouns and verbs.**

adjudicate, adjudicator.

administer (preferred to administrate), administrator (but administratrix, fem. legal), administrative, administration, administrable (not *administratable*).

admit, admissible, admission, admittance. *Admit* to should be reserved for meaning "allow physical entry" (e.g. "She admitted him to her room"); in the meaning "confess" (e.g. "She admitted to letting him in"), *to* is redundant and should be omitted.
Admit of means "allow room for" (e.g. "The evidence admits of no other interpretation").

admonish, admonition (preferred to admonishment).

ad nauseam (italics) = to a sickening extent; the Latin form should be avoided.

adolescent *See* **baby.**

adopt, adopter, adoption, adoptive (describing the parents of an adopted child), adoptee (describing the adopted child). *See also* **adapt.**

adrenalin (preferred to *adrenaline* in ordinary writing; the usual North American term for the hormone is *epinephrine*).

adsorption *See* **absorption.**

adulate, adulator.

adulterate = spoil by adding a foreign or poisonous element;
adulteration = act of adulterating; **adultery** = extra-marital sexual relations; **adulterer** = someone who commits adultery (for *adulteress*, see **gender**).

adv. is the abbreviation of adverb. *See* **adverb**.

advance (noun) = forward movement, progress, loan (in anticipation of income); **advancement** = promotion, furthering (of a cause).

advantage, advantageous.

advent should be reserved for a coming that is of great importance or significance, and not used merely as a grand alternative to the neutral **arrival**. E.g.:
"A profusion of flowers heralded the advent of spring."
"A whistle announced the arrival of the train."
When it describes the coming or second coming of Christ, *Advent* has an initial capital letter.

adventitious = happening by chance or accident; **adventurous** = involving adventure.

adventure = exciting experience, remarkable occurrence; **venture** (noun) = (speculative) business undertaking.

adverb Most adverbs are formed by adding *-ly* to an adjective (e.g. happily, quickly, slowly, tearfully). Some retain the spelling of the adjective, in at least in one meaning, but may also have an *-ly* form (with a different meaning):

Adverb with adjective spelling	*Different adverb*
direct (straight)	directly (= immediately)
enough	
far	
fast	
hard (= energetically)	hardly (= scarcely)
high (= at a height)	highly (= very, favourably)
late (= behind time)	lately (= recently)
low	
much	

near (= close)   nearly (= almost)
straight

The two adverbial forms cannot be interchanged. E.g.:

"a *hard* apple" (adjective)
"she worked *hard*" (adverb)
"She *hardly* worked" (different adverb)

See also **-ly**.

adverse = unfavourable; **averse** = unwilling, opposed to, against. Both words take *to* in adjectival constructions. E.g.:

"Slippery fallen leaves on the road contributed to the adverse driving conditions."
"She was averse to driving a car on the slippery road."

advert (noun) is colloquial for advertisement, and should be avoided; **ad** with the same meaning is even less acceptable. The verb is **advertise**; the different verb **advert** = refer to.

advise (verb), advisable, adviser (preferred to advisor), advisory, advice (noun).

advocate *See* **barrister**.

-ae- This vowel sound, in words from Greek or Latin, should be written (and printed) as separate letters, not as the ligature æ (e.g. Aesop, Caesarian, formulae, haemoglobin), although æ is retained in Old English. In a few modern words, the vowel has been reduced to a single *e* (e.g. coeval, ether, medieval, hyena). *See also* **-oe-**.

aeon is the preferred spelling (not *eon*).

aerial *See* **antenna**.

aerie The preferred spelling is **eyrie** (= an eagle's nest).

aerobic = capable of life only in an oxygen-containing environment; **aerobics** = type of physical exercise.

aeroplane is generally being replaced by **aircraft**. An *aeroplane* is a fixed-wing aircraft, whereas the term *aircraft* can include rotating-wing machines (such as a helicopter). *Plane* (not *'plane*) is now an accepted short form; *airplane* is an Americanism, to be avoided.

aerosol (note spelling).

aesthetic = to do with standards of beauty and perfection in arts and crafts; **ascetic** = spartan, deliberately lacking in comfort. E.g.:

"Many modern designs are more utilitarian than aesthetic."
"The ascetic life of a monk did not appeal to him."

aetiology (not *etiology*). *See also* **-ae-**.

affect = to have an effect on; **effect** (verb) = to bring about, produce, accomplish; **effect** (noun) = the result of an action, impression produced. E.g.:

"Moisture affects the conductivity of carbon."
"Moisture effects a colour change in cobalt salts."
"The effect of moisture is to alter the colour."

affectation = pretence, adoption of an unreal or unnatural appearance; **affection** = love, attachment. E.g.:

"His cultured accent was an affectation to disguise his humble background."
"His affection for language is reflected in his precise enunciation of English."

affinity *with* or *between* people or things, not affinity *for* or *to*. *Affinity for* is correct in scientific usage.

affirm = to state or declare that something is true; **confirm** = to ratify or corroborate an existing statement (already taken to be true). *See also* **allege**.

afflict = to distress, cause to suffer, torment; **inflict** = to impose suffering or punishment; **inflect** = to turn off course, to bend in, to modulate (the voice). The corresponding nouns are *affliction, infliction* and *inflexion* (*see also* **-ection**). E.g.:

"Several of the people in the village were afflicted with leprosy."
"My uncle inflicted his holiday photographs on us."
"In English, the voice is often inflected to a higher pitch at the end of a question."

affluent = abundant, well provided; it should be avoided as a synonym for the simpler *rich* or *wealthy*.

affranchise, affranchisement.

affront (noun) = deliberate insult; **effrontery** = cheek, impudence.
E.g.:
"The manager knew his remarks would be an affront to the
company's chairman."
"The manager correctly guessed that, at the annual office party, his
effrontery would be overlooked by the chairman."

Afghanistan The derived adjective and noun is *Afghan* (not *Afghani*).

aficionado (italics) = enthusiast; the Spanish form should be avoided.

aforementioned is archaic for (as) **mentioned before**; it is retained in
legal contexts but should be avoided in ordinary writing.

aforesaid is archaic (and legal) for **previously mentioned**, which should
be used.

Afrikaans is the language; **Afrikaners** are the people. *See also* **Dutch
words**.

Afro-English etc. (with a hyphen).

after, afterbirth, after-care, after-effect, afterlife, aftermath,
afternoon, after-thought.

aftermath, originally meaning a second crop of grass or an unpleasant
consequence, is now used of any result or after-effect.

afterwards is preferred to **afterward**.

age, aging (preferred to ageing).

agenda is singular (even though it is the Latin plural of *agendum*); its
plural is *agendas*.

aggravate = to worsen, increase (an evil). The sense to *tease* or *irritate*
is colloquial. The verb should not be used to mean *spoil*, *upset* or
endanger. E.g.:
"Hot water merely aggravates the condition" is correct;
"He turned up the volume to aggravate his neighbour" is colloquial.
"His attitude aggravated their friendship" is incorrect.

aggression (= an opening act of hostility), aggressive (= initiating hostility, attacking), aggressiveness (= displaying aggression). The key ideas of aggression are displaying hostility and acting first. Thus such expressions as "continuing aggression" and "an aggressive response to their attack" are strictly incorrect.

aghast (note spelling).

agitate, agitator, agitation.

agnostic = someone who believes that the existence of God cannot be proved; **atheist** = someone who denies the existence of God.

agony, agonize.

agree, agreeable, agreement. *Agree* is traditionally an intransitive verb taking the preposition *with*, *on* or *to*, although the word can be used transitively. E.g.:
"I agree with your comments on the text" (intransitive),
"We must agree on an agenda" (intransitive),
"I agree to your commenting on the text" (intransitive),
"I agree your figures" (transitive);
the last form should be used sparingly.

agriculture, agriculturist (preferred to agriculturalist).

aid = to help, assist; **aide** = an assistant.

aide-mémoire (italics) = reminder; the French form should be avoided.

aim *at* a target; **aim** *to* achieve something (= intend). E.g.:
"The wicketkeeper aimed the ball at the stumps."
"The charity aims to provide food for starving children."

ain't should not be used for **am not** in formal writing. *See* **non-standard English**.

air, airborne, air-conditioning, aircraft, airfield, airflow, airgun, airman, airless, airlift, airline, airliner, airport, air-pump, air raid, airship, airtight, air-to-air (missile), airworthy, airworthiness.

aircraft names should be typeset in roman face with an initial capital letter; e.g. Concorde, Boeing 747, Hurricane, Messerschmitt, Vulcan.

Names given to individual aircraft should be italicized, e.g. *Spirit of St Louis; Lucky Lady*. See also **aeroplane**.

airplane is an Americanism for **aeroplane**; *aircraft* is the preferred current term.

aisle = gangway in a church; **isle** = island (most commonly part of a proper name, such as *Isles of Scilly*).

akin *to* (not akin *with*).

à la (italics) = in the manner/style of (e.g. *à la* Strauss); the French term (an abbreviation of *à la mode de*) should be avoided.

à la carte (italics, with a grave accent) = with each dish of a meal priced separately on a menu; **table d'hôte** (italics, with a circumflex) = with a whole meal at a fixed price.

a large extent seldom means more than **much** or **most**, which are preferred. **To a large extent** usually means merely **mostly**.

albedo (pl. albedos).

albeit *See* **howbeit**.

albino (pl. albinos), albinism.

albumen = white of an egg; **albumin** = a particular protein that occurs in blood, muscle, etc.

ale = drink made by fermenting a watery mash of malt (germinated barley), with the yeast on top; **beer** = drink made by a similar process to that used for ale but with added hops (for flavour) and the yeast at the bottom of the brew; **bitter** = light non-sweet beer; **lager** = extra-light beer, traditionally kept for six months before use; **mild** = dark beer, sweeter than bitter and with no hops; **pilsner** (sometimes abbreviated to **pils**) = lager-type beer, originally from Pilsen in Czechoslovakia; **porter** = dark beer made using roasted malt; **stout** = extra-strong porter. *Porter* is archaic, as (according to the *OED*) is *ale* although the word has long been preserved in the terms *light* or *pale ale* and *brown ale* (usually bottled versions of bitter or mild with added gas) and in the draught bitters proprietarily called *India(n) Pale Ale* (IPA). The revived interest in "real" ales has also revived *ale* from its archaic status. The American term **malt liquor** is usually applied to a strong, gassy, light beer sold in cans; bottled strong, dark beer is called **barley wine** in Britain.

alexia = loss of the power to read; **dyslexia** = inability to learn to read (properly).

alfalfa is an alternative (and American) name for the fodder crop *lucerne*, which is preferred.

alfresco (one word preferred) = in the open air; the Italian expression should be avoided.

alga (pl. algae).

alias (pl. aliases).

alibi (pl. alibis) is a defence based on the plea that the accused was elsewhere at the time of the alleged offence; it should not be used to mean merely *excuse*.

alien, alienate, alienable (not *alienatable*), alienator, alienation. The adjectival expression is *alien to* (not *from*).

-alist or **-ist** Apart from well-established words such a *conversationalist*, the tendency is for the short form to be preferred. E.g.:

agriculturist	not *agriculturalist*
educationist	not *educationalist*
horticulturist	not *horticulturalist*

Sometimes the two forms have different meanings (e.g. *naturist* and *naturalist*).

alive = living; **live** (adj.) = energized (e.g. a live electricity cable, live ammunition), not recorded (e.g. a live performance), living (e.g. a live specimen).

alkali (pl. alkalis), alkaline.

all- Most compound adjectives with the prefix *all-* are hyphenated; e.g. all-American boy, all-day event, walk on all-fours, all-in wrestling, all-night garage, all-out effort, all-over roof, all-powerful ruler, all-risks policy, all-round sportsman (an all-rounder), all-time low.

all alone, like **all by her/him/itself**, is usually a tautology (omit *all*).

allay = to relieve or calm; **alleviate** = to mitigate, give temporary relief. The former is usually permanent, the latter is always temporary. E.g.:
"Appointment to the permanent staff allayed his fears of redundancy."
"The soothing lotion alleviated the itching of the rash."

allege = to claim that something is true; **affirm** = confirm or ratify (the truth of something); **assert** = to declare with (apparent) proof; **explain** = to make understandable, account for. E.g.:
"My husband alleges that I was not at home when he telephoned."
"I can affirm that Wendy was at home when her husband telephoned."
"Wendy asserted that she was at home and the window-cleaner confirmed what she said."
"She explained what the window-cleaner was doing near the telephone."

allegiance = loyalty to a person; **alliance** = pact or treaty between nations.

allegro (pl. allegros).

allergic should be reserved for reference to a true (medical) allergy, and not misused to express dislike or antipathy.

alleviate, alleviator.

alliance *See* **allegiance**.

all in = exhausted; **all-in** = inclusive, taken as a whole. E.g.:
"By the time we had climbed the hill we were all in."
"I bought the day's travel and meals for an all-in price of £17."

all in all (e.g. "All in all it is a good result") is, like **by and large**, a cliché to avoid.

allot, allotted, allottable, allotment.

all over Consider the following sentences:
"He tipped his cup and spilled tea on the chair."

"He knocked over a bottle and spilled milk over the floor."
"He tripped over a bucket and spilled water all over the floor."
"The song became popular all over the world."
The first three, using *on*, *over* and *all over*, correctly convey the idea
of an increase in volume spilled with increasingly serious
consequences. In the fourth sentence, *all over* means *throughout*, a use
to be avoided in formal writing.

allow *See* **permit**.

all ready *See* **already**.

all right is the preferred form of alright.

All Saints' Day, All Souls' Day (but All Souls College, Oxford).

all together *See* **altogether**.

allude, allusion *See* **illude**.

allure = to entice, attract as by a lure (noun); **lure** (verb) = to attract
someone or something to his/its disadvantage, to entrap.

alluvium (pl. alluvia).

almanac (not *almanack*).

almost is an adverb and should not be used to qualify a thing, for
which use **virtual** (or *near*). E.g.:
"The virtual (or near) certainty that . . . "
Avoid **almost never** (use *hardly ever* or *very seldom*). *See also* **already**.

alms (= charity) is a singular word. The related adjective (meaning
charitable, or to do with alms) is the unlikely word *eleemosynary*.

aloes (= a bitter drug), although a plural form, is regarded as singular
(e.g. "Aloes is used on the fingers to discourage nail-biting").

alone = unaccompanied, single, on one's own; **lone** = solitary,
isolated. The meanings overlap, although the former tends to be used
of people and the latter of things (and is usually preceded by *a*). E.g.:
"She preferred to eat alone, not with the crowd."
"All he contributed to the discussion was a lone idea about
schedules."

A person who prefers to be alone is a *loner*. Alone can also mean *only*, as in "She alone knew he was lying". *See also* **lonely**.

alongst is archaic for **along**, which should be used.

a lot of *See* **lots of**.

alpha, alpha-numeric (characters on computer displays), alpha particle (= a helium nucleus), alpha rays (streams of alpha particles).

alphabetization Words in a list or index should be alphabetized by considering each word letter by letter to the first comma (or other punctuation mark), ignoring spaces, apostrophes, accents, diacritical marks and hyphens.

Names that include *de, van, von* and the like, should be listed under the most commonly used form of the name. Thus the German statesman Otto von Bismarck should appear as *Bismarck, Otto von*, whereas the Dutch painter Vincent van Gogh should be under *Van Gogh, Vincent*, preferably with a cross-reference from *Gogh, Vincent van*.

M', Mc and *Mac* are listed as if they were spelled *Mac*. Thus the political scientist *McBain, Howard Lee* precedes the Scottish king *Macbeth*, who precedes the American senator *McCarthy, Joseph* (in each instance the letters after the *Mc* or *Mac* determine the alphabetical order). Exceptions to this rule are African names beginning with *M'*; they are listed in strict alphabetical order: *M'Ba, Mbandaka, M'bour, Mdina*, and so on.

Abbreviations are alphabetized as if they were spelled out (e.g. *S.* is alphabetized as San, and *St* is alphabetized as Saint). Therefore the heading *St Clair, Arthur* is listed before *Saint Clair, Lake*, which precedes *St Denis, Ruth* and the Dutch island *Saint Eustatius*. Again, in each instance the first letters of the word after Saint determine the alphabetical order.

If the same spelling occurs two or more times, alphabetize the words by category in the order persons, places and things. Thus, in a series headed Washington, the person *Washington, George*, precedes the place *Washington, state*, and the latter precedes *Washington, Treaty of* (thing).

The order of listing for persons of the same name is determined by rank; saints, popes, emperors, kings, followed by titled nobility, such

as crown prince, duke or count, baron, baronet, and so forth.
Monarchs of the same name are listed numerically and alphabetically
by country: *Charles X*, King of France (and all the other French
Charleses) appears before *Charles III*, King of Naples, who in turn
precedes *Charles III* of Spain. In family articles, alphabetize people
with identical names chronologically (by birth date).
Identical place-names are alphabetized in order of population.

already is an adverb; **all ready** is adjectival. E.g.:
"They are all ready there" (i.e. all of those people are ready);
"They are already there" (i.e. even by this time they are there).
Almost and *all most* are also adverb and adjective, respectively.
Compare "It is all most useful" and "It is almost useful".

alright should be avoided; use **all right**.

altar = table for offerings in a church or temple; **alter** = to change.

altercation = a (verbal) quarrel, not a (physical) fight.

alternate(ly) = by turns; **alternative(ly)** = in a way that offers a
choice. E.g.:
"The lights flashed alternately red and green."
"Show a red light, or alternatively show a green one."
As a verb, **alternate** = to take it in turns. *See also* **alternative**.

alternative involves the use of *or* or *and*; **choice** involves the use of
between or *of*. E.g.:
"The alternative is to walk or to run."
"The alternatives are to walk and to run."
"The alternatives are walking and running."
But note "The choice is between walking and running."
and "He had the choice of walking and running."
The word *alternative* should, strictly, be used to describe one of two
possibilities; e.g. "You can choose between the two alternatives, tea
and coffee" (not "tea or coffee"). Increasingly usage permits more
than two possibilities; e.g. "The vending machine offered six
alternatives, from which I chose coffee." In this example, you would
strictly choose *among* the six (or make a choice *from among* the six),
not *between* them.

although It does no harm if, with a few exceptions, **although** is used consistently instead of **though**, and many publishers' style sheets insist on this. Exceptions include the combinations **as though** (often better put as *as if*), **even though**, and inverted constructions such as "Harmless though it seems . . .". Phrasing such as "Do not change it, though" (= "But do not change it") is clumsy and should be avoided.

alto (pl. altos).

altogether = entirely, wholly; **all together** = together in time, place or thought, as one body. E.g.:
"The team's performance deteriorated altogether" (completely);
"The team lost heart all together" (each member at the same time).

amateur – non professional, not done/performed for payment; **amateurish** = inept, to a poor standard.

amazing = causing amazement (i.e. great surprise and wonder); in its overworked guise this word seldom means more than **surprising**. E.g. in "She ate an amazing amount – two portions!" mere *surprising* would probably be emphatic enough. *See also* **surprise**.

ambidextrous (preferred to ambidexterous).

ambivalent = having in mind simultaneously two irreconcilable desires. It should be kept as a psychoanalytical term, and not used as a pretentious synonym of *with mixed feelings* nor as an incorrect one of *ambiguous.*

amenable *to* requires a noun; it should not be followed by a verb. E.g.:
"She is amenable to persuasion" is correct; "He was amenable to listen" is incorrect.

amend – to improve something (that is imperfect); **emend** = to remove errors from a passage of text or a numerical calculation. E.g.:
"He amended the design to make the photographs more prominent."
"She emended the text before it was typeset."
The corresponding nouns are *amendment* and *emendation.*

America, strictly = North America and South America (also called The Americas). The people who live there are Americans. North

America = Canada and the United States (USA), although it is sometimes taken to include also Central America (Mexico *et al*). In English text, *American* usually describes anything pertaining to the United States (as opposed to, say, Canadian), and may be abbreviated to US.

Americanisms English – that is, British English – contains various words from the Americas. These include some derived from Carib, Inuit (Eskimo), North American Indian and South American Indian languages. E.g.:

avocado	hickory	pecan	tamarack
barbecue	hurricane	pemmican	tanager
cannibal	igloo	petunia	tapioca
canoe	jaguar	peyote	tapir
cashew	kayak	piranha	terrapin
caucus	llama	poncho	tobacco
chilli	maize	potato	toboggan
cocoa	moccasin	puma	tomahawk
chipmunk	moose	quetzal	tomato
chocolate	musquash	quinine	totem
coyote	pampas	raccoon	toucan
coypu	papaya	rumba	wampum
curare	papoose	sequoia	wapiti
hammock	parka	skunk	wigwam

Others were taken or modified from the languages of voluntary or involuntary immigrants (for instance, from Africa), sometimes via Portuguese or Spanish. E.g.:

banana	chaps	jazz	sleigh
banjo	cola	limbo	tango
bongo	hamburger	okra	tote
boss	hokum	voodoo	prairie
caribou	hoodlum	pretzel	zombie

Modern America has also supplied some words of its own. E.g.:

blurb	commuter	hobo	lifestyle
bobcat	gerrymander	jive	lunch
bunkum	gimmick	know-how	motel

maverick	stunt	teenager	tuxedo
stetson			

or influenced English spelling (such as the terms *analog, disk* and *program* as used in computer technology). Words in all but the last group are standard English. Words in this last group, the use of totally American expressions (such as "candy store" for "sweet shop", "presently" for "at present" and "truck" for "lorry") and even words that have fallen into disuse in English but are still current in North America (such as "closet" for "cupboard", "gotten" for "got" and "raise" for "rise" in pay) are examples of Americanisms, which should be avoided in normal English writing.

When the Americans and British have different words for the same thing, ignorance of each other's terms generally leads merely to an absence of understanding. Thus what is in the United States termed a *beltway* is called a *ring road* in Britain, *janitor* (USA) is *caretaker* (UK), and *straw boss* (USA) is *assistant foreman* (UK); an Englishman who does not know what a straw boss is will be at a loss if he comes across the term. But when the same spelling means different things in the two countries, misunderstanding can be total (because a person in each country thinks that he *does* know what the other intends). Thus an American in Britain who ordered chips would be surprised to receive French fries, just as a Briton in the United States who asked for a cot for the baby would wonder why he was given a camp bed.

American spellings should be used only in direct quotation and for the names of American organizations, buildings, and so on (e.g. Secretary of Defense, Farmer-Labor Party). *See also* **Americanisms; quotations**.

American states *See* **US states**.

Amerindian The preferred term is **(North/South) American Indian**.

amiable = agreeable or good-natured (of a person); **amicable** = friendly (of relationships or arrangements). E.g.:

"Amiable people generally have amicable relationships."

amid, amidst *See* **mid**.

amoeba has the preferred plural **amoebas** (not *amoebae*).

amok is the preferred spelling (not *amuck*).

among should be used consistently instead of **amongst**. *See also* **between**.

among other reasons/things should be avoided; the usual meaning is "along with other . . .", "apart from other . . .", "besides" or, most often, "in addition to other. . .".

amoral = non-moral, lacking in morals; **immoral** = wicked, corrupt. E.g.:
"Someone of amoral upbringing may develop immoral tendencies."

amortize (= spread initial cost over many repayments).

amount applies to mass or bulk (or money), not to number. E.g.:
"A large amount of timber" but "A large number of tables".

amp. is the abbreviation of ampere.

ampersand (&) should be avoided in ordinary text unless it is part of a direct quotation (e.g. "The company of Jones & Co."). Do not use *&c.* for *etc.*

amuck *See* **amok**.

an *See* **a** *or* **an**.

anaesthesia, anaesthetic, anaesthetize.

analogous = having analogy, resembling in certain circumstances or effects, parallel; **similar** = having a resemblance or likeness, of like kind. Both words are used with *to*. E.g.:
"The action of the elbow joint is analogous to that of a hinge."
"The bones of the fingers are similar to those of the toes."

analogue = something of like appearance or function; **analogy** = point of correspondence between things that are otherwise different. E.g.:
"The elbow and hinge are analogues, because they allow movement in only one plane."
"The past participle of *strive* is *striven*, by analogy with *drive* and *driven*."
Increasingly in computer technology, *analog* is being spelled in the American way. *See also* **data; disc; programme**.

analysis (pl. analyses), analyse, analyst, analytic(al).

anatomical/biological/medical terms are not spelled with an initial
capital letter unless they include a proper noun or adjective; e.g.
Adam's apple, Fallopian tube, Golgi apparatus, Huntington's chorea,
islets of Langerhans.

ancient refers to the remote past — it is the opposite of modern;
antiquated refers to something that is no longer used or is no longer in
style/fashion; **antique** refers to objects from former times; **archaic**
refers to things that were used in the past and are used now only in
historical reconstruction; **obsolete** refers to things that are no longer
used because they have been superseded (supposedly by something
better); **obsolescent** refers to things that are becoming obsolete.

Ancient Egyptians/Greeks etc. need an initial capital letter on
Ancient.

ancillary (not *ancilliary*).

and Avoid beginning a sentence with *and,* although it is not forbidden;
never begin a paragraph with *and.* Do not use a comma before *and* at
the end of a list (unless the last-but-one item on this list comprises two
things linked by *and*). *See* **punctuation** (comma).

and/or should be avoided in ordinary writing; e.g. "He will give it to
his brother and/or sister" is better put as ". . . to his brother or sister,
or to both of them."

and which, if used, should be preceded by another *which* clause; e.g.
"The dog, which had bitten him and which continued to bare its teeth,
stood its ground." Usually the second *which* in such constructions can
be omitted.

anecdote = short account (about an event or person); **antidote** =
medicine to counteract/treat poisoning.

anemone (note spelling).

anent is archaic for **about** or **concerning**, either of which should be
used.

aneurysm is the preferred spelling (not *aneurism*).

Anglo-Indian = somebody of mixed British and Indian parentage (although the term formerly meant a Briton living in India).

angry *at* things or events; **angry** *with* people. E.g.:
"She was angry at the damage, and with the other driver for having caused it."

angst is a term in psychology and psychiatry; it is better left there and not used as a synonym for ordinary anxiousness or anxiety.

annalist = somebody who compiles annals; **analyst** = somebody who makes an analysis.

annex (verb) = to take over, add on; **annexe** (noun) = an addition.

annoyed *at* a thing or occurrence; **annoyed** *with* a person. E.g.:
"I was annoyed at the error and with myself for making it."

annunciation = proclamation, announcement; **enunciation** = method of or strictness in pronunciation.

anon is archaic for **soon**, which should be used; **anon.** is the abbreviation of anonymous.

anorexia The preferred adjective is **anorectic** (not *anorexic*).

another should not be used for plain **other**; e.g. "some way or another" is incorrect. Neither misuse **another** for **one other**; e.g. "There is only another page to go" is also incorrect. **Another** should not be used for a second number unless it is identical to the first one. E.g.:
"Nearly 3,000 people attended the meeting and another 3,000 waited outside" is correct;
"About 10,000 people died of starvation and another 30,000 are suffering from malnutrition" is incorrect (say "... an additional 30,000 are" or "... 30,000 others are").

-ant or **-ent** *See* **-ance** or **-ence.**

antagonist *See* **protagonist.**

ante- = before (in place or time); **anti-** = against (opposed to). E.g.:
antechamber, antedate, antenatal (= prenatal), ante-room; and

anti-aircraft, antibiotic, anticline, anticlockwise, antidote, antifreeze,
anti-hero, antimatter, antiparticle, anti-Semitic, anti-Semitism,
antitoxin.
The spelling of anticipate (which *see*) appears illogical.

antedate *See* **predate.**

antenna = a radio or radar aerial, has the plural *antennas*; **antenna** =
a "feeler" of an insect or other animal, has the plural *antennae*.

anti- *See* **ante-.**

anticipate = to act before someone else, notice a need and act in
advance. It should not be used to mean merely **expect**; e.g. "I
anticipate that the article will be finished by Friday" is incorrect.

antipathy = strong dislike bordering on hatred; **antithesis** (pl.
antitheses) = opposite of. E.g.:
"I have an antipathy to firearms."
"The demonstration was the antithesis of non-violence."

antiquated *See* **ancient.**

antique *See* **ancient.**

Anti-Semitic *See* **Semitic.**

antonyms = words of opposite meaning (e.g. *hot* and *cold*); **synonyms**
= words of the same meaning (e.g. *gorse* and *furze*). *See* **homonym;
synonym.**

anxious = worried, feeling or displaying anxiety; the word should not
be used to mean merely impatient or eager, particularly if it is
pleasurable expectation. E.g.:
"The convicted man was anxious to hear the sentence of the court"
(correct);
"She was anxious to receive the prize" (incorrect).
Note: anxious *to* do something, anxious *for* something to occur, and
anxious *about* something (e.g. "anxious to hear", "anxious for news"
and "anxious about the outcome").

any more is always two words (not *anymore*).

anyone = anybody (which is preferred) should be distinguished from **any one**, as in "The poison can kill anyone (anybody)" and "The poison could kill any one of us". *Anyone, anybody, no one, nobody, some one* and *somebody* are all singular and conventionally represented by a masculine pronoun, unless specifically female. Some publishers, however, insist on the "he or she" formula. *See* **gender**.

anything/something can be replaced by **any thing/some thing** when contrasted with any person or the pronouns in the preceding entry; e.g. "He will buy anything" and "He will not paint people or animals but he will paint any thing you ask him to" (better as "... anything else..." or "...any object...").

anyway = in any case, and is often a non-essential part of a sentence; **any way** = in any manner, by any method. E.g.:
"I did not use the illustration − it was poorly drawn anyway."
"She can do the illustration any way we like."

ape, aped, aping, apish.

apex (pl. apexes).

aphis (pl. aphides, although *aphis* is increasingly being used also as the plural form).

apiary = place for keeping bees; **aviary** = place for keeping birds.

apocope = cutting off of the end of a word to form a new one in its own right (not merely a recognized abbreviation). For a list of examples and advice about their use, *see* **shortened words**. *See also* **abbreviations**.

apostrophe = punctuation mark or figure of speech. The punctuation mark indicates the omission of letters or possession (genitive case); e.g. "can't" (omission), "John's book" (possession). *See also* **ellipsis; punctuation** (apostrophe).

apparatus (pl. apparatuses).

appease, appeasement.

appendix, meaning an addition to a book, has the plural *appendixes*; as a term in medicine, it has the plural *appendices*.

appetite, appetize, appetizer, appetizing.

appliqué, appliquéed, appliquéing.

apposite = appropriate, apt, suited to its purpose; **opposite** = opposed, directly contrary, face to face.

apposition is an additional descriptive but non-essential word or phrase, usually written in commas after the noun it describes; e.g in "My son, the local doctor, lives there", the phrase "local doctor" is in apposition to "My son".

appraise = to evaluate; **apprise** = to inform, make award; **apprize** (archaic) = to (estimate the) value (of).

appreciate (= gratefully acknowledge, increase in value) should not be overworked to mean *admit*, *realize* or *understand*. All of the following are incorrect:

"I appreciate you have had problems."
"You must appreciate my position."
"I am glad you finally appreciate what you have done."

Examples of correct usage are:

"She appreciated what I had done for her."
"The antique chair has already appreciated in the three years since I bought it."

apprehend, apprehension, apprehensive, apprehensible. **Apprehend** = grasp or seize (a person or an idea); **comprehend** = understand; **reprehend** = blame.

apprehensive = dreading something that is to come; **timid** = lacking self confidence; **timorous** = timid but shrinking (habitually) because of lack of courage.

appro *See* on appro.

appropriate, as an adjective, is overused. Take the appropriate action and try *right, suitable, fitting* or *proper*, for a change.

approve = confirm, think well of, ratify (noun *approval*); **endorse** = to note on a document or to assign (in writing), give one's name to, sanction (noun *endorsement*).

approximate(ly) = very close(ly). It should not be used when *about* or *roughly* will do; nor should it be applied to figures that are not approximate (but exact). The absurd expression *very approximate* should be avoided; it means, if anything, *not* very approximate.

apt *See* **liable**.

aquarium (pl. aquariums).

aqueduct (not *aquaduct*).

Arabia The preferred adjective and noun for the people is *Arab* (not *Arabic*, which should be reserved for the language, or *Arabian*, except in names such as Arabian desert). *See also* **Arabic words; Middle East**.

Arabic numerals are the "ordinary" numbers 1,2,3,4,5,6,7,8,9 and 0. *See also* **numbers and counting; roman numerals**.

Arabic words that have contributed to the English vocabulary include several that incorporate the definite article *al-* (admir*al*, *al*chemy, *al*cohol, *al*cove, *al*embic, *al*gebra, *al*kali). Many other words can be traced to Arabic origins − possibly by way of India, Persia or Turkey or even via French or Spanish. Sometimes they present spelling difficulties, so here, for interest and as a spelling check, is a list of examples:

alfalfa	crimson	howdah	minaret
arsenal	dhow	jar	mocha
burnous	divan	jasmine	monsoon
cadi	djellaba	jerboa	mosque
caftan	douane	jumper	muezzin
camphor	elixir	kebab	mufti
candy	fakir	kismet	mullah
caracal	fez	lemon	mummy
carafe	gain	lilac	nadir
carat	gazelle	loofah	orange
caraway	giraffe	lute	popinjay
carob	ghoul	macramé	quintal
caviare	harem	magazine	racket
cipher	henna	marabou	realgar
coffee	hookah	mattress	saffron

saker	sirocco	tamarind	wadi
saluki	soda	tarboosh	yashmak
sash	sofa	tare	zenith
sequin	sugar	tariff	zero
sheikh	sumac	turban	
sherbet	tabby	vizier	

arbitrate, arbitrator (= someone who impartially and with given authority resolves a dispute), arbiter (= someone who comments on matters of taste or gives an expert opinion in a dispute), arbitrary, arbitration. *See also* **mediate**.

arbor = spindle for holding a rotating tool or workpiece; **arbour** = bower of trees, tree-shaded area.

arc (noun) = part of a circle, spark between two electrodes; **ark** = (wooden) chest, Noah's vessel.

archaeology is the preferred spelling (not *archeology*).

archaic *See* **ancient**.

archaisms are old-fashioned words that should by now have passed on, but are sometimes preserved as a single use in a cliché or used in "precious" writing. Several common examples, such as *betwixt, nigh* and *wont*, are included in this Dictionary, usually with the advice to avoid them. *See also* **non-standard English**.

archipelago (pl. archipelagos).

Arctic has an initial capital letter when it is used for the region round the North Pole (which also has initial capital letters); e.g. "the weak Arctic sunshine", "the cold Arctic seas". **Arctic Circle** also has initial capital letters.

aren't should not be used for **are not** in formal writing.

Argentina The derived adjective and noun is *Argentine* (not *Argentinian*).

argot, often regarded as the same as **cant**, is a type of slang restricted to a particular group of people, such as criminals. *See* **non-standard English; slang**.

argue, arguing, arguable, argument.

arise has the past tense **arose** and past participle **arisen**. *See also* **raise**; **rise**. Arise = happen, come into being (e.g. "Several new claims have arisen since we last discussed the matter"); it no longer has the meaning of **rise** in the sense of come/get up (e.g. "I rose at dawn", not "I arose at dawn").

armadillo (pl. armadillos).

aroma is usually precious for **smell** or **odour**, either of which is preferred.

around should be avoided as a substitute for **about** (e.g. "It was built around the 1800s" is better put as "... about the 1800s") and not used for **round** (e.g. "He passed the salt around the table" should be "... round the table"). In general, *around* should refer to something moving or placed in an extensive area (e.g. "The horses galloped around the moors") whereas *round* should indicate motion in a circular path (e.g. "The horses galloped round the final bend").

arouse = engender, give rise to, stimulate, wake from sleep; **rouse** = stir from dormancy or inaction. E.g.:
"The national music aroused feelings of patriotism."
"The sudden threat roused him into action."

arpeggio (pl. arpeggios).

arrange, arranging, arrangeable, arrangement.

arrant = complete, utter; **errant** = straying, wandering. E.g.:
"He regularly speaks arrant nonsense."
"They are searching for the errant cattle."

arras = hanging tapestry screen; **arris** = horizontal, triangular rail of a fence, sharp-edged stone; **arête** = sharp rocky ridge (on a mountain).

arrest, arrestable, arrestment (rare).

arrogate *See* **abrogate**.

art, artistic, arty-crafty (= pretentiously artistic), artful (= deceitful, cunning), artless (= innocent, naive). *See also* **inartistic**.

art deco/art nouveau (no initial capital letters).

artefact is the preferred spelling (not *artifact*). **Artefact** = something made by a human being; **artifice** = crafty trick (and is thus pejorative).

article *See* **a** or **an**.

artificial describes a copy or model (of something real); **synthetic** describes a manufactured version (of something that occurs naturally). E.g.:
"The room was decorated with artificial flowers."
"Industry uses synthetic diamonds as abrasives."
Man-made should be avoided as a synonym of *synthetic* on sexist grounds (*see also* **gender**).

artificial satellites Italicize their names and use Arabic numerals; e.g. *Early Bird, Comsat, Telstar, Skylab 2*.

artist = someone who draws, paints, sculpts, etc.; **artiste** = a professional entertainer.

artless = innocent, ingenuous, naive, "uncrafty"; **ignorant** = lacking in knowledge (often used pejoratively).

as should not be misused for **because**, a use that often leads to ambiguity. E.g. "He could not read as he was lying in bed" is capable of two interpretations (or four with the additional ambiguity of *lying*). *See also* **than**.

ascend, ascender, ascendant, ascendance, ascendancy, ascension.

ascent = a going up; **assent** = agreement, consent. E.g.:
"The first successful ascent of Everest took place in 1953."
"She will not give her assent to her daughter's marriage."

ascetic *See* **acetic; aesthetic**.

ascribe = assign, reckon; **attribute** (verb) = to impute, consider as belonging. The meanings overlap and the words are near synonyms.

ascus (pl. asci).

as far as...is/are concerned should be avoided as an alternative to a simpler preposition such as **for**; e.g. "There are some attractive clothes as far as the younger age groups are concerned" is better put as "... clothes for younger people".

as follows is the correct form of introducing one or several listed items. E.g.:

"The most popular choice is as follows: English."
"The most popular choices were as follows: English, Biology and History" (not *"as follow"*).

Asia The derived adjective and noun is *Asian* (not *Asiatic*).

aside from should be avoided in the sense *except* or *apart from*.

asinine (note spelling).

asperate *See* **aspire**.

asphalt (not *ashphalt*, *asphalte*).

asphyxia, asphyxiate, asphyxiation.

aspire, aspirant (who aspires), aspirate (= breathe, pronounce the letter *h*), aspirator (= apparatus for producing a flow of gas), aspiration (= hope, breathing, pronouncing an *h*, or action of an aspirator); **asperate** (= roughen), asperity (= roughness, extreme coldness).

ass is the preferred name for the wild animal of the horse genus (*Equus*); its domestic cousin is usually called a **donkey**. *See also* **horse**; **mule**.

assassin, assassinate, assassination (each with four *ss*).

assay (verb), an archaic word for **try**, now means testing metals' ores; **assay** (noun) = a (scientific) test; **essay** (verb) = to attempt, to try; **essay** (noun) = an attempt (archaic), a prose composition.

assert *See* **allege**.

assess, assessable, assessor.

asset = valuable possession, advantage; **assets** = property.

assign, assignee (preferred to assignor), assignment, assignation. An *assignment* is an allotted task; and *assignation* is an arranged meeting (often furtive, sometimes amorous).

assimilate *See* **simulate**.

assist, assistant (preferred to assister; assistor, legal). Assist someone *in* doing something, not assist someone *to do* something.

assume = adopt, (take for granted); **presume** = to take as true without definite proof, (take upon oneself, take for granted). These verbs are often interchangeable, especially in their secondary meanings. E.g.:
"He assumed the role of dictator."
"He saw your car outside and so presumed you were there."
"He saw your car outside and so assumed you were there."
Assumption and **presumption** are also similar in some of their meanings.

assure, assurable, assurer (who gives assurance), assuror (an insurance underwriter). *See also* **insure**.

asterisk (*) *See* **footnotes**.

astern *See* **abaft**.

asthma, asthmatic.

as though *See* **although**.

astonish *See* **surprise**.

astound *See* **surprise**.

astronaut = member of the crew of a space vehicle; **cosmonaut** = Soviet astronaut.

astronomical terms Constellations, planets, stars and other named celestial bodies have an initial capital letter(s); e.g. Great Bear (= Ursa Major), Venus, Earth, Sun, Moon, Dog Star, Orion Nebula, Milky Way (*see also* **Earth; Moon**).
Messier numbers are typeset with no space before the catalogue number (e.g. M42); New General Catalogue numbers do have a space (e.g. NGC 332).

-asy *See* **-acy** or **-asy**.

asymmetry, asymmetric(al). **Asymmetry** = lack of symmetry; **dissymmetry** = asymmetry, or the symmetry of right and left hand, of an object and its mirror image.

at should not be used for *in* in the construction "She was born in England/London/Kensington/Cromwell Road". Note also "He went to university *in* London", "He studied *at* Queen Mary College" and "He graduated *from* the University of London".

at an earlier date seldom means more than **earlier**, which is preferred; **at an early date** usually means **soon**, which also is preferred.

atheist *See* **agnostic**.

atom bomb is the preferred form (editorially speaking) of **atomic bomb**.

atomic *See* **nuclear**.

atomize, atomization.

atrium (pl. atria).

atrocious should be reserved to describe an *atrocity* (= a brutal, barbaric or extremely wicked act), and not used to mean merely poor quality or bad (as in "The player made an atrocious mistake").

attaché (acute accent).

attain = to reach, gain, achieve; **accomplish** = to perform (a task), succeed in (an undertaking). E.g.:
"To attain the target amount you must accomplish something every day."

attend, attendant, attendance.

attended *by* another person; **attended** *with* another thing or things.

at the end of the day is a modern cliché (equivalent to the older ones "when all is said and done" and "when it comes down to it") meaning, if anything, *finally* or *ultimately*. They should all be avoided. *See also* **basically**.

at the present time, like **at this moment in time**, = now (or today), which is preferred.

attire, like **garb**, is precious for **clothes** or **dress**, either of which is preferred.

attorney *See* **barrister**.

attribute (verb) *See* **ascribe**.

attune = make to correspond, arrange in a suitable way; **tune** = put in tune or (figuratively) put in accord with, adjust something to a required form or state. Thus the usual meaning of the former overlaps with the figurative meaning of the latter. E.g.:
"He found it difficult to attune his views to hers";
"She decided to tune her attitudes to those of the rest of the group."

audible, audio.

auditorium (pl. auditoriums).

au fait (italics) = acquainted, instructed; the French term should be avoided.

auger = tool for boring; **augur** = Roman fortune-teller.

aught = anything, in any way (archaic); **ought** = should. E.g.:
"I doubt that it will come to aught."
"Ought it to come to anything?" (= "Should it come . . .")

au naturel (not *natural*) = naked, raw or plainly cooked. The French term should be avoided.

aunt = sister of one's parent and, by extension, wife of one's uncle.

aural = pertaining to the ear or hearing; **oral** = pertaining to the mouth, the voice or speaking. *See also* **oral**.

auspicious = with good omens for success, favourable, of good auspices; the word should not be used as a synonym of memorable (as in the cliché "auspicious occasion").

Australia and New Zealand have English as their official language. Early British settlers in these countries adopted some words from the local people (particularly names of indigenous animals), and these are now part of English. For example, Australian Aborigines donated boomerang, budgerigar, dingo, kangaroo, koala, kookaburra, wallaby, wallaroo and woomera, whereas kauri, kiwi, mana, moa and tuna (eel) are Maori words, and lei, taboo, tattoo and ukulele are from various Pacific island languages.

autarchy = despotism, absolute sovereignty; **autarky** = national (economic) independence; **autocracy** = government by a single absolute ruler; **autonomy** = self-rule or self-government.

authentic, authenticate, authenticator.

authoress Most female authors prefer to be called *authors*, although *lady author* (like *lady doctor*) is accepted by some. *See also* **gender**.

authority, authorize, authorization, authoritative (not *authoritive*), authoritarian. **Authoritative** = with the approval/sanction of authority (e.g. "The headmaster's authoritative ruling was accepted by everybody present at the meeting"); **authoritarian** = using authority regardless of people's rights, heavy-handed (e.g. "Many teachers resented the headmaster's authoritarian manner, which failed to acknowledge their points of view"). An expert is an **authority** on something; someone in power has authority over someone else – he or she has authority *to* do something or *for* doing something. E.g.:

"He is an authority on silver snuffboxes."
"She has authority over the other workers."
"She has authority to organize their work."
"She has the authority for checking their work."

autobahn (pl. autobahns, not *autobahnen*). *See also* **motorway**.

automaton (pl. automatons, preferred to automata).

automobile is no longer the usual American word for car (for which the usual word now is *car*). It is retained in such expressions as automobile industry which, in both Britain and the United States, is being replaced by automotive industry (although this is a wider term, including lorries (ever more commonly being called *trucks* in English) and sometimes agricultural and earth- moving vehicles).

auxiliary (not *auxillary*).

avant-garde, avant-gardism.

avenge another person (take vengeance on behalf of someone else); **revenge** oneself upon (take revenge on).

average (= arithmetic *mean*) of a set of *n* numbers is their sum divided by *n*. The **mode** is the number that appears most frequently in the set. The **median** is the number that has exactly the same number of values larger than it than there are values smaller than it. Average should apply to a quantity, not to a person (e.g. "The English drink an average of 50 gallons of tea per person every year", not "The average Englishman drinks 50 gallons of tea each year").

averse *See* **adverse**.

avert, avertible, aversion.

aviary *See* **apiary**.

avocation = ancillary occupation, side-line; **vocation** = main occupation, calling.

await is transitive; **wait** is intransitive. E.g.
"We await the arrival of spring."
"We cannot wait indefinitely."

awake, awaken, wake, waken These four verbs should be inflected as follows:

awake	awoke	awaked (not *awoke* or *awoken*)
awaken	awakened	awakened (not *awoken*)
wake	woke	woken
waken	wakened	wakened

Simplification can be achieved by using only two verbs: *wake* and *wake up*, which inflect the same way.

award = something given as a result of a judgement or arbitration, possibly after a trial or competition (e.g. a football referee can award a free kick, an Ombudsman can award compensation); **reward** = something given in recognition (e.g. an insurance company may offer a reward for the recovery of stolen property).

awe, awesome, awful, awe-inspiring. *Awful/awfully* have been so grossly overworked as pejorative terms that *awe-inspiring* now has to be used of things that inspire awe. As the Fowlers said: "*Awfully nice* is an expression than which few could be sillier."

axel = jump in ice-skating; **axil** = angle between a leaf-stalk and its stem; **axle** = spindle holding a wheel or wheels.

axis (pl. axes).

ay = yes; **aye** = always (both archaic). *Ayes* is the plural of *ay* ("The ayes have it").

aye-aye (Madagascan lemur).

B

-b- or **-bb-** Words ending in -*b* preceded by a single vowel double the *b* before the suffixes -*able*, -*ed*, -*er*, -*ery*, -*ing*, -*ish*, and -*y* (which begin with, or are, a vowel). E.g.:

club	clubbable, clubbed, clubbing
drab	drabber, drabbish
grab	grabbed, grabber, grabbing
knob	knobbed, knobby
snob	snobbery, snobbish
web	webbed, webbing, webby

The *b* remains single if preceded by a double vowel or a vowel followed by an *r*. E.g.:

barb	barbed
boob	boobed, booby
curb	curbed, curbing
daub	daubed, dauber, daubing

baccy = tobacco (slang); **bakkie** = pick-up truck (in South Africa).

bacillus (pl. bacilli).

backache, backbender, backbite, back-boiler, backbone, backbreaking, backchat, back-cloth, backcross, back door (noun), back-door (adj.), back-draught, backdrop, back-end, backfire, back-formation, back garden, background, backhand, back-handed, back-hander, backlash, back-list, backlog, back-number, back-pedal, backrest, back room, back-scratcher, back seat, backside, backslide, backstage, backstitch, backstroke, backtrack, backwash, backwoods (man), back yard.

back-formation is a new word created by removing a suffix or, much more rarely, a prefix from an existing one, and there are many well-established examples (mostly verbs) in English, such as

burgle (from *burglar*)	diagnose (*diagnosis*)
commentate (*commentator*)	donate (*donation*)
devolute (*devolution*)	edit (*editor*)

escalate (*escalator*) salve (*salvage*)
laze (*lazy*) scavenge (*scavenger*)
liaise (*liaison*) sidle (*sideling*)
peddle (*pedlar*) teethe (*teething*)
reminisce (*reminiscent*) televise (*television*)

Some more recent back-formations are frowned on by purists (e.g. *baby-sit, couth, enthuse, lech, locomote, negate, peeve, sculpt, self-destruct, spectate*), and these are best avoided.

back-slang = form of slang in which words are pronounced backwards or given their totally opposite meaning (e.g. *cool* = look, *yob* = boy; *bad* or *wicked* = good). *See also* **slang**.

backward can be an adjective (e.g. "a backward child") or an adverb (e.g. "move backward"), although **backwards** is the preferred form of the adverb. *See also* **-wards**.

bacterium (pl. bacteria).

baggage is a singular word, meaning suitcases and so on taken by passengers travelling by air or sea; **luggage** is also singular, used by travellers by land (car, coach or train). *Baggage* used to mean *luggage* is an Americanism. A plural can be achieved by the construction "items of luggage/baggage".

bail (noun) = money or other security lodged with a court to secure the temporary release of a prisoner before trial, or one of the crosspieces on cricket stumps; **bail** (verb) = to provide or release on bail, to remove water from a boat; **bale** (noun) = a large bundle; **bale** (verb) = to make bales, or (with *out*) to parachute from an aircraft. A person who bails water is a *bailer*; a person or a machine that makes bales is a *baler*. These are the preferred forms, although *bale* is an alternative spelling of the verb *bail* (but not vice versa). *Bale* is also an archaic word for *evil* (*see* **baleful**).

bailey = part of a castle; **bailie** (or baillie) = Scottish magistrate.

baited = supplied with a lure (e.g. "fish-hooks baited with maggots") or teased (e.g. "She continually baited him with references to his previous mistakes"); **bated** = diminished, lessened (e.g. "We waited for the announcement with bated breath").

Bahamas The derived adjective and noun is *Bahamian*.

Bahrain The derived adjective and noun is *Bahraini*.

balance, balanceable. Balance should not be used to mean *remainder* or *rest*, e.g. "I shall make the first three articles; you must make the balance" is incorrect. **Balance** (verb) = to put in equilibrium, to apportion equally; **balance** (noun) = equilibrium, scales for weighing; **unbalance** (verb) = to put out of equilibrium; **imbalance** (noun) = lack of equilibrium. *Unbalance* should be avoided as a noun, and *imbalance* should be avoided as a verb. *Unbalanced* often means mentally unstable. *Inbalance* should never be used — particularly because it could be confused with *in balance*.

balcony = railed off and elevated platform projecting from the outside wall of a building, reached by a window or French window; **gallery** = railed off and elevated platform projecting from the inside wall of a building, a long narrow room. The "layers" of seats in a theatre are called *stalls* (ground floor), *dress circle, balcony* and *gallery* (uppermost level).

bale *See* **bail**.

baleful = evil, hurtful, malignant; **baneful** = poisonous, harmful, destructive. Both words now have an old-fashioned ring to them.

balk (noun and verb) is the preferred spelling of **baulk** (except in billiards and snooker).

ballot, balloted, balloting.

balmy = mild, refreshing, soothing (e.g. "a balmy breeze"); **barmy** = frothy or mad (e.g. "a barmy mixture of yeast", "a barmy idea").

bamboo (pl. bamboos)

Bangladesh The derived adjective is *Bangladeshi*; the people (as a nation) are *Bangalees*; many of them (as an ethnic group) are *Bengalis*.

banister = a (usually wooden) upright that supports the handrail of a (usually indoor) staircase; **banisters** = the whole rail and its (wooden) supports; **baluster** = a (usually stone) upright that supports a (usually outdoor) coping or rail; **balustrade** = the whole rail and its (stone) supports.

banjo (pl. banjos)

banzai = Japanese battle-cry; **bonsai** = technique/art of growing miniaturized trees in containers.

baptize, baptism, Baptist, baptistry (not baptistery).

bar, used to mean *but* or *except*, is at best a colloquialism and should be avoided. E.g.: in "They all came bar the twins", *bar* should be *except*.

Barbados The derived adjective and noun is *Barbadian*.

barbarian = an uncivilized, rough or tasteless person. The derived adjectives **barbaric** and **barbarous** are virtually synonymous, meaning brutal, cruel, harsh, uncivilized or wild, although the latter is somewhat nastier than the former.

barbecue (not any of the many variants).

bare (verb) = to uncover, expose (e.g. "He bared his chest"); **bare** (adj.) = uncovered, naked (e.g. "He displayed his bare chest"); **bear** (verb) = suffer, endure, carry or give birth to (e.g. "She bears pain in silence"; "He bears arms for the queen"; "Most animals bear their young in spring"); **bear** (noun) = large furry mammal (e.g. "Bears are reputed to like honey"). For past tenses and participles, *see* **bear**.

barely, hardly and **scarcely** are negative terms (meaning almost not) and should not therefore be used with another negative. E.g. (with correct examples first):
"I could barely walk" (not "couldn't barely walk")
"He can hardly speak" (not "can't hardly speak")
"Scarcely anybody heard her" (not "nobody scarcely heard her")
See also **double negative.**

bar mitzvah, bat mitzvah.

barmy *See* **balmy.**

baron holds a **barony**; **baronet** holds a **baronetcy**.

barque is the preferred spelling of **bark** (a sailing vessel).

barrel, barrelled, barrelling, barrelage.

barrister = somebody who is qualified to plead at the bar in any court of law (called an **advocate** in Scotland). **Solicitor** = somebody who advises and acts for clients in legal matters, and prepares cases for barristers; he or she may represent a client in a lower court. **Lawyer** is another name for a solicitor, also called (especially in the USA) an **attorney**.

base (adj.) = of little value, inferior, sinful (as in "base metal", "base instincts"); **bass** (adj.) = low in pitch (as in "bass clef", "bass notes"); **bass** (noun) = fish, deep-voiced singer or fibrous string.

basically is often included in a sentence for no purpose (e.g. in "Basically, there are three options . . ." or "There are basically three options . . .", delete *basically*).

basinet = light metal helmet; **bassinet** = (old-fashioned) pram or cradle.

basis (pl. bases).

bass *See* **base**.

bated *See* **baited**.

bath (verb) = wash in a bath; **bathe** = moisten with liquid, wash a wound, swim (in the sea). E.g.:
"Please bath the dog."
"Please bathe the dog's injured paw."
The past tenses are spelled the same (e.g. "I bathed the dog"; "I bathed the dog's paw"), but pronounced differently.

baton – a stick, staff, truncheon; **batten** – a strip of (sawn) timber.

battalion (with two *t*s and one *l*).

battle-axe, battle-cry, battledress, battlefield, battleground, battleship.

baud = unit of speed in data transmission (equivalent to one "piece" per second); **bawd** = brothel-keeper or prostitute.

baulk *See* **balk**.

bayonet, bayoneted, bayoneting.

bay window sticks out from a wall; **bow window** is a curved bay window.

bazaar = (Eastern) market; **bizarre** = strange, odd, extravagant.

BC (abbreviation of before Christ) usually comes after the relevant date.

bear (verb, meaning "give birth to") has the past tense **bore** and past participle **born**. When **bear** = to carry, the past tense is still **bore** but the past participle is **borne**.

beat (verb) has the past tense **beat** and preferred past participle **beaten** (not *beat*).

beau (pl. beaux).

beauty, beautiful, beauteous (avoid), beautify.

because should not be misused for **that**, e.g. "The importance of science is because it broadens the mind" should be "The importance... is that it broadens the mind". Avoid beginning a sentence with *because*. See also **as; for**.

become has the past tense **became** and past participle **become**.

bedbug, bedclothes, bedcover, bedfellow, bed-jacket, bedpan, bedpost, bedridden, bedrock, bedroom, bedside, bed-sitter (-sitting-room), bedsore, bedspread, bedstead, bedtime.

bedouin (= desert-dwelling Arab) does not need an initial capital letter – neither does *bushman* (Australian) nor *nomad*, although *Bushman* (of a particular South African group) does.

bedspread (or **counterpane**) is a coverlet for a bed, placed over the blankets; **duvet** (or **continental quilt**) is covering filled with feathers, kapok or plastic foam, usually with a removable cover, used on a bed instead of blankets; **eiderdown** (or **quilt**) is a similar covering used on top of the blankets.

beef has the plural **beefs** when it means kinds of beef, cuts of meat; it has the plural **beeves** when it means cattle or oxen.

beer See **ale**.

beforehand (one word).

befriend = act as a comforter to; it does not mean "to make friends with", for which use *make friends with*.

beg, beggar.

begin has the past tense **began** and the past participle **begun**. *See also* **commence; start**.

beg the question *See* **question**.

behest is archaic for *command*, *request* (as in the cliché "at his behest"); either of the modern alternatives should be used.

behindhand, = in arrears (with), can usually be replaced by the simpler **behind** (as in "I am behindhand with my work").

behove is archaic for *to be fit* or *proper for* (used impersonally with *it*: e.g. "It behoves me to pass judgement in this matter"); the alternative spelling **behoove** is now an Americanism; **behoof** is archaic for *behalf* or *benefit*. All three words should be avoided.

beige (not *biege*).

Belgium The derived adjective and noun is *Belgian*.

belief *in* something, not belief *of*.

believe, believable. *See also* **make-believe**.

bellicose = warlike, liable to wage war; **belligerent** = waging war. E.g.:
"The new republic was worried by its neighbour's bellicose attitude."
"The neighbouring country continued its belligerent action with daily air raids on the capital."

bellows (noun) is a plural word; "a pair of bellows" achieves a singular construction.

below *See* **above; beneath**.

bend (verb) inflects *bend – bent – bent*.

beneath = lower than; it should not be misused for **under** (as in "Miners work beneath the ground", which is incorrect).

benefactor (not *beni-*).

benefit, benefited, benefiting.

benzene = liquid hydrocarbon (a single substance, which is the basis of aromatic organic chemistry); **benzine** = mixture of petroleum hydrocarbons (used as a general solvent), and containing no benzene; **benzoin** = natural hard resin from various south-east Asian trees.

bequeath, bequeather (= testator), bequest.

bereave is a little-used verb meaning to deprive, cause to be orphaned or widowed; its preferred past tense and participle is **bereaved**, although *bereft* is retained as an adjective (as in the cliché "bereft of beauty"). It should be remembered, however, that someone can become bereft only of something he or she once possessed; the woman of the cliché is bereft of beauty only if she was once beautiful (if she was never beautiful she is merely *plain* or perhaps even *ugly*).

beseech is archaic for **entreat** (which also now sounds old-fashioned) and precious for **ask**; the simple **beg** usually serves instead. If *beseech* must be used, the old past tense and participle *besought* is probably more in keeping than the more modern form *beseeched*.

beside = at the side of; **besides** = as well, in addition to (but not *other than*). Both words are used incorrectly in these examples:
"There were two girls beside the twenty men there" (in which *besides* = *in addition to* is intended);
"The reaction must have been caused by something besides an acid" (in which *other than* is intended). *See also* **by**.

best known etc. is hyphenated when it precedes a noun (e.g. "best-known designer", "best-loved hymn") but unhyphenated when following a verb (e.g. "design for which she is best known").

bet (verb) has the preferred past tense and participle **bet** (not *betted*).

bête noire (italics) = pet aversion, bugbear; either of the English forms is preferred to the French expression.

bethink (past tense and participle **bethought**) is archaic for to reflect or remind (oneself), and should be avoided.

better is the comparative of **good** (of which the superlative is **best**) and so requires *than* and both the things/persons being compared; e.g. "Evergreen trees provide better protection" – better than what? Note also **better** = person who bets (not *bettor*), often called a *punter*.

between applies strictly to only two persons or things, and they should be linked by *and*. E.g.:

"Between 20 and 30 people came" is correct;
"Between 20 to 30 people came" is incorrect;
"The guests included between 20–30 men" is incorrect.
For more than two alternatives, **among** is preferred. E.g.:
"He shared the wine among all the guests, but divided the cheese between only two of them."
According to some authorities, *between* can be used to express the relation of one thing to many surrounding ones individually; *among* expresses a relationship to them collectively and vaguely. E.g.:
"The area between the three trees."
"A giant among men."
See also **among; in between**.

betwixt is archaic for **between**, which should be used. The tautologous **betwixt and between** should not be used.

bevel, bevelled, bevelling.

beverage can nearly always be replaced by **drink**, which is preferred.

Bhutan The derived adjective and noun is *Bhutanese*.

bi-, as a prefix, takes a hyphen only as an aid to reading and pronunciation (*bi-iliac* is the usually quoted example). Before a vowel, it may become *bin-* (e.g. binaural, binocular). For *bi* or *di* as prefixes meaning *two*, *see* **numerical prefixes**.

biannual = half-yearly; **biennial** = two-yearly. *Half-yearly* (or *twice a year*) and *two-yearly* (or *every two years*) should be used to prevent possible confusion.

bias, biased, biasing (preferred to biassed, baiassing).

Bible (capitalized) when referring to the Old Testament or New Testament, but **biblical** (uncapitalized).

biblical citations should take the form of book, chapter and verses (inclusive); e.g. "Genesis 3:4–8" (Book of Genesis, Chapter 3, verses 4 to 8 inclusive). The preferred style for numbered books is I Kings, II Kings.

bicentenary = 200th anniversary; **bicentennial** = to do with (every) 200 years; **centenary** = 100th anniversary; **centennial** = to do with (every) 100 years. *Centennial* (as a noun) is an Americanism for *centenary*.

biceps is a singular word; both the Latin plural *bicipites* and the "English" *bicepses* would confound many readers – perhaps "two (or several) biceps muscles" achieves a more acceptable plural construction. The same comment can be made about **triceps**.

bid (verb) has the preferred past tense and participle **bid** (not *bad, bade* or *bidden*).

bight = wide bay, bend in a rope; **bite** (noun) = wound made by teeth, a piece bitten off.

bigot, bigoted.

bijou (pl. bijoux) = a trinket, "toy"; the French term should be avoided.

bike is slang (or at least colloquial) for **bicycle**, and should be avoided.

bill *See* **act**.

billet, billeted, billeting.

billiards is a singular word; "games of billiards" achieves a plural construction.

billion = 1,000 million in the United States (a number formerly known as a *milliard* in Britain); originally a billion = 1 million million in Britain, but is increasingly being used in the American sense. Therefore, to prevent possible ambiguity, use "thousand million" or "million million". Scientific texts may use 10^9 and 10^{12}. *See also* **trillion**.

bin- *See* **bi-**.

bind has the past tense and participle **bound** (not *binded*); *bounden* is retained as an archaic adjective (as in the cliché "bounden duty").

binoculars (noun), like *spectacles*, is a singular word. *Binocular* is the adjective (= two-eyed), as in "binocular vision".

biological nomenclature *See* **Latin classification**.

birdbath, birdcage, bird-lime, birdseed, bird's-eye view, bird's-foot (trefoil), bird-song, bird-table.

Biro (= ball pen) is a trade name and should have an initial capital letter; note *ball pen* (which avoids the trade name) is preferred to *ball-point pen*. *See also* **trade names**.

birth control, birth date, birthday, birthmark, birthplace, birth rate.

birth date = date on which somebody was born (date of birth); **birthday** = anniversary of somebody's birth.

bisect *See* **dissect**.

bison (pl. bison) = species of European or North African ox (the European animal is also called **wisent**); **buffalo** (pl. buffaloes) = species of ox found in southern Africa (− Cape buffalo) or Asia (= water buffalo). The use of *buffalo* for the North American bison is an Americanism, and should be avoided except in historical contexts (e.g. "An American buffalo hunter").

bit = abbreviation of binary digit, one of the two characters (0 or 1) in the binary notation used by digital computers. A group (of usually eight) bits is a **byte** (which *see*).

bite (verb) has the past tense **bit** and preferred past participle **bitten** (not *bit*) − except in the cliché "the biter bit". *See also* **bight**.

bitter *See* **ale**.

bivouac, bivouacked, bivouacking, bivouacker.

bizarre *See* **bazaar**.

black (no capital letter) is the preferred term for dark-skinned people from, or originally from, Africa, the United States or the West Indies. The term Coloured (with a capital letter) should be reserved for South

African people of mixed ancestry. The word Negro and its derivatives should be avoided. *See also* **native**.

black-and-blue, black-and-tan (and Black-and-Tan(s)), black-and-white, black art, blackball, black belt, blackberry, blackbird, blackboard, black box, blackcap (bird), black cap (judge's headgear), black-coated, black comedy, Black Country, blackcurrant, Black Death (plague), black eye, Blackfoot, blackguard, black-hearted, black humour, blackjack, blacklead, blackleg, blacklist (verb), blackmail(er), Black Maria, black market(eer), black mass, blackout (noun), black powder, black pudding, Black Rod, black sheep, Blackshirt, blacksmith, black spot, blackthorn, black velvet, Black Watch, blackwater fever, black widow.

blame, blameable. Blame somebody *for* something, not blame something *on* somebody; *put the blame on* somebody is, however, correct.

blanch = to make or become white; **blench** = to shrink from, flinch. The words are only coincidentally interchangeable (e.g. when given a fright, someone might blanch *or* blench − or both). A valid alternative to *blench* is *bleach*, although this word should be used only of objects, not people; the usual gardening and culinary term is *blanch*.

blancmange (note spelling).

blanket, blanketed, blanketing.

blasé (acute accent).

blatant = falsely noisy or showy, obviously contrived (for effect); **flagrant** = outrageous, shockingly objectionable. The words are close in meaning. E.g.:
"I saw him in the restaurant yet he said he stayed at home all day because he was ill; he told me a blatant lie."
"She deliberately lit a cigarette although she knew that smoking is forbidden in the works kitchen; it was a flagrant breach of regulations."

bleach See **blanch**.

bleed inflects *bleed — bled — bled*.

blench *See* **blanch**.

blend with (not blend *into*).

blessed is the preferred past tense and participle of the verb *bless* (not **blest**).

blitz (noun and verb) is now accepted English (German *Blitzkrieg* = lightning war).

bloc = a group of people or nations; **block** = a (usually cuboidal) piece of solid material, etc.

blond (masc.) and **blonde** (fem.) retain their genders in English.

blood bank, blood-bath, blood-brother, blood cell, blood count, blood-curdling, blood donor, blood feud, blood group, bloodhound, blood-letting, blood-lust, blood orange, blood-poisoning, blood pressure, bloodshed, bloodshot, blood sports, bloodstain, bloodstock, bloodstream, bloodsucker, blood supply, blood test, bloodthirsty, blood transfusion, blood vessel.

bloom = an individual flower, especially on a plant grown for its flowers; **blossom** = a collection of flowers, especially ones that will lead to fruit (roses are blooms, apple trees bear blossom).

blow (verb) has the past tense **blew** and past participle **blown**.

blue, blueing, bluish, blueprint.

blurb = publisher's and advertiser's term for a short description of a book, usually on its jacket (originally American slang, but not now condemned by the *OED*).

bn is an abbreviation of billion (which *see*).

boat = any small vessel, or a ferry or other passenger-carrying vessel that sails in shallow or sheltered water (or, in the navy, a submarine); other, larger, vessels are called **ships**. The distinction is preserved in various compound words, e.g. ferryboat, fishing-boat, lifeboat and rowing-boat, but depot ship, lightship, steamship, warship.

boat-builder, boat-deck, boat-hook, boathouse, boatman, boat people, boatrace, boat-racing, boat-train.

boatswain is a perfectly good spelling, although the alternatives *bosun* or *bo'sun* better reflect the pronunciation.

bodge *See* **botch**.

bogey = designated number of golf strokes for a hole or course; **bogie** = wheeled undercarriages; **bogy** = goblin; **bougie** = candle, surgical instrument.

bole = tree trunk; **bowl** = basin, deep dish or wooden ball.

bona fide(s) = in good faith, genuine(ness); the Latin term should be avoided. If the noun form must be used, it is singular. E.g.:
"Her bona fides is without doubt."

bonhomie (italics) = pleasant (good) nature; the French term should be avoided.

bon mot(s) (italics) = "clever" saying, witticism; the French term should be avoided.

bonnet, bonneted, bonneting.

bonus (pl. bonuses).

book-binder, bookcase, book club, book-end, bookie, bookkeeper, booklet, booklouse(-lice), bookmaker, bookmark, bookseller, bookshelf, bookshop, bookstall, book-token, bookworm.

booklet = small book with the pages fixed in the binding (often saddle-stitched, with wire staples like a slim magazine, rather than sewn); **leaflet** = a single (unstitched) leaf or page of printed matter, possibly folded; **pamphlet** = small book with the pages stitched but not bound (i.e. with no separate cover); **brochure** = slightly "posh" name for a pamphlet or leaflet (usually advertising) promoting a product or service).

born = brought into life; **borne** = carried, or given birth to (past tense and participle of *to bear*). E.g.:
"He was born in a caravan at the seaside."
"The cup was borne aloft by the winning captain."
"My dog has borne three litters of puppies."

born *in* is preferred to **born** *at* (in biographical text).

borrow = have temporary use of an object or money (the object is *borrowed* or *on loan*, the money is a *loan*); **lend** = to make an object or money temporarily available to someone else (the object/money is *lent*). If A borrows from B, B lends to A. *Borrow* and *lend* are verbs; *loan* is a noun.

Börse = West German Stock Exchange.

bortsch is the preferred spelling of **borsch** (Russian beetroot soup).

bosom is an archaic euphemism for **breast**, which is preferred.

botch (= make or repair badly) is preferred to **bodge**.

both should not be misused for **each**; e.g. "There is a large building on both sides of the street" is incorrect for "... on each side of the street" (unless it is a building with a street through the middle of it).

bouillon *See* **bullion**.

bounce, bouncy, bounceable.

bourgeois, bourgeoisie.

bourrée (acute accent).

Bourse = French Stock Exchange.

boutique (not italics).

bowdlerism *See* **non-standard English**.

bowl *See* **hole**.

bowls (the game) is a singular word; "games of bowls" achieves a plural construction.

bow window *See* **bay window**.

boycott, boycotted, boycotting.

b.p. is the abbreviation of boiling point.

bra is now an accepted short form of brassière.

bracket = structure for supporting or holding (up); **brackets** = square brackets []; round brackets ( ) are properly called **parentheses; braces** are { }. For use of parentheses, *see* **punctuation** (parentheses).

brain-child, brain drain, brainpower, brainstorm(ing), brain-teaser, brains trust, brain-wash(ing), brainwave.

braise = to cook (using steam, in a closed pan); **braze** = to join metal using heat and a high-melting solder; **brazier** = someone who brazes, a worker in brass, a container for hot coals.

brand names *See* **capitalization; trade names**.

brand-new (with hyphen; not *bran-new*).

brasier The preferred spelling is **brazier**.

brassière (not italics).

bravado = behaviour that is boastful, ostentatiously bold or seemingly courageous; **bravery** = genuine courage (in adversity), heroism; **bravura** = brilliant but showy performance. E.g.:
"His offer to climb the tall tree was an act of bravado he soon regretted."
"She was awarded a medal for her bravery in rescuing a drowning child."
"The juggler ended his act with a bravura sequence using flaming torches."

bravo The *OED* prefers **bravoes** as the plural in the rare use of the word to mean "hired ruffian, desperado" but **bravos** when it is a cry of approval. It is simpler, and no less correct, to use **bravos** for both (incidentally, the plural of *desperado* is *desperados*).

breach = breaking of a rule etc., a split, a gap in fortifications; **breech** = rear end of a gun barrel (as in breech-birth); **breeches** = knee-length trousers.

breadth = width; **broad** = wide, coarse or dialectal (e.g. a broad river or a broad accent); **broadness** = coarseness (not *breadth*).

break (verb) has the past tense **broke** and part participle **broken**. The related adjective is *broken* (not *broke*). *See also* **brake**.

breath is the noun; **breathe** is the verb.

breathalyse, breathalyser (with an *s*).

breech/breeches *See* **breach**.

breed (verb) inflects *breed – bred – bred*.

brethren is archaic for **brothers**, except in certain religious contexts, and should be avoided.

briar The preferred spelling is **brier**.

bribe, bribable, bribery.

bric-à-brac (with hyphens, grave accent).

brief = lasting a short time, concise (of a speech etc.); **short** = of little duration (=brief), but also = of little length (opposite of long); e.g. "a brief interlude", "a short article" and "a short stick".

briefs *See* **knickers**.

brier is the preferred spelling of **briar**.

bring inflects *bring – brought – brought*. See also **fetch**.

bring to a conclusion = **conclude**, which should be used.

brioche = small round cake; *broche* = piece of meat; **brochette** = small piece of meat or the skewer it is cooked on. Only the second term retains enough Frenchness to still require italicization.

Britannia, Britannica (not *Britania, Britanica*).

British = to do with Britain, i.e. Great Britain, i.e. The United Kingdom of Great Britain and Northern Ireland (as opposed to French, American, Irish, etc.); or = to do with the British Isles (the United Kingdom and the Republic of Ireland). *British* should not be used when English (or Welsh or Scottish) is more accurate or intended. A derived noun is **Briticism** (or Britishness), the name given in North America to imported English words (the converse of an *Americanism*).

broach (verb) = to pierce, break into, introduce; **broach** (noun) = a tapering tool; **brooch** = ornamental pin (originally for fastening clothes).

broad etc. The adjectives broad, deep, high, long and wide form the nouns *breadth*, *depth*, *length* and *width*; only *height* does not have the *-th* ending.

broadcast (verb) has the past tense and participle **broadcast** (not *broadcasted*).

broccoli (note spelling).

brochure *See* **booklet**.

bronchus (pl. bronchi).

bronco (pl. broncos).

Bronze Age (initial capital letters).

brooch *See* **broach**.

brother-in-law *See* **in-laws**.

browse = to read desultorily, to feed on leafy vegetation. *See also* **peruse; scan**.

brunch *See* **lunch**.

budget, budgeted, budgeting.

buffalo (pl. buffaloes). *See also* **bison**.

buffet (verb) buffeted, buffeting.

bug = mistake or malfunction in a computer program. The removal of such errors is termed debugging. *See also* **insect**.

build inflects *build* – *built* – *built*.

bulk refers to volume or mass; it should not be misused for **most** (which refers to numbers).

bull *See* **cattle**.

bullion = bulk precious metal (gold, silver), often cast in the form of ingots; **bouillon** = meat broth, soup.

bullock *See* **cattle**.

bulrush (not *bullrush*).

bumptious (note spelling).

buoy, buoyage, buoyant, buoyancy.

bur = prickly seed-head that sticks to fur or clothing; **burr** = rough edge left on metal after cutting, a dental drill; **burin** - engravers tool.

bureau (pl. bureaux), bureaucracy, bureaucrat(ic)

bureaucratic English, or officialese, = convoluted, verbose and often unhelpful language used by some civil servants and other bureaucrats; it is one of the worst kinds of **jargon** (which *see*).

burger = abbreviation of hamburger; **burgher** = foreign townsman. *Burger* is given by the *OED* as colloquial and of mainly American usage; it is currently fully entrenched in English and looks as if it is here to stay − but so have many other now defunct words.

burgh is the usual Scottish term for **borough**.

Burma The derived adjective and noun is *Burmese*.

burn Preferred past tense and participle is **burned** (not burnt), although *burnt* is retained as an adjective (e.g. "burnt offering").

burst *See* **bust**.

bus (pl. buses), bused, busing. *Bussed, bussing* = kissed, kissing (archaic) in English; in North America *bussing* describes the compulsory transport of black and white children to give a better racial balance in schools.

bushman *See* **bedouin**.

business = commercial or industrial undertaking, trade or profession; **busyness** = state of being busy (a spelling introduced to distinguish between the two words).

bust used as a verb (with the past tense and participle *bust* or *busted*) is an Americanism, retained in British English only in such expressions as *bust-up*. The correct English verb is **burst**, which inflects *burst − burst − burst*.

butte (two *t*s, despite the pronunciation which rhymes with *flute*).

buy inflects *buy – bought – bought*.

buzz-word *See* **vogue words**.

by *See* × (multiplication sign); **with and by**.

by-election (preferred to bye-election), bygone(s), by-lane, by-law (preferred to bye-law), byline, byname, bypass, by-play, by-product, by-road, bystander, byway, byword.

by and large *See* **all in all**.

bye (noun) = secondary issue, extra (e.g. at cricket). The preferred form of the phrase meaning "in passing" is *bye the bye* (not by the by) although the apparent anomaly can be avoided by using *by the way*. Note also *goodbye* and its colloquial abbreviation *bye-bye*.

byte (in computers) = eight bits (a *bit* is one binary digit).

C

c. (italic) is the abbreviation of *circa* (= about), and is preferred to *ca*.

°C = degrees Celsius (formerly centigrade). *See* **Celsius**.

-c to -ck- Words ending in *-c* usually have an added *k* before a suffix beginning with a vowel (or a *y*), to preserve the hard sound of the *c*. E.g.:

colic	colicky
frolic	frolicked, frolicking (but frolicsome)
garlic	garlicky
mimic	mimicked, mimicking
panic	panicked, panicking, panicky
picnic	picnicked, picnicker, picnicking
traffic	trafficked, trafficker, trafficking

cabriole = curved ("Queen Anne") furniture leg; **cabriolet** = carriage or motor car with a folding hood.

cacao = tropical American seed-bearing tree; **cocoa** = extract from seeds of cacao tree used to make the drink cocoa and to make chocolate; **coca** = South American shrub whose leaves contain a stimulant; **coco** = palm tree that bears coconuts.

cache is now used to mean any hiding place, not merely an underground one (for provisions).

cachet = distinguishing mark; **cachou** = scented sweet (to perfume the breath); **cashew** = tropical tree or its nut..

cactus (pl. cacti).

caddie = someone who carries someone else's golf clubs; **caddy** = container for tea.

Caesarean (section), in surgery, not *Caesarian*.

café (acute accent).

caffeine (note *-ei-* spelling).

caftan is the preferred spelling (not *kaftan*).

cage, caged, caging, cagey, cagily, cageyness (preferred to caginess).

calamine = naturally occurring zinc oxide, used in a lotion for treating minor burns; **camomile** (preferred to *chamomile*) = a flowering plant of the daisy family.

calculate, calculator, calculable (and incalculable, not -*atable).*

calculus = a "stone" in the body (pl. calculi) such as a kidney stone, or a system of mathematics (pl. calculuses).

calendar = chart or book of dates; **calender** = to make smooth; **colander** (preferred to *cullender*) = perforated vessel for straining food. A machine that calenders is also a *calender*; a person who calenders is a *calenderer*. (A *calender* is also a Persian or Turkish dervish.)

calf (pl. calves).

calibre = diameter of a bullet or shell, internal diameter of a tube (such as a gun barrel), status or importance (of a person). *See also* **calliper**.

calico (note spelling).

caliph is the preferred spelling (not *calif, kalik, khalif*).

calligraphy is pretentious for **handwriting** (and incorrect unless the writing is artistically beautiful).

calliper (preferred to caliper) = a metal leg splint which enables a disabled person to walk, or a technical term in papermaking for the thickness of paper or board (plural callipers), usually expressed in microns or millimetres. **Callipers**, = compasses for measuring internal or external dimensions, is a plural word; "a pair of callipers" achieves a singular construction.

callus (pl. calluses) = patch of hard skin, corn; **callous** is the corresponding adjective, with the additional figurative meaning of unfeeling, unsympathetic, hard (in attitude), cruel.

Calvary = site of Christ's crucifixion; **cavalry** = troops mounted on horses.

calyx (pl. calyces) is the preferred spelling (not *calix*).

camel There are two kinds: the one-humped *Arabian* camel (from northern Africa) and the two-humped *Bactrian* camel (from central Asia). A **dromedary** is a kind of Arabian camel, originally bred for racing and riding.

camellia (although pronounced to rhyme with *steelier*).

cameo (pl. cameos) = precious stone or shell carved in relief; **intaglio** (pl. intaglios) = design carved in relief in any material (and a method of printing).

camomile *See* **calamine**.

can implies an ability to do something; **may** implies permission to do something or reflects doubt (= **might**). E.g.:
"The boy can ride a bicycle" (has the ability to).
"May the boy ride his bicycle to school?" (has he permission to?).
"They may get to school early" (there is a possibility that).

canal, canalize, canalization.

canapé = toast or pastry case with a savoury filling; **canopy** = "roof" projecting, supported or suspended over a throne etc., or an aircraft cockpit cover.

cancel, cancelled, canceller, cancelling, cancellation.

candelabra, although originally a plural word, has the plural candelabras. **Candelabra** = branched candlestick; **chandelier** = branched pendant light.

cannibal, cannibalize, cannibalization.

canoe, canoeing, canoeist.

canon = churchman; **cañon** = ravine; **cannon** = gun, shot at billiards; **canyon** = ravine (preferred to cañon).

cant = jargon, often applied to that spoken by criminals. *See* **jargon**; **non-standard English**.

can't should not be used for cannot in formal writing.

canto (pl. cantos).

canvas = strong, coarse cloth; **canvass** = to solicit support (for).

canyon *See* **canon**.

capable *See* **able**.

capacity *See* **ability**.

capers, like *chives*, was originally a singular word (e.g. "Chives is a plant of the onion family"), although some dictionaries now list *caper* and *chive* as singulars. **Pease** (pl. peason) was once similar and gave rise to *pea* as another singular form, which has to be given the plural *peas*; the old singular survives in various compounds, such as pease-blossom and pease-pudding. *See also* **lens**.

capitalization Unnecessary capitalization should be avoided, and if in doubt do not capitalize.

1. *The state, government, politics:*
The rules are best illustrated by examples: the state, state control; Parliament; the Government (a specific one, but no capital when used adjectivally; e.g. government control); the House of Commons; the Labour Party; the Conservative Party (etc.); Prime Minister or President when followed by the name of the office holder − prime minister, president when referring to the office or constitution; Communist Party (but communism).

2. *Gods, religions:*
Again, examples:
God, but he, his, him of God or Jesus ("pagan gods"); (The) Bible, but biblical; hell; Devil of The Bible; Roman Catholic (but catholic taste); Buddhism; Christianity; Protestant(ism); Puritan (but puritan morals); the established Church (but "an old stone church").

3. *Titles and ranks:*
Capitalize titles and ranks when followed by a proper name; e.g. Field Marshal Lord Alexander, Pope John, President Carter, Prince Charles, Queen Victoria. Also capitalize titles when they stand for the office holder's name; e.g. the Pope, the President, the King of France (but kings and queens in the general sense, the king, several American

presidents, Roman Catholic popes), Professor of Chemistry, the Minister of Health. Spell out all ranks the first time they are used. Thereafter continue to use them in full, except for those with an abbreviation here:

Navy: Able Seaman (AB), Petty Officer (PO), Chief Petty Officer (CPO), Sub-Lieutenant, Lieutenant-Commander, Commander, Captain.

Army: Private, Lance-Corporal (L/Cpl), Corporal, Sergeant, Warrant-Officer (WOI and WOII; note that CSM and RSM are appointments, not ranks), Second-Lieutenant, Lieutenant, Captain, Major, Lieutenant-Colonel, Colonel, Brigadier, Major-General (pl. Majors-General), Lieutenant-General, General, Field Marshal.

Air Force: Aircraftman (note no "s"), (AC2, AC1, LAC, SAC), Corporal, Sergeant, Flight Sergeant, Warrant-Officer (WO), Pilot Officer, Flying Officer, Flight Lieutenant, Squadron Leader, Wing Commander, Group Captain, Air Commodore, Air Vice-Marshal, Air Marshal.

4. *Proper names:*

William Shakespeare, the Bard of Avon; the Mother of Parliaments; Father, Mother, etc. when used in speech as a form of address. The particles de, de la, du, des, van, von, etc. are generally lower case except at the beginning of a sentence. There are, however, some exceptions; e.g. Charles de Gaulle but De Gaulle, Thomas De Quincey and De Quincey.

"Dutch" names, where appropriate, appear as Van unless preceded by a Christian first name or initial; e.g. Vincent van Gogh but Van Gogh. Some North Americans with Van use a capital "V".

5. *Geographical areas:*

Do not capitalize points of the compass except as an abbreviation; the north of England, south-eastern England (not southeastern or southeast), in a north-westerly direction (not northwesterly), in the east of the county (but Western civilization, the wisdom of the East). *See* **compass directions**. Note also the following examples:

the Continent	South-East Asia (political)
the Lake District	South India
the Netherlands (not Holland)	the Soviet Union (not Russia)
North America	the United States (not America)

Northern Ireland	the West Country
North India	Western Australia
the Orient; the Occident	West Germany
South America	the West Indies

Western, Eastern, Central or Northern Europe when discussed as a
political/social/cultural entity — but uncapitalized when used as an
ordinary adjective.

6. *Trade names:*
Trade names should always be capitalized; although some have
become generic terms and may, with care, be used uncapitalized (e.g.
nylon, polythene). *See* **trade names**. *See also* **aircraft names; car
names; locomotive and train names; ships' names; space rockets and
missiles**.

7. *Adjectives and nouns derived from proper names:*
Capitals should be used for adjectives derived from proper names; e.g.
Victorian, French, Junoesque. But where the connection has become
remote, use lower case:

alpine	roman (type)
chelsea bun	venetian blind
china clay	victoria (a carriage)
french window	wellington boots

In adjectives with prefixes, the prefix is generally uncapitalized; e.g.
anti-Hitlerian, pre-Columbian (but note Pre-Raphaelite Brotherhood),
trans-Atlantic, mid-Atlantic (but the American Mid-West). *See also*
named effects and laws.

8. *Eras in history and historical events:*
Note the following examples:

the Boston Tea Party	the Ottoman Empire
the British Empire	the Renaissance
Byzantine	the Roman Empire
Carboniferous	the Seven Years War
Classical	the South Sea Bubble
the Dark Ages	the Wars of the Roses
the Middle Ages	World War I (not First World War)
early Minoan	World War II

9. *Other points of capitalization:*
Few major periodicals have the definite article as part of their titles, except *The Times, The Economist, The Bookseller, The Listener*. Planets, stars, constellations and so on are capitalized (*see* **astronomical terms**). In named effects and laws, capitalize the person but not the law; e.g. Newton's law, Pascal's principle (*see* **named effects and laws**).
Taxonomic groupings except species, race and variety are capitalized (*see* **Latin classification**).
Names of chemical elements are uncapitalized, e.g. arsenic, zinc.

capo (pl. capos).

capsize (not *-ise*).

carafe (note spelling).

carat = measure of purity of gold (24-carat is pure gold, 9-carat is therefore 9/24 gold and 15/24 another metal, such as copper) or weight of gemstones (1 carat = 0.2 grams); **caret** = editor's and proofreader's mark that indicates the position of an omission in text (the mark ˆ); **carrot** = a vegetable.

carburettor (note spelling).

carcass is the preferred spelling (not *carcase*).

care about = be concerned or worried about; **care for** = look after, take care of, like; **care to** = want to, like to. E.g.:
"She cares about the quality of her work."
"She cares for her invalid mother at home."
"She seldom cares to go out in the evening."

careen = turn on one side (as a ship's hull for cleaning or repair); **career** (verb) = move rapidly/recklessly.

carefree = without a care, unworried; **careless** = without taking care, unheeding, sloppy. E.g.:
"Her work was good, despite her carefree attitude to it."
"Her work was poor because of her careless approach to it."

caretaker = someone who looks after (empty) premises such as a school or offices; **care-taker** = anyone who looks after and raises a child (originally a sociological term). The hyphen is necessary in the latter (new) word to distinguish it from the former. Such a care-taker may be a parent, guardian, permanent child-minder and so on.

cargo (pl. cargos)

caribou (pl. caribous) = North American name for the reindeer (*Rangifer tarandus*).

Carib words that have become part of English are included in the examples under **Americanisms**. Note the spelling **Caribbean** (not *Carribean*).

caries, the medical term for *decay*, is a singular word (e.g. "Dental caries is the most common disorder in the Western world"); "cases of caries" achieves a plural construction (e.g. "Cases of caries are increasingly common in children under five"), although "Caries is increasingly common..." would serve as well). The adjective is **carious** (not *carous*).

car names should be given initial capital letters (and typeset in roman face); e.g. a Ford Escort, Volkswagen Golf. Names of individual cars should be italicized; e.g. *Bluebird*.

carousal = (noisy) drinking bout; **carousel** = merry-go-round, rotary conveyor (the pronunciations are ca-row-sal and carra-sel).

carpal = to do with the wrist; **carpel** = leafy part of a flower.

carte blanche (italics) = a free hand, full discretion; the French term should be avoided.

carton = (thin) cardboard box; **cartoon** = drawing (usually humorous).

cask = small barrel; **casque** = helmet.

cashew *See* **cachet**.

casino (pl. casinos).

cassock = long garment worn by clergy or choristers; **hassock** = small stool or cushion for kneeling on in church.

caster = someone who casts, a casting machine; **castor** = oil-bearing plant, small wheel, beaver, sugar sprinkler (although fine sugar is usually known as *caster* sugar).

casual = informal, off-hand; **causal** = that causes, being the cause.

catabolism is the preferred spelling (not *katabolism*).

catacomb = underground burial place (often in plural as *catacombs*); **catafalque** = platform for displaying a body (while it is lying in state); **cenotaph** = memorial to the dead (but not a tomb).

cataclasm = violent break, disruption; **cataclysm** = deluge, violent upheaval.

catalysis, catalyse, catalyst.

catarrh (note spelling).

catastrophe = disaster of great magnitude; it should not be used of events that are merely *serious* or *severe*.

catch (verb) inflects *catch – caught – caught*.

Catholic should not be used when Roman Catholic is intended, particularly at the first mention; catholic (with no initial capital letter) = wide-ranging, universal (e.g. "a person with catholic tastes in music").

cat-o'-nine-tails (note hyphens and apostrophe).

catsup The preferred spelling is **ketchup**.

cattle is plural (e.g. "The cattle are lowing"); "a herd of cattle" achieves a singular construction. The sexes have various names, depending on age and fertility. A male is called a *bull* if it is uncastrated (and used for stud), or a *bullock* or *steer* if castrated (and used for meat). A female is a *cow* if she has had a calf, or a *heifer* if she has not. The young of either sex, under 12 months old, is a *calf*. An *ox* (pl. *oxen*) is – or was – a castrated male used as a draught animal.

caucus (p. caucuses).

cause = the (non-human) factor responsible for an event or outcome;

reason = (human) justification of an action or belief, a distinction that is not always preserved. E.g.

"Heavy rain was the cause of the landslide."
"Her wish to see her mother was the reason she went."

cauterize, cautery (an instrument or chemical that cauterizes), cauterization.

cavalry *See* **Calvary.**

cavil, cavilled, cavilling, caviller.

cayman (pl. caymans)

cc is the abbreviation of cubic centimetre, which for ordinary liquids is equivalent to a millilitre (ml).

-ce and **-cy** are noun endings which generally are not interchangeable. E.g.:

agent	agency	diligent	diligence
avoid	avoidance	ignorant	ignorance
belligerent	belligerence	intelligent	intelligence
clement	clemency	latent	latency
decent	decency	magnificent	magnificence
different	difference	vacant	vacancy

For a few words, both the *-ce* and *-cy* forms exist and have the same meaning:

consist	consistence, consistency
inconsistent	inconsistence, inconsistency
irrelevant	irrelevance, irrelevancy
resilient	resilience, resiliency
valent	valence, valency

For yet others, the two forms have different meanings:

depend	dependence (= be dependent on in general)
	dependency (= a country that is dependent on another)
emerge	emergence (= a coming out)
	emergency (= unexpected happening)

excellent   excellence (= state of being excellent)
                excellency (= diplomatic title)

-ce or **-se** In words that can have either ending, the noun forms generally end in *-ce* and the verbs end in *-se*:

nouns	verbs
advice	advise
device	devise
licence	license
practice	practise

cede, ceder (who cedes); the tree is a **cedar**.

-cede is the usual verb ending (e.g. concede, intercede, recede) except in *exceed*, *proceed* and *succeed*, and the often misspelled *supersede*.

cedilla = an accent which, in French, softens the sound of *c* before the vowels *a, o* and *u*, as in *garçon*. In Turkish, it converts a sibilant *s* to the sound *sh*, as in *Gelişm*.

-ceed *See* **-cede.**

celebrate, celebrator, celebrant (who celebrates, say, mass), celebrity (who is celebrated).

celibate = unmarried (usually applied to men); **chaste** = abstaining from sexual intercourse, although not necessarily virgin (usually applied to women).

cello (pl. cellos), cellist.

Celsius temperatures (abbreviation °C) should now generally be used in "scientific" texts, rather than centigrade temperatures (which are numerically identical).

Celtic words have contributed to the English language, mainly by way of Gaelic, Irish, Scottish and Welsh − in addition to a huge influence and borrowings from French (*see* **French words**). The following examples form an interesting list:

banshee (female fairy)	Irish *bean sidhe*
bard (poet)	Gaelic *bàrd*
bog (marsh)	Gaelic *bogach*

brogue (shoe)	Gaelic *brog*
cairn (pile of stones)	Gaelic *càrn*
ceilidh (folksong/dance meeting)	Gaelic
colleen (girl)	Irish *cailín*
coracle (boat)	Gaelic *curach*
corgi (dog)	Welsh *cor ci*
corrie (hollow)	Gaelic *coire*
cromlech (stone circle)	Welsh *crom llech*
dolmen (tomb)	Cornish *tolmen*
drumlin (long mound)	Gaelic *druim*
flummery (trifle(s))	Welsh *llymru*
galore (abundance)	Irish *go léor*
glen (valley)	Gaelic *gleann*
leprechaun (little imp)	Irish *luchorpán*
loch (lake)	Gaelic *loch* (Irish) *lough*
menhir (standing stone)	Breton *men hir*
pikelet (cake)	Welsh *bara pyglyd*
plaid (cloth)	Gaelic *plaide*
poteen (illicit whiskey)	Irish *poitín*
shamrock (plant)	Irish *seamróg*
shillelagh (club)	Irish (place-name)
slob (stupid person)	Irish *slab*
slogan (catch word)	Gaelic *sluagh gairm*
Tory (now Conservative)	Irish *tóraighe*
trousers (garment)	Gaelic *triubhas*
whisky (drink)	Gaelic *uisge beatha*

cement = binding agent consisting of an anhydrous powder that sets solid after the incorporation of water (and by extension any adhesive); **concrete** = rock-like solid made from a mixture of sand, gravel (aggregate) and cement; **mortar** = substance used to bind together bricks or masonry, made from sand and cement (or, formerly, sand and lime). Cement is not a synonym of concrete or mortar.

cenotaph *See* **catacomb.**

censer = incense vessel; **censor** = official who can suppress part (or whole) of a letter, film, play, book, etc.; **censure** = to condemn, blame.

centenary/centennial *See* **bicentenary**.

centi- is the metric prefix for a hundredth ($\times 10^2$), as in *centimetre*.

centigrade *See* **Celsius**.

central, centralize, centralization.

centre of a circle; **middle** of a line. Middle is less precise and can apply
to time; e.g. "middle of the field" is vaguer than "centre of the field",
"middle of the week" cannot be changed to "centre of the week".
Avoid **centre round**; use **centre on** (or **centre in** for exactness or
precision). Other forms are **centred** and **centring**, but note **centering**
for an arch.

century is named after the last of its 100 years. For instance, 1900 was
the last year of the nineteenth century; 2000 will be the end of the
twentieth century; and the twenty-first century will not begin until
2001. Thus the nineteenth century consisted almost entirely of the
1800s; the 1900s make up the twentieth century. (This is because there
was no year 0 AD, a fact that should be remembered when calculating
the ages of people who were born BC and died AD.) Used adjectivally,
century names have a hyphen; e.g. "built in the eighteenth century"
but "an eighteenth-century house". Abbreviated forms such as "in the
15th century" and "a 20th-century building" should be avoided in
formal writing.

ceramics (= the making of pottery etc.) is singular; **ceramics** (= pots
etc.) is plural.

cereal = a grain crop (barley, millet, oats, rice, rye, wheat etc.); **serial**
= story or radio/television drama that appears as regular separate
episodes. *See also* **grain**.

ceremonial (adj.) describes a ceremony or other formal occasion;
ceremonious describes a person or people when they behave as they
might at a ceremony (even if this is inappropriate). E.g.:
"The Queen's coronation was a colourful ceremonial occasion."
"He donned his robes of office and made a ceremonious entrance."

certainty = the state of being certain or having conviction; **certitude**

= the state of having conviction – i.e. the former can mean the latter, but the latter shares only one meaning with the former. E.g.:

"It was a certainty that the tidal wave would engulf the ships in the harbour."

"Despite the mood of the meeting, he expressed his views with certitude."

cervix (pl. cervixes, not *cervices*) has the adjective *cervical*. It can apply to the neck (e.g. cervical ribs, cervical vertebrae) or to the neck of the womb (e.g. cervical cancer).

cession = handing over (to another); **session** = period of time, meeting.

Chad The derived adjective and noun is *Chadean*.

chafe, chafing (= wearing by friction); **chaff**, chaffing (= bantering, teasing).

chairperson *See* **gender**.

chambré (italics) = at room temperature.

chameleon (note spelling).

chamois has the same form in the singular and plural. When applied to a type of soft leather, the word can also be spelled **shammy** (in accord with its pronunciation in this meaning).

champagne = the sparkling wine; **champaign** = a plane, flat open ground.

change, changeable, changeling.

chandelier *See* **candelabra.**

channel, channelled, channelling.

chaperon (not *chaperone*).

character, characteristic, characterize.

Charollais (breed of cattle).

chassis has the plural **chassis** (only the pronunciation changes).

chaste *See* **celibate**.

château (pl. châteaux).

chauvinism *See* **gender**.

cheap is an adjective meaning *inexpensive*; **cheaply** is an adverb meaning *inexpensively*. E.g.:
"She bought a cheap pair of shoes."
"She has new shoes, which she bought cheaply."
On the cheap is slang, and should be avoided.

check-in, check-list, check-out, check-up (all nouns); but check in, check out, check up as verbs.

chequer, chequered, chequering (= patterned with squares). Avoid using *checkered* etc. (although *checker* is correct meaning someone who checks goods and so on).

cherub (pl. cherubs, preferred to cherubim).

chickenpox (one word).

chicory (*Cichorium intybus*) has long, smooth pale yellow leaves and a slightly bitter taste; its roots are roasted as a coffee additive/substitute. **Endive** (*Cichorium endivia*) has curly or wavy leaves. Both are used in salads (and, in this context, have their meanings reversed in the United States).

chide, an archaism for *scold*, has the preferred past tense and participle **chided** (not the original *chid* and *chidden*).

chilblain (not *chillblain*).

child *See* **baby**.

childbirth, childhood, childlike, child-minder, child-proof.

childish = puerile, not suitable/becoming for an adult; **childlike** = having the innocence/candour/good qualities of a child.

chilli (pepper) has the plural **chillies**.

chimera = is the preferred spelling of the fabulous beast and the only one for the shark-like fish (not *chimaera*).

China The derived adjective and noun is *Chinese* (the term *Chinaman* should not be used to describe somebody from China).

Chinese words that have found a permanent place in English include:

cheongsam	ketchup	pekinese	tea
chop suey	kowtow	sampan	typhoon
chowmein	kung fu	silk	wok
cumquat	lychee	soya	yin
kaolin	mandarin	tai chi	yang

chiropody = medical treatment of the feet (by a *chiropodist*); **chiropractic** = treatment of disorders by manipulation of the spinal column (by a *chiropractor*).

chirrup, chirruped, chirruping.

chisel, chiselled, chiselling.

chives *See* **capers**.

chivvy is the preferred spelling (not *chivy* or *chevy*).

choice *See* **alternative**; **option**.

choir, chorister. *See also* **quire**.

choose, choosy. **Choose** has the past tense **chose** and past participle **chosen**.

chop = cut of meat including a piece of (rib) bone, usually lamb (sheep) or pork (pig); **cutlet** = small cut of (lean) meat with no bone.

chord = harmonious set of notes, line joining points on a curve; **cord** = strong string (and spinal cord, umbilical cord, vocal cords).

chordate = any member of the group (phylum) of animals that includes vertebrates; **cordate** = heart-shaped; **cordite** = propellent explosive made mainly from gun-cotton ("nitrocellulose").

chorus, chorused, choral (to do with a chorus or choir), chorale (a piece of music), chorister.

chou (pl. choux) = cabbage, decorative "rose" made of ribbon; **choux** = light, rich pastry.

Christian name can be an objectionable term to a non-Christian person and is best avoided. Of the alternatives, *first name* is preferred to *forename* or *given name*, except in official documents or for peoples who traditionally state their family name or surname first.

chronic = long-term, long-standing; **acute** = of sudden onset, short-term.

chukka = type of boot; **chukker** = period of play at polo.

chute is the preferred spelling (not *shoot*) for the sloping trough for conveying things.

cine- is preferred to **kine-** as a prefix (e.g. cinematograph).

cipher (= zero, monogram) is the preferred spelling of **cypher**.

circumcise, circumcision.

circumflex = an accent, as in *fête*.

circumstances *In the circumstances* and *under the circumstances* are now both acceptable phrases when used correctly. *See* **under the circumstances**.

circus (pl. circuses).

cirrhosis (note spelling).

cist = prehistoric burial chamber; **cyst** = lump, growth or sac.

cite = refer to, quote; **site** = place, position.

civil, civilize, civilizable, civilization.

clack = sharp sound (like two pieces of flat wood struck together); **claque** = hired applauders. *See also* **click**.

clad *See* **cloth**.

claim to be requires an object to refer to the claimant; it does not mean to **assert**. E.g.:

"She claims to be happy" (correct, the happiness is possibly hers).
"They claim to be rich" (correct, the richness is possibly theirs).
"You claimed the work to be late" (incorrect, *late* refers to *work*, not *you*, and the sentence should be rephrased as "You asserted that the work was late").

clamour, clamorous.

clang, clanger, clangour, clangorous. The verb inflects *clang –
clanged – clanged*. *See also* **cling**.

classic = typifying the best, first class; **classical** = relating to or in the
manner of ancient Greece or Rome, the opposite of romantic or
popular. E.g.:
"She wore a classic gown made of black silk."
"The church was designed in the classical style and built of local
materials only fifty years ago."

clay, clayey.

cleanliness = the routine or habit of keeping something clean;
cleanness = the state of being clean. E.g.:
"The maintenance of strict cleanliness reduces the risk of
contamination."
"After the contamination, the cleanness of the apparatus was in
question."

cleave There are two different verbs of opposite meaning with this
spelling. One = to divide, split, hack apart; the other = to stick (to),
unite. The first has the past tense **clove** and past participle **cloven**,
although *cleft* is also retained as an adjective (e.g. "a cleft stick"). The
second verb has the past tense and participle **cleaved**.

clench *See* **clinch**.

clerihew is a four-line verse (usually a pair of rhyming couplets that do
not scan), often describing a person and his or her achievements. E.g.:
"Alexandre Leclair
Was an optician extraordinaire;
He changed the looks of many French lasses
By prescribing contact lenses instead of glasses."

clever = ingenious, adroit, quick-witted; it should strictly not be used
to mean knowledgeable, well educated, well informed (as in "He must
be a clever man to know Latin grammar").

cliché = a stereotyped expression, a well-worn and thus overexposed
idea. Clichés should be avoided like the plague, if you see what I

mean. Often they are refuges of **archaisms** (which *see*). The adjective is *clichéd*. *See also* **inseparable pairs; metaphor**.

click = a short, sharp sound; **clique** = exclusive group of people. *See also* **clack**.

client = someone who commissions a lawyer, estate agent or some such – i.e. purchases a professional service (although a doctor has *patients*); **customer** = someone who purchases goods or a tradesman's services; thus a consultant has clients, a plumber and a grocer have customers. A group of customers may properly, if a little affectedly, be referred to as **clientele**.

climatic = to do with climate; **climactic** = to do with a climax; **climacteric** = to do with a critical period (usually the menopause).

clime is archaic for climate (as in the cliché "sunnier climes"); *climate* should be used.

clinch = to embrace, to settle (a deal); **clench** = to close tightly (teeth or fist); to secure a nail or rivet.

cling inflects *cling – clung – clung*. *See also* **clang**.

close *See* **shut**.

cloth (noun = textile material, fabric) has the plural *cloths* (e.g. "cloths for wiping the top of the table"); **clothe** (verb) = to dress, cover (with fabric) (e.g. "clothed in silk"); **clothes** (plural noun) = garments (e.g. "he wore his best clothes"). The verb **clothe** has the preferred past tense and participle **clothed**, although *clad* is retained in certain technical terms (e.g. "tile-clad elevation").

club, clubbable.

clue – hint (at a solution to a problem); **clew** = part of a sail.

coal-dust, coal-face, coalfield, coalfish, coal gas, coalman, coal-mine, coal tar.

coarse (adj.) = rough, base, unrefined; **course** (noun) = track or ground to be covered (e.g. racecourse, golf course, course of action), series of lessons/lectures (e.g. A-level course), dishes (e.g. a meal of three courses), doses of medicine (e.g. a course of antibiotics), a row of laid bricks or dressed stones (e.g. damp course).

coastal = to do with the coast (e.g. "coastal defences" against the action of tides); **costal** = to do with the ribs (e.g. "costal muscles" used in breathing).

coaxial, coeducation(al), coefficient, coequal, coeval, coexist(ence), coextensive, coheir(ess), cotangent. Most other words with the prefix *co-* have a hyphen.

coca *See* **cacao**.

coccus (pl. cocci); its compounds have similar plurals.

coccyx (pl. coccyxes).

cockatoo (pl. cockatoos).

coco *See* **cacao**.

cocoa *See* **cacao**.

coconut (not *cocanut*).

codeine (note *-ei-* spelling).

codex (pl. codices).

codicil *See* **corollary**.

coelom (pl. coelomata). Note also coelacanth, coelenterate.

coequal should be avoided in favour of plain **equal**.

coeval (not *coaeval*).

cogitate is an affected synonym for **ponder** and an inaccurate one for **think**.

cohere, coherent, cohesion (= sticking together), coherence (= consistency, logical connection).

coiffure (italics) = hairstyle or the more familiar hair-do; the French term should be avoided.

coign *See* **quoin**.

coir *See* **quire**.

colander *See* **calendar**.

colic, colicky.

collaborate = work (willingly) with someone else for a common purpose; it is pejorative, with implications of treason, if the collaboration is with an enemy. **Corroborate** = (provide evidence to) confirm someone else's claim/statement. *See also* **collusion**.

collapse, collapsible.

colleague = someone who works with a professional person, such as a doctor, solicitor, teacher, and so on. Strictly it should not be used for someone who works with a tradesman or manual worker (who is termed a fellow-worker or workmate). *See also* **client; skilful**.

collect, collector, collectable. **Collect** = gather, bring together; it should not be misused for **fetch** (which *see*).

collective words often pose problems about number − are they singular or plural? Group collectives, such as *audience, class, committee, company, congregation, corporation, council, crew, department, family, firm, gate* (at a sporting event), *government, majority, minority, personnel, population, staff, team*, and so on may be regarded as singular or plural, depending on context. Singular is better when referring to the collection as a whole (e.g. "The department was held to be responsible"); plural is better when the emphasis is on the individual members (e.g. "The council were given front-row seats"). But once the choice has been made, it should remain consistent throughout the text. The use of a pronoun to refer to such a collective may force the verb into singular or plural. E.g.:

"The family was unable to agree about its holiday."
"The family were told to take off their coats."
(One cannot say "The family was told to take off its coat".

Words for groups of similar things, people or animals, such as *flock* (of birds), *heap* (of things), *herd* (of animals), *horde* (of people), *pack* (of dogs/wolves), *pile* (of sand, stones etc.), *shoal* (of fish), and so on, are singular. E.g.:

"The herd of antelopes has begun to migrate."
"A flock of gulls is flying overhead."

So-called distributive collective words (such as *folk, people*) and generalizing collectives (usually occupations such as *the clergy*, *the police*) are regarded as plural. E.g.:

"The people are upset."
"The police have taken action."

Nouns of "mass" or class collectives (uncountable nouns for groups of different things that together form a category) are singular – indeed they have no plural. Examples include *baggage*, *clothing*, *crockery*, *cutlery*, *furniture*, *garbage*, *glassware*, *hardware*, *ironmongery*, *kitchenware*, *luggage*, *machinery*, *software* (computers), *stationery*. E.g.:

"All baggage is weighed."
"No cutlery has been washed."
"Much stationery was missing."

Expressions such as "items of clothing" and "pieces of furniture" achieve a plural construction, if needed.

collision occurs when a moving object hits a stationary one; **collusion** occurs when two or more people conspire to deceive or defraud (straightforward open co-operation is *collaboration*). E.g.:

"My car was dented in a collision with a tree."
"The witnesses' accounts were identical down to the last detail, suggesting collusion between them."

colloquialism = non-formal English, usually reserved for speech and to be avoided in formal writing. *See also* **non-standard English; slang**.

collusion = (secret) agreement in order to deceive; it should not be used as a synonym for co-operation, which may be open and praiseworthy. *See also* **collaborate; collision**.

colon *See* **punctuation**.

colony, colonial, colonize, colonization. **Colony/colonials** should not be applied to former British overseas territories or their citizens (*colonial* is pejorative). Some nations are properly called *Dominions*, many are republics and *Commonwealth* countries. Hong Kong (until 1996) has the official status of a Crown Colony.

colophon = publisher's symbol, usually printed on book jackets, spines and title pages. A letter symbol is also known as a **logo** (short for *logogram* or *logo type*).

coloration (and discoloration); other words (except decolorize) derived from *colour* keep *-ou-*.

comatose = affected with coma, unconscious; **comose** = hairy, tufted, resembling the head of a comet.

combat = a fight between enemies; a **contest** or **competition** may be between neutrals or friends (at worst they are rivals). Other forms are combated, combating, combative.

combust, combustible, combustion. *See also* **inflammable**.

come has the past tense **came** and past participle **come**.

comic describes someone or something that is deliberately funny; **comical** describes someone or something that is unintentionally funny or amusing. E.g.:
"He wrote a comic sketch for the student review."
"Her make-up ran in the rain, giving her face a comical expression."

comma *See* **punctuation**.

commando (pl. commandos).

comme il faut (italics) = as it should be, proper; the French expression should be avoided.

commemorate, commemoration (a double *m* and then a single *m*).

commence should be reserved for the beginning of a formal ceremony or procedure; otherwise **begin** or **start** should be used. *See also* **start**.

commentate, commentator, commentary.

commercialese = pejorative term for the jargon of business and commerce, particularly in letter-writing, with its abbreviations such as *inst.*, *prox.* and *ult.* and use of expressions such as *in respect of*, *per*, *re*, and so on. It is universally and soundly condemned by advocates of good style in writing. *See also* **jargon**.

commissionaire (note spelling).

commit, committed, committing, committee, commission (= act of committing, authority to commit), commitment (= obligation, order for sending to prison), committal (= pledge, order for sending to trial).

common *See* **mutual**.

commoner is the noun; **more common** should be used as the comparative of **common**. *See also* **comparative and superlative**.

Common Market *See* **Economic Community**.

common names (of plants and animals) *See* **Latin classification**.

common sense is the noun form, **common-sense** is the adjective; *commonsense* should be avoided.

Commonwealth is an acceptable short form of *Commonwealth of Nations*, the former *British Commonwealth (of Nations)*.

communiqué (acute accent).

Comoros The derived adjective and noun is *Comorian*.

comparable = can be compared with; **compatible** = can coexist with, congruous. E.g.:

"They went to different schools and were taught in different ways but their examination results are comparable."
"They tried living together but found that they were not compatible."

comparative and superlative forms of short (monosyllabic and disyllabic) adjectives are usually formed by adding *-er* and *-est* (or *-r* and *-st* if the adjective ends in *e*):

    small, smaller, smallest
    large, larger, largest.

Adjectives ending in a consonant usually have a double consonant in the comparative and superlative:

    big, bigger, biggest
    hot, hotter, hottest

Adjectives ending in a *y* change the *y* to an *i*:

    funny, funnier, funniest
    happy, happier, happiest

Most polysyllabic adjectives have *more* and *most* to form the comparative and superlative:

> beautiful, more beautiful, most beautiful
> uncooperative, more uncooperative, most uncooperative

Irregular comparatives and superlatives have to be learned. Common examples include:

> bad, worse, worst
> good, better, best
> little, less, least
> old, elder, eldest (although older, oldest also exist).

compare *to* (= to liken something to something else) has a different meaning from **compare** *with* (= to point to resemblances and differences between two things); **contrast** = to note only differences. E.g.:

"I could compare his handwriting to an infant's scribbles."
"Compare the galley proof with the typescript."
"Contrast the attitudes of the English and the Americans."
Other forms are comparable, comparative, comparison.

compass = instrument for finding directions, or a different instrument for drawing circles (also called a *pair of compasses*).

compass directions The basic terms north, south, east and west (without capital letters, abbreviated to N, S, E, W, without full points) give rise to northern, northerly and northward(s) (*see* **-wards**), and similar forms for the other directions. Compounds have hyphens. E.g.:

"In north-eastern China" (not north-east)
"A south-westerly direction" (not south-west).

Note compounds such as a "north-facing window" (preferred to northerly-facing or northward(s)-facing).
Exceptions are established national or political units, which are usually also distinguished by capitalization. E.g.:
South Africa (the nation), but southern Africa (the southern part of the continent in general).
South-East Asia (politically), but south-eastern Asia (generally).

Note that a *southerly* (from the south) wind blows a sailing vessel in a *northerly* course (to the north).

compatible *See* **comparable.**

compendium *See* **anthology.**

compère (with accent). The term *commère* for a woman compère should be avoided.

competent *See* **able.**

competition *See* **combat.**

complacent = self-satisfied; **complaisant** = obliging. E.g.:
"He thinks he knows everything about the job — he is so complacent."
"Ask George if he will help — he is usually complaisant."

complement = that which fills or completes, an integral part or portion; **compliment** = flattering comment. E.g.:
"When the typist returns from holiday we shall have a full complement of staff."
"The boss paid a compliment to the staff by commenting on their good time-keeping record."
See also **supplement.**

complete and utter is a tautology and should be avoided. E.g. in "He made a complete and utter fool of himself", delete *complete* or *utter* (and the *and*).

complex (adj.) = made up of many parts, intricate; it is often used as a synonym for **complicated**, which can have the additional meaning *confused* (e.g. "a complex problem with a complicated solution").
Complex (noun) = group of psychological symptoms, a group of buildings (e.g. "sports complex").

complexion is one of the few words that should be spelled *-exion* (not *-ection*).

compose, composer (of music), compositor (of type), composition (= the result of composing either music or type), composure (= calmness of temperament).

compound words Most compound words are formed from adjective-noun combinations (e.g. blackboard, hardcore) or noun-noun combinations (e.g. cupboard, schoolboy). But, to quote G.H. Vallins, "when two nouns really coalesce to become one (armchair, bookcase), when they are linked by a hyphen (plate-rack, pen-holder), and when they remain separate are questions that in the present state of usage are past the wit of man to answer." Here are some general rules: Hyphens should be used as little as possible, and then only when needed to avoid confusion in sound or comprehension. E.g.:

> re-cover and recover
> re-creation and recreation
> re-count and recount
> re-form and reform
> re-enter and co-operate (to prevent the same two vowels occurring together).

Use hyphens for compound adjectives, the parts of which, if not separated, could lead to miscomprehension. E.g.:

> hot-metal typesetting
> fried-fish shop
> good-sized house
> red-hot poker
> poverty-stricken town
> red-brown dust.

A hyphen is not needed for an adverb-adjective combination when the meaning is clear. E.g.:

> a richly endowed church
> the rumour was ill founded
> a beautifully phrased sentence
> a fully grown bear (but full-grown bear preferred)
> a swiftly flowing stream

A hyphen is often needed for a verb-adverb combination used as a noun. E.g.:

> make-up   mark-up   paste-up   take-off

but note: breakdown, getaway, handout, layout.

A hyphen is needed for numbers and fractions when they are spelled out. E.g.:

twenty-eight	fifty-four	one-and-a-half
two-thirds	fifteen-sixteenths	two-and-a-half

A hyphen is needed to avoid repetition in such expressions as:

> single- or double-jointed
> a two-, three- or four-colour process
> forward- and rear-facing windows.

A hyphen is usually desirable in compounds of which the first element ends with a vowel and the second element begins with a vowel (e.g. aero-elastic, sea-urchin), or in which the first element ends with the same consonant as that beginning the second element (e.g. part-time). Exceptions include words used so commonly that the hyphen can be ommitted (e.g. coeducation, earring, radioactive). Many unhyphenated two-word compound nouns take hyphens when they are used attributively. E.g.:

> boiling-point measurement
> engine-room officer
> freezing-point determination
> melting-point temperature
> nickel-silver alloy
> right-angle(d) triangle
> test-tube baby

Note: In text for typesetting where an obligatory hyphen happens to come at the end of a line, mark it " = " to distinguish it from a non-obligatory hyphen of a word break. E.g.:

> "... and they co =
operated in marking up the copy".

See also **well-**; **word breaks**.

comprehend, comprehensive, comprehensible (= understandable, preferred to *comprehendible*), comprehensive (= wide-ranging, complete). *See also* **apprehensive**.

comprise = consist of, contain, include, be composed of; e.g. "The staff comprises nine people". *Comprise* should not be used to mean to form, or to make up; e.g. "Nine people comprises the staff" is incorrect. *See also* **consist of**.

compromise (not *-ize*, noun and verb).

compulsion = irresistible urge or action (adj. *compulsive*); **impulse** = spontaneous (but resistible) thought or action (adj. *impulsive*).

compute is now acceptable for what a *computer* does; it should not be used as a synonym for **calculate** or **estimate**, particularly if performed by a human being. Similarly **computation** should be avoided when **calculation** is intended. The verb for to convert (a system) to computer use/control is **computerize**.

concave = domed in, like the inside of a spoon; **convex** = domed out, like the outside of a spoon. The corresponding nouns are *concavity* and *convexity*.

concensus The correct spelling is **consensus** (derived from *consent*, not *census*).

concerned *in* or *with* = having to do with; **concerned** *for* or *about* = worried. E.g.:
"He was not concerned in the crime."
"Arithmetic is concerned with numbers."
"The pupils were concerned for the teacher after his accident."
"He was concerned about the consequences of his actions."

concertina, concertinaed, concertinaing.

concerto (pl. concertos, not *concerti*).

conch (a shell), (pl. conchs).

conclave = private or secret assembly; **enclave** = area of land surrounded by foreign territory.

concrete *See* **cement**.

concreter = someone who concretes, part of a sugar refinery.

concur *with* someone *in* something; e.g. "He concurs with me in praising your work." Other forms are concurred, concurring, concurrent, concurrence.

condole (with) = be in sympathy (with); **console** = comfort. E.g.:
"She condoled with me when I lost my job."
"I could not console her when she lost her engagement ring."
The corresponding nouns are *condolence* and *consolation*.

condominium = joint sovereignty. The word is being imported (from the United States) as a name for a jointly owned and occupied building, usually split into flats (apartments).

conducive *to* (not conducive *of*).

conduct, conductor (all uses).

confer, conferred, conferring, conferrable; but conferment, conference.

confetti is singular (despite being the Italian plural of *confetto*).

confidant (fem. confidante) = someone to whom one entrusts a confidence (secret); **confident** = exhibiting or feeling confidence (assurance). Both words derive from **confide** (which *see*), but reflect two meanings of *confidence*.

confide *in someone* (= confess); **confide** something *to* someone (= entrust).

confirm See **affirm**.

conga (pl. congas) = a dance; **conger** = an eel.

congenial = of the same taste, sympathetic, kindred; **congenital** = present at birth; **genial** = affable, cheering, kindly; **genital** = pertaining to generation or reproduction, of the genitals.

Congo The derived adjective and noun is *Congolese*.

conjure, conjuror (preferred to conjurer for the performer).

connect, connection (not *-exion*). See also **-ection**.

connive = ignore something known to be wrong; **contrive** = artfully influence the outcome. E.g.:
"The teacher connived at the children's noisy outburst."
"Henry usually contrives to be at the front of the queue."
The corresponding nouns are *connivance* and *contrivance*.

connoisseur (note spelling).

connote = to imply/mean secondarily; **denote** = to indicate/mean primarily. E.g.:

"In modern journalism, the term *fun-loving* usually connotes *promiscuous*."

"In chemistry, the word *ebullition* denotes *boiling*."

conquer, conqueror.

conscience takes only an apostrophe (not *'s*) to form the possessive (e.g. "for conscience' sake").

conscientious (note spelling).

conscious is better put as **aware** (of) in such constructions as "He became conscious that it was raining."

consensus is the correct spelling (not *concensus*).

consequent takes the preposition *on* (e.g. "He was charged with the crime consequent on his confession"). The phrase has a stilted ring to it, and the simpler "... *as a result of* his confession" or "... *after* he confessed" is preferred. *See also* **following** (which should be avoided as an alternative to *consequent on*).

conserve, conservation, conservationist (not *conservationalist*).

consider (= regard as) does not need an additional "as" or "to be". E.g.:

"I consider style important" is sufficient and correct (not "consider as important" or "consider to be important").

considerable should be avoided when being used to mean *great* or *large* (e.g. " a considerable number of people"), thus reserving it to mean "worthy of consideration".

consistent = compatible, fixed, uniform – hence **consistently** = uniformly, without exception; **persistent** = on-going, enduring, continuous – hence **persistently** = continuously, without interruption.

consist of = to be made up of; **constitute** = to make up; e.g. "A whole consists of the parts; the parts constitute the whole.";

consist in = have its essence in; e.g. "The popularity of the book consists in its humour."

consommé (acute accent).

consortium (pl. consortia).

constrain = to compel someone (to do something); **restrain** = to hold back someone (or oneself). E.g.:
"She constrained him to go to the meeting."
"She restrained him from interrupting the meeting."

constructional = pertaining to construction; **constructive** = helpful (opposite of *destructive*). E.g.:
"The building collapsed because of a constructional fault."
"The building inspector made constructive suggestions about how to maintain the schedule."

consult, consultant, consultancy.

consume = to use up (= destroy), not merely to *use*. **Consume** (applied to human beings) is, like **partake of**, precious for **eat** or **drink**, which are preferred.

contact (verb) = to touch, bring into contact; some people do not approve of its use to mean *communicate* (as in "He contacted me last week"), although it is an almost exact synonym for the idiomatic *get in touch with*.

contagion/contagious *See* **infection/infectious**.

contemplate, contemplative (not *contemplatative*).

contemporary (not *contempory*).

contemptible = worthy of derision, despicable; **contemptuous** = scornful, haughty. E.g.:
"His efforts at building a wall were contemptible."
"When asked about the quality of the work, the builder gave a contemptuous reply."

content (noun) refers to the type of material in a container; **contents** refers to all of it. E.g.:

"It was a large basket and the major content was fruit."
"The basket held fruit and the entire contents were rotten."
See also **preface.**

contest *See* **combat.**

contiguous *See* **adjacent.**

continental quilt *See* **bedspread.**

continual = always going on, although not necessarily without interruption; **continuous** = non-stop, unbroken in time or sequence. E.g.:

"The monsoon season brings continual rain."
"The mechanism provided for a continuous movement from floor to ceiling."

continuation = a "going-on", resumption, that which continues; **continuity** = the state of being continuous, unbroken, uninterrupted. E.g.:

"They agreed to meet again tomorrow for a continuation of their discussion."
"They agreed to talk all night to preserve the continuity of their discussion."

continuo (pl. continuos, not to be confused with *continuous*).

contra (= against) forms compounds without a hyphen except in the medical terms contra-indication and contra-suggestible.

contractions end with the final letter of the word when it is spelled in full, and so do not need a full point. E.g.:

Ave	Bt or Bart	Ct	cwt	Dr	Fr
ft	hr	Ltd	Mlle	Mme	Mr
St (street and Saint; plural SS for Saints)			yd		

The usual style for dates is not 1st, 2nd etc. but 1 January 1986. Verbal contractions (e.g. *can't* for *cannot*, *shan't* for *shall not*) should be avoided in formal writing. *See also* **abbreviations** (particularly under measurements and units).

contralto (pl. contraltos, not *contralti*).

contrast *See* **compare**.

contretemps is a singular word meaning **mishap** (usually involving embarrassment); it does not mean *argument* (as in "We had a contretemps about who should pay the bill"). The French term should be avoided.

contribute, contributor, contribution.

control, controlled, controller, controlling, controllable.

controvertible (not *-ible*).

conundrum (pl. conundrums).

convenience takes only an apostrophe (not *'s*) to form the possessive (e.g. "for convenience' sake").

converse, conversation, conversationalist. **Converse** is precious for **talk**, which is preferred. *See also* **inverse**.

conversion factors *See* **units**.

convert, converter, convertible (not *-able*), conversion.

convey, conveyer (who conveys), conveyor (which conveys).

convince = make someone believe something, give them conviction; **persuade** = make someone do something, using persuasion. E.g.:
"He could convince me that black was white."
"He could persuade me to do anything he wanted."
The derived adjectives are *convincing* and *persuasive*.

cony is the preferred spelling (not *coney*), except in Coney Island.

co-operate, co-operation, co-operative (with hyphens); but note non-co-operation (two hyphens) and uncooperative (no hyphen).

co-ordinate, co-ordination (with hyphens); but note uncoordinated (no hyphen).

copper = pink metal (used for electrical conductors and coinage); **copra** = the dried "flesh" of the coconut (used as a source of vegetable oil); **copro-** is a prefix meaning faecal or filthy.

copyright (noun) = the legal right to publish or reproduce a work (text, drama, music, film or television); **copyright** (verb) has the past tense and participle **copyrighted; copywrite** = to write copy (text), particularly for advertising or the press.

cord See **chord.**

core = central part; **corps** = group of (uniformed) people; **corpse** = dead body. **Corps** has the same form in both singular and plural.

co-respondent = the person named in a divorce action as the alleged adulterer's extramarital partner; **correspondent** = a person who writes a letter or newspaper report.

corgi (pl. corgis).

corn is an American term for **maize**, and a common term elsewhere for any cereal crop. **Corn on the cob** is a seed-head of maize, also known as **sweet corn**. *See also* **grain**.

cornflour/cornflower See **grain.**

corollary = conclusion drawn from something already proved, a natural consequence; **rider** = amendment or supplement to a proposition or document; **codicil** = rider to a will.

corpulent is a euphemism for fat, as are *adipose, portly, rotund, stout* and *well-built* (of which the last seems to be the least offensive to fat people). *Well-covered* is colloquial for *fat; well-endowed* is colloquial for *buxom.* **Obese** is the medical term for *overweight*, often used in everyday language to mean very fat, grossly overweight.

corpus (pl. corpora).

corps *See* **core.**

corpse *See* **core.**

corrasion = term in geology that describes local land erosion; **corrosion** = gradually eating or wearing away (as of a metal by acid or rust).

correct, correction, corrector (who corrects), corrective (which corrects), correctness, correctitude (archaic for correctness of manner/conduct).

correspond, when making comparisons, takes *to*; when it means to write, it takes *with*. E.g.:

"An annual bonus of £5,200 corresponds to £100 a week."
"My daughter corresponds with a boy in Germany."

correspondent *See* **co-respondent.**

corrigenda (sing. corrigendum) = list of corrections in a book. Strictly they should consist of last-minute changes by the author to statements in the text as originally written and printed. *See also* **errata.**

corrigible (not *-able*).

corroborate = confirm (the truth of something); **verify** = discover the truth of something. E.g.:

"My account of the accident was corroborated by one of the other witnesses."
"It was impossible to verify his claim to the inheritance."

corrupt, corruptible, corrupter, corruption.

cortège (grave accent).

cortex (pl. cortices).

cosmonaut *See* **astronaut.**

cosset, cosseted, cosseting.

cost (verb) inflects *cost – cost – cost.*

cosy (not *cozy*).

cotter = retaining pin; **cottar** - villein.

couch = long upholstered seat (originally with a half-back and an arm at one end), as used by doctors and so on; **divan** = long seat with no back or ends, now used mainly of a bed (with no headboard); **settee** = long upholstered seat with a back and ends (arms); **sofa** = settee (but with an old-fashioned ring to it).

counsel (verb = to advise, noun = barrister), counselling, counsellor (adviser), but councillor on a **council.**

counter (= opposite, duplicate) generally forms compounds without a hyphen except in counter-attack, -attraction, -claim, -clockwise, -espionage, -intelligence, -offensive, -productive, -revolution, -tenor; note also Counter-Reformation.

counterfeit (note -*ei*- spelling).

counterpane *See* **bedspread**.

counting *See* **numbers**.

countless should not be used to describe something that can (or could) be counted; often **many** is all that is intended.

country names, adjectives from Adjectives derived from country names are commonly formed by adding -*n* or -*ian* to the name of the country (e.g. an Angolan, Jordanian). Often the same word serves as a noun for the name of the people (e.g. Angolan, Angolans; a Jordanian, Jordanians). There are many exceptions (e.g. Dutch, French, Swedish/Swede), and many of the less familiar ones are included in this Dictionary.

coup = sudden successful move, take-over of the government; **coupe** = shallow bowl; **coupé** = two-seater closed (hard-topped) car; **coupee** = salute to a dancing partner. All form the plural by adding *s*.

coup de grâce (italics) = finishing stroke; ***coup de main*** (italics) = sudden successful attack; ***coup d'état*** (italics) = violent (subversive) take-over of government; the French terms should be avoided, but *see* **coup** (non-italics). If used, the plurals are *coups de grâce* etc.

course *See* **coarse**.

courtesy = polite behaviour, act of respect; **curtsy** = act of obeisance, usually by a standing woman bending her knees.

court martial (noun, pl. courts martial), court-martial (verb).

cousin = child of an uncle (parent's brother) or aunt (parent's sister), also called *first-cousin*; **second-cousin** = child of parent's first-cousin; **first-cousin once removed** = child of first-cousin; **first-cousin twice removed** = grandchild of a first-cousin. In each case, the term is defined from the standpoint of the person using the expression. *See also* **family relationships**.

covert (noun) = bushes etc. that provide shelter for birds such as partridges and pheasants; **covey** = group of birds such as partridges.

cow See **cattle**.

cowrie is the preferred spelling (not *cowry*). *See also* **karri**.

cozy The preferred spelling is **cosy**.

crackpot See **mad**.

crape See **crêpe**.

crave is too strong a word to serve as a synonym for **ask** or **beg**; a **craving** is an irresistible desire, not merely a *liking* for something.

craven = cowardly, lacking courage; **graven** = engraved, carved.

crèche (grave accent).

credence = belief or trust; **credibility** = quality of being believable; **credulity** = quality of being ready to believe anything.

credible = believable; **creditable** = praiseworthy, to someone's credit; **credulous** = gullible; **credit-worthy** = of sufficient financial status or reputation to be given credit.

credit, creditor, credited, credit card. **Credit** (verb) = to believe, trust, lend on trust or for a fee; **accredit** = to accept or prove to be true, vouch for, provide with credentials.

credo (pl. credos).

creep inflects *creep – crept – crept*.

crematorium (pl. crematoria).

crêpe (as in crêpe paper, crêpe Suzette), although **crape** is preferred for the fabric.

crescendo (pl. crescendos).

crevasse = a deep, often wide fissure in a glacier; **crevice** = any cleft, rift or small fissure, a split.

cringe, cringed, cringing.

crisis (pl. crises).

criss-cross (hyphen).

criterion (pl. criteria).

critic, criticism, critique, criticize. A **critic** = someone who produces a **criticism** or **critique** (i.e. a knowledgeable review of the quality/merit of a work), often also termed a *review* or *survey*. Because the verb **criticize** is now more often used to mean *find fault* (rather than *give a balanced judgement*), the words *critic* and *criticism* have also attracted negative connotations.

crochet (needlework), crocheted (pronounced "kro-shayed"), crocheting.

crocus (pl. crocuses, not *croci*). *See also* **gladiolus; narcissus**.

croissant (not italics).

crosier is the preferred spelling of **crozier**.

cross-references to other headwords or articles in alphabetically arranged matter such as a dictionary, encyclopaedia, glossary or index should be distinguishable typographically. A common style is to set *see* or *see also* in italics and the title referred to in small capitals or bold face; e.g. *see* CAPITALIZATION, or *see also* **capitalization**. *See* should be used to direct the reader directly to the location of the information being sought. E.g.:

    trade names *See* **capitalization**

See also should be employed to direct the reader to additional or ancillary information. E.g.:

    trade names should be spelled with an initial capital letter. *See also* **capitalization**.

The abbreviation *cf.* (*confer*) means "compare (with)" and should, strictly, direct the reader to contrasting information and be distinguished from *see* or *see also* as previously defined, although it is nearer the latter than the former.

croûton (italics).

crow (verb) has the preferred past tense and participle **crowed** (not *crew*).

crucial = decisive, testing, critical (from *crux* = turning point); it should not be used to mean merely **important**.

crucify, crucifix, crucifixion.

crumble is what some rocks, dry soil, bread or cake does (to form *crumbs*); **crumple** is what cloth does (to loose its smoothness, as in "a crumpled tablecloth").

crumpet = round cake made from dough containing yeast, baked (on a baking sheet) on one side only and with holes in the top; **drop scone** = small thick pancake, containing baking powder and turned during baking so that it is cooked on both sides; **muffin** = round doughy cake cooked on both sides; **pancake** = very thin, large "cake" made with eggs and flour (batter) and fried on both sides; **pikelet** = crumpet; **scone** = small cake made from an unsweetened mixture containing flour or oatmeal and baking powder, usually baked in an oven; **Scotch pancake** = drop scone; **teacake** = round flat bun made from a sweetened mixture containing yeast, often with added fruit (currants or sultanas). Crumpets, muffins and teacakes are usually toasted before being eaten; pancakes may be served with sweet or savoury dishes.

crutch = a prop or support (as used by the lame); **crotch** = the fork of the body.

crux (pl. cruxes).

crystal, crystallize, crystallization.

-ction *See* **-ection**.

cubical = shaped like a cube; **cubicle** = small room or cupboard.

cudgel, cudgelled, cudgelling.

cue, cueing. **Cue** = a hint, stick for striking a ball at billiards, pool or snooker; **queue** = a line of people waiting, pigtail. *See also* **clue**.

cul-de-sac (pl. cul-de-sacs, not *culs-de-sac*).

cuneiform (note spelling).

cullender *See* **calendar**.

cupful (pl. cupfuls).

curb This spelling should be used for the verb, **kerb** for the noun (kerbstone).

cure, curing, curable.

curio (pl. curios).

currant = a small fruit; **current** = a flow of air, electricity or water. *Current* is also an adjective meaning contemporary, up-to-date.

currency *See* **money**.

curriculum (pl. curricula).

curse = to wish someone evil; **swear** = to take or utter an oath, to use swearwords. E.g.:
"May you rot in hell" is cursing someone;
"God damn it!" is swearing.
Contempt of God or Jesus is also termed *blasphemy*.

curtsy *See* **courtesy**.

cuscus = millet grain, Indian grass fibre; **cus-cus** = Malaysian marsupial; **couscous** = North African dish of steamed wheat flour and meat.

customer *See* **client**.

cutlet *See* **chop**.

cut-off (adj. and noun), meaning the point at which something ceases to apply or happen, is a vogue term (e.g. "We cannot spend any more time on the task − we have reached the cut-off point"). *See* **vogue words**.

cyclopaedia *See* **encyclopaedia**.

cymbal = metal percussion instrument; **symbol** = emblem or sign. Users of each are called **cymbalists** or **symbolists**.

cypher The preferred spelling is **cipher**.

cypress = evergreen tree or shrub (*Cupressus*); **Cyprus** = eastern Mediterranean island nation (derived adjective and noun *Cypriot*).

cyst *See* **cist**.

czar The preferred spelling is **tsar**.

Czechoslovakia The derived adjective and noun is *Czechoslovak* (not Czechoslovakian); the words *Czech* and *Slovak* should be reserved for the two major languages.

D

-d- or **-dd-** Monosyllabic words ending in *-d* preceded by a single vowel double the *d* before *y* or a suffix beginning with a vowel. E.g.:

bid	biddable
bud	buddable, budded, budding, buddy
cad	caddish
nod	nodded, nodding, noddy
prod	prodded, prodder, prodding
red	redden, redder, reddish
rod	rodded, rodding
trod	trodden

The *d* remains single if preceded by a long or double vowel. E.g.:

broad	broaden, broader, broadest
hard	harden
laud	laudable, laudatory
load	loaded, loading
mood	moody
proud	prouder, proudest
speed	speeding, speedy
thread	threadable, threaded, threading

With polysyllabic words, the choice of *-d-* or *-dd-* depends on where the accent falls. If it is on the last syllable, the rule is as for monosyllabic words; e.g. applauded, beholding, contender, forbidden, overridden, subtending. If the last syllable is unaccented, the *-d-* is not doubled; e.g. fluidic, periodic, timidity, wickedest. Neither is the *d* doubled, in monosyllabic or polysyllabic words, before suffixes that begin with a consonant; e.g. handful, hardly.

dado (pl. dados).

daffodil (two *f*s and one each of *d* and *l*).

dagger (†) *See* **footnotes**.

dago (pl. dagos), but avoid.

dahlia (plant named after Anders Dahl).

Dáil (with accent) = Irish parliament.

daily = of or on each day; **diurnal** = opposite of nocturnal, occupying one whole day (e.g. "a planet's diurnal rotation").

damage (noun) occurs to a thing; **injury** occurs to a person.

dare has the preferred past tense and participle **dared** (not *durst*).

dare say should be spelled as two words (i.e. not *daresay*).

darts (the game) is a singular word; "games of darts" achieves a plural construction.

dash *See* **punctuation**.

data can be singular in computer technology (*see* **plurals**).

date, datable.

dates *See* **time**.

datum (pl. data, which *see*).

day-bed, day-book, day-boy, day-break, day-dream, day-girl, daylight, day-long, day-school, daytime.

de, as part of a French proper name, usually has no initial capital letter (except at the beginning of a sentence); e.g. Charles de Gaulle. In many other languages it is capitalized; e.g. Cecil B. De Mille. Follow the style of the name's owner, if this is known.

deacon, deaconess, deaconship, diaconate.

deadly = (capable of) causing death; **deathly** = resembling death. E.g.:
"The berries contain a deadly poison."
"Eating the berries gave her a deathly pallor."

dead reckoning, originally a nautical term, means a method of reasoning based on estimation/calculation, rather than on (precise) measurement/observation. Its result can be (and often is) imprecise – it is not "dead on".

deaf-and-dumb (adj.) should not be used to describe someone who is a **deaf-mute** (noun).

deal inflects *deal − dealt − dealt*. When it has a preposition, write deal *in* goods or commodities, but deal *with* people, a topic.

death-bed, death-blow, death-cap, death duties, death's door, death's-head, death-rate, death-trap, death-watch, death wish.

debacle (no accents).

debar = to prohibit, prevent; **disbar** = to expel from the (legal) bar.

debate, debatable.

debauch = to corrupt, lead astray; **debouch** = issue forth (especially from a confined space into a larger one).

debit, debited.

debonair (note spelling).

debris (no accent).

debt, debtor.

debug *See* **bug**.

debut, debutant(e).

deca- is the metric prefix for ten times ($\times 10$), as in *decametre*.

deceive, deception, deceptive, deceit, deceitful. **Deceitful** = intended to deceive; **deceptive** = which deceives (perhaps unintentionally). E.g.:
"The child was reprimanded for her deceitful behaviour in blaming her sister."
"The deceptive coloration of the insect made it almost invisible against the mottled background."

decent = proper, seemly, modest; **descent** = going down, ancestry; **dissent** = disagree(ment), giving rise to dissension (not *dissention*).

deci- is the metric prefix for a tenth ($\times 10^{-1}$), as in *decilitre*.

decided (adj.) = definite, clear, without question; **decisive** = positive, showing a clear decision. E.g.:
"The designer's drawing skills gave her a decided advantage."
"The editor took decisive action and rejected the manuscript."

decidedly = without doubt, definitely; **decisively** = without hesitation, conclusively. E.g.:

"It is decidedly colder on the northern face of the mountain."
"He grabbed his coat and decisively strode out into the snow."

decimal, decimalize, decimalization.

decimate = to destroy one in ten (i.e. 90 per cent survive); strictly, it does not mean to wipe out entirely, maul or cut up. The noun is **decimator**.

déclassé(e) (two acute accents) = having lost social position; the French expression should be avoided.

decline, declinable, declension (of nouns), declination (of stars).

decolorize, decolorization.

décor (acute accent).

decorate, decorator, decorative.

decorous = seemly, with decorum; **decorative** = providing decoration; **decorated** = having decoration.

decry = state one's strong disapproval of something, disparage; **descry** = catch sight of something (from a distance), catch on.

deduce = infer, draw a (logical) conclusion; **deduct** = take away, subtract. The verbs are not confused as often as the adjectives **deducible** (= may be inferred) and **deductible** (= may be taken away). And to add to the confusion, the two verbs share the same noun: **deduction**. E.g.:

"From the size of the paw prints and their spacing, the zoologist was able to deduce that they were made by a leopard."
"The identity of the animal was deducible from its paw prints."
"I persuaded the salesman to deduct his commission and so lower the price."
"The commission was deductible from the price."
Both the zoologist and the salesman made deductions.
See also **induce**.

deep-rooted, deep-seated.

deface, defaceable.

defecate, defecation (but faecal, faeces).

defect, defective, defector.

defective = imperfect (in quality); **deficient** = insufficient (in quantity). E.g.:

"I had to return my new hi-fi to the shop because the pick-up was defective."

"I could not finish building the model because the kit was deficient in screws and adhesive."

defend, defender, defendant, defence, defensible (= that may be defended; defendable in law); defensive (= intended to defend). E.g.:

"I had to agree that she had a defensible point of view."

"They planted a defensive thorn hedge round the stockade."

defer, deferred, deferring, deferrable, deferrer, deferral (all with two *r*s), but deference, deferment, deferential.

define, definable.

definite = certain, precise; **definitive** = final, beyond change or criticism. E.g.:

"Her book expresses her definite views on singing."

"Her book has become the definitive work on singing."

definitely (not *definately*). *See* **really**.

deflect, deflection (not *deflexion*).

defuse = remove a fuse or tension; **diffuse** (verb) = spread (thinly and) widely. E.g.:

"The bomb disposal squad defused the shell."

"Concessions will have to be made by both sides to defuse the confrontation between the unions and the management."

"George's cigar smoke gradually diffused through the whole room."

degrade, degradable, degradation.

de-ice (remove ice), de-iced, de-icing.

déjà vu (italics, two accents).

de La, as part of a French proper name, usually has a capital letter only on *La* (except at the beginning of a sentence, when the *De* also has a capital); e.g. Jean de La Fontaine. Other languages vary; e.g. Walter de la Mare, Lord De La Warr. Follow the style of the name's owner.

delay *See* **dilate**.

delegate *See* **regulate**.

delicatessen (note spelling).

delimit = to impose a limit (not to remove one)

delineate, delineable (not *delineatable*), delineation.

deliver, deliverer, deliverance (from evil), delivery (of coal).

delusion = a (lasting) belief that the false is true; **illusion** = a false conception of an idea or circumstances, deceptive appearance (illusions are believable, delusions are believed). *See also* **illude**.

de luxe (two words, not *deluxe*) should be avoided when *luxurious* is meant (*see* **luxuriant**).

delve is archaic for **dig**, which is preferred.

demarcation is the preferred spelling (not *demarkation*).

demean = to lower in dignity/reputation, to humble oneself, to conduct oneself; **demeanour** = bearing (towards others); **demesne** = a landed estate.

demi- Little-used prefix meaning *half* (as in demigod, demijohn, demisemiquaver); more common are *hemi-* and *semi-*. *See also* **numerical prefixes**.

demise = death (which is preferred); it should not be used to mean merely *decline* (as in "A gradual increase in vandalism has accompanied the general demise of discipline in the schools").

demobilize, demobilization.

demon, demonic (not *demoniacal*).

demonstrate, demonstrable (not *demonstratable*), demonstrator, demonstration. **Demonstrate** = to show, reveal, or to support/protest publicly; **remonstrate** = to object or protest through argument. The meaning of the latter is rapidly being taken over by the last meaning of the former. The associated nouns are *demonstration* (colloquial abbreviation *demo*) and *remonstrance*.

demonstrative pronouns *See* pronoun.

demount = remove something from its mounting (such as a photographic transparency); **dismount** = unmount, get off a horse (or other animal). Then the transparency is *demounted*; the person on foot is *unmounted*.

demur, demurred, demurring, demurral, demurrage. **Demur** *at* or *to* = hesitate (because of uncertainty), object to; **demure** = sober, modest, grave (noun demureness). E.g.:
"She demurred at the invitation to go the party."
"She wore a demure, high-necked dress to the party."

denarius (pl. denarii) is the Latin origin of the abbreviation **d** for the old (and now defunct) British penny.

denationalize, denationalization.

denizen is old-fashioned, and informal, for **inhabitant** (as in the cliché "denizens of the deep"); *inhabitant* is preferred.

denote *See* connote.

dénouement (acute accent)

deny, deniable, denier, denial. **Deny** = to assert the falsity of a statement; **refute** = to prove the falsity of an accusation or theory.

deodorize, deodorizer.

département (of France).

depend, dependable, dependence, dependant (one who depends on another for support), dependent (conditional on, contingent). *Depend* linked to a condition requires the preposition *on* (preferred) or *upon* (e.g. "It depends whether we have enough time" is incorrect); when *depend* = *hang down* the preposition is *from*.

depict, depicter, depiction.

deplete = to empty, exhaust, use almost entirely; **reduce** = to make less.

deplore people's attitudes or actions, but not the people themselves.

depolarize (not -*ise*).

deposit, depositer (who deposits), depository (to whom a deposit is made, or in which a deposit is made), deposition (= the act of depositing or the act of deposing).

depot (no accents).

depraved = bad, corrupt, evil (noun *depravation*); **deprived** = suffering because of a lack of basic necessities (noun *deprivation*). E.g.:
"The person who committed this horrible crime must be totally depraved."
"Children living in the camps are deprived of a proper education."

deprecate = to plead earnestly against; **depreciate** = to belittle, fall in value (opposite of *appreciate*). E.g.:
"I deprecate the modern tendency to resort to violence to settle differences."
"He depreciates all my contributions to the project."
"Contrary to the usual rising trend in house prices, property in this district has depreciated this year."

depress, depressant, depressible.

depute, deputy, deputize.

derange, derangement, derangeable.

deride, derider, derision, derisible (= laughable), derisory (= scoffing, deserving derision, ridiculously small), derisive (= expressing derision). E.g.:
"His attempts at pottery were derisible."
"Her comments about his pottery were derisory."
"She made derisive comments about his pottery."

de rigueur (italics) = required by custom or etiquette; the French term should be avoided.

descend, descendant (who or which is descended from), descendent (which descends or is descending), descender, descendible.

descent *See* **decent**.

descry *See* **decry**.

desert = arid region; **deserts** = something deserved; **dessert** = pudding. All three words are singular; the first and third add an *s* for the plural, the second has the same spelling for the singular and the plural.

desertification, a comparatively new word meaning the formation of desert (through ecological mismanagement), is preferred to **desertization**.

desiccate, desiccation (not *dessicate, dessication*).

desire, desirable (= worthy of desire, wanted), desirous (of) (= full of desire (for)).

desman (pl. desmans).

desolate = barren, forlorn, uninhabited; **dissolute** = immoral, loose.

despatch The preferred spelling is **dispatch**.

desperado (pl. desperados).

desperate (not *desparate*) = feeling beyond hope, in despair, fraught with danger; **disparate** = different in character or quality. E.g.:
"They had not eaten for four days and were desperate for food."
"The twins looked almost identical but held disparate views about the way they should dress."

despise, despicable (not *dispise* or *despisable*).

despite is preferred to **in spite of**.

despite the fact that = **although**, which should be used.

despoil = to plunder (it does not mean to spoil or damage).

dessert *See* **desert.**

destined = meant, certain, foreordained; it does not mean merely *intended* (it has more to do with *destiny* than *destination*). E.g.:

"The prince was destined to become king one day if he outlived his father." (correct)
"The old books were destined for the rubbish bin but I sent them to the jumble sale instead." (incorrect)

destiny = unalterable outcome (of a course of action/events); **destination** = place at which somebody or something arrives.

destroy, destroyer, destruction, destructible.

detect, detector, detection, detective, detectable.

detent = mechanical catch; **détente** (with acute accent) = improvement in formerly strained diplomatic relations.

deter, deterred, deterring, deterrable, deterrent, determent.

detour (no accent).

detract (from) = take away (from); **distract** (from) = divert attention (from). E.g.:

"Misspellings detracted from the quality of the article."
"Misspellings distracted the reader from the point being made."

de trop (italics) = unwanted or superfluous, either of which is preferred.

develop, developed, developing, developer, development, developable.

developing countries This term is preferred to *undeveloped* or *underdeveloped countries*.

deviate, deviation, deviant (preferred to deviator).

device *See* **devise.**

Devil (capital letter if synonymous with Satan), devilish, devilment, devilry.

devise (verb), deviser (who devises), devisor (who bequeaths), devisee (who receives a bequest); **device** is the noun. *See also* **divide.**

devitalize (not *-ise*).

dextrous (= nimble-fingered) is the preferred spelling of **dexterous**.

diacritical marks *See* **accents and diacritical marks**.

diagnose, diagnosis (pl. diagnoses). **Diagnosis** is the identification of a fault or disorder (from its symptoms or from test results); **prognosis** is the prediction of the course of a disorder and its probable outcome (from experience of similar conditions).

diagram, diagrammed, diagrammatic, diagrammatize.

dial, dialled, dialling, dialler.

dialect = (usually regional) variety of a language, often with some words unique to its vocabulary; **dialectal** = to do with dialect; **dialectic(s)** = branch of logic concerned with methods of reasoning; **dialectical** = to do with dialectics. *See also* **accent**.

dialogue (= conversation between two people) is a vogue word and should be avoided in figurative use (*see* **vogue words**).

dialysis (pl. dialyses), dialyse, dialyser.

diamanté (italics, acute accent).

diaphragm, diaphragmatic (the *g* is silent in the first word but pronounced in the second).

diarrhoea (spelling of other *-rrhoea* words is analogous).

Diaspora (= the dispersion of Jews outside Palestine or Israel) should not be capitalized in its modern (vogue) use to mean any or all people at large.

diatribe = invective, vicious criticism; the word should not be used for merely any verbose statement.

dice (noun) is now the accepted form of both the singular and the plural; the use of *die* as a singular of *dice* is archaic (except in such expressions as "the die is cast"). The adjective is *dicey*.

dichotomy = separation into opposite/contrasting categories; it should not be used to mean merely **ambivalence** or **dilemma** (which see).

dictum (pl. dicta).

die *of* is preferred to **die** *from* (e.g. "They died of the plague").

dietitian is the preferred spelling of **dietician**.

differ, meaning *to be different*, requires the preposition *from*; when it is used to mean *disagree*, it can take *from* or *with*. E.g.:
"The possession of retractable claws is the main way in which cats differ from dogs."
"I differ with you on that point."
Do not use differ *to*. See also **diverge**.

different *from* is increasingly becoming preferred usage to **different** *to*; do not use different than.

difficulty requires *in* before a verb. E.g.:
"She had difficulty in making herself understood."

diffraction = splitting of light into (coloured) bands by passing a beam close to an edge or through a narrow slit (verb *diffract*); **dispersion** = splitting of light into spectral colours by passing a beam through a prism or grating (verb *disperse*); **refraction** = bending of light rays (possibly with the formation of colours) by passing them from one transparent medium to another (verb *refract*). Even physicists sometimes confuse these terms (which can also be applied to other forms of radiation and to sound).

dig inflects *dig* − *dug* (preferred to digged) − dug. See also **delve**.

digest, digester, digestible, digestion.

digit, digitize, digitization, digital.

digraph See **ligature**.

dike The preferred spelling is **dyke**.

dilapidated (not *delapidated*).

dilate, dilatable, dilation (but dilatation in medicine), dilator (not *dilatator*); all derive from *dilate* = to make/become wider. The words dilatory, dilatorily and dilatoriness derive from *delay* = put off (in time).

dilemma involves a choice between two equally undesirable alternatives. The word should not be used to describe merely any difficult choice or problem.

diminish = to lessen; **minimize** = to make as little as possible. E.g.:
"Knowing what he has done does not diminish my respect for him."
"Tell her gently so as to minimize the shock of the bad news."

dinghy = small (rowing or sailing) boat; **dingy** = gloomy, grimy.

dingo (pl. dingoes).

dinner = main meal of the day, formally eaten in the evening (although to many people *dinner* is a mid-day meal; a smaller evening meal is called *supper*). A person who eats dinner in a restaurant is a *diner. See also* **lunch**.

diphtheria (note -*phth*- spelling).

diphthong *See* **ligature**.

diplomat = someone who represents a government or state; **diplomate** = someone who has been granted a diploma.

direct (adj.) = straight, straightforward. The logical related adverb is **directly**, but this means *immediately* and so *direct* has to do duty also as the adverb meaning *straight*. E.g.:
"She made a direct approach to the problem" (adjective);
"He felt unwell and went directly to bed" (adverb);
"They flew direct to Frankfurt, with no break at Paris" (adverb).

directions *See* **compass directions**.

dirigible = steerable; as a noun it is applied to early airships.

dis- *See* **negative prefixes**.

disadvantaged is sociologist's jargon; like **underprivileged**, it seldom means more than *poor* (e.g. "the disadvantaged sector of society" = "poor people").

disagree *See* **differ**.

disapprove = not approve, consider to be bad or wrong; **disprove** = prove to be incorrect. E.g.:

"I disapprove of young girls being allowed out late at night."
"Her handling of her assailant disproved your theory that young girls cannot take care of themselves."

disarmed = having had arms (weapons) taken away; **unarmed** = not bearing arms; **disarming** = charming, winsome.

disarrange, disarrangement.

disassemble = to take to pieces, to strip (down a machine); **dissemble** = to disguise, to hide one's feelings. E.g.:

"We had only an hour to disassemble the machine, fix it, and put it back together again."
"They used to add curry to the dish to dissemble the flavour of the bad meat."

disassociate The preferred spelling is **dissociate**.

disaster, disastrous (not *disasterous*). *See also* **misfortune**.

disbar *See* **debar**.

disbelief = state of not believing; **disbelieve** = to refuse to accept as truth; **disbeliever** = someone who rejects belief in something (having given it due consideration); **unbeliever** = someone who does not believe, often merely through disinterest.

disburse, disbursement. **Disburse** = pay out (money); **disperse** = scatter, spread widely. E.g.:

"The finance committee disbursed the proceeds of the fund-raising campaign."
"By the time mounted police arrived, the demonstrators had dispersed into the side streets."

disc is the preferred spelling of **disk** (although both are correct English); American spelling favours *disk* as, increasingly, do computer engineers (who call a small computer disk a *diskette*).

discern, discernible.

disclose = to declare, reveal; **expose** = to unmask, put in jeopardy. E.g.:

"She opened her coat to disclose a bright red dress."
"The blackmailer threatened to disclose his victim's guilty secret."
"The victim decided to expose the blackmailer."

discoloration (but discolour, discoloured).

discomfit = thwart, disconcert, defeat in battle; **discomfort** = to disturb, upset; **discomfiture** = a defeat.

discotheque is the preferred spelling (not *discothèque*); the colloquial abbreviation **disco** should be avoided in formal writing.

discover = to come across or find (out) something that already exists; **invent** = to make something new, to originate (something that did not previously exist); e.g. "Scheele discovered chlorine" but "Nobel invented dynamite".

discreet = prudent, circumspect, using care with (personal) information (its opposite is **indiscreet**); **discrete** = separate, individual, distinct (its opposite is **indiscrete** = continuous, homogeneous). E.g.:

"The manager is a discreet father-figure to his staff."
"A sugar lump is composed of small discrete crystals."

discriminating = discerning, selective in an experienced way; **discriminatory** = unfair, biased. E.g.:

"She is usually discriminating in her choice of clothes."
"He was often discriminatory in preferring to employ men rather than women."

discus (pl. discuses) = disc-shaped object thrown by an athlete; **discuss** = to debate, examine in detail.

disfranchise is the preferred form of **disenfranchise**.

dishevel, dishevelled.

disinterested = impartial; **uninterested** = not interested. E.g.:

"The umpire should be a disinterested party who can be trusted to favour neither side."
"I am totally uninterested in the game of cricket."

disk *See* **disc**.

dislodge, dislodgement.

dismiss, dismissible.

disorganize, disorganization.

disorient (preferred to disorientate), disorientation. *See also* **orient.**

dispassionate = calm, without passion; **impassioned** = showing passion, highly enthusiastic; **impassive** = unemotional, apathetic. E.g.:
"Throughout the trial he put his client's case in a dispassionate way."
"At the end of the trial counsel made an impassioned plea for clemency."
"Throughout the trial the defendant maintained an impassive expression."

dispatch is the preferred spelling of **despatch** (noun and verb).

dispel, dispelled, dispelling

dispense, dispenser, dispensable (not *-ible*), dispensary, dispensation. *See also* **dispose.**

dispersal = the act of dispersing, distributing, spreading out; **dispersion** = the result of dispersing, distributing, spreading out. E.g.:
"Rapid dispersal of troops is essential if they come under air attack."
"The dispersion of pigment was uneven, making the paint streaky." *See also* **diffraction.**

dispose = arrange in a particular way, adjust − its noun is *disposition*; **dispose of** = give/throw away − its noun is *disposal*; **dispense with** = do without.

disprove *See* **disapprove**.

disqualified = with a qualification removed, banned; **unqualified** = having no qualification. E.g.:
"He was convicted of a motoring offence and disqualified from driving a car."
"Unqualified people are not allowed to practise medicine in Britain."

disremember should be avoided as a synonym of *forget*; **misremember** = to remember incorrectly.

disrepair = state of needing repair/mending; **misrepair** = to repair incorrectly/badly.

disruption *See* **eruption**.

dissatisfied = discontented, disappointed; **unsatisfied** = not satisfied/fulfilled. E.g.:
"We were extremely dissatisfied with the service at the hotel."
"The demand for hotel rooms at the resort is still unsatisfied."

dissect, dissection (not *disect, disection*, although bisect, bisection are correct). **Dissect** = cut/split into pieces; **bisect** = divide in two.

dissemble *See* **disassemble**.

dissent *See* **decent**.

dissimulate = conceal, disguise, pretend the opposite; **simulate** = copy, imitate. E.g.:
"The thief dissimulated the diamonds by putting them in the crushed ice."
"The jeweller simulated diamonds with zircons and synthetic garnets."

dissociate is the preferred form of **disassociate** in ordinary text, and the only form in chemistry.

dissolute *See* **desolate**.

dissolve, dissolvable (which is preferred to *dissoluble*, but equivalent to *soluble* in this sense).

dissymmetry *See also* **asymmetry**.

distaste, distastable, distasteful.

distend, distension (not *distention*), distensible.

distil, distilled, distilling, distillation, distillery.

distinct = separate, individual, unique; **distinctive** = characteristic, distinguishing; **distinguished** = eminent, famous (person). E.g.:
"She assumed a distinct air of indifference."

"I noticed the distinctive smell of petrol."

"The chairman greeted our distinguished visitor."

distract has the past tense and participle **distracted**, although **distraught** is retained as an adjective. *See also* **distrait.**

distrait (italics) = absentminded; **distraught** = agitated (in mind). The former should be avoided.

distribute, distributer (who distributes), but distributor (in a car).

disused = no longer used (although formerly used); **unused** = not been used (yet), or unaccustomed; **misused** = used incorrectly; **ill-used** = used badly, ill-treated.

ditto Do not use the symbol " or the abbreviation *do*, even in tabular matter.

diurnal *See* **daily.**

divan *See* **couch.**

diverge = to move apart; **divergent** = getting farther apart. These two words do not mean the same as *differ* and *different*. E.g.:

"The editor and designer held divergent views" is incorrect if their views were different.

divide, divisible (preferred to dividable), division, divider (who or which divides, generally), divisor (maths). *See also* **devise.**

divorcee is the preferred spelling for both sexes (not *divorcé* or *divorcée*).

djellaba is the preferred spelling for the Arab robe (not *djellabah, jellaba*).

do (verb) has the past tense **did** and past participle **done**. Do (noun) has the plural do's (as in *do's and don'ts*).

do should not be used as an abbreviation of ditto.

docket, docketed, docketing.

doctor, as a verb, has to work extremely hard. It can mean treat medically ("I doctored myself"), spay or castrate ("I had my dog doctored"), patch up ("I doctored the crack in the window") interfere

with ("I doctored his drink"), or falsify ("I doctored the accounts").
Most uses are colloquial and should be avoided in formal
writing.

doctrine = principle or belief; **dogma** = doctrine laid down with
authority; **doctrinaire** = theoretical, carried to a logical but
unworkable extreme; **dogmatic** = asserting positively, overbearing.

dodo (pl. dodos).

doff = take off (a hat); **don** = put on (clothes). Both words are
old-fashioned.

dog biscuit, dog-cart, dog-collar, dog-days, dog-eared, dogfight,
dogfish, doghouse, dog-Latin, dogleg, dog-rose, dogsbody, dog star,
dog's-tooth (plant, ornament), dog-tooth (canine tooth), dog-watch,
dogwood.

doggie = a (little) dog; **doggy** = to do with a dog or dogs.

dogma (pl. dogmas).

doily is the preferred spelling (not *doyley*).

dolman (pl. dolmans) = robe or mantle, type of sleeve; **dolmen** (pl.
dolmens) = prehistoric stone slab or tomb.

dolour, dolorous.

dolphin = long-snouted aquatic mammal (family Delphinidae);
porpoise = blunt-nosed aquatic mammal of similar overall appearance
(genus *Phocaena*); both are classified in the same order as whales
(Cetacea). *Dolphin* is also the name of two species of brightly coloured
marine fish.

domestic = pertaining to the home; **domesticated** = modified to be
home-loving; e.g. a dog is a domestic animal, a tame water buffalo is
a domesticated animal.

dominating = masterful; **domineering** = bullying; **predominant** =
outstanding, principal; **dominant** = prevailing, outstanding, opposite
of recessive. The correct form is dominated *by*, not dominated *with*.

dominoes (the game), although strictly plural, is usually treated as a singular form (e.g. "Dominoes is a game for two or four players"). When referring to the playing-pieces, the word is an ordinary plural (e.g. "Most modern dominoes are made of plastic").

don *See* **doff.**

don't should not be used for **do not** in formal writing. As a noun, it has the plural **don'ts** (as in *do's and don'ts*).

dope, doper, dopy.

dose, dosage, dosimeter.

dote, dotage.

double entendre (italics) = double meaning (often indecent); the pseudo-French form should be avoided.

double negative Two negatives in a single sentence cancel each other, leaving a positive. E.g.:

"He will not eat nothing." = "He will eat something."
"The model appeared without no clothes on." = "The model appeared with some clothes on."
"I was left without hardly any money." = "I was left with quite a lot of money."

Double negatives should therefore be avoided, unless they are used deliberately for effect (e.g. "The model was not unattractive").

doubling of letters (before suffixes). *See* **-b** or **-bb-; -d-** or **-dd-; -l-** or **-ll-; -m-** or **-mm-; -n-** or **-nn-; -p-** or **-pp-; -r-** or **-rr-; -s-** or **-ss-; -t-** or **-tt-.**

doubt, used in a positive statement, requires *whether* or *if*; in a negative statement, it takes *that* or *but that*. E.g.:

"I doubt whether she will finish on time."
"I have no doubt that she will finish on time."

dovecot is the preferred spelling (not *dovecote*), and reflects the correct pronunciation.

dowel, dowelled, dowelling.

downbeat, downcast, down-draught, downfall, down-hearted, downhill, down-market (adj.), downpour, downright, downstairs, downstream, down time, down town, downtrodden, downward(s), downwind.

down-market is salesman's jargon, usually to describe goods of low price and/or inferior quality; it should be avoided in formal writing. The opposite is **up-market**.

doyley The preferred spelling is **doily.**

dozy, dozier, doziest.

drachm = unit of apothecaries' weight; **drachma** = Greek money.

draconian = harsh, severe, swingeing; **draconic** = to do with a dragon. *Draconian* should not be overworked to describe something that is merely a mild measure or punishment.

draft = plan, preliminary sketch, group of men (drawn from others); **draught** = a pull, something drawn (pulled), current of air, depth of a ship's keel. A **draughtsman**, however, draws lines, not pulls things; a **drayman** carries things in a truck or cart, originally pulled by *draught* horses.

dragée (acute accent).

dragoman (pl. dragomans).

drama, dramatize, dramatization.

drastic = severe, strongly-acting, vigorous (e.g. "drastic measures"); the word should not be used to mean merely *large* (as in "a drastic waste of paper").

draughts (the game) is a singular word; "games of draughts" achieves a plural construction.

draw (verb) has the past tense **drew** and past participle **drawn.**

drawers, an old-fashioned term for knickers, is a plural word; "a pair of drawers" achieves a singular construction.

dreadful should be reserved for things or circumstances that invoke dread (= great fear), and not used of something that is merely *unpleasant* or *disagreeable* (as in "she looked dreadful in her new dress").

dream (verb) The preferred past tense and participle is **dreamed** (not *dreamt*).

drink (verb) has the past tense **drank** and the past participle **drunk**.

drive (verb) has the past tense **drove** and the past participle **driven**.

drivel, driveller, drivelled, drivelling.

dromedary *See* **camel**.

drug names Generic names (approved names) should normally be used, not trade names or proprietary names (e.g. write diazepam, not Valium; soluble aspirin, not Disprin). If trade names must be used, they should have an initial capital letter (*see* **trade names**).

dry, drier (not *dryer*), driest (adjectives), drily, dryish. **Drier** is also the preferred spelling of the noun (not *dryer*).

duel, dueller, duellist, duelling.

due to, like **owing to**, are adjectival and strictly should not be used as prepositions equivalent to *because of* or *on account of*. E.g.:
"I was late due to a delay on the railway" is better put as "I was late because of a delay on the railway".

duly = in (a) due manner; **dully** = in a dull manner. E.g.:
"He summoned a waiter who duly came to our table."
"I called to him but he just looked up dully from the book he was reading and said nothing."

duplicate, duplicator, duplication (= act of making a copy or duplicate), duplicity (= double-dealing, deception).

during the course of = **during**, which should be used.

during the period from = **from**, which should be used.

Dutch words assimilated into English seldom cause difficulty, because most are well established and familiar. So, more for interest than instruction, here is a list of words — many to do with the sea and ships — that came to Britain via the Netherlands:

boor	easel	sketch	tarpon
brandy	foist	skipper	trigger
caboose	gin	sledge	waffle
cruise	kit	sloop	wagon
deck	landscape	splice	yacht
decoy	loiter	splinter	
dock	maelstrom	split	
drill	marlin	spool	

Other Dutch words, such as *boss* and *sleigh*, probably arrived in Britain via North America; still others travelled from South Africa by way of the Afrikaans language, such as:

aardvark	boomslang	rand	trek
apartheid	commandeer	spoor	veld
boer	klipspringer	springbok	wildebeest

duty, dutiable.

duvet *See* **bedspread**.

dwarf (pl. dwarfs).

dwell is archaic for to **live** (somewhere), which should be used. When **dwell** means linger or remain, it has the preferred past tense and participle **dwelled** (not *dwelt*).

dwelling is a slightly old-fashioned term for a building in which somebody lives, but like **home** it has the advantage of general imprecision and is much preferred to the bureaucratic **accommodation**. *Dwelling* can also be applied to less sophisticated homes, from a cave to a mud hut. More precise terms include **bungalow** (a single-storey building), **house** (a building of at least two storeys), **flat** (a self-contained part of a larger building), **maisonette** (similar to a flat, often on two floors, and with its own street-level entrance) and **bed-sitter** (a single room, usually with shared washing and cooking facilities). One can also live with somebody else in **lodgings** (colloquially **digs**), and any of these can be euphemistically described as **living quarters**. The American term **apartment** is gaining ground as a synonym of *flat*, but **condominium** (for a group of owner-occupied apartments whose owners share certain overall costs) has yet to catch on in Britain as a word or a venture.

dyad, or double, = a pair of words that are almost always found together. *See* **inseparable pairs**.

dye, dyed, dyeing, dyeable (of cloth).

dyke is the preferred spelling of **dike**.

dynamo (pl. dynamos).

dys- *See* **negative prefixes**.

dysentery (not *dysentry*).

dysfunction is medical; **malfunction** is general.

dyslexia The preferred adjective is **dyslectic** (not *dyslexic*).

E

-e When suffixes are added to words that end in a silent *e*, some words drop the *e* and some retain it. If the suffix begins with a vowel, the *e* is usually dropped:

age	aging
cringe	cringing
debate	debatable
dote	dotage
immune	immunize
intrigue	intriguing
love	lovable
move	moving
pledge	pledging
prude	prudish
range	ranging
tinge	tinging

(exceptions *hoeing, mileage, shoeing, tiptoeing* and *probeable* – to distinguish it from *probable* – and some people would also make *ageing* and *rateable* exceptions). The *e* is also dropped by most words that form an adjective by adding a *y*:

bone	bony
cage	cagy
craze	crazy
doze	dozy
ice	icy
race	racy
sponge	spongy

(exceptions *bluey, dicey, gluey* and *holey*).

If the suffix begins with a consonant, the *e* is retained:

acknowledge	acknowledgement
blame	blameless
change	changeling
home	homely

hope	hopeful
judge	judgement
lone	lonely
time	timeless
unique	uniqueness

(exceptions *duly, fledgling, truly*).

The *e* is also retained if preceded by a *c* or *g* and followed by *a* or *o*:

engageable	marriageable
changeover	replaceable
knowledgeable	traceable

See also **spelling; suffixes**.

each and **every** require singular verbs when they precede the words they refer to; e.g.: "The team made errors and each member is to blame for the defeat; every member later admitted his responsibility." When *each* follows the word it refers to it requires a plural verb; e.g. "The members each have to carry part of the blame." A preference for plural verbs and pronouns can be expressed by substituting *all* (or *both*) for *each* (or *every*): "The team made errors and all the members are to blame for the defeat; all subsequently admitted their responsibility." *See also* **both; either**.

each other applies to two persons or things; **one another** applies to three or more; e.g. "The two boys argued and then hit each other; all four parents arrived and shouted at one another." The possessive forms are **each other's** and **one another's**.

earache, ear-drum, ear-like, earmark, earphone(s), ear-piece, earplug, earring.

Earth, the planet, should be spelled with an initial capital letter (*see* **astronomical terms**).

earthly = to do with the planet Earth; **earthy** = to do with the soil; **earthen** is an archaic form of *earthy*, retained in such expressions as "an earthen floor" and in the compound word *earthenware*.

earthnut = pignut (plant of the carrot family); **groundnut** = peanut (plant of the pea family).

Earth satellites *See* **artificial satellites**.

east, eastern, easterly, etc. *See* **compass directions; eastern; Far East; Middle East**.

eastern refers to the eastern part of any place, e.g. "the eastern part of Surrey", "eastern Europe" (although it is usually the *east* end/side of a city); **oriental** refers to anywhere east of the Middle East, and is virtually synonymous with *Asian*.

Eastern Hemisphere (initial capital letters).

easy-going (hyphen).

eat has the past tense **ate** (not *eat*) and past participle **eaten**. (*Ate* is pronounced to rhyme with *get*.)

eatable *See* **edible**.

echo (pl. echoes), echoing, echoer, echo-location, echo-sounder, echo-sounding.

éclair (acute accent).

éclat = brilliant success, showy fame; the French term should be avoided.

eclectic = freely chosen from available sources, non-exclusive; it does not mean specially selected to include only the best.

economic = pertaining to (the) economy; **economical** = pertaining to economics; neither word should be used to mean **inexpensive** or **cheap**.

Economic Community (abbreviation **EC**) is the current name for what was formerly called the **European Economic Community (EEC)**, and originally called the **Common Market**.

economy, economize.

ecstasy, ecstatic (note spelling).

-ection is the preferred spelling to **-exion** in such words as confection, connection, deflection, reflection (thus avoiding such combinations as "deflexion of a section" and "in connexion with the election"). Words that should be spelled *-exion* include complexion, genuflexion and inflexion. Note also crucifixion, fluxion. *See also* **reflect**.

Ecuador The derived adjective and noun is *Ecuadorian*.

eczema (note spelling).

-ed or **-t** Modern usage generally favours *-ed* rather than *-t* as the ending of past tenses and past participles of verbs that can have either form. Only three verbs have the *-t* form preferred in some dictionaries (*burn, smell* and *spill*), and this guide recommends consistency and the *-ed* spelling in all cases. The *-t* forms are, however, sometimes retained as adjectives. E.g.:

bereave	bereaved (but bereft as adj.)
burn	burned (but burnt as adj.)
dream	dreamed
kneel	kneeled
lean	leaned
leap	leaped
learn	learned
smell	smelled
spell	spelled
spill	spilled (but spilt as adj.)
spoil	spoiled (but spoilt as adj.)

See also **suffixes.**

edema The preferred spelling is **oedema.**

edge, edging, edgy.

edible = can be eaten without harm, fit to eat; **eatable** = presented in a way that tempts one to eat. The opposites are *inedible* and *uneatable*.

edifice rarely means more than simply **large building**, which is preferred.

educate, educator, educatory, educatable, educative, education, educational, educationist (not *educationalist*).

educe, educible.

-ee is a suffix added to a noun to denote a person to whom something is done or given. More-or-less established examples include:

appointee	employee	evacuee	internee
detainee	escapee	grantee	lessee

| mortgagee | nominee | trainee | trustee |

Newly invented words of this type (such as *returnee*) should be avoided.

EEC *See* **Economic Community.**

e'er is a (poetic) abbreviation of **ever**, and should be avoided; **ere** is archaic for **before**, and should also be avoided.

effect, effecter (who effects), effector (which effects). *See also* **affect.**

effeminate is properly applied to a man who is womanish, unmanly; it is not a synonym of **feminine** (see **female**). The corresponding term, applied to woman, is *mannish*.

effete = worn out, exhausted; it does not mean *effeminate* or *sophisticated*, and is probably best avoided.

efficient = achieved without waste, capable; **proficient** = executed to an accepted (defined) standard; e.g. "His writing was extremely small, making efficient use of the paper, but it revealed that he was not proficient in the use of English." **Efficiency** and **proficiency** are sometimes similarly confused. *Efficient* has also been confused with **effective** (= producing the desired/required effect) and **effectual** (= able to produce an effect) and even **efficacious** (= producing the required (medical) result, with implied rapidity); e.g. "The machine ceased to be efficient so the mechanic poured in some oil which, although effective in reducing friction, was not effectual in reducing fuel consumption; when swallowed by the mechanic, the same oil was efficacious in relieving his constipation."

effrontery *See* **affront.**

EFL is the abbreviation of English as a foreign language (as taught to overseas students living temporarily in Britain); **ESL** = English as a second language (as taught to non-English residents of Britain whose first language is not English).

e.g. is the abbreviation of *exempli gratia* (for example). It should not be confused with **i.e.** (= *id est*, that is). E.g.:

"We may have a choice of transport, e.g. bus, train or taxi."
"The key to the country's progress is the development of an infrastructure, i.e. a network of good roads and railways."

egoism = theory that self-interest is (or should be) the basis of morality − an adherent is an *egoist*; **egotism** = overuse of the pronoun *I*, talking about oneself too much − someone who does so is an *egotist*.

-ei- or **-ie-** The child's rule of thumb is: "I before E except after C". It is not an inflexible rule; the following words have *i* before *e*, after *c*, and therefore break the rule:

ancient	omniscience, omniscient
coefficient	prescient
conscience	proficient, proficiency
deficient	science
efficient, efficiency	specie, species
glacier	stupefacient
inefficient, inefficiency	sufficient, sufficiency

All the following words have *-ei-* not immediately after *c* in their spelling:

beige	feign	meiosis	seizure
being	feint	neigh	sheikh
blueing	foreign	neighbour(ing)	shoeing
caffeine	forfeit	neither	singeing
casein	freight	nonpareil	skein
canoeing	gneiss	obeisance	sleigh
canoeist	heifer	plebeian	sleight
codeine	heigh-ho	poltergeist	surfeit
counterfeit	height(en)	protein	surveillance
cuneiform	heinous	reign	swingeing
deign	heir, heiress	rein(deer)	their(s)
dyeing	hoeing	Seidlitz	tyreing
eider(down)	inveigh	(powder)	veil
eidograph	inveigle	seigneur	vein
eight, eighty	kaleidoscope	seine	weigh, weight
etc.	leisure	seismic etc.	weir
either	madeira	seize	weird

eiderdown *See* **bedspread.**

Eire, like Southern Ireland, should not be used for the Republic of Ireland or, simply, Ireland. **Northern Ireland** is the correct term for the Irish part of the United Kingdom (formally the United Kingdom of Great Britain and Northern Ireland), for which the term **Ulster** should not be used.

either applies to one of two (persons or things) and is singular; e.g. "There are two applicants: either (of them) is suitable." If the choice is not between two but among three or more, use *any* or *any one* (two words); e.g. "Five teams competed: any (one of them) could have won."
Do not misuse *either* for **each**; e.g. "There are houses on either side of the street" is incorrect; say "... on each side of the street" or "on both sides of the street". (But "There are no houses on either side of the street" is correct and slightly better than "There are houses on neither side of the street", which is an example of a sentence that is an unfulfilled promise.) *See also* **alternative**.

eject, ejector.

eke (out) = to make something last by adding to it (not to make it last by "stretching" or husbanding it, without supplement). E.g.:
"He eked out his meagre wages with money he earned by working as a barman in the evenings."

élan (italics) = dash, impetuousness; the French form should be avoided.

elapse = to pass, expire; **lapse** (verb) = to err, fail, fall (temporarily) into disuse (e.g. time may elapse, a person's manners may lapse).

elder is the comparative (and *eldest* the superlative) of *old* as applied to the ages of people, with the emphasis on priority by birth (e.g. "your elder sister", "my eldest son"); **older** (and *oldest*) are usual in all other instances (e.g. "a much older man", "the oldest car at the rally"). In comparisons employing *than*, the form *older* is used (e.g. "you are older than me").

elect, elector (fem. electress), election.

electric describes something powered by electricity (e.g. *electric central heating, electric kettle, electric motor*); **electrical** describes something to do with electricity in general (e.g. *electrical engineering, electrical* *industry*); **electronic** describes something that uses valves, transistors or silicon "chips" (e.g. *electronic calculator, electronic flash*).

electrolysis, electrolyte, electrolyse, electrolytic.

elegy = poem, funeral song; **eulogy** = lavish written or spoken praise. The corresponding verbs are elegize, eulogize.

element, elemental (= pertaining to the elements, either the chemical ones or the classical earth, air, fire and water), elementary (= basic, primary). E.g.:
"Reactive metals, such as sodium and magnesium, are rarely seen in their elemental form."
"Every student should take an elementary science course."

elevator, in British English, should be reserved for a machine for lifting goods (e.g. *freight elevator, grain elevator*); a machine for people is a **lift** (= *elevator* in American).

elf (pl. elves).

elicit = to draw out, evoke; **illicit** = unlawful, improper. E.g.:
"The interviewer found it difficult to elicit a response from the candidate."
"The police wanted to interview him about possible illicit dealings in gold bullion."

eligible = meeting the requirements for appointment/election/ selection; **legible** = clear, easily read; **illegible** = written or printed so badly as to be incapable of being read (*see* **unreadable**).

eliminate = to remove something from something; **isolate** = to separate something from among other things; **exclude** = to ignore/shut out completely.

elision = omission of a sound, usually a vowel, in pronouncing a word or words; the missing component is indicated by an apostrophe (e.g. can't, didn't, he'll, I'm, Len's arrived, won't). Elided words should be avoided in formal writing. *See also* **ellipsis**.

élite, élitist (acute accent).

elk = large deer of northern Europe and Asia (*Alces alces*), the North

American race of which is called a **moose**. Americans use the term *elk* for a different animal, the wapiti or North American elk (*Cervus canadensis*). *See also* **caribou**.

ellipsis (pl. ellipses). Omissions in a quotation, list or mathematical series are indicated by three full points, preserving any adjacent punctuation. E.g.:

"On the first day of Christmas … a partridge in a pear-tree."
January, February, …, November, December.
$x_1, x_2, x_3, \ldots, x_n$
See also **elision**.

El Salvador The derived adjective and noun is *Salvadoran*.

else when paired with a pronoun such as *anybody* (anyone), *everybody* (everyone), *nobody* (no one), *somebody* (someone) or *who* forms the genitive (possessive) **else's** (e.g. "anybody else's book", "who else's book is torn?").

elucidate, elucidator.

elude *See* **illude**.

elusive = difficult to understand/capture; **illusive** = not as valuable/real as it seems. E.g.:

"To me, atomic theory will always be elusive."
"His trite explanation proved to be illusive when he was questioned more closely."
See also **delusion**.

embalm, embalming, embalmment, embalmer.

embargo (pl. embargoes).

embarrass, embarrassment (with one *b*, two *rs* and two *ss*).

embed, embedded, embedding.

embezzle, embezzlement.

embrocation = healing lotion, liniment; **imbrication** = set of overlapping shapes (like tiles on a roof or scales on a fish).

embryo (pl. embryos).

emend *See* **amend**.

emerge, emergent, emergence (= act of emerging), emergency (= happening that emerges unexpectedly).

emigrant and **immigrant** The correct use of these words depends on where you are standing. If you are in Britain, an incoming Nigerian is an immigrant and an outgoing Englishman, who intends to settle in Nigeria, is an emigrant. To a Nigerian in Nigeria, the appellations would be reversed. Both people are **migrants** (as are animals that move long distances, whether they be coming or going). The corresponding verbs are **emigrate**, **immigrate** and **migrate**.

émigré (acute accents).

eminent *See* **immanent**.

emollient = something that softens the skin, a lotion; **emolument** = pay for holding an office, salary.

emotion gives rise to the adjectives *emotional* and *emotive*. The former is used to mean displaying emotion, the latter to mean stimulating emotion. E.g.:
"Her sensitive singing produced an emotional response in those who heard it."
"The crowd stirred to the emotive sound of military music."

empanel, empanelled, empanelling.

empathy = agreeing with/sharing somebody's feelings; **sympathy** = feeling of sorrow for somebody in trouble/distress.

emphasis (pl. emphases), emphasize.

emporium (pl. emporia).

empty = containing or carrying nothing; **vacant** = unoccupied, expressionless; e.g. "An empty cupboard in a vacant flat."

emulate = to try to equal or better (not merely to **imitate**). E.g.:
"He emulated his boss and assembled two machines in an hour."
"He imitated his boss and was dismissed for insubordination."

en- or **in-** The *en-* form is preferred to *in-* as the prefix of *enclose*, *encrust* and *endorse*; the words *ensure* and *insure* coexist with different meanings (*see* **insure**); the *in-* form is preferred for *inquire*.

enable = to make able; it does not mean to make possible. E.g.:
"The completion of the work on time enabled us to keep to the schedule" is correct;
"... enabled the schedule to be kept" is incorrect.

enamel, enamelled, enamelling, enameller.

en bloc (italics) wholesale, as a unit; the French form should be avoided.

enclave *See* **conclave**.

enclose/enclosure are preferred to **inclose/inclosure** (but Inclosure Acts, historically).

encrust (preferred to incrust), incrustation (preferred to encrustation).

endemic is an adjective that describes a disease affecting most members of a population in a particular locality; **epidemic** (noun and adj.) applies to a disease that temporarily affects many people in a region; **pandemic** (noun and adj.) refers to a disease that occurs throughout a large area. E.g.:
"Myxomatosis is endemic among the rabbits of Australia."
"The new strain of Asian flu has reached epidemic proportions in Britain this winter."
"Scientists predict that AIDS may become a worldwide pandemic unless a cure or vaccine is discovered soon."

endive *See* **chicory**.

end product, like **end result,** is nearly always tautologous for simply *product* or *result*, which should be used.

endocrine etc. is preferred to **endochrine** etc.

endorse (preferred to indorse), endorsable, endorsement. *See also* **approve**.

endure, endurable.

enema (pl. enemas, not *enemata*).

energy, energetic, energize.

enervate = to sap the strength or energy of, to devitalize; it does not mean to put nerve into, invigorate.

enforce, enforceable.

enfranchise (not -*ize*).

English, in one form or other, is the language spoken by nearly 450 million people throughout the world (and is second only to Mandarin). It is the mother tongue in Australasia, Britain, Ireland and most of North America; a principal language in many African countries; and a second language on the Indian subcontinent and in much of south-eastern Asia. The type of English advocated for formal use is often termed standard English, but it is easier to give advice about what to avoid or what not to say than to define what is standard. For this reason, *see* **non-standard English.** *See also* **Americanisms; Australia and New Zealand; received English; slang.**

engrain (preferred to ingrain), ingrained (preferred to engrained).

enigma (pl. enigmas).

enliven is preferred to **liven up.**

en masse (italics) = all together, in (as) a body; the French form should be avoided.

enormity = serious crime, great wickedness. The word should not be used to mean hugeness, large size; e.g. "The enormity of the supertanker . . ." is incorrect.

enough *See* **adequate.**

enquire The preferred spelling is **inquire** (and **inquiry** is preferred to **enquiry**).

enrol, enrolled, enroller, enrolling, but enrolment.

en route (italics) = on the way; the French form should be avoided.

ensue, ensuing.

en suite (italics) = in a set, forming a unit (with); the French form, beloved of estate agents, should be avoided in formal writing.

ensure *See* **insure.**

entente (italics) = understanding or agreement between nations.

enterprise (not -*ize*).

enthral, enthralled, enthralling, enthraller, but enthralment.

enthuse should be avoided as a verb meaning **show enthusiasm** (for). *See* **back-formation.**

entitle(d), = name(d), is preferred to **title(d).**

entomology = the study of insects; **etymology** = the study of words.

entrance (noun) = the act of going in; **entry** = the result of going in; both = the way in. E.g.
"He made an entrance to gain entry."

entrap, entrapped, entrapping, but entrapment.

entrecôte (circumflex).

entrée (acute accent).

entrepôt (circumflex).

enumerable = countable; **innumerable** = uncountable, and should not be used instead of **many** of things that can (or could) be counted.

enunciate, enunciator, enunciation. *See also* **annunciation.**

envelop is the verb; **envelope** is the noun.

enviable = (capable of) arousing envy; **envious** = showing/feeling envy. E.g.:
"She had an enviable reputation for speed and accuracy."
"He was envious of her ability to work quickly and accurately."

environs is a plural word; it has no singular.

envisage = to imagine/visualize something planned but not created, to view. The word should not be used as a grandiose way of saying to *think*, *describe*, *estimate*, and so on. Examples of misuses include: "I envisage that the article will occupy two pages" (use *estimate/expect*); "The article envisaged two applications of . . ." (use *described*); "He envisaged that train fares might rise" (use *thought/predicted*).

envoi (preferred to *envoy*) = concluding part of a poem; **envoy** = diplomatic messenger.

envy = desire to have what somebody else has (adj. *envious*); **jealousy** = resentment that somebody else has something that one feels should be one's own (adj. *jealous*). E.g.:

"I was envious of Tina's new fur coat."
"I was jealous when Tina was promoted and I was not."

eon The preferred spelling is **aeon**.

epaulet (not *epaulette*).

épée (acute accents).

ephemera is singular (pl. ephemeras).

epidemic *See* **endemic**.

epigram = concise witty or sarcastic statement; **epilogue** = concluding part of a book or play; **epitaph** = inscription on a tombstone; **epithet** = an apt, descriptive term.

epilogue *See* **epigram**.

episcopal = to do with bishops; **Episcopalian** = to do with the Scottish Episcopalian Church.

epitaph *See* **epigram**.

epithet *See* **epigram**.

epitomy, epitomize.

eponym = someone who gives his name to a place or institution, now applied to any word formed from a person's name. E.g.:

> *boycott* (Charles Boycott)
> *braille* (Louis Braille)
> *clerihew* (Clerihew Bentley)
> *guillotine* (Dr J. Guillotin)
> *hansom cab* (Joseph Hansom)
> *lynch* (Capt. W. Lynch)
> *mansard roof* (François Mansard)
> *maverick* (S.A. Maverick)

pasteurize (Louis Pasteur)
pinchbeck (Christopher Pinchbeck)
sandwich (4th Earl of Sandwich)
shrapnel (General H. Shrapnel)
silhouette (Etienne Silhouette)
zeppelin (Count von Zeppelin).

equable = even, regular, unflappable; **equatable** = can be equated, regarded as equal; **equitable** = just, fair (note the spelling of *equitable*, which derives from *equity*). E.g.:

"He is renowned for his equable temperament even under stress."
"Jane's contribution is not equatable with that of Susan, who has worked much harder."
"To pay Jane and Susan the same amount would not be equitable."
See also **inequity.**

equal, equalled, equalling, equalize, equalization, equalizer. **Equal** takes *to*, not *as* or *with*. *See also* **coequal.**

equality does not need *as* before the word it qualifies; e.g. in "His version was equally as good", delete *as*.

equator (no initial capital letter when it refers to 0° latitude).

equinox (pl. equinoxes).

equip, equipped, equipping, equipment, equipage (archaic).

equitable *See* equable.

equivocate, equivocator.

-er *See* **comparative and superlative; -or; suffixes.**

eradicate = to root out (and thus destroy); **irradicate** (rare) = to root, fix firmly; **irradiate** = to expose to radiation such as light or X-rays.

erase, erasion, erasure (preferred). **Erase** = rub out, scrape away; **raze** = destroy completely, level with the ground, sweep away.

ere is archaic (and poetic) for **before**, which should be used. *See also* **e'er.**

erect, erector (who erects), but erector muscle.

errant *See* **arrant**.

errata (sing. erratum) = list of corrections in a book. Strictly they should consist of typesetting errors in the printed book which the author failed to correct on proof. *See also* **corrigenda**.

erstwhile is archaic for **former**, which should be used.

eruption = a breaking out (like a pimple or volcano); **irruption** = a breaking in (as of the sea through a broken sea wall); **interruption** = something that breaks (in) between; **intervention** = coming between two people or parties; **disruption** = a shattering, interruption.

escalate, used to mean *suddenly increase* or *intensify* (e.g. "His remarks escalated their differences"), is a vogue word and should be avoided (as should *escalation*). *See* **vogue words**.

Eskimo (pl. Eskimos, not *Eskimoes, Esquimaux*). North Americans and linguists prefer the term **Inuit**.

esoteric = intelligible only to the initiated, secret; **exoteric** = intelligible to the uninitiated, commonplace.

especially *See* **specially**.

esprit de corps (italics) = loyalty to a group (of which one is a member), high morale, pride/faith in a cause. There seems to be no English term for this "typically English characteristic"; nevertheless, the French term should be avoided.

Esquire (usually abbreviated to **Esq.**) is a formal, old-fashioned form of address equivalent to ordinary *Mr*. If used, it follows the man's name: *John Smith, Esq*.

-ss As a feminizing suffix, *see* **gender**.

essay *See* **assay**.

-est *See* **comparative and superlative; suffixes**.

estimatable = can be estimated; **estimable** = worthy of esteem; **inestimable** = too large to be estimatable. E.g.:

"There is insufficient information to make the cost estimatable."
"His estimable contribution enhanced the quality of the work."

"We could not thank her enough for her inestimable contribution to the work."

estimate (noun) = knowledgeable guess (of cost, worth, quantity required, etc.), or the figure arrived at; **estimation** = the act of making an estimate; judgement of worth. Both are made by an **estimator**. E.g.:

"I can make an estimate of the time the task will take."

"In my estimation the task will take three weeks."

Possible confusion can be avoided by using the verb to estimate. E.g.:

"I cannot estimate how long the task will take."

"I estimate that the task will take three weeks."

et al, the abbreviation of *et alia, et alii*, etc. (meaning "and other persons"), should be avoided in narrative text. *See also* **et cetera**.

etc. is the abbreviation of **et cetera** (which *see*).

et cetera is nearly always used as its abbreviation etc. This term should be avoided in formal text — use a phrase such as "and so on" instead. If etc. must be used, remember that it means "and other similar things" and therefore should not, strictly, be appended to an incomplete list of people (*see* **et al**), animals or plants. Also good style requires a comma before *etc*. E.g.:

"There were various makes of cars: Fords, Fiats, Bentleys, and many others" is correct;

"There were many makes — Fords, Fiats, Bentleys, and so on" is also correct;

"There were many cars: Fords, Fiats, Bentleys, etc." is acceptable but should be avoided;

"There were several of the senior managers: Jones, Smith, Brown, Green, etc." is strictly incorrect.

eternal *See* **temporal**.

ethics = set of moral principles, theory of good behaviour or conduct; **morals** = standards of behaviour/conduct in practice. E.g.:

"A doctor can usually be relied upon to comply with the ethics of the medical profession."

"He continues to criticize what he regards as the low morals of modern society."

etiology The preferred spelling is **aetiology**.

étude (italics) = study; the French form should be reserved for use as a musical term.

étui (= a needle-case, which is preferred).

etymology *See* **entomology**.

eulogy, eulogize. *See also* **elegy**.

euphemism *See* **non-standard English**.

European Economic Community (EEC) *See* **Economic Community.**

evade, evadable (= can be evaded), evasion (= act of evading, hedging), evasive (= difficult to pin down), evasiveness (= quality of being evasive). E.g.:

"He will not pay any tax if he finds that it is evadable."
"When asked about his income tax he gave evasive answers."
"You cannot expect him to give a straight answer − he is known for his evasiveness."

even should be placed next to the word it qualifies; misplaced it can lead to ambiguities similar to those created by a misplaced **only** (which *see*). Consider how the position of *even* affects the meaning when it is inserted into the sentence "Children are writing books":

"Even children are writing books" (let alone adults);
"Children are even writing books" (let alone reading them);
"Children are writing even books" (let alone essays).

even though *See* **although**.

ever, intensifying a noun or pronoun, does not take a hyphen (e.g. "Best ever result", "Largest ever found", "Was the poorest ever", "Who ever told you?", "What ever happened?"). If **ever** is used to generalize a pronoun, it joins it to form one word (e.g. "Come whenever you like", "Whatever interests you", "It is wrong, whoever told you", "It will take time, however you do it").

every is singular (e.g. "Every draughtsman has his own drawing-board"). *See also* **each**. **Everybody, everyone, everything** are similarly also singular (e.g. "Everybody is welcome to his share"). **Everyday**

(one word) is an adjective (e.g. "A delay in getting through is an everyday occurrence"); in other contexts, **every day** (two words) should be used (e.g. "Delays occur every day").

evince = to show or prove something (using argument or evidence), and should not be used merely as a synonym for show; **evoke** = to summon, call forth.

evocative = reviving memories, stimulating emotions; **provocative** = stimulating interest, causing annoyance/anger (usually with mischievous intent). E.g.:

"The evocative smell of wood smoke reminded her of home."
"He responded angrily to the provocative remark about his ability."

evolve, evolvable, evolution.

ex- (prefix) The preferred term is **former** (which *see*).

exacerbate = make worse; **exasperate** = annoy to distraction. E.g.:
"The herbal remedy only exacerbated his illness."
"She was exasperated by his childish behaviour."

exalt, exalter. **Exalt** = elevate in rank or status, praise, fill with pride; **exult** = rejoice.

excavate, excavator.

exceed See **accede.**

except is archaic when used for **unless**; e.g. in "He will not go except I go with him", *unless* should be used. See also **accept; bar.**

exceptionable = to which exception may be taken, open to objection; **exceptional** = which is an exception (hence *unexceptionable* = unobjectionable; *unexceptional* = not worthy of special note). E.g.:
"In my opinion his derogatory comments about your work were quite exceptionable."
"His praise for your work was quite exceptional."

excessive = in excess; **excessively** = in an excessive manner, immoderately; **exceedingly** = greatly, very much, extremely. E.g:
"She is excessively proud of her exceedingly good looks."

exchange, exchangeable.

excise, excisable.

excite, excitement (= state of being excited emotionally), excitation (= act of exciting, usually in science), excitable, exciter (= who or which excites, but excitor nerve).

exclamation mark (!) should be avoided in formal writing except in direct quotation (e.g. *Hello, Dolly!*, Westward Ho!) and reported speech (e.g. "Damn!" he said, "We're lost.").

exclude *See* **eliminate**.

excreta (not *excretia*) is a plural word.

excuse, excusable.

execute, executer (who executes something), executioner (who executes somebody), executor (who executes a will; fem. executrix).

exemplary = serving as a model to be imitated (e.g. "His exemplary behaviour became a standard for the others"); **excellent** = having/showing excellence, of best quality. The former word should not be used for the latter.

exempt (adj.) = not liable; **immune** = not liable to infection/danger; **excused** = free from blame/guilt/responsibility.

exercise = make use repeatedly of one's muscles, improve through practice, enforce a right; **exorcize** = drive out an evil influence (by invoking a deity).

exert, exertion.

ex gratia (italics) = as an act of grace, i.e. without prejudice (as in "an *ex gratia* payment"); the Latin term should be avoided.

exhausting = causing exhaustion; **exhaustive** = full, complete, thorough; **exhaustible** = can be exhausted. E.g.:
"Finding the goats involved an exhausting climb."
"Finding the goats involved an exhaustive search."
"Petroleum is an exhaustible resource."

exhibit, exhibitor, exhibition, exhibitionist. An *exhibitor* displays an *exhibit* at an *exhibition*; an *exhibitionist* draws attention to himself by exaggerated behaviour or by exposing himself.

exigent = urgent, pressing, rigorous; **exiguous** = small, scanty.

-exion *See* **-ection**.

exist, existent, existence, but extant.

exit, exited (exit = he/she goes out; exeunt = they go out).

ex officio (italics) = by virtue of office, i.e. as a consequence of having another appointment/position (as in "an *ex officio* member of the committee"); the Latin term should be avoided.

exorbitant (not *exhorbitant*).

exorcize, exorcism.

expand, expansive, expansible (not *expandable*).

expatriate (not *expatriot*).

expect, expector, expectable, expectant, expectancy, expectation. *See also* **anticipate**.

expectorate is a euphemism for **spit**, which today rarely gives offence as a word.

expedient (adj.) = advantageous, fitting; **expeditious** = quickly, prompt. E.g.
"When the police arrived, I thought it expedient to make an expeditious departure."

expel, expelled, expelling, expellent.

experiment, experimenter.

expertise (note spelling).

expiate, expiatable.

expire, expiration (of breath), expiry (of life or a fixed term).

explain *See* **allege**.

expletive = an oath, swearword or (violent) exclamation, usually followed (in writing) by an exclamation mark. E.g.:
"Damn! I have laddered my best pair of tights!"
See also **exclamation mark**.

explicit = stated directly (not merely implied), fully expressed; **implicit** = implied (although not stated), entirely/unquestioningly relying on.

explode, explosive, explodable (preferred to *explosible*), explosion.

explosion = a bursting outwards, often used to describe the bang made by a chemical explosion (verb *explode*); **implosion** = a bursting inwards (verb *implode*).

export (verb) = to send out (goods to another country); **import** (verb) = to bring in (goods from abroad); the goods are **exports** or **imports**; **import** (noun) = the meaning of an action or statement (e.g. "Her remarks had a greater import than I first thought").

expose *See* **disclose**.

exposé (acute accent) should be avoided when **exposure** will serve as well.

expound = explain in great detail, not merely explain.

express, expresser, expressible, expression.

expropriate = to dispossess (take away someone's property); **misappropriate** = to take (dishonestly) for oneself, to put to wrong/illegal use.

extant = still existing, surviving (*see also* **exist**).

extempore (usual adv.), extempory (usual adj.), extemporize, extemporization.

extend, extender, extensible (preferred to *extendible*), extension (not *extention*), extensor muscle. **Extended** = stretched, made larger (e.g. "an extended tour"); **extensive** = wide-ranging, comprehensive (e.g. "an extensive search").

exterminate = destroy completely, and should therefore apply to the whole of a group, not merely part of it (e.g. "The insecticide exterminated most of the dog's fleas" is incorrect).

extol, extolled.

extort, extortion, extortionist (preferred to extortioner).

extract, extractor, extractable, extraction. **Extract** = draw or pull out using force (e.g. extract a cork or a confession); **extricate** = free from entanglement (e.g. extricate a sheep from a thorn hedge).

extreme(s), extremely. The latter is a useful alternative to the overworked intensifier *very*.

exult *See* **exalt**.

eyeball, eyebath, eye-bolt, eyebrow, eyeful, eyeglass, eyelash, eyeless, eyelid, eye-opener, eyepiece, eyesight, eyesore, eye-strain, eye-tooth, eyewash, eye-witness. Note also eyed, eyeing.

eyrie (= an eagle's nest) is the preferred spelling (not *aerie*).

F

-f/-fe For plurals of words ending in *-f* or *-fe*, *see* **plurals**.

°F = degrees Fahrenheit. *See* **Fahrenheit**.

fable = fictitious story (sometimes of known authorship), often with animals as characters and generally with a moral; **legend** = traditional story with an assumed historical basis, usually involving "real" people (even though possibly fictitious); **myth** = traditional story, usually involving supernatural "people" (gods) or creatures (mythical beasts) and their influences on mortals; **saga** = usually heroic adventure story, often from Iceland or Ireland, originating in medieval times. The derived adjectives from the first three are *fabulous, legendary* and *mythical* which, like the nouns, should be used with care in their figurative senses; fabulous should not be used to mean *excellent* (as in "The rock group gave a fabulous performance"). **Legend** is also a printer's term for an annotation, label or caption.

façade (cedilla).

facet, faceted, faceting.

facia = dashboard of a car, shopkeeper's nameboard; **fascia** = board beneath roof-eaves.

facility = ease, amenity; **faculty** = knack, ability, university department. E.g.:

"He has a facility for drawing" implies he has a pencil;
"He has a faculty for drawing" means he is good at it.

facsimile (pl. facsimiles).

factious = relating to a faction (a group with a vested interest);
fractious = fretful, unruly, peevish. E.g.:

"The government refused the opposition party's factious demands."
"The parents ignored the child's fractious behaviour."

factitious = contrived, arranged, engineered (but nevertheless existing); **fictitious** = unreal, sham, counterfeit (non-existent). *See also* **fictional**.

factor, factorize, factorization.

factotum (pl. factotums).

faeces, faecal (but defecate, defecation).

Fahrenheit temperature (abbreviation °F) should normally be restated in Celsius (°C). If the text requires both, express them thus: 37°C (98.6°F).

faience (note spelling).

fail = not succeed in an attempt; **failure** = lack of success in an attempt. Neither word should be used as a mere negative (i.e. if no attempt has been made). E.g.:
"The train failed to start because no driver was available." (incorrect)
"The car failed to start because the battery needed recharging." (correct)

faint = weak, unclear, to lose consciousness; **feint** = false or distracting movement. In *feint rule*, meaning the narrowest line printed on a sheet of paper, the latter spelling is used with the former meaning.

fait accompli (italics) = something already done, an accomplished fact; plural *faits accomplis*. The French terms should be avoided.

faker = someone who fakes; **fakir** = religious (usually Hindu or Muslim) mendicant or ascetic.

fall (verb) has the past tense **fell** and past participle **fallen**.

fallacious = illogical, wrong; **false** = not true, not genuine. E.g.:
"His belief that swallows hibernate in old buildings is fallacious."
"His claim that he has swum the Channel is false."

fallacy is a false idea or belief (not a lie or deliberate deception, which is a **falsehood**). E.g.:
"He believed that eating garlic would prevent him from catching any infection, but since he contracted influenza he knows this to be a fallacy."
"He told the police that his name was Peter Watkins, but he knew this to be a falsehood."

fallible (not *-able*).

fallout (noun, one word).

falsehood = an untruth, a lie; **falseness** = deception, treachery, disloyalty; **falsity** = false assertion, quality of being false. E.g.:

"His excuse for being late proved to be a falsehood."

"He was found out through the falseness of his former friend."

"Inconsistencies revealed the falsity of his argument."

falsetto (pl. falsettos).

familiar, familiarize, familiarization. **Familiar** *to* = known to/by (e.g. "The printing process is familiar to me"); **familiar** *with* = having an understanding/working knowledge of (e.g. "I am familiar with the process").

family name usually means the same as **surname** (as opposed to Christian name, first name or forename). Family names are sometimes used as forenames or second (Christian) names. Thus a boy whose grandfather's name is *John Halford* might be given the name *David Halford Jones*. *See also* **Christian name; second name**.

family relationships give rise to many terms, from great-grandparents to great-grandchildren six generations later. Marriage complicates the terminology by introducing "in-laws" (the immediate relatives of one's husband or wife) into the relationships. *See also* **cousin; half-brother; in-laws; step-**.

famous = well known for "good" deeds; **infamous** = well known for "bad" deeds, notorious.

fantasy is the preferred spelling (not *phantasy*). **Fantastic** = unreal, fanciful; its use to mean *excellent* is colloquial and should be avoided.

faraway is an adjective (e.g. faraway places); **far away** is an adverb (e.g. they moved far away).

Far East includes Cambodia, China, Indonesia, Japan, Korea, Malaysia, Singapore, Taiwan and Vietnam (the countries of eastern and south-eastern Asia).

farrago (pl. farragoes).

Farsi *See* **Iran**.

far-sighted(ness) *See* **long sight**.

farther is the comparative of *far* and applies to distance in length or time. **Further** is also the comparative of *far*, but means *additional*. E.g.:

"Birmingham is farther than Brighton from here."
"The article needs further editorial work."

fascia *See* **facia**.

fascinated *by* a person; **fascinated** *with* a thing or event.

fat *See* **corpulent**.

fatal = leading to/causing death, disastrous; **fateful** = determined by fate. E.g.:

"He swallowed a fatal dose of poison."
"Turning back proved to be a fateful course of action."
The former word has been overworked and is consequently devalued. E.g.:

"When I'm on a slimming diet, just the sight of a cream cake is fatal."

father has an initial capital letter when used as a form of address (e.g. "Dear Father, thank you for the birthday present") or as part of a title (e.g. Holy Father, Father Time, Father Murphy).

fault, fallible (not *faultable*).

faun = Latin rural deity; **fawn** (noun) = young deer, a light yellow-brown colour; **fawn** *on* (verb) = to flatter in a servile way, to be obsequious.

fauna may have the plural *faunas* in biological texts (*see* **plurals**).

faux pas (italics) (pl. *faux pas*) = (an embarrassing) mistake (literally "false step"); the French form should be avoided. The English idiom is to *commit a faux pas*, or *make* a mistake.

feasible (not *-able*) = possible, practicable (it does not mean likely, probable). *See also* **viable**.

feckless = irresponsible; **reckless** = lacking any caution. E.g.:

"My feckless son just sits around and refuses to look for a job."
"My reckless son drives a fast car without wearing a seat-belt."

feed (verb) inflects *feed – fed – fed*.

feel inflects *feel – felt – felt*.

feint *See* **faint**.

feldspar is the preferred spelling of **felspar**.

fem. is the abbreviation of female or feminine.

female describes the sex of an organism; **feminine** describes the characteristics of a female (the corresponding terms are *male* and *masculine*); **feminist** = somebody who champions women's rights. **Female** should not be used as a noun synonymous with *girl* or *woman*. *See also* **gender**.

femme fatale (italics) *See* **hussy**.

femur (pl. femurs, not femora).

fence, fencible.

feral = wild (after having been tame), uncultivated; **ferule** = cane, flat stick used for corporal punishment; **ferrule** = strengthening metal ring or a rubber cap at the end of a stick.

ferment = to use yeast to convert sugar into carbon dioxide (which makes bread dough rise) and, if prolonged, alcohol (as in brewing and wine-making); **foment** = to apply a hot poultice to inflamed skin, such as a boil. Both words can be used figuratively to mean "to stir up (trouble)".

ferret, ferreter, ferreted, ferreting.

fertilize, fertilizer, fertilization (all uses).

fetch = to go some distance, find or retrieve something, and move it where required; **bring** = to move something from near at hand to where required. E.g.:

"Please go upstairs and fetch my book."
"Please bring me the book you are holding."

fetch off should not be used for **remove** (e.g. "That wine would fetch the varnish off the table" is incorrect usage). *See also* **bring**.

fête, fêted (circumflex).

fetid is the preferred spelling (not *foetid*).

fetus The preferred spelling is **foetus**.

few = opposite of many; **a few** = "opposite" of none. E.g.:
"Few of the audience had heard the song before" (not many had heard it);
"A few of the audience had already heard the song" (which was new to many but not to all).

fewer *See* **less**.

fez (pl. fezzes).

fiancé (masc.), fiancée (fem.) (acute accent).

fiasco (pl. fiascos).

fibreglass, fibre-optic (adj.), fibre optics (noun).

fictional = related to fiction; **fictitious** = not genuine, counterfeit, "made up". The meanings overlap. *See also* **factitious**.

fiddle (noun) is both colloquial for violin and the preferred term for the instrument to people who earn their living by playing one; **fiddle** (verb) = to play the violin or, in slang, to cheat or swindle. Thus in formal writing it is safer to use *violin* or *play the violin*.

fidget, fidgeted, fidgeting, fidgety.

fight (verb) inflects *fight – fought – fought*.

Fiji The derived adjective and noun is *Fijian*.

Filipino = people and language of the Philippines (pl. Filipinos).

fillet, filleted, filleting.

fill in = to complete, insert into a gap; **fill out** = to enlarge or extend to a desired size/limit; **fill up** (often better merely as *fill*) = to add something to a "container" until it is full. E.g.:
"Fill in your name in the space provided."

"Fill out the row of plants until it is ten feet long."
"Fill (up) the glass with water."

filly *See* **horse.**

filter = a device for separating a solid from a liquid; **philtre** = a love potion.

fimbria (pl. fimbriae).

final, finalize, finalization. **Final** (noun) = deciding event in sport or athletics; **finale** = conclusion of a play or piece of music.

financial = to do with finance/money; **fiscal** = to do with government money/the treasury. E.g.:
"I am finding it increasingly difficult to meet my financial commitments."
"For taxation purposes, the fiscal year usually begins in April."

find (verb) inflects *find – found – found.* **Find** = happen upon (by chance), recover (after deliberately looking for); **locate** = place something in its proper position, settle (to live/work in a place), discover the position of. The latter should not be used as a grand way of saying the former. E.g.:
"See if you can find some firewood." (correct)
"See if you can locate the pin in the hole." (correct)
"See if you can locate a phone box." (incorrect)

fine, finable.

Finland The derived adjective is *Finnish* and the noun (for the people) is *Finn.*

fiord is the preferred spelling of **fjord.**

fire-alarm, firearm, fireball, fire-bomb, firebrick, fire brigade, fireclay, fire-damp, fire-dog, fire-engine, fire-escape, fire extinguisher, fire-fighter, firefly, fire-guard, fire hydrant, firelight, fire-lighter, fireman, fireplace, fireproof, fireside, fire-water, firewood, firework.

first Both numbers 1 and 2 from a list should be referred to as the *first two* (not the *two first*). Similar style applies to *first three, first four,* and so on. **Last** follows the same rule. *See also* **latter.**

first aid (noun), first-aid (adj.), first-class (adj.), firstborn, first-floor (adj.), first-fruit, firsthand (adj.), first-rate, First World War (but use World War I).

firstly should be avoided; use instead **first** (second, third, and so on are preferred to *secondly, thirdly*, and so on).

first name *See* **Christian name**.

First World War The preferred style is World War I.

fiscal *See* **financial**.

fish usually has the plural *fish* ("They bought six fish"). When listing several types or species, use the plural *fishes* "Cod and herring are the main fishes caught").

fistula (pl. fistulas).

fit (verb) inflects *fit – fitted – fitted*.

fizz, fizzes, fizzed, fizzing.

fjord Use the spelling **fiord**.

fl. is the abbreviation of *floruit* (Latin, meaning "flourished") and of guilder(s) (from the Dutch *gulden florijn* = golden florin).

flaccid *See* **placid**.

flagrant *See* **blatant**.

flak = anti-aircraft fire, or (figuratively) repeated criticism. The spelling **flack** does not exist in standard English.

flambé (italics), *flambéed, flambéing*.

flamenco (pl. flamencos).

flamingo (pl. flamingoes).

flammable *See* **inflammable**.

flan = open sponge-cake base, usually containing fruit; **pasty** = pastry envelope with a savoury filling; **pie** = pastry case with fruit or savoury filling and a pastry lid; **pizza** = bread base with a savoury topping usually based on cheese; **quiche** = open pastry case with a savoury filling usually containing eggs; **tart** = open pastry case usually with a fruit filling; **turnover** = pastry envelope with a fruit filling. These are the usual meanings, although a pie may also be cooked in a dish (not lined with pastry) with just a lid of pastry or, in a cottage pie or shepherd's pie, of potato. There are also various local variants and names, such as a *clanger* (a type of pasty, sometimes with a fruit-filled part as well as a savoury-filled part). *See also* **canapé**.

flannel, flannelled, flannelling, flannelly, flannelette.

flare = very bright light (e.g. a magnesium flare), or a widening (e.g. "The flare at the end of a trombone is called the bell").

flaunt = to display ostentatiously or proudly; **flout** = to disobey (a law or rule) openly and scornfully.

flèche (grave accent).

fledge, flegling.

flee inflects *flee – fled – fled. See also* **fly.**

fleshly = to do with the flesh (in the carnal/sexual sense); **fleshy** = plump, pulpy. E.g.:
"He took every opportunity to indulge his fleshly desires."
"He preferred pale, fleshy women to thin, tanned girls."

fleur-de-lis (pl. fleurs-de-lis).

flex, flexible, flexion (not *-ection*).

flier is the preferred spelling of **flyer.**

fling inflects *fling – flung – flung.*

floe = floating ice (pl. floes); it should not be confused with **flows.**

flong = a stereotype mould (not *flonge*).

floor relates to a part of a building; each floor occupies a **storey** (the preferred spelling, not *story*), which generally relates to height. E.g.:
"Two floors of the ten-storey building are vacant."
In Britain and elsewhere in Europe, floors are usually numbered as *Ground, First, Second, Third*, and so on. The usual system in North

America is *First Floor, Second Floor, Third Floor, Fourth Floor* and so on. The numbering of storeys is the same on both sides of the Atlantic, with the first storey at street level.

flora may have the plural *floras* or *florae* in biological texts (*see* **plurals**).

floruit (Latin, meaning "he/she flourished") has the abbreviation *fl.* (italics, with a full point).

flotation = keeping something afloat, floating a business (not *floatation*).

flounder (verb) = to struggle or make a mistake; **founder** = to sink, stumble. E.g.:
"The would-be rescuer floundered in the mud."
"The ship was holed and foundered on the rocks."

flout *See* **flaunt**.

flow *See* **floe**.

flu (not *'flu*) should be avoided as an abbreviation of **influenza** in formal writing. Nor should it be confused with **flue** (in a chimney).

fluid, fluidize, fluidity.

fluoresce, fluorescence, fluorescent.

flux, fluxion.

fly (verb) has the past tense **flew** and past participle **flown**; **fly** (insect) has the plural *flies*; **fly** (an old type of carriage) has the plural *flys*. Other forms are flying, flier (not flyer). *See also* **flee**.

fly agaric, fly ash, flyaway (adj.), fly-bitten, fly-blown, fly-by, fly-by-night, flycatcher, fly-fishing, fly-half, fly-kick, flyleaf, flyover, flypaper, fly-past, flyposting, fly-sheet, fly-spray, flytrap, fly-under, flyweight, flywheel.

flyover = road elevated to cross over another one; **overfly** = to fly over (in an aircraft); **underpass** = road that tunnels under another one; **pass under** = to cross beneath.

foal *See* **horse**.

focus (pl. of noun is foci), focused, focusing (preferred to *focussed*, *focussing*).

foetus (pl. foetuses), foetal.

foggy = with or hidden by fog; **fogy** (pl. fogies) = somebody with old-fashioned ideas.

föhn (with an umlaut, preferred to foehn).

folio (pl. folios) = a page in a book or manuscript; abbreviations f. and ff. In a book, a right-hand folio (page) is called the *recto* side, and a left-hand one is the *verso*. *Folio* is also a printer's term for a page-number; rectos have odd numbers, versos have even ones.

folk is a plural word, and so the double plural **folks** should be avoided. *See also* **people**.

folk-dance, folklore, folk-song.

following should not be misused for **after** or **as a result of**; e.g. "I found an assistant following a newspaper advertisement" is ambiguous, and "Rationing did not immediately end following World War II" is incorrect. The former should have *as a result of*; the latter *after*.

foment *See* **ferment**.

fondue (italics).

font (of type in printing) The preferred spelling is **fount** (although still pronounced *font*).

fontanelle is the preferred spelling (not *fontanel*).

foot (pl. feet) In attributive constructions, the singular form should be used (e.g. "a six-foot wingspan" but "a wingspan of six feet", "its wings were six feet across").

foot-and-mouth disease, football, foot-brake, footbridge, foot candle, foot-fault, Foot Guards, foothill, foothold, footlight(s), footloose, footnote, footpath, footplate, foot-pound(al), footprint, foot-rot, footsore, footstep, footstool, footway, footwear.

footnotes The usual symbols to indicate footnotes are *, †, ‡ (asterisk, dagger or obelisk, and double-dagger), in that order, and are doubled for additional references (**, ††, ‡‡). If the number of references in one table or on one page exceeds six, use superscript numerals. If there are many references, number them sequentially and list them at the end of the section or chapter.

for- Words with the prefix *for-* include forbear (which *see*), forbid (forbade, forbidden), forever, forfend, forgather, forget, forgive, forgo (which *see*), forlorn, forsake, forswear, forward(s). *See also* **fore-**.

forasmuch (one word).

forbear (verb) = abstain, voluntarily avoid, exhibit forbearance; **forebear** (noun) = ancestor. The verb has the past tense **forbore** and past participle **forborne**.

forbid has the past tense **forbade** and past participle **forbidden**. **Forbidding** = discouraging (e.g. "a forbidding attitude"); **foreboding** = suggesting unpleasantness to come (e.g. "his attitude filled me with foreboding").

force, forceful (= vigorous, powerful, exerting/exhibiting force), forcible (= brought about by force, having force). E.g.:

"The spokesman made a forceful speech at the meeting."
"The protesters made a forcible entry to the meeting."

force majeure (italics).

forceps Unlike callipers, knickers, scissors, shears, trousers and so on (which are plural words), *forceps* can be either singular or plural, although the plural form is much more common.

fore- Words with the prefix *fore-* (meaning "before" or "in front of") include forearm, forebear, forebode, forecast, forecastle, foreclose, forecourt, fore-edge, fore-end, fore-father, forefinger, forefront, forego, foreground, forehand, forehead, foreland, foreleg, forelock, foreman, foremast, foremost, forenoon, forerunner, foresaid, foresail, foresee, foreshadow, foreshore, foreshorten, foresight, foreskin, forestall, foretaste, foretell, forethought, forewarn, foreword (of a book). *See also* **for-**.

forecast The preferred past tense and participle is **forecast** (not *forecasted*).

foreign words and phrases should be avoided wherever possible – if they are not well known, they require translation (hence Stephen Potter's recommendation, in a One-Upmanship context, "to confuse, irritate and depress [an opponent] by the use of foreign words, fictitious or otherwise, either singly or in groups"). Many are listed and defined in this Dictionary, usually with the advice to avoid the foreign form.

Many words once regarded as foreign have become totally assimilated into the English language. Indeed, where would English-speakers be without such useful words as chauvinist, gourmand, martinet (from French); loafer, plunderer, swindler (German); bandit, brigand, pedant, ruffian (Italian); desperado, guerrilla (Spanish)? Probably they would still be using the older (and shorter) words such as cheat, liar, outlaw, rogue and thief.

Foreign words that have become part of standard English should be typeset in roman face; others should be set in italics, with any necessary accents. Some, although totally assimilated and normally set in roman, retain their accents as an aid to pronunciation (e.g. café, fiancée, précis). This advice to avoid the use of foreign words is not intended to be xenophobic; and it can be argued that **jargon** (which *see*) confuses as much as overuse of non-English expressions. For lists containing foreign words that have become part of standard English, *see also* **Americanisms; Arabic words; Celtic words; Dutch words; French words; German words; Hebrew words; Indian words; Italian words; Latin words; Portuguese words; Scandinavian words; Spanish words; Russian words**.

forename *See* **Christian name**.

forensic = to do with the law or courts, hence *forensic medicine* = *medical jurisprudence*. The expression *forensic evidence* is tautologous, and usually means *scientific evidence*.

for ever, for evermore (two words) are the preferred spellings (not *forever, forevermore*).

foreword *See* **preface**.

forfeit, forfeited.

forget, forgettable, forgetting, forget-me-not.

forgive, forgivable. **Forgive** has the past tense **forgave** and past participle **forgiven**.

forgo (= to relinquish, to do without), forgoing, forgone; **forego** (= to go before), foregoing, foregone.

form (noun) = shape, document with blanks to be filled in, school class, customary behaviour, etc; **forme** = assembled type (in a *chase*) ready for printing or stereotyping.

formal, formalize, formalization.

formally = in a formal way; **formerly** = as before, in the past.

format (verb), formatted, formatting.

former is preferred to the prefix **ex-** in such expressions as "former president John Jones", "his former wife", "her former boss" (not *ex-president, ex-wife, ex-boss*). *See also* **late; latter**.

formula (pl. formulas, except in some mathematical texts which use formulae).

forsake has the past tense **forsook** and past participle **forsaken**.

forte (a person's strong point).

forth is an old-fashioned word for onwards (e.g. "go forth and multiply"); **fourth** is the ordinal number from 4 (e.g. "she came fourth in her class").

for the reason that = **because**, which should be used.

fortuitous = accidental, by chance; **fortunate** – favoured, lucky, prosperous. E.g.:
"Although he accused me of contriving our meeting, it was entirely fortuitous."
"I was extremely fortunate to be able to meet him."

forum (pl. forums).

forward can be an adjective (e.g. "a very forward child") or an adverb (e.g. "move it forward"), although **forwards** is the preferred form of the adverb. *See also* **-wards**. For the nautical usage of *forward*, *see* **abaft**.

fossil, fossilize, fossilization.

foul = dirty, filthy, obscene; **fowl** = bird (particularly a duck or chicken).

founder *See* **flounder**.

fount *See* **font**.

fourth *See* **forth**.

fovea (pl. foveae).

fowl *See* **foul**.

fracas has the same form in the singular and plural (although the pronunciation changes from "frak-ah" to "frak-az").

fractious *See* **factious**.

fragile = easily broken (of an object, because it is brittle, like glass); **frail** = easily broken (of a person, because he or she is weak/unhealthy).

framework, used to mean *circumstance* or *limitation* (e.g. "We will only negotiate within the framework of the existing guidelines"), is a vogue word and should be avoided. *See* **vogue words**.

franchise (not *-ize*).

fraternal, fraternize, fraternization.

fraught is archaic for **filled** (except in the cliché "fraught with danger/difficulties"); *filled* or *laden* should be used. **Fraught** survives in colloquial use as an adjective meaning *upset* or *anxious*.

free-and-easy, freeboard, free-born, free-for-all, freehand, freehold, free-lance, freeman, freemason, free-range, freestone, free-thinker, free trade, free-wheel, free will.

freeze has the past tense **froze** and past participle **frozen**.

French words One of the functions of the Académie Française is to examine "new" words and sanction official acceptance or rejection for the French language. English imports (termed Briticisms) are almost always banned in French (such as *le shopping, le weekend*). The English language, on the other hand, has never had an official review of foreign candidates for its vocabulary – these survive or not depending on the vagaries of usage. Thus words such as *café, leotard* and *pâté* are probably with us for ever, because they have no simple English equivalents – indeed they *are* English. At the time of writing, the British fashion trade (for example) employs *blouson* and *cagoule* for two types of lightweight jackets; only time and usage (or lack of it) will determine their fate. English dictionaries also contain many French words that have outgrown their usefulness, and often have better understood English equivalents; their inclusion can give straightforward descriptive text an arty-crafty or pretentious flavour. Examples, just from those beginning with *m*, are manège, mélange, métier and milieu; this Dictionary includes many more of the latter type, usually with advice to avoid them. *See also* **foreign words and phrases; Latin words.**

fresco (pl. frescoes).

fresh should be used with care to mean **new** or **renewed**; e.g. "They agreed to fresh talks" is incorrect, whereas "fresh bread" and "fresh fall of snow" are correct.

freshwater (adj.), fresh water (noun), but seawater (adj. and noun).

friable = easily crumbled, or = can be fried (not the spelling *fryable*), so that only context distinguishes the two meanings.

fridge *See* **refrigerate.**

frier The preferred spelling is **fryer.**

frightful/frightfully should be reserved for things or circumstances that invoke fright or fear, and not used as an intensifier (= **very**) or of something that is merely **unpleasant** or **disagreeable** (as in "I have a frightful cold", "I thought the talk was frightfully boring").

frolic, frolicked, frolicking, but frolicsome.

fry, fried, frying, fryer (not *frier*). *See also* **friable**.

fuchsia (plant named after Leonard Fuchs).

fuel, fuelled, fuelling.

-ful Quantities and measurements ending in *-ful* form the plural by adding *s*; e.g. *cupfuls, handfuls, spadefuls, spoonfuls* (not *cupsful* etc.).

fulcrum (pl. fulcrums).

fulfil, fulfilled, fulfilling, fulfilment.

fuller's earth, so-named because it was used for fulling (cleaning and finishing) cloth, does not have an initial capital letter.

full-length = not shortened; **full-scale** = not reduced in size/scope. E.g.:
"The bride wore a full-length wedding dress."
"After the wedding, there was a full-scale reception for a hundred guests."

fullness is the preferred spelling (not *fulness*).

full point/full stop *See* **punctuation**.

fulsome = nauseous, excessive, insincere; it no longer means merely abundant or ample.

fumatory is a little-used word for a room or building in which fumigation is carried out; **fumitory** is a wild flower.

fumigate, fumigator, fumigation.

funeral, funereal (= like or appropriate to a funeral), funerary (= pertaining to a funeral).

fungus (pl. fungi), fungous (adj.), fungal (another adj., preferred to *fungoid*).

funnel, funnelled, funnelling.

fur, furred, furring, furry.

furore (not *furor*, which is an Americanism).

further *See* **farther**.

fuse, fusible (but fissionable in nuclear physics). **Fuse** should be used for all meanings (not *fuze*).

G

gabardine = durable (worsted) cloth; **gaberdine** = old name for a long loose cloak.

gabbro (pl. gabbros).

Gabon The derived adjective and noun is *Gabonese*.

Gaelic = to do with (ancient) Ireland or Scotland (the *Celts*); **Gallic**. = to do with France or the French (the *Gauls*). Coincidentally, **gallic** (in botany/chemistry) = to do with *galls*. *See also* Celtic words.

gaff = fish-spear or hook for landing large fish; **gaffe** = blunder, especially a social one.

gage = token of defiance, challenge, pledge; **gauge** = specific measurement or measuring instrument.

gall bladder, gallstone.

gallery *See* **balcony**.

Gallic *See* **Gaelic**.

Gallicism = use of French (or pseudo-French) words in English, often condemned in this Dictionary; *see* **French words**. *See also* **foreign words and phrases**.

gallop, galloped, galloper, galloping (**galop** is the dance).

gallows is usually regarded as a singular word; "sets of gallows" achieves a plural construction.

gambit = an opening move that involves an apparent sacrifice but for long-term gain; **gamut** = musical scale, whole range, scope (as in Dorothy Parker's sarcastic comment about an actress: "She ran the whole gamut of her emotions from A to B").

gamble/gambling is applied to games of chance involving stakes, and by extension to any venture with an element of risk. **Gaming** has now an old-fashioned ring except when applied to a casino's *gaming tables*.

gambol, gambolled, gambolling (compare **gamble**, gambled, gambling).

game is now used generally to refer to any animals or birds killed for sport, large exotic ones being termed *big game* – it is no longer limited (in England) to deer, grouse, hares, partridges and pheasants (*see also* **quarry**); **gamy** = having the flavour of hung game; **gammy** = lame (preferred to the spelling *game*).

gamut *See* **gambit**.

gaol, gaoler. The preferred spellings are **jail**, jailer (although *gaol* is the official term).

garlic, garlicky.

garot = duck, tourniquet; **garotte** (preferred to *garrotte*) = ligature round the neck (to strangle criminals).

gaseous = of the nature of gas; **gassy** = full of gas. E.g.:
"The Earth has a gaseous atmosphere."
"Lemonade is a gassy drink."

gasoline *See* **petrol**.

gâteau (pl. gâteaux).

gaucho (pl. gauchos).

gaudy, gaudiness, gaudily.

gauge, gauging, gaugeable (compare **gage** (= pledge), gaging).

gay (= merry, bright, lively) should be avoided because of possible ambiguity with the modern usage meaning *homosexual* (adj. and noun). Derived words include gayness, gaiety, gaily.

gazebo (pl. gazebos).

gazette, gazetted, gazetteer. *See also* **anthology**.

gecko (pl. geckos).

gelatin is the preferred spelling (not *gelatine*).

gelding *See* **horse**.

gemma (pl. gemmae).

gender should be applied only to words, not to girls, women or female animals. *See also* **female**. Grammatical gender has largely passed from English. Sex-defining words do have two forms, of natural male and female gender. E.g.:

boy	girl	his	hers
he	she	man	woman
him	her	Mister (Mr)	Mistress (Mrs)

Other words, describing people, that retain gender usually denote occupation, position or (family) relationships.

   It is regarded as sexist by some people to emphasize the difference between men's and women's roles by using many of these words. Their habitual use by men is often branded as chauvinist. There are also many other compounds ending in *-man* or *-woman* (e.g. businessman, chairman, policeman, salesman). Some of these, particularly those lacking a *-woman* form (such as craftsman, draughtsman, fireman, foreman), have been objected to on sexist grounds, giving rise to compromise words such as *chairperson*. Where this might be a sensitive area, terms with a masculine preference should be avoided and "neutral" ones substituted, or the offending words recast to circumvent the problem (e.g. *fireman* becomes *fire fighter*, *policeman* becomes *police officer*, *workman* becomes *worker*). Masculine pronouns can often be avoided by making the sentence plural (e.g. "The applicant must sign his name before he begins to write" becomes "Applicants must sign their names before they begin to write").

genealogy (not *-ology*).

general, generalize, generalization.

generate, generator.

genet = civet-cat; **jennet** = small Spanish horse.

genial/genital *See* **congenial**.

genie has the plural genii; **genius** has the plural geniuses (not *genii*).

genitive *See* **gerund; punctuation** (apostrophe).

genius has the plural *geniuses* when it means a person of great mental ability, and the plural *genii* when it means a demon or spirit. Similar to the second meaning is **genie**, from the Arabic (plural) word **jinn**.

genteel = over- or affectedly polite (pejorative); **gentle** = mild, soothing (opposite of harsh, rough); **Gentile** = non-Jewish.

genteelism *See* **non-standard English**.

genuflect, genuflexion (not *-ection*).

genus (pl. genera). *See also* **Latin classification**.

geographical names *See* **compass directions; capitalization**.

gerbil is the preferred spelling of **jerbil**.

geriatric = concerning the health/welfare of elderly people (it does not mean *elderly* or *senile*); **geriatrics** = medical care of the elderly; **gerontology** = study of the processes of aging; **gerontocracy** = government by the aged.

germ (= a pathological micro-organism) is, like *microbe*, a term no longer used in science, which prefers more specific words such as *bacterium, fungus, virus* or the all-embracing *pathogen. Germ* is retained, more in botany than in zoology, for the (fertilized) cell from which a new individual develops.

German words assimilated into English include:

blitz	hinterland	plunder	spanner
carouse	kindergarten	poltergeist	swindle
dachshund	lager	poodle	waltz
dollar	loafer	quartz	zinc
ersatz	nickel	rucksack	
glockenspiel	noodle	snorkel	

Germany For the post-1945 nations, use **East Germany** (for the German Democratic Republic) and **West Germany** (for the Federal Republic of Germany).

gerrymander is the preferred spelling (not *jerrymander*).

gerund is a verb form ending in *-ing* used as a noun (e.g. "the coming of winter", "a strange happening occurred"). Difficulties sometimes arise when the gerund is preceded by a pronoun or noun, which should have a genitive (possessive) form. E.g.:

"I looked forward to *his* coming" (not *him* coming, because I looked forward to the *coming*, not to him);

"He was annoyed at *its* breaking so soon" (not *it* breaking);

"She dreaded *John's* laughing at her" (not *John* laughing);

"She objected to *one's* smoking";

"I watched my *child's* gradual growing up";

"I watched my *children's* gradual growing up".

The last three, although strictly correct, seem stilted in comparison with:

"She objects to one smoking" (or "... to my smoking", or just "... to smoking");

"I watched my child gradually growing up";

"I watched my children gradually growing up".

This form of construction is being increasingly used, although the possessive is still preferred for a pronoun or proper name before a gerund. Also a gerund, like the participle it resembles, is in danger of being made unrelated to its "subject" (*see* **participles, related and unrelated**).

get, gettable, get-at-able. Get (inflexion *get − got − got*) = to obtain, procure, acquire, attain to, receive, reach − which are preferred. *See also* **got**.

Ghana The derived adjective and noun is *Ghanaian*.

ghastly = resembling death (of the same derivation as *ghost/ghostly*), shocking, appalling; the word should not be used in a derogatory way (to mean *unpleasant*). E.g.:

"After the accident he had a ghastly complexion" (correct);

"Have you seen that ghastly shirt he is wearing" (incorrect).

ghetto (pl. ghettos).

gibbet, gibbeted, gibbeting.

gibe *See* **jib**.

giga- is the metric prefix for a thousand million times ($\times 10^9$), as in *gigahertz*.

gigolo (pl. gigolos).

gild = to cover with gold; **guild** = group of tradespeople, a society; **gilt** = covered with gold; **guilt** = sinfulness, state of a lawbreaker or wrongdoer. The preferred past tense and participle of **gild** is **gilded** (not *gilt*).

gipsy The preferred spelling is **gypsy**.

give, givable. **Give** has the past tense **gave** and past participle **given**.

given name *See* **Christian name**.

glacé (acute accent).

gladiolus (pl. gladioli).

glamour, glamorous, glamorize.

glance = look at briefly/quickly (a positive action); **glimpse** = catch sight of briefly/quickly (a passive response). E.g.:

"I glanced at her while she was not looking at me."
"I glimpsed her as she walked past the open door."

glasses (= spectacles) is a plural word; "a pair of glasses" achieves a singular construction.

glue, glued, gluing, gluey.

glycerin is the preferred spelling (not *glycerine*); the substance is termed *glycerol* in chemistry.

gnaw has the preferred past tense and participle **gnawed** (not *gnawn*).

gnu (pl. gnus); but the preferred term is **wildebeest** (pl. wildebeest).

go has the past tense **went** and past participle **gone**.

gobbledegook is a descriptive term for jargon, particularly that of officialdom and technology. *See* **jargon**.

God has an initial capital letter when referring to the deity of monotheistic religions such as Christianity, Judaism and Islam. For other gods (as in "the Egyptian god Ra" or "the Greek god Zeus"), no capital letter is required.

godchild, god-daughter, goddess, godfather, God-fearing, god-forsaken, godhead, godless, godlike, godmother, godparent, godsend, godsent, godson, Godspeed.

goffer = heated iron for crimping hair; **gopher** = North American burrowing rodent, kind of wood.

going, as in the informal "the going rate for the job", is a poor substitute for **current**, which should be used.

gold (adj.) describes something made of gold (e.g. a gold ring); **golden** describes something that is a gold colour (e.g. a golden sunset).

golf-club (hyphen) is used for hitting a golf ball at a golf club (no hyphen) or golf course.

good (comparative *better*, superlative *best*), goodness, goodliness. Compounds include good afternoon, goodbye, good day, good evening, good-for-nothing, Good Friday, good-hearted, good-humoured, good-looking, good morning, good-natured, good night, good-sized, goods-train, goods van, goods yard, good-tempered, goodwill/good will (which *see*). *See also* **better**. **Good** is the opposite of *bad*; **well** is the opposite of *ill*; both can be the opposite of *unattractive*. E.g.:

"The workmanship is good" (good = unbad, i.e. high-quality);
"That food smells good" (good = attractive, i.e. appetizing);
"My son is now well again" (well = unill, i.e. healthy);
"The books look well on the shelf" (well = attractive).

good idea It is a good idea to avoid this expression.

goodwill = established custom/popularity of a business, often ascribed a monetary value (as an asset) when the business is sold; **good will** (adj. good-will) = kindly regard, well-wishing. E.g.:

"The price of the shop includes allowances for the stock and the goodwill."
"Much of his popularity stemmed from the fact that he was a man of good will."

Increasingly, the one-word spelling is being used for both meanings.

gossip, gossiper, gossiped, gossiping.

got is the past tense and participle of *get*. As a substitute for have, possessed, acquired, attained, arrived (at), achieved, and so on it should be avoided. *See also* **get**.

gourmand = lover of eating, a glutton; **gourmet** = connoisseur of wine or good food.

govern, governor, government.

gracile is rare, and literary, for **slim** or **slender** (which are preferred); it should not be confused with **graceful** (= elegant, becoming) or **gracious** (= courteous, sympathetic, refined). E.g.:

"Everybody admired the fashion model's gracile figure."
"Everybody commented on her graceful manner of walking."
"Everybody noted the gracious way she accepted the prize."

graffito (pl. graffiti).

grain (the seeds from a cereal crop) is ground to make **meal** which, after the husks are removed, becomes **flour**. **Corn** is an imprecise term for a cereal crop or its grain, but in American English is the term for **maize**. **Oatmeal** is the meal from oats; **flour** (unqualified) usually means wheat flour. **Cornflakes** and **cornflour** (= cornstarch) are made from maize (and **cornflower** is a blue-flowered plant that often grows in cornfields).

gram is the preferred spelling of gramme, and in normal writing should be abbreviated to gm (not *g*); note also milligram (mg), kilogram (kg).

grammar = systematic collection of the "rules" of a language and how it is used; **linguistics** = scientific study of words and their origins; **semantics** = branch of linguistics concerned with the meanings of words; **syntax** = branch of linguistics concerned with the arrangement and relationship of words in a sentence.

gramophone has come to refer to the earlier breed of machines (the first of which were called *phonographs*, now an Americanism); the modern version is *record player*.

granddad, grand-aunt, grandchild(ren), granddaughter, grandfather, grand master, grandmother, grand-nephew, grand-niece, grandparent, grandson, grand-uncle.

grand-parental = relating to grandparents; a new adjective coined by analogy with *parental*, it fills a gap in the vocabulary. E.g.:
"Aging parents take on a grand-parental role with their children's children."
Grandparenting (= acting as grandparents) is less acceptable, probably because *parenting* (on which it is presumably based) has yet to gain universal acceptance.

grant, granter (who grants), grantor (who makes a grant in law).

grapefruit has the same form in the singular and plural.

grateful = feeling gratitude, thankful; **gratified** = pleased, satisfied, indulged.

gratis (italics) = without charge, free; the Latin term should be avoided.

grave (noun) = an accent (as in *crèche*), or a burial place; **grave** (verb) = to engrave, has preferred past tense and participle **graved**, although **graven** is retained as an archaic adjective (e.g. "a graven image"). *See also* **craven**.

graze, grazer (an animal), grazier (a keeper/breeder of grazers).

grease, greasy.

Great Britain consists of England, Scotland and Wales; the *United Kingdom* consists of Great Britain and Northern Ireland. *Eire* should be referred to as the Republic of Ireland. The terms *English* and *England* should not be used when *British* and *Britain* are intended. *See also* **British; Eire**.

grief is the noun; **grieve** is the verb, giving *grievance* and *grievous* (not *grievious*).

griffin = fabulous beast (a winged bird-lion); **griffon** = kind of dog, bird of prey (vulture); **gryphon** = griffin.

grill = to cook under direct heat, to cross-examine; **grille** = metal grating.

grind (verb) inflects *grind − ground − ground*.

grind to a halt is a cliché for to **end** or **stop**, either of which is preferred.

grisly = causing horror or terror, ghastly; **gristly** = having or like gristle; **grizzly** = grey, grey-haired (= *grizzled*), as in *grizzly bear*.

grissini (Italian crispbread in the form of thin sticks) is a plural word, although like *lasagne*, *spaghetti* and other pasta names it is usually regarded as singular in English.

gristle = cartilage; **grizzle** = cry fretfully or self-pityingly.

groin = groove between lower abdomen and thigh, or an arch between ceiling vaults; **groyne** = breakwater.

grotto (pl. grottoes).

group terms *See* **collective words**.

grovel, grovelled, grovelling, groveller.

grow has the past tense **grew** and the past participle **grown**.

guana = iguana, lizard; **guano** = sea-bird excrement.

guarantee is the only spelling of the verb and the preferred spelling of the noun (not **guaranty**). Other verb forms are *guaranteed* and *guaranteeing*, and a person who gives a guarantee is a **guarantor**.

guerrilla is the preferred spelling (not *guerilla*).

guild *See* **gild**.

guilder (abbreviation fl. = florin) is preferred to the Dutch form *gulden* for the money of the Netherlands.

guilt *See* **gild**.

gullible (not *-able*).

gunboat, gun-cotton, gun dog, gunfire, gun-lock, gunman, gun-metal, gunpoint, gunpowder, gunroom, gun-runner, gunship, gunshot, gunsmith.

guttural (not *gutteral*).

Guyana The derived adjective and noun is *Guyanese*.

gybe *See* **jib**.

gymnasium (pl. gymnasiums, not *gymnasia*).

gypsy is the preferred spelling (not *gipsy*).

gyro (pl. gyros).

H

habitable = "live-in-able"; **habitat** = usual place or region in which an animal or plant lives; **inhabit** = to live in; **inhabitable** = habitable; **uninhabitable** = "not live-in-able". *Habitable* is usually applied to dwellings, *inhabitable* to regions, *uninhabitable* to both.

habitué (italics, acute accent) = frequenter, regular attendant; the French form should be avoided.

Habsburg is the preferred spelling (not *Hapsburg*).

hadj, haji (preferred to hajj, hajji).

haematite, haematology, haemoglobin, haemophilia, haemorrhage and other *haem-* words retain the first *a* in English (i.e. not *hem-*, which is an Americanism).

hairbreadth, hair's breadth, hairbrush, haircut, hair-do, hairdresser, hair-line, hair-net, hair-oil, hairpin, hair-rising, hair shirt, hair-space, hair-splitting, hairspring, hair-style, hairtrigger.

hale is archaic for **vigorous, healthy** − as in the cliché "hale and hearty" − and should be avoided; **hail** = frozen rain, a form of greeting (also archaic).

half may be singular or plural, depending on context. E.g.:

"Half (of) the text is unreadable."
"Half (of) the people are missing."

In the first example, *half* denotes an amount (of a singular word, *text*); in the second example, *half* denotes a number (of a plural word, *people*). In each case, *of* is optional. The singular word *half* has the plural *halves* (e.g. "Buy two halves of cucumber"). Compounds ending in *-half* usually have *-halfs* as their plurals (e.g. right-half, right-halfs). *See also* the following entry.

half a dozen (noun), half-and-half, half an hour, half-back, half-baked, half-binding, half-blood (pejorative), half-bound, half-breed (pejorative), half-brother, half-caste (pejorative), half-cock, half-day, half dozen (adj.), half-empty (adj.), half-hearted, half holiday, half-hour, half-litre, half-mast, half measure, half moon, half nelson, half past, half pay, halfpenny, half-pint, half-pound, half-price, half-sister, half-term, half-timbered, half-time, half-title, halftone, half-truth, half-volley, half-way, half-wit(ted), half-yearly.

half-brother or **half-sister** is the child of one's parent who has remarried − i.e. half-brothers or half-sisters have one parent in common. *See also* **family relationships; step-**.

hallo *See* **hello**.

Hallowe'en is the preferred spelling (not **Halloween**).

halo (pl. haloes).

hand forms part of three common idioms: **at hand** = soon to happen; **on hand** = available, ready for use; **to hand** = within reach. E.g.:
"The day of reckoning is at hand."
"A good general always keeps reinforcements on hand."
"You should organize your work-bench so that all the tools are to hand."

handful (pl. handfuls).

handicap, handicapped, handicapper, handicapping.

handkerchief (pl. handkerchiefs).

handsome = attractive, good-looking (of a man); **hansom** = two-wheeled carriage (once used as a cab), named after Joseph Hansom.

hang, hanger (who or which hangs), hangar (for aircraft), hangman (who executes criminals), hanger-on (pl. hangers-on). A picture or pheasant is *hung*, a criminal is (or was) *hanged*. The two meanings of the verb inflect *hang − hung − hung* and *hang − hanged − hanged*.

Hapsburg The preferred spelling is **Habsburg**.

hara-kiri = a Japanese form of suicide (not *hari-kari*).

harangue, harangued, haranguing, haranguer.

harass, harassed, harassing, harassment (not the common misspelling *harrass*).

hard (adj.) = unsoft, difficult. The logical related adverb is **hardly**, but this means *scarcely* and *hard* is therefore also used as an adverb meaning *energetically, with difficulty*. E.g.:

"The plastic table had a hard shiny surface" (adjective);

"She hardly knew him" (adverb);

"He hit the table hard enough to break it" (adverb).

There is a lot of difference between a loaf that is hard-baked and one that is hardly baked.

See also **barely, hardly** and **scarcely.**

hard-and-fast, hardback, hard-baked, hard-bitten, hardboard, hard-boiled, hard cash, hardcore (noun), hard core (adj.), hard-headed, hard-hearted, hard hit, hard labour, hard-line (adj.), hard luck, hard-nosed, hard-of-hearing, hardship, hard shoulder, hardtrack, hardtop, hard up (noun), hard-up (adj.), hardware, hard-wearing, hardwood, hard-working.

hardly none (= hardly not one) is incorrect for **hardly any**. Avoid using *hardly* in any negative construction (*see* **barely, hardly** and **scarcely**).

hare-brained *See* **mad.**

harmonize, harmonization.

harmony is produced by combining notes to form chords; **melody** is a succession of notes that form a tune.

hassock *See* **cassock.**

hate, hatable.

haul, hauler (who or which hauls), haulier (whose job is to carry goods).

haute couture = high fashion, and *haute cuisine* = high-class cookery (both italics); the French terms should be avoided.

have inflects *have* – *had* – *had*.

he (and *him, his*) is the common gender pronoun in normal usage, even if the noun referred to could be a girl or woman (e.g. "A baby needs feeding when he is hungry", "A young child often counts on his fingers"). Sexist objections can be overcome by using *he or she* (or *him or her*, *his or her*), but this construction is clumsy and soon palls with repetition; it is best avoided. An alternative solution is to avoid gender by recasting in the plural (e.g. "Babies need feeding when they are hungry", "Many young children count on their fingers"). *See also* **gender**.

headache, headband, headboard, head-dress, headgear, head-first, head-hunting, headhunter, headlamp, headland, headlight, headline, headlong, headman, headmaster, headmastership, head mistress, head-note, head off (verb), head-on, headphones, headpiece, headquarters, head-rest, headroom, headscarf, headset, headship (preferred to headmastership), headsman, head start, headstock, headstone, headstrong, head teacher, headway, headwind.

headlines *See* **journalese**.

headquarters may be regarded as singular or plural.

hear inflects *hear – heard – heard*.

heartache, heart attack, heartbeat, heart block, heartbreak(ing), heartbroken, heartburn, heart disease, heart failure, heartfelt, heartless, heartrending, heart-searching, heart's ease, heartsick, heartsore, heartstring, heart-throb, heart-to-heart, heartwarming, heartwood.

heave has the preferred past tense and participle **heaved**, although *hove* is retained as a (nautical) adjective and verb form (e.g. "hove to").

Heaven (initial capital) = the dwelling-place of God; **heaven(s)** = region in which the Sun, Moon, stars and so on (heavenly bodies) can be seen.

Hebrew *See* **Semitic**.

Hebrew words taken into English sometimes give trouble with plurals. As a rule, words of long standing take a normal "English" plural in -*s* (e.g. cherub/cherubs, seraph/seraphs, shibboleth/shibboleths), whereas rarer or more recent acquisitions retain the Hebrew plural in -*im* (e.g. goy/goyim, kibbutz/kibbutzim, teraph/teraphim). The combination of Hebrew and German which became **Yiddish** has also influenced English (with such words as bagel, golem, kibitzer, kosher, matzo, mazuma, nosh) and American (whose slang expressions schlep, schlock, schmaltz, schmo, schmuk, schnorer, shemozzle, and so on can also be encountered in Britain).

hectic, strictly, = affected by fever; many authorities regard its use to mean *rushed* or *extremely busy* as colloquial. *See also* **livid**.

hecto- is the metric prefix for a hundred times ($\times 10^2$), as (shortened) in hectare.

hedge, hedging.

heifer (note -*ei*- spelling) *See* **cattle**.

heinous (not *heinious*).

heir = someone who inherits or succeeds to an estate/title; **heir apparent** = heir whose claim cannot be superseded; **heir presumptive** = heir whose claim can be superseded after the birth of a child with a superior claim.

helix (pl. helices).

hello is the preferred spelling, although **hallo** and (more rarely) **hullo** are still used.

help (verb) someone *to* do something (the omission of *to* in this construction is usually regarded as an Americanism).

hemi- *See* **numerical prefixes**.

hence = from here, and so does not need another *from* (i.e. "from hence" is incorrect). **Hence** also = *from now* ("two years hence") and *for this reason* ("... hence my interest").

henceforth = from this time/point on; except in legal contexts, it should be avoided.

hendiadys = two words (often adjectives) joined by *and* used to convey a more complex idea. E.g.:

fast and furious	= furiously fast
hale and hearty	= heartily hale

nice and comfortable	= nicely comfortable
short and sweet	= sweetly short
well and truly	= truly well

Many of these are also examples of *dyads* (*see* **inseparable pairs**).

hepta- or **sept-** *See* **numerical prefixes**.

heredity (noun), hereditary (adj.), hereditable (= inheritable, which is preferred), heritable (= inheritable).

hereof, heretofore and **hereunto** are archaisms, still employed by the legal profession, for *of this*, *before* and *until this*, which should be used.

hernia (pl. hernias, not *herniae*).

hero (pl. heroes).

heroin = drug derived from opium; **heroine** = female hero.

hers (no apostrophe); *see* **one's**.

hesitate, hesitancy (= state of mind causing someone to hesitate), hesitation (= act of hesitating). E.g.:
"He could not decide whether to go ahead with the work, and the ever-increasing cost of the delays added to his hesitancy."
"Without hesitation, he authorised work to continue."

hew has the preferred past tense and participle **hewed**, although *hewn* is retained as an adjective (e.g. "hewn logs"). All are archaic for **chop/chopped** (down).

hexa- or **sex-** *See* **numerical prefixes**.

hiatus (pl. hiatuses).

hiccup (preferred to **hiccough**), hiccuped, hiccuping.

hidalgo (pl. hidalgos).

hide (verb) has the past tense **hid** and preferred past participle **hidden** (not *hid*).

hideous, hideousness (not *hideosity*).

hie, hied, hieing (*hie* is archaic for go quickly).

hieroglyph *See* **ideograph**.

high (adj. and adv.) is the opposite of low (e.g. high voice, flying high); **highly** (adv.) = extremely (e.g. highly emotional state).

highbrow, highchair, high-class, high explosive, high fidelity (hi-fi), highflown, high-flying, high frequency, high jump, high-handed, highland(s), highlight, high-pitched, high pressure, high priest(ess), high-rise, high road, high school, high seas, high-spirited, high water, highway, highwayman.

hijack (preferred to **highjack**), hijacker, hijacked, hijacking.

hind leg, hindmost, hindquarters, hindsight.

hinder, hindrance.

Hindi *See* **Indian words**.

hinge, hinged, hinging.

hippopotamus (pl. hippopotamuses).

hire, hireable, hireling (= someone who is hired), hiring (= contract of hire). **Hire** = to pay for the short-term use of an item or service (e.g. hire a suit, a barman for the day, or a car for a week); **rent** = to pay for long-term use (e.g. rent a house, a stretch of river for its fishing rights); **lease** = a form of renting with certain legal implications, usually for a specified period (e.g. a three-year lease on a shop).

his *See* **he**.

historic = famous, important (in history); **historical** = of the nature of history — e.g. "A historical novel by a historic author." For the use of the indefinite article before *historic* and other words beginning with *h*, *see* **a** or **an**.

hitchhike, hitchhiker.

hither is archaic for **to here** (as in the cliché "come hither"), as **hitherto** is for **up to now**; both should be avoided.

HMS (roman capitals with no full points) is the abbreviation of Her Majesty's Ship. Ships' names should be typeset in italics (e.g. HMS

Beagle, HMS *Victory*) and, after the first mention, can be referred to simply as *Beagle*, *Victory* (not *the Beagle*, *the Victory*).

Ho. is the abbreviation of House, but should be avoided.

hoard (noun) = store, collection of goods/provisions/treasure; **horde** = band of nomads, group of people.

hocus, hocused, hocusing.

hodgepodge *See* **hotchpotch**.

hoe, hoeing.

hoi polloi (italics) (= ordinary people) literally means *the many* and purists claim that *the hoi polloi* (= the the many) should not be allowed − all the more reason for avoiding the Greek expression.

hold (verb) inflects *hold − held − held*.

hold up = lift up (with the hands), delay, stop and rob (carry out a hold-up); **uphold** = maintain, defend. E.g.:
"The captain held up the cup for the crowd to see it."
"The spokesman asserted he would uphold the law."

hole, holey (= with holes), holeable.

Holland is only part of the Netherlands, although often used for the whole country; strictly, **Netherlands** should be used.

holocaust = destruction by fire (*the Holocaust* refers to genocide of the Jews during World War II); the word should not be used for any other type of **disaster**.

hologram = three-dimensional photograph taken and viewed using lasers; **holograph** = handwritten document, in the writing of the signatory.

holy, holier, holiest, holiness, holily (= with holiness).

home is a useful general term for a dwelling, lacking as it does the restrictive precision of bungalow, caravan, flat, house, and so on − although some authorities disagree. *See also* **accommodation.**

home-brew(ed), home-coming, home-grown, homeland, homeless, homely, home-like, homeliness, home-made, homesick(ness), homespun, homestead, home town, homeward(s), homework.

homesickness = longing for home and its associations; **nostalgia** originally had the same meaning, but now more often means a longing for times past and their associations.

homicide = the killing of one person by another; **murder** = deliberate killing of another; **manslaughter** = unintentional killing of another; **suicide** = killing oneself. Definite types of murder include *fratricide* (= killing one's brother), *genocide* (= killing a race of people), *infanticide* (= killing one's child), *matricide* (= killing one's mother), *patricide* or *parricide* (= killing one's father), *sororicide* (= killing one's sister) and *regicide* (= killing a monarch). A recent introduction from psychology is the term **parasuicide** = an apparently attempted suicide in which the "victim" does not really mean to die.

homoeopathy (not *homeopathy*).

homogeny, homogenize, homogeneous (= of constant composition, not *homogenous* = of common descent).

homonyms are two or more different words that are pronounced the same, often a source of confusion to learners of English. True homonyms are also spelled the same (words that merely sound the same are *homophones*; words merely spelled the same are *homographs*). Examples of the latter type are the future-forming verb *will* (= shall), the noun *will* (= testament) and the proper name *Will* (short for William); the nouns *seal* (= a tight closure) and *seal* (= an aquatic animal); and two remarkable verbs of opposite meaning, *cleave* (= to split apart) and *cleave* (= to stick together). To qualify as homonyms, the words must be of different origin and derivation; thus the various substantive meanings of *hand* (including the part of the arm below the wrist, a workman or seaman, and a unit for measuring the height of a horse) are not homonyms because they are derived from the same etymological source. Homonyms with different spellings (properly called homophones) are much more common.

Homonyms that might cause confusion are listed separately in this Dictionary. *See also* **antonym; pun.**

Homo sapiens (italics, initial capital letter).

Honduras The derived adjective and noun is *Honduran*.

Hong Kong (two words).

honour, honourable (= worthy of or motivated by honour), honorific; **honorary** (= conferred as an honour, or holding an office without reward or without performing the usual obligations).

honours A person is *awarded* a Nobel Prize, a VC or an OBE; *made* a CBE; *granted* a knighthood; *created* a life peer or a DBE. *See also* **capitalization** (Titles and ranks).

hoof (preferred plural *hoofs*).

hookah = Eastern tobacco pipe with a water trap, a hubble-bubble; **hooker** = small boat, rugby player, or prostitute (slang).

hope = desire (with expectation of achievement) for something good, optimistic anticipation ("the power of being cheerful in circumstances which we know to be desperate" – G.K. Chesterton). Strictly therefore the use of the word, and its corresponding verb, in a negative or pessimistic sense is at best colloquial (e.g. "I hope his application fails"). *See also* the next entry.

hopefully = in a hopeful manner. It does not mean *it is hoped that* or *let us hope*; e.g. "With the prospect of explaining his ideas to a group of intelligent people, he went to the meeting hopefully" is correct; "Hopefully it will not rain today" is incorrect. *See also* **optimistic; regretfully; thankfully**.

horrible/horribly should be reserved for things or circumstances that invoke *horror*, and not used of something that is merely **unpleasant** or **disagreeable** (as in "I made a horrible typing mistake"). *See* **horror**.

horrid originally meant bristly (as the poetic word *horrent* still does), but it has taken on the colloquial meaning of nasty, detestable (as in "Teacher was horrid to me at school today"). The word, which does not mean *horrible* (*see* **horror**), is probably best avoided.

horror = extreme repugnance and revulsion, a meaning it has largely retained even in *horror film*, although with additional associations of fear and dread. The same cannot be said of some of its derivatives, victims of journalism's "shock-horror". The basic meanings are:

horrible = capable of evoking horror; **horrify** = cause horror (in someone); **horrific** = directly exciting horror. *Horrible* should not be used merely to mean disagreeable or destestable (as in "Did you eat any of that horrible salad?"). *Horrific* should not be employed merely to emphasize what follows it, with the sense *significant* (as in "Changing the goalkeeper at halftime could have horrific consequences"). *Horrify* should not be diluted to mean stir the emotions/conscience − except the emotion of horror (as in "Horrifying statistics highlight the increase in parking offences"). When horrific scenes follow a terrorist bomb explosion in a busy street, many headline writers find they have devalued the currency of *horror* and its derivatives (and promptly write about "unspeakable horror"). *See also* **horrid**.

hors-d'oeuvre(s) (italics).

horse has various names, depending on its age, sex and fertility. A fertile male, used for stud, is a *stallion*; a castrated male (used for riding and racing) is a *gelding*. A fertile female is a *mare*; a young female is a *filly*. The young of either sex, under 12 months old, is a *foal* (and between the 1 January and 31 December after its birth is a *yearling* in racing circles); under four years old it is a *colt*. A small horse, less than 14.2 hands high, is a *pony*. *See also* **mule**.

horseback, horse-box, horse-chestnut, horseflesh, horsefly, horsehair, horse-leech, horse-mackerel, horseman(ship), horseplay, horsepower, horse-race, horse-raddish, horseshoe, horseshoe-shaped, horsetail, horsewhip, horsewoman, horsy.

horticulturist is the preferred form (not *horticulturalist*).

hotchpotch is the preferred spelling (not *hodgepodge*).

hospice, an archaic word for a place of rest for travellers (often kept by monks or nuns), is a useful reintroduction for "a special hospital for the terminally ill".

hospitalize, a convenient if American-sounding short way of saying "put or take into hospital", can now be found in some English dictionaries; the action is **hospitalization**.

host = large number of people; it should not be applied to things (e.g. "He raised a host of objections" is incorrect).

hostelry is archaic for **inn** and precious for **pub** (or *public house*).

house-agent, house arrest, houseboat, housebreaker, house-dog, house-flag, housefly, household(er), housekeeper, housemaid, housemaster, house party, houseproud, house-surgeon, house style, house-to-house, housetop(s), housewarming, housewife, housework.

howbeit is archaic for **nevertheless**, which should be used. The similar **albeit** (= although it be, even if) does remain in currency.

however is, to purists, among the most misused (or, at least, misplaced) words. It should be placed in a sentence immediately after the significant thing/idea being emphasized. Examples are difficult to construct without a preceding sentence or clause. Suppose the initial sentence is "Most editors drink more beer than do designers", then, of the following sentences,

1. "However, most designers eat more food"
2. "Most designers, however, eat more food"
3. "Most designers eat more food, however",

(1) contrasts the whole of the two sentences, (2) contrasts "editors" and "designers" (as was probably intended) and (3) contrasts "beer" and "food". Note also the obligatory comma or commas when *however* is used with the meaning of *nevertheless*. When it is used as an adverb meaning *no matter how*, it needs no comma. E.g.:

"However fast he runs, he will never catch a rabbit."

See also **ever**.

howsoever/whosoever/whomsoever (each one word). *See also* **ever**.

hullo *See* **hello**.

human should be reserved as an adjective; **human being** is the preferred noun form. **Humankind** overcomes the objections to **mankind** (which *see*). **Humanize** is the verb (not -*ise*). **Humane** = kind. *See also* **race**.

hummus = (Greek) dish made from puréed chickpeas or lentils; **humus** (noun) = organic content of soil; **humous** (adj.) = to do with humus.

humour, humoured, humouring, humorous, humorist.

hung *See* **hang.**

hurt inflects *hurt – hurt – hurt* (there is no form *hurted*).

hussy (original meaning *housewife*) is an old-fashioned and derogatory term once applied to any woman from a *flirt* or *prostitute* to a *mistress* or *adultress* (*see* **gender**). The genteel *femme fatale* and coarser *trollop* are also colloquialisms. The Victorian euphemism "No better than she ought to be" often conveyed the intended meaning, for which there seems to be no acceptable modern equivalent.

hydrolysis, hydrolyse.

hydrometer = instrument for measuring the specific gravity (density) of a liquid; **hygrometer** = instrument for measuring the humidity of a gas (such as air).

hyena is the preferred spelling (not *hyaena*).

hygiene, hygienic.

hyper- = over, above, involving an excess; **hypo-** = under, below, involving a deficiency (e.g. hypertension = high blood pressure, hypotension = low blood pressure).

hyperbole Figure of speech which uses (often gross) exaggeration for emphasis; e.g.: "He made countless errors" (no matter how many errors he made, given enough time they could be counted). The device, even used deliberately, could leave the reader with the impression that the writing is imprecise.

hypercritical = over-critical; **hypocritical** = pretending to be better than one is, insincere, false (from *hypocrisy* = behaving in a way contrary to one's true character).

hyphen, hyphenation (not *hyphenization*). *See* **compound words; word breaks.**

hypnosis, hypnotism, hypnotize, hypnotic.

hypocrisy, hypocrite.

hypothesis (pl. hypotheses).

I

ibid. (italics) is the abbreviation of *ibidem* (= in the same place).

-ible *See* **-able** and **-ible**.

-ic/-ics *See* **suffixes**.

Iceland The derived adjective is *Icelandic* and the noun (for the people) is *Icelander*.

ideal, idealism, idealize, ideology, ideological.

idée fixe (italics) = fixed idea, obsession; the French form should be avoided.

identical *with* (not identical *to*).

identify = establish the identity of; it should not be used to mean *find* or *discover* (e.g. "We must identify a new approach to the problem" is incorrect).

ideogram = another name for an **ideograph**.

ideograph = letter, character or symbol that stands for a thing, not for a spoken sound (e.g. an Egyptian hieroglyph); **logogram** = symbol for a complete word (e.g. an ampersand, & = *and*); **idiograph** = private symbol or trademark (such as a monogram). *See also* **monogram**.

idiom, in the sense of an established, usually colloquial expression characteristic of a language but incapable of literal interpretation, adds colour to English but should be avoided in "serious" or formal writing, particularly in text for translation into other languages. Some English readers may be unfamiliar with a particular idiom and, more importantly, idioms cannot be translated literally (they are metaphorical) and so place an unnecessary burden on co-edition translators – hence the well-known story that the expression "out of sight, out of mind" was once translated as "invisible idiot". The term idiom can be limited to a phrase and not be applied to a single word that takes on a new meaning. For example *battle-axe*, originally a formidable weapon, has come to mean also a formidable, haranguing woman. The expression *to lean over backwards for someone* is, however, true idiom because its meaning − not its literal one − is to go to extreme lengths to accommodate/please someone, and cannot be attributed to an existing or new meaning of any of the individual words in the phrase.

idiosyncrasy, idiosyncratic.

idle, idled, idling, idly.

idol, idolator, idolatry, idolize.

idyll, idyllic (preferred to *idyllian*).

-ie- *See* **-ei-**.

i.e. is the abbreviation of *id est* (= that is). It should not be confused with **e.g.** (which *see*).

if and when usually includes two redundant words (either *if and* or *and when*); *if* or *when* alone is sufficient. *See also* **tautology**.

if need be works with the present or future tense; the past requires *if need were*; e.g. "He corrects the work, if need be", "He will correct the work, if need be" but "He corrected the work, if need were". The last sounds so stilted, it might be better phrased as "He corrected the work as (or when) necessary".

if not Avoid ambiguous use of this term; e.g. "He made the fastest, if not the most accurate, changes to the text" might be damning with faint praise. The sentence should be written "He made the fastest, and the most accurate, changes..." if that is what is meant. (The other meaning requires "... the fastest, but perhaps not the most accurate, changes...").

igloo (pl. igloos).

ignite, ignitable, igniter.

ignoramus (pl. ignoramuses).

ignorant *See* **artless**.

il- *See* **negatives prefixes**.

ileum = part of the small intestine (adj. *ileac*); **ileus** = intestinal obstruction (adj. *ileac*); **ilium** = the hip-bone (adj. *iliac*).

ill/illness is generally preferable to **sick/sickness** when referring to poor health; *sick* is used in references to vomiting. E.g.:

"He was ill for a long time."
"She died after a brief illness."
"The smell of petrol makes me feel sick."
"I was sick after eating some oysters."

A sufferer of a long-term illness can also be described as *sick*. E.g.:

"She nursed her sick child for three weeks."
"I was off sick for a fortnight."

Unwell is generally used of a mild illness ("I left early because I was feeling unwell"), and **poorly** (= unwell) now sounds old fashioned ("He did look poorly").

ill-advised, ill at ease, ill-bred, ill-conditioned, ill-disposed, ill effects, ill-fated, ill-favoured, ill-gotten, ill health, ill humour, ill-humoured, ill-judged, ill luck, ill-mannered, ill nature, ill-natured, ill-omened, ill-tempered, ill-timed, ill-use (= ill-treat, not misuse), ill will.

illegal *See* **unlawful**.

illegible *See* **unreadable**.

illegitimate *See* **unlawful**.

illicit *See* **elicit**.

illiterate = unable to deal with words (read and write); **innumerate** = unable to deal with numbers.

illude = to deceive, trick; **allude** = to refer to (casually); **elude** = to evade. The corresponding nouns are *illusion* (*see* **delusion**), *allusion*, and *elusiveness*. The adjective from *illude* is *illusory* (preferred to *illusive*); from *elude* it is *elusive* (preferred to *elusory*).

illustrate, illustration, illustrator.

im- *See* **negative prefixes**.

image, imagine (= conjure up mental images), imagination (= repository of mental images), imaginary (= existing in the imagination), imaginative (= capable of having or stimulating imagination). The last two should not be confused. E.g.:

"The illustration depicted imaginary creatures from Mars."
"The illustration made imaginative use of colour."

imago (pl. imagines).

imbibe is precious for **drink** and euphemistic for **drink alcohol**; it should be avoided.

imbrication *See* **embrocation**.

imbroglio (pl. imbroglios).

imbue (with) = permeate, fill; **instil** (in) = to infuse, introduce into. E.g.:

"His reassurance imbued the staff with confidence."
"Confidence was instilled in the staff by his reassurance."

imitate, imitator. *See also* **emulate**.

immanent = pervading, inherent; **imminent** = impending, threatening; **eminent** = famous. E.g.:

"Adaptation for survival is an immanent characteristic of most organisms."
"Because of pollution, the extinction of several organisms is imminent."
"These statements were made by an eminent biologist."

immaterial = irrelevant, unimportant; **unmaterial** = not composed of matter (a meaning that is generally no longer applied to *immaterial*). E.g.:

"The slight differences in size were immaterial."
"A ghost is an unmaterial manifestation."

immature = not fully formed/developed; **premature** = arriving too soon. A premature baby is often also immature.

immeasurable = beyond measure (figuratively); **unmeasurable** = incapable of being measured (physically). Like *countless* and *innumerable*, *immeasurable* should not be used to describe things that can/could be measured. E.g.:

"She made an immeasurable contribution to the project" is acceptable;

"We had to walk an immeasurable distance to the village" is unacceptable.

immigrant/immigrate *See* **emigrant**.

imminent *See* **immanent**.

immiscible (but note mixable).

immobile, immobilize, immobilization.

immoral *See* **amoral**.

immortal, immortalize, immortalization.

immovable (but immoveable in law) = cannot be moved (although once could be); **irremovable** = cannot be removed (having become established). E.g.:

"The rusty bolt was immovable."
"The wine stain was irremovable."
See also **mobile**.

immune *See* **exempt**.

immunity, immunize, immunization. **Immunity** = freedom from disease, harm or liability; **impunity** = freedom from penalty or punishment. E.g.:

"Scientists have developed a new vaccine that confers total immunity to whooping cough."
"Scientists should not be allowed to experiment on living animals with impunity."

impact should be reserved for actual or figurative collisions, and not used as a stronger word for *effect* or *impression*.

impassable = cannot be passed; **impassible** = non-feeling, impassive. E.g.:

"Snow blocked the valley and made it impassable."
"His response was impassible, and his face expressionless."

impassioned/impassive *See* **dispassionate**.

impecunious is a euphemism for **short of money** or the colloquial **hard up**; it should be avoided.

impede, impediment (= hindrance), impedance (= resistive property of a conductor passing an alternating electric current).

impediment = hindrance, physical defect; **obstacle** = obstruction. E.g.:
"She had difficulty in communicating because of a speech impediment."
"The defenders slowed the attackers' advance by putting obstacles on all major roads."

impel, impelled, impelling, impellent.

imperceptible (not *-able*).

imperial = concerning an empire or emperor; **imperious** = domineering, overbearing. E.g.:
"The imperial aspirations of British and Spanish explorers of the Americas."
"He alienated the staff by his imperious attitude."

imperil, imperilled, imperilling.

impetus (pl. impetuses).

impinge, impinged, impinging.

implausible (not *-able*).

implicit *See* **explicit**.

imply *See* **infer**.

important is a grossly overworked word; chief, main, principal, significant could be used for a change. And if the intended meaning really is *of import*, an explanation of why or in what way should follow. For **importantly,** *see* **thankfully**.

impossible/improbable *See* **possible** and **probable**.

impracticable = cannot be fulfilled or dealt with, unmanageable;
impractical = unpractical (which avoid), all right in theory but not in practice.

impresario (pl. impresarios).

imprimatur = licence to print or publish, a sanction (approval);
imprimature is obsolete for **impression** (of a book).

improve, improvable, improvement.

improvident = lacking provision for the future or foresight;
imprudent = ill-advisedly bold, incautious. E.g.:
"His unwillingness to save money proved to be improvident when he lost his source of income."
"His investment in the new company proved to be imprudent when it collapsed after a few months."

improvise, improviser (who improvises, in general), improvisator (who improvises at speaking or playing a musical instrument), improvisation.

impulse *See* **compulsion**.

in (no full point) is the abbreviation of inch (and inches).

in Avoid using this word for **within**, a use that can lead to ambiguity; e.g. "I can have a bath in four minutes" and "Please edit this text in four days" would both benefit from *within* for *in* to convey the senses intended. Also avoid using **in** for *into*; "He jumped in the lake" and "She walked in the room" both require *into* for *in*. In is preferred to *at* in the construction "She was born in England/London/Kensington/Cromwell Road".

in- *See* **negative prefixes**.

inaccessible (not -*able*).

inadmissible (not -*able*).

inadvisable = not recommended; **unadvisable** = not open to advice. E.g.:
"I thought that the proposed change to the schedule was inadvisable."

"I tried to pass on the information to the manager, but he proved to be unadvisable."

in all probability = **probably,** which is preferred.

in any case should be avoided; use **anyway** (not *any way*).

inapt *See* **inept.**

inartistic = poor at appreciating art, lacking an artistic viewpoint; **unartistic** = lacking the talent/ability of an artist. E.g.:
"I found the exhibition of sculpture boring because I am inartistic."
"I find drawing a lifelike face impossible because I am unartistic."

in as much as, in so far as are preferred (as four separate words) to *inasmuch as* and *insofar as.*

inaudible (not *-able*).

in between (preposition) is usually a tautology (e.g. in "It was a colour in between blue and green", delete *in*); **in-between** (adj.) = intervening (e.g. "It was an in-between colour, neither blue nor green"); **in-between** (noun) = someone or something between two (specified) states/qualities (e.g. "He was neither man nor boy, merely an in-between") and should be avoided. *See also* **between.**

in-built, originally an Americanism, = **built-in,** which is usually to be preferred.

incapable relates to a permanent lack of ability; **unable** relates to a specific inability in terms of situation or time; e.g. "He was incapable of climbing the ladder because he had two artificial legs" (i.e. he never could) and "He was unable to climb the ladder because he had sprained his ankle" (but would be able to do so when his ankle healed).

incentive = that which incites to action (with the idea of reward for success); **inspiration** = that which inspires, stimulation (not necessarily for reward other than self-satisfaction); **instigation** = the act of inciting, impulse (with authoritarian overtones); **motivation** = that which motivates, makes move/happen (with no or merely neutral overtones). *See also* **induce.**

in charge of = in authority over; **in the charge of** = under the authority of. E.g.:

"The babysitter was in charge of the child."

"The child was in the charge of the babysitter."

incidentally (not *incidently*).

incise, incision.

inclose/inclosure The preferred spellings are **enclose/enclosure** (but Inclosure Acts, historically).

include, inclusive, includible. *Include* should not be used to mean made up of, consist of, comprise – that is, to describe a complete group; *include* can refer only to an incomplete group.

incognito (pl. incognitos).

incompatible (not *-able*).

inconceivable, like *unimaginable* and *unthinkable*, are extreme words that have rapidly come into vogue. They should not be devalued merely to emphatic synonyms of such words as *impracticable*, *unacceptable*, *undesirable*, *unnecessary*, *unlikely* and *unwanted*.

incontinent = lacking self-control; **incontinently** = immediately.

incorrect (not *uncorrect*) is the opposite of *correct*; **uncorrected** is the opposite of *corrected*.

incorrigible (not *-able*).

increase = to make larger/more numerous; **maximize** = to make as large/much as possible. E.g.:

"We must increase productivity if we are to maximize profits."

incredible = unbelievable; **incredulous** = unbelieving. The corresponding nouns are *incredibility* and *incredulity*. *See also* **credence; credible**.

incubate, incubator, incubation.

incur, incurred, incurring.

indefensible (not *-able)* is preferred to **undefendable**.

indefinite, indefinitely (not *indefinate, indefinately*).

indefinite article *See* **a** or **an**.

indelible (not *-able*).

independent (not *-ant*) is the spelling of both the adjective and the noun, unlike *dependant* (noun) and *dependent* (adj.).

indestructible (not *-able*).

Indian words Many words have entered the English vocabulary from the Indian subcontinent, often by way of the army or the British raj. Hindi, itself based on the Urdu word for India, has provided the most and there are others direct from Sanskrit and other modern languages of the subcontinent. As a check list of spellings (and for interest), here are some examples.

From Hindi:

bandana	dinghy	kukri	shampoo
bangle	dixie	loot	Sikh
bungalow	dungarees	mahout	sitar
cheetah	gavial	mina (bird)	thug
chintz	guru	mugger	toddy
chit	gymkhana	(crocodile)	tom-tom
chukka	jodhpurs	pundit	top
chukker	juggernaut	pukka	raj
chutney	jungle	punkah	verandah
cot (bed)	kedgeree	puttee	wallah
dekko	krait	sari	

From Sanskrit: brahmin, mantra, raga, sandal(wood), stupa, yoga.
From Tamil: catamaran, cheroot, curry (food), mulligatawny, pariah, pappadam.
From Urdu: khaki, nabob, purdah, pyjamas, sepoy, shawl, tandoor, tandoori.
Others: gala-azar (Assamese), jute (Bengali), coir, copra, teak (Malayalam), mongoose (Marathi), panda (Nepali).
See also **Malay words.** For American Indian words, *see* **Americanisms.**

indict = to accuse; **indite** = to write.

indigestible (not *-able* or *undigestible*) = that cannot be digested; **undigested** = that has not been digested.

indiscipline (absence of discipline) but **undisciplined** (of someone lacking discipline).

indiscreet/indiscrete *See* **discreet**.

indiscriminate = heedless, lacking care; **undiscriminating** = lacking discrimination, lacking judgement. E.g.:
"Her appearance suffered from the indiscriminate use of make-up."
"She was undiscriminating in her choice of clothes for the formal occasion."

indispensable (not *-ible*).

indispose, indisposition (not *indisposedness*). **Indisposed** is precious when used to mean **slightly unwell**.

indite *See* **indict**.

individual (noun) should not be used to mean **person** (as in "a certain individual").

indivisible (not *-able*).

indoor is the adjective, **indoors** is the adverb. E.g.:
"Squash is an indoor activity."
"Squash is played indoors."
Outdoor and **outdoors** are similar.

indorse The preferred spelling is **endorse**. *See also* **approve**.

induce = to bring on or into being, draw an inference (inductively); **induct** = to introduce; **inducement** = incentive, motive, that which induces; **induction** = bringing or drawing in, installation in office. *Induce/induction* also have technical meanings in electricity. *See also* **deduce**.

industry, industrial (pertaining to industry − of the e.g. engineering or manufacturing kind), industrious (diligent). E.g.:
"Many industrial processes still rely on a large number of industrious workers."

inedible *See* **edible**.

ineducable (not *uneducatable*).

ineffective = not producing the required effect; **ineffectual** = unable to produce an effect. E.g.:
"The advertising campaign was ineffective in persuading people to buy the product."
"His pleading was ineffectual – nobody believed him."

inept = without skill, unfit, fatuous, futile; **inapt** = inappropriate, unsuitable, unaccustomed to; **unapt** = inapt. These are close meanings that can, however, be distinguished. E.g.:
"The art student made a surprisingly inept attempt at drawing a face."
"The young art student was an inapt candidate for the senior designer's position."

inequity = inequality, unfairness; **iniquity** = immorality, wickedness. E.g.:
"Some people object to the inequity of the way the law is applied to the rich and the poor."
"They claim that the poor are punished for the slightest misdemeanour, whereas the rich get away with great iniquities."
The corresponding adjectives are *inequitable* and *iniquitous*.

inestimable *See* **estimable**.

in excess of seldom means more than **more than**, which is preferred.

inexplicable (= incapable of explanation) is preferred to **unexplainable**.

infallible (not *-able*).

infamous *See* **famous**.

infant *See* **baby**.

infection/infectious refer to a disorder (disease) that can be passed from one person to another – by whatever means; **contagion/contagious** refer to a disease that is passed on by contact (with an infected person, a carrier, or anything contaminated by pathogens); **infestation** is a disorder or circumstance that involves a "take-over" by insects, worms, parasites, and so on. An infestation that causes a disorder may or may not be infectious/contagious.

infer = to deduce, derive (as a consequence); **imply** = to hint, suggest, signify, express indirectly. One infers something *from* a statement, but implies something *with* (or *by*) a statement: what A implies, B infers. Note also the forms inferable, inferred, inferring, inference.

inferior *to* (not inferior *than*).

inferno (pl. infernos).

infiltrate = introduce (insidiously) a few items into a larger whole (such as a few men among a body of enemy troops or an idea into someone else's mind), to permeate; **insinuate** = introduce subtly or stealthily (such as oneself into favour or a thing into place), to suggest obliquely. Infiltrate does not need *into* (e.g. "The spy infiltrated the enemy camp"); insinuate needs *that* (e.g. "Are you insinuating that I am lying?").

infinitive, split *See* **split infinitive**.

inflammable (= capable of being set afire) is preferred to **flammable**. **Non-inflammable** (preferred to **non-flammable**) strictly means not capable of supporting flame although combustible − that is, treated in such a way that combustion cannot take place. Something that simply will not burn is **incombustible**. Thus petrol is inflammable, cotton fabrics can be made non-inflammable, and asbestos is incombustible.

inflate, inflater, inflatable.

inflect, inflective, inflexion. *See* **afflict**.

inflexible (not -*able*).

inflexion (not -*ection*).

inflict *See* **afflict**.

inform = to give or pass information to; it should not be used to mean *advise*, *ask*, *instruct* or simply *tell*.

informant = someone who provides specific information or knowledge; **informer** = someone who provides information (usually about another) to the police or other authority.

infra-red (but ultraviolet).

infrequent is preferred to **unfrequent** (but use *un*frequented, not *in*frequented).

infusible (not *-able*) (= unmeltable).

-ing *See* **gerund; suffixes.**

ingenious = clever (at contrivance); **ingenuous** = naive, innocent. **Ingenuity** is common to both, although **ingenuousness** is better of the latter. The French term **ingénu(e)** (unsophisticated or artless person) should be avoided.

inhabitable *See* **habitable.**

inherent = intrinsic, permanently existing in or as part of something; **innate** = inborn, native, natural; **congenital** = present at birth (although possibly of earlier origin); **inherited** = derived from a parent or predecessor.

inheritable is preferred to **hereditable.**

inhuman = cruel, unfeeling, lacking in humanity; **unhuman** = non-human (which is preferred). E.g.:
"The guards were censured for their inhuman treatment of the prisoners."
"The footprints were made by an unhuman creature."

initial, initialled, initialling.

initiate = admit someone to a select group (often with some sort of ceremony), make someone aware of the basic principles of a subject; the word should not be used merely as a synonym of *begin*. E.g.:
"He performed the rites that would initiate him into the secret society" (correct);
"The receipt of an order initiated the manufacturing process" (incorrect),
which is better put as "Manufacturing began after receipt of the order".

in-laws is a convenient colloquialism for the relatives of one's husband or wife. **Brother-in-law** (pl. brothers-in-law) is the brother of your husband (or wife), often extended to mean also your sister's husband and even your sister-in-law's husband. **Sister-in-law** (pl. sisters-in-law) is your husband's (or wife's) sister, your brother's wife, or your brother-in-law's wife. **Father-in-law** is your spouse's father, and **mother-in-law** is your spouse's mother.

in lieu = instead, which is preferred.

in most instances = usually, which is preferred.

innate *See* **inherent**.

innings (at cricket) has the same form in the singular and plural. Baseball solves the problem by having *inning* as the singular (and *innings* as the plural).

innocuous *See* **inoculation**.

innovation = something newly introduced; it is therefore tautologous to write "To the local people, the motor car was a new innovation" (delete *new*). **Innovative** should not be used as a modish alternative to **new** or **original**.

innumerable, like countless, should strictly be used only of things that cannot be counted (e.g. "The over-punctuated text contained innumerable commas" is incorrect). *See also* **enumerable**.

innumerate *See* **illiterate**.

inoculation (with one *n* and one *c*, because it originally meant the insertion of a plant graft into a bud or eye: *in-oculus*); note also **vaccination** (with two *c*s, from *Vaccinia* = cowpox) and **immunization** (with a *z*). Finally, note the spelling **innocuous** (with two *n*s and one *c*), meaning harmless.

in order that should be followed by *may* or *might*; e.g. "In order that no delay *will* occur" is incorrect.

in order to should not be used when plain *to* will do; e.g. in "I had to leave home an hour earlier than usual in order to meet the plane", the simpler ". . . than usual to meet the plane" works better.

-in or -ine As an ending of scientific or technical terms taken into more general use, *-ine* tends to be shortened to *-in* (e.g. adrenalin, gelatin, glycerin, lanolin, vitamin are the preferred forms); these spellings also reflect the preferred pronunciations.

inquire is the preferred spelling, not **enquire** (similarly **inquiry** is preferred to **enquiry**).

in rare cases is more briefly expressed as **rarely**.

in regard to, like *in relation to* and *in respect of*, seldom means more than **about**, which is preferred.

insanitary = unhealthy, unhygienic, likely to cause ill-health; **unsanitary** = lacking sanitation. E.g.:
"The army nurses fought a constant battle against sepsis in the insanitary wards of the field hospital."
"Their primitive homes were unsanitary, lacking any provision for the disposal of domestic or human waste."

insect is, strictly, an arthropod animal of the class Insecta. A typical mature insect has six legs, two antennae and three chief body parts (head, thorax and abdomen), although some of these features may be lacking at earlier (e.g. larval) stages. There are several other classes of arthropods, such as arachnids (spiders and their allies), crustaceans (including shrimps, crabs and so on), diplopods (millipedes) and chilopods (centipedes), all of which have more than six legs. It is therefore incorrect to refer to members of these other classes as *insects*. The general American term **bug** (for insect) should be avoided except in reference to insects of the order Hemiptera, the true bugs (most of which feed by sucking sap or blood).

insensible = unconcious, lacking feeling/emotion; **insensitive** = incapable of reacting to sensation, unfeeling/unemotional. The latter is preferred to the former in their second meanings. **Nonsensical** = lacking in (common) sense, absurd. E.g.:
"The blow to the head knocked her insensible."
"She seemed insensitive to pain."
"Her proposal to omit the checking stage was a nonsensical suggestion."

inseparable pairs of words – often of similar meaning and many of which form clichés – should be avoided in formal writing. Known technically as *dyads*, many are archaic, and some are idiomatic and thus puzzling if taken literally. They are also irreversible – it is unnatural, and un-English, to say *change and chop* or *choose and pick*. A few common examples include:

bits and pieces	might and main
chop and change	odds and sods
cut and thrust	part and parcel
fair and square	pick and choose
fast and furious	pink and dimples
fine and dandy	rack and ruin
goods and chattels	short and sweet
hale and hearty	spick and span
heart and soul	sweetness and light
home and dry	thick and fast
hue and cry	time and tide
kith and kin	toss and turn
leaps and bounds	trials and tribulations
live and learn	well and truly

See also **hendiadys; tautology**.

inside of should be avoided; use plain **inside** (unless *inside* is a noun – e.g. "the inside of the box").

insidious (not *insiduous*) = spreading stealthily and secretly, possibly also treacherously; **invidious** = offensive, possibly also unjust; **perfidious** = treacherous (as in the French description of Britain as "perfidious Albion").

insignia is a plural word (Latin singular *insigne*).

insignificant = unimportant; it does not mean **small**.

insinuate = to imply in an underhand way, to hint at a flaw or fault in something; it is a pejorative term and should not be used as a synonym for the neutral **suggest**. **Insinuation** and **suggestion** are similarly related. *See also* **infiltrate**.

insipid, insipidness (not *insipidity*). *See also* **sapid**.

insist, insistent, insistence.

in situ (italics) = in (original) position; the Latin form should be avoided.

in so far as is preferred to *insofar as* (*see* **in as much as**).

insolate = to expose to sunlight; **insulate** = to isolate, block from a source of electricity, cold or sound.

insoluble describes something that cannot be dissolved or cannot be solved; it is preferred to **unsolvable** in the latter sense.

inspect, inspector, inspection.

inspiration *See* **incentive**.

in spite of is better put as **despite** or **although** (*see* **despite the fact that**).

instability (= state of lacking stability), but **unstable** (= not stable).

instal, instals, installed, installing, installation, instalment.

inst. is a business abbreviation of **instant**, = this month, which should be avoided (write "your letter of the 5th of this month" not "of the 5th inst.").

instant = a very short time, now; **moment** = a slightly longer but nevertheless short time, very soon. E.g.:
"It will take me only an instant" (= very short time);
"Please do it this instant" (= now);
"It will only take me a moment" (= short time);
"I'll do it in a moment" (= soon).

instantaneously = at the same time/instant, simultaneously; **instantly** = at once, at this instant, now. E.g.:
"The door banged and he dropped the saucer instantaneously."
"Please pick up that saucer instantly."

instigation *See* **incentive**.

instil, instilled, instilling, instillation, instilment (not to be confused with installation, instalment; *see* **instal**).

instinct, instinctive (= done/controlled by instinct, inborn, innate), instinctual (to do with instinct). The meanings of the two adjectives are much the same. E.g.:

"Suckling by a newborn baby is an instinctive reflex response."
"The suckling response in babies is instinctual."

Instinct is an innate ability, inherited by human beings and other animals − indeed one definition of non-human creatures hinges on the fact that much animal behaviour is totally instinctive. **Intuition**, on the other hand, is purely a human attribute. It requires insight and is a product of the intellect which involves reasoning, unlike the automatic functioning of instinct. E.g.:

"He excelled at snooker with little or no coaching − he had a natural instinct for it."
"His intuition told him to play the blue ball, which turned out to be the correct choice."

instructional = giving instructions, educational; **instructive** = giving information, informative. E.g.:

"The students learned the technique by watching an instructional video film."
"The students found the video film instructive."

insure = to make an arrangement for the payment of money in the event of loss or injury; **ensure** = to make sure.

intaglio (pl. intaglios). *See* **cameo; printing processes**.

intangible (not *-able*).

intelligence = innate mental (thinking) capacity; **intellect** = mental development; **intelligent** = quick-witted, "bright"; **intellectual** = thinking, "brainy".

intelligible (not *-able*).

intend, intendant, intendancy, intent (adj., or noun = purpose), intention (= purpose) (not intension, a term in logic).

intense = concentrated, extreme, dense, with strong emotion; **intensive** = thorough, unremitting, exhaustive. E.g.:

"Even the glass melted in the intense heat."
"Meeting the deadline required an intensive effort by all the staff."

inter- = between, among; **intra-** = within; **infra-** = below, less than; **intro-** = into, inwards. E.g.:

> interfere, international, interrupt;
> intracellular, intramuscular, intravenous;
> infra-red, infrasonic, infrastructure;
> introduction, introgression, introspective.

inter, interred, interring. *See also* **internment.**

inter alia (italics) = among other things; the Latin form should be avoided.

intercept, intercepter (preferred to interceptor), interception.

interchange, interchanging, interchangeable.

interesting is a word that, unqualified, raises the questions "to whom and in what way?" Puzzling, dramatic, unusual, important (used correctly), titivating, intriguing, full of character, strange, exotic, curious, worthy of further investigation – all are better, if somewhat wordier, alternatives.

interface = common boundary between two fluids or other states of matter, an apparatus that links two electronic devices (such as an IBM terminal and an ICL computer). The word should be reserved for such technical meanings and not used to mean any common ground or boundary between any two of anything. *See* **vogue words**.

interject = interrupt (as an abrupt contribution to a conversation); **interpose** = interject; **interpolate** = insert something (into a text or conversation) or estimate a value from other, surrounding values; **extrapolate** = to extend (by estimation) a given set of values into an unestablished area, to infer; **intersperse** = place things between or among others. E.g.:

> "The chairman had hardly begun his speech when a heckler interjected a remark about high directors' fees."
> "Given the values for June and December, I interpolated those for September."
> "We extrapolated the graph and estimated the probable maximum value."
> "The flower bed contained begonias interspersed with marigolds."

interment = burial (of a corpse); **internment** = confinement of an alien (in time of war). The corresponding verbs are *inter* and *intern*.

intermezzo (pl. intermezzi).

in terms of is a cliché generally to be avoided.

intern *See* **internment**.

interpret, interpreter, interpretable, interpretation, interpretative (preferred to *interpretive*).

interrelate, interrelated, interrelation, interrelationship.

interrogative pronouns *See* **pronouns**.

interrupt, interrupter, interruption.

interstate = between two or more (political/territorial) states; **intestate** = having made no will (testament).

interval = length or period of time between two events; it should not be used merely to mean any period of time. E.g.:

"The schedule extended for two years, an interval regarded as too short" is incorrect;

"Between receipt of copy and dispatch of film is an interval of four months" is correct.

in the circumstances *See* **under the circumstances**.

in (the) close proximity = **close** or **near**, either of which is preferred.

in the event that = **if** (which is twelve letters shorter).

in the nature of should be avoided for *about*, *like* or *approximately*.

in the neighbourhood of = **near** or **round about**, either of which is preferred.

in the order of and **in the region of** should not be used to mean *about* or *approximately* (as "Its length was in the order of 20 metres", "It cost in the region of £10,000").

into is the usual preposition ("We went into the room", "I entered into a contract"); **in to** is a preposition (*in*) and part of an infinitive (*to*), as in "You came in to see her."
See also **onto**.

intolerable = unbearable; **intolerant** = unwilling to endure something, likely to oppose those who differ or disagree. E.g.:

"How can you put up with the intolerable heat in this room?"

"Louise is very intolerant of people who like the room warm."

in toto (italics) = entirely, completely (it does not mean in total or on the whole); the Latin form is often misused or misunderstood, and is therefore best avoided.

intramuscular, intra-uterine, intravenous.

intrigue, intrigued, intriguing, intriguer.

intrude = force (oneself/something) in; **obtrude** = thrust forward (unwelcomely); **protrude** = stick out. E.g.:

"Ann insists on intruding when we are trying to have a private conversation."

"Ann always obtrudes her views into the conversation."

"Ann needs orthodontic treatment because her teeth protrude."

The corresponding adjectives are *intrusive* (= butting in, unwelcomely), *obtrusive* = very noticeable, and *protrusive* = jutting out.

intuition *See* **instinct**.

inundate, inundation.

inure (not *innure*).

in vacuo (italics) = in a vacuum; the Latin term should be avoided in ordinary writing.

invalid (adj.) = not valid; **invalid** (noun) = someone who is ill. **Invalidated** = made not valid, made void; **invalided** = regarded as an invalid or unfit for duty; use **invalidation** of the former, **invalidity** of the latter.

invaluable *See* **valuable**.

inveigh = speak loudly against something; **inveigle** = tempt, entice or persuade someone into doing something.

invent, inventor, invention. *See also* **discover**.

inverse = the direct opposite of something in order or direction, an inverted state or condition; **converse** = something (or an action) that is the exact opposite; **obverse** = counterpart/opposite of any fact; **reverse** = the opposite or contrary of something. All these words are close in meaning; *reverse* or *opposite* should be used when in doubt. Consider:

"His manner was the reverse of co-operative."

"The possession of flair without experience is the converse of the possession of experience without flair."

"The inverse of 1, 2, 3 is 3, 2, 1."

"He claims that men are more sensitive than women, whereas the obverse is often true."

(Technically, *reverse* = back, or non-head side, of a coin; *obverse* = front, or head side, of a coin.)

invert, inverter.

inverted commas English is one of the few languages in which inverted commas (or quotation marks) take the form of ' and ' or " and " (with the initial mark literally one or two inverted commas, resembling the figure 6 in shape, and the final mark identical with a normal comma or apostrophe). When checking printed proofs, editors and proof-readers should ensure that the initial mark is typeset correctly (especially if the typesetter is a non-English company) because in some other languages the initial mark may be identical with a comma and not inverted (i.e. ' and ' or " and "). Still other languages use totally different marks (such as << and >> in Greek). *See also* **punctuation** (apostrophe); **punctuation** (quotation marks).

invest, investor, investment.

investigate, investigator, investigation.

in view of the fact that = **considering** or **because**, which are preferred.

invincible (not *-able*).

invisible (not *-able*).

invite is a verb; it should not be used as a noun to mean **invitation** (e.g. "I accepted her invite to the party" is incorrect).

in vitro, in vivo (italics).

involve is overused and should be deleted or replaced by a more precise verb. E.g.:

"The additional time involved will be two days" (delete *involved*).

"The cost involved in building the house" (say "The cost of building the house").

"Much labour has been involved in cleaning" (say "Much labour has been expended on cleaning").

"The injury involved her leg" (say "She injured her leg" or "The impact broke/bruised/cut/fractured/gashed/grazed/hurt/lacerated/numbed/paralysed/severed her leg").

inward can be an adjective (e.g. "an inward movement") or an adverb (e.g. "move inward slightly"), although **inwards** is the preferred form of the adverb. *See also* **-wards**.

ion, ionic, ionize, ionization (and de-ionize). **Ionic** (with a capital *i*) refers to Ionia or a style of Greek architecture.

-ionaire or **-ionnaire** This suffix varies, and the variants have to be learned (e.g. commissionaire, millionaire, questionnaire).

ipso facto (italics) = **thereby**, which should be used.

ir- *See* **negative prefixes**.

Iran The derived adjective and noun is *Iranian*, which is preferred to *Persian* except in historical contexts (and expressions such as Persian carpet). The Iranian/Persian language is *Farsi*. The preferred name for what used to be called the *Persian Gulf* is simply *The Gulf*.

Iraq The derived adjective and noun is *Iraqi*.

irascible (one *r*, and not *-able*).

iridesce, iridescent, iridescence, iridium (the metallic element).

iris (pl. irises).

Irish *See* **Celtic words; Gaelic; Scotland**.

Iron Age (initial capital letters).

ironic(al) = suggesting or expressing irony; it should not be overworked to mean *strange*, *paradoxical* or merely *unusual*.

irradicate *See* **eradicate**.

irreconcilable, irreconcilement.

irreducible (not *-able*).

irregardless merely means **regardless**, which should be used.

irregular verbs *See* **verbs**.

irrelevant (not *-ent*).

irreligious = (deliberately) ignoring religious beliefs; **unreligious** = not holding/belonging to a religious faith. E.g.:

"I was offended by his repeated irreligious use of Christ's name."
"I admire church architecture although I am quite unreligious."

irrepairable = cannot be repaired, and **irreparable** = cannot be made good (from *repair* and *reparation* respectively) are now virtually synonymous.

irreplaceable (note *-eable*).

irrepressible (not *-able*).

irresistible (not *-able*).

irresponsible = rash, feckless; it does not mean *not responsible*. E.g.:

"Throwing the bottle out of the car window was an irresponsible act."
but "Because of his mental state, he was not responsible for his actions."
See also **unresponsible**.

irreversible (not *-able*).

irruption *See* **eruption**.

-is Words of Greek origin ending in *-is* generally form the plural in *-es*. E.g.:

amanuensis	amanuenses
analysis	analyses
basis	bases

catharsis	catharses
crisis	crises
ellipsis	ellipses
hypothesis	hypotheses
oasis	oases
parenthesis	parentheses
synthesis	syntheses
thesis	theses

-ise *See* **-ize** *or* **-ise**.

Islam is the preferred term for the religion of Muslims. **Muslim** (adj., preferred to *Moslem*) describes the people, **Islamic** (adj.) describes the religion, culture, and so on.

isle *See* **aisle**.

isn't (= is not) should be avoided in formal writing.

isolate *See* **eliminate**.

Israel The derived adjective and noun is *Israeli*. *See also* **Semitic**.

issue (verb) takes *to* not *with* (e.g. write "Pens were issued to the staff" not "The staff were issued with pens", although " . . . were issued pens" is correct).

-ist *See* **-alist**.

isthmus (pl. isthmuses).

Italian words in English relate mostly to the arts (particularly music) and to food. Long-standing nouns ending in *-o* tend to take the "English" plural in *-s* or *-es* (fresco, grotto, motto and volcano take *-es*). The following words form the plural with *-i*: graffito, incognito, libretto, literato, ovolo, scherzo, virtuoso. Words ending in *-a* generally form the plural with *-s*; e.g. breccia, gondola, pasta, piazza, pizza, plaza, trattoria, vista (although lira has the plural lire). They should be distinguished from words of Latin origin ending in *-a* that form the plural *-ae* (although some assimilated Latin words also form plurals in *-s*) and Latin words that are already plural (e.g. candelabra, plectra, spectra, strata).

Other Italian words that have become assimilated into English
include:

arcade	cello	malaria	sonata
balcony	colonel	manifesto	sonnet
ballot	concert	nepotism	spaghetti
bandit	confetti	opera	squadron
bravo	corridor	parapet	stanza
brigand	dilettante	pastel	stiletto
bronze	ditto	pedantry	stucco
bust	domino	piano	studio
cameo	duet	picturesque	tarantula
canto	fiasco	regatta	terra-cotta
caprice	gazette	replica	traffic
caress	gelatine	ruffian	umbrella
caricature	infantry	salami	zany
carnival	influenza	scenario	
cartoon	lava	sentinel	
casino	macaroni	sequin	

See also **plurals.**

italic, italicize, italicization.

italics Italicize the names of ships (but keep HMS in roman type);
names of newspapers, journals and magazines; titles of books, plays,
films, radio and television programmes, operas, ballets, poems, and
names of musical works (*see* **musical works**). Italicize also all foreign
words and phrases that have not become part of everyday English (*see*
foreign words and phrases). Avoid italics for emphasis; do not italicize
the names of foreign streets or buildings, names of hotels or houses.
In the Latin nomenclature for plants and animals, only the names of
genera, species and varieties/races should be italicized (*see* **Latin
classification**). In genetics, letters representing genes should be set in
italics (e.g. gene pairs *R'* and *r'*), but their products should be in
roman face (e.g. R'r' antibodies). Do not italicize physical features of
the Moon, planets, and so on. The following chemical prefixes are
italicized: *cis-, trans-, dextro-, laevo-, n-, sec-, tert-, ortho-, o-, meta-,
m-, para-, p-, meso-.* In a block of text (such as a caption) typeset in
italics, any words that would normally be italicized should be typeset
in roman face.

item, itemize, itemization. The verb **list** is preferred to *itemize*.

it goes without saying, like *needless to say*, is usually not worth saying.

its = genetive of *it*; **it's** = short form of *it is* or *it has* and should be avoided in formal writing. *It's* should not be confused with *its* (as common an error as *her's* for *hers*). *See also* **one's**.

ivy (pl. ivies), ivied (= covered in ivy).

-ize or -ise The ending *-ize* and *-ization* are generally preferred to *-ise* and *-isation*. The following list of exceptions includes obvious as well as less obvious examples (with any related noun in parenthesis). It also includes verbs ending in *-yse*. A simple rule of thumb is that if the verb can form a noun ending in *-ation*, then the verb should be spelled *-ize*; if an *-ation* noun is not possible, spell the verb *-ise* (exception *improvise*).

advertise (advertisement)
advise (advice)
analyse (analysis)
apprise
arise
baptise (baptism)
catalyse (catalysis)
chastise (chastisement)
circumcise (circumcision)
comprise (comprisal)
compromise
demise
despise (despisal)
devise (device)
dialyse (dialysis)
disfranchise (disfranchisement)
disguise
electrolyse (electrolysis)
emprise
enfranchise (enfranchisement)
enterprise

excise (excision)
exercise
franchise
hypnotise (hypnotism)
improvise
incise (incision)
merchandise
paralyse (paralysis)
patronise (patron)
premise
prise (verb)
promise
reprise
revise (revision)
summarise (summary)
supervise (supervision)
surmise
surprise
televise (television)
vasectomise (vasectomy)

J

jackanapes, jackass (= male ass; laughing jackass = Australian bird), jackboot(ed), jackdaw, jack-in-the-box, jack-knife, jack-of-all-trades, jack-o'-lantern, jack plug, jackpot.

jacket, jacketed, jacketing.

Jacobean = pertaining to James I or his reign; **Jacobian** = pertaining to the mathematics of Karl Jacobi; **Jacobin** = member of a (French) revolutionary society; or type of (Dominican) friar; **Jacobite** = follower of James (i.e. James II, Henry James or Jacobus Baradaeus).

jail/jailor are the preferred spellings (not *gaol/gaoler*, except in official use).

jam (noun) = blockage, or fruit preserve; **jamb** = upright part of a door.

japan (verb), japanned, japanning.

jargon has been defined by Eric Partridge as "the technicalities of science, the professions, the Services, trades, crafts, sports and games, art and Art." It is to be assiduously avoided in ordinary writing − it is bad style to talk shop to the uninformed reader. An editor might blench at being asked to cut two-thirds from a piece of highly technical text, yet this (contrived) 100-word sentence:

> "Should the relative humidity of the ambient atmosphere in the machine's working environment decrease below the optimum level, the flexibility co-efficient of the base material of the punched paper tape and similarly that of the punched cards decreases, thus destabilizing their dimensions and inducing a degree of curvature; on the other hand, among the likely consequences of a higher than optimal ambient relative humidity is an inverse effect on the stretch co-efficient of the substrate of the punched cards with the result that their linear dimensions exceed the design parameters of the output device and cause its transport mechanism to malfunction."

can be edited to the following 34-word version (cited in slightly different form by Gowers as an example of anti-jargon):

> "If the air in the computer room is too dry, paper tape may become brittle and cards may shrink and curl; if the air is too damp cards may expand and jam the card-reader."

without any loss of information but with a considerable increase in impact and understanding. *See also* **non-standard English; slang.**

jejune = barren, meagre, puerile; it is sometimes taken to mean unsophisticated or naive, a use that should be avoided.

jerbil The preferred spelling is **gerbil**.

jerrymander The preferred spelling is **gerrymander**.

jettison, jettisoned.

jewel, jewelled, jewellery (*jewelry* is an Americanism).

Jewish *See* **Semitic.**

jib (verb) = to balk, refuse, show objection; **jibe** is a spelling to be avoided either for **gybe** (= to swing a sail from one side to another) or for **gibe** (= to scoff (at), taunt, flaunt).

jigger (flea) The preferred spelling is **chigoe** (known as *chigger* in the United States).

jingo (pl. jingos), jingoism (= British chauvinism). **Jingo** is an archaic mild oath, as in E.E. Cummins'
> "in every language even deafanddumb
> ...by gorry
> by jingo by gee by gosh by gum".

jinn *See* **genius.**

journalese = type of language favoured by popular (and sometimes less popular) newspapers. One reason for it is the desire to capture the reader's attention, often by the overuse of colourful words and superlatives (the "shock-horror" syndrome). Another reason is the need for brevity because of lack of space, particularly in headline writing, which often leads to the use of consecutive nouns ("Vicar in love-tug mercy dash"). Thus short words are pressed into service as synonyms for long ones; an investigation becomes a *probe*, a limitation a *ban* or *curb*, reductions are *cuts*, to resign is to *quit*, to criticize is to *slam*, and to discredit is to *gun for*. All-noun headlines can be ambiguous, especially if a noun has the same form as a verb. A recent headline "Police chase death" was meant to convey that somebody had died during a car chase involving the police, not that the boys in blue were pursuing the old man with the scythe. Puns may be used in journalese writing to catch attention or amuse (as in the classic misquotation of Keats: "Amid the Alien Porn").

journey = travels by land or air; **voyage** = travels by sea; **trip** = a short journey or voyage.

judgement (but strictly judgment in law).

judicial = relating to a court of law or a judge; **judicious** = of sound judgement, wise, prudent.

judo = sport in which the object is to use the minimum force to unbalance an opponent and hold him or her to the ground; **jujitsu** (no hyphen) = traditional Japanese method of unarmed self-defence; **karate** = traditional Japanese method of unarmed combat that uses the hands, elbows, feet and legs to chop, kick and "smash" an opponent; **kendo** = stylized form of Japanese fencing using bamboo staves (instead of swords); **sumo** = traditional Japanese wrestling. Judo is a modern sport, sumo continues to be a popular spectator sport in Japan. Kendo was a method of training, and jujitsu and karate were originally meant to maim or kill an opponent; all three were part of **Bushido**, the feudal code of Japanese samurai warriors.

jujitsu *See* **judo**.

junction = a joining of roads or railway lines, a joint; **juncture** = a joining of events.

junta is the preferred spelling (not **junto**). This useful Spanish word has no short English equivalent, and should be pronounced in the English fashion (not *hun-ta*).

jurist = expert on law and legal matters; **juror** = member of a jury.

justify = to excuse (give an excuse for), to exonerate; **rectify** = to correct. There is a world of different between justifying a mistake and rectifying it.

juvenile = young, youthful; **puerile** = childish. An old man can have juvenile appetites and behave in a puerile way to satisfy them. *See also* **childish**.

K

k is an abbreviation of the metric prefix *kilo-* (which *see*); **K** is the abbreviation of kelvin (the unit of temperature on the "absolute" temperature scale) and is increasingly being used as an abbreviation of *thousand* when referring to sums of money (e.g. a salary of £15,000 a year may be referred to as £15K) or computer memory storage capacity (e.g. a 128K RAM machine), although originally in computers $1K = 2^{10} = 1,024$.

kaftan The preferred spelling is **caftan**.

kale (a type of cabbage) is the preferred spelling, not *kail*.

kaleidoscope (note *-ei-* spelling).

kangaroo (pl. kangaroos).

karate *See* **judo**.

karri = Australian eucalyptus tree ("blue gum"); **kauri** = New Zealand "pine" tree; **cowrie** (preferred to *cowry*) = Asian and African mollusc and its shell.

katabolism The preferred spelling is **catabolism**.

keep (verb) inflects *keep − kept − kept*.

Kelt/Keltic The preferred spellings are **Celt/Celtic** (although the *k* pronunciation is the more usual).

ken is archaic for **knowledge** (as in the cliché "beyond/within his ken"); *knowledge* should be used.

kendo *See* **judo**.

kerb (= kerbstone) is the preferred spelling of **curb** (as a noun).

kerosene (not *kerosine*) is usually known as paraffin in Britain and is the name of similar petroleum hydrocarbons used as a fuel for gas turbine (e.g. "jet" aircraft) engines.

ketchup is the preferred spelling (not *catsup*).

keyboard, keyhole, key man, key-ring, keyword.

khaki (note spelling).

kibbutz (pl. kibbutzim).

kidnap, kidnapper, kidnapped, kidnapping.

kilo- is the metric prefix for a thousand times ($\times 10^3$), as in *kilometre*; **kilo** (pl. kilos) is an abbreviation of kilogram.

kilogram has the abbreviation kilo (pl. kilos) or kg.

kimono (pl. kimonos).

kin is old-fashioned for **relatives**, which is preferred.

kind should be regarded as singular (**kinds** being plural). E.g.:
"Some new kind of approach to the design is required."
"Some new kinds of designs are required."
See also **type of**.

kine- The preferred prefix is **cine-** (e.g. cinematograph).

king-sized (hyphen).

kneel has the preferred past tense and participle **kneeled** (not *knelt*).

knickers = women's undergarments (also called *briefs, panties* or *pants*); underpants = men's undergarments (also called *briefs* or *pants*); **trousers** = outer garments (for men or women); **shorts** = short-legged or legless outer garments (for men or women); **slacks** = old-fashioned term for *trousers*. All are plural words; "a pair of..." achieves a singular construction.

knight-errant (pl. knight-errants). *See also* **arrant**.

knit has the preferred past tense and participle **knitted**, although *knit* is used as frequently.

knot = nautical mile per hour (used for speeds of aircraft and ships); "a speed of 15 knots per hour" is therefore incorrect (write "speed of 15 knots").

know has the past tense **knew** and past participle **known**.

knowledge, knowledgeable.

Koran (initial capital letter).

krona (pl. kronor) is Swedish money; **krona** (pl. kronur) is Icelandic money; **krone** (pl. kroner) is Danish or Norwegian money.

kudos is a singular word.

Kuwait The derived adjective and noun is *Kuwaiti*.

L

-l- or **-ll-** Words ending in *-l* preceded by a single vowel double the *l* before suffixes that begin with a vowel. E.g.:

annul   annulled, annulling
counsel   counselled, counselling, counsellor
distil   distillable, distillation, distilled, distiller, distillery,
         distilling
tranquil   tranquillize, tranquillizer, tranquillity
(exception *parallel*, paralleled, paralleling).

Words with a long or double vowel preceding *-l* do not double the *l* before such suffixes. E.g.:

appeal   appealed, appealing
foul   fouled, fouling
spoil   spoiled, spoiling, spoiler
repeal   repealed, repealing
travail   travailed, travailing
(exception *initial,* initialled, initialling).

The *l* remains single before the suffix *-ment*. E.g.:

bedevil   bedevilment
enrol   enrolment
fulfil   fulfilment

Most words ending in *-ll* drop an *l* before the suffixes *-ful*, *-ly*, *-ment*, *-some* or other elements that begin with a consonant. E.g.:

all   albeit, almost, already, also, although, altogether,
        always
chill   chilblain
dull   dully (not *dull-ly* = *dullly*)
full   fulfil, fully, fulsome
install   instalment
skill   skilful
will   wilful

The *l* remains double, however, before the suffix *-ness*. E.g.:

chill	chillness
dull	dullness
ill	illness
shrill	shrillness
still	stillness

See also **suffixes**.

laager = camp or encampment; **lager** = light beer (*see also* **ale**).

label, labelled, labelling.

labium (pl. labia).

labour, laboured, laborious.

lace, lacy.

lachrymal, lachrymation, lachrymatory, lachrymose (not *lacrimal*, etc.).

lack *See* **absence**.

lackadaisical (= affected, listless) persists, whereas *lackaday* and *lackadaisy* have dropped out of circulation.

lacrimal etc. The preferred spelling is **lachrymal** etc.

lacuna (pl. lacunae).

lade (= to load with cargo) has the past tense and participle *laden*.

ladybird, lady-in-waiting (pl. ladies-in-waiting), lady-killer, ladylike, lady-love, ladyship, lady's maid. Most modern writers avoid using **lady** for *woman* in terms such as *woman doctor, woman traffic warden*, but *see* **gender.**

laid *See* **lay; lie.**

laisser-faire, laissez-faire (italics) survive as a short way of saying "government abstention from interference with individual action" (*Concise OED*).

lama = Buddhist priest; **llama** = South American camel-like mammal.

lamé (acute accent).

lamina (pl. laminae).

lamp-black, lampholder, lamplight(er), lamp-post, lampshade, lamp-shell.

land-agent, land-bridge, land-crab, landfall, land-grabber, landholder, landlady, land-line, land-locked, landlord, landlubber, landmark, land-mine, landowner, landscape, landslide, landslip, landsman, landward(s), land-yacht(ing).

languid = sluggish, lacking vigour, listless; **limpid** = clear, not turbid, untroubled.

languor = inertia, lassitude (adjectives languorous, languid; verb languish); **langur** = (sacred) Indian monkey.

lanolin is the preferred spelling (not *lanoline*).

Laos The derived adjective and noun is *Laotian*.

lapel, lapelled.

lapse *See* **elapse**.

large should not be used to qualify breadth, depth, distance, height or length (for which use **great**).

large number of = many; **large share of** = most. The shorter forms should be used.

larger than *See* **as large as**.

largess is the preferred spelling (not *largesse*).

largo (pl. largos).

lariat = rope for tying up animals (it is not a **lasso**, which is a throwable rope with a noose at the end).

larva (pl. larvae).

larynx (pl. larynges).

lasso (pl. of noun is lassos, 3rd. person singular present of verb is lassoes), lassoed, lassoing. *See also* **lariat**.

last can be ambiguous if used for **preceding**; e.g. "... referred to in the last four chapters" is strictly wrong if what is meant are the four before the one in which the statement is made ("the last four" are the four that end the whole book). **Last** describes the final item in a series, **latest** refers to the most recent (which may or may not turn out to be the last). For *last two* etc., *see* **first**. *See also* **latter**.

late = dead (as in "the late king"); it should not be used to mean *former* of someone who has relinquished an office or position (e.g. "the former president" is still alive but no longer in office, "the late president" is dead). *See also* **former**.

lath = thin strip of wood; **lathe** = machine for turning wood or metal.

Latin classification (of plants and animals). Initial capital letters (but not italics) are used for phyla, orders, classes and families, but no initial capital for their anglicized equivalents; e.g. Arthropoda, arthropods; Crustacea, crustaceans.
For both botanical and zoological classifications, genera, species and subspecies/varieties/races are typeset in italics; all other divisions are set in roman face. All but species and subspecies/variety/race have an initial capital letter. Thus the Indian elephant belongs to family Elephantidae of the order Proboscidea; it is genus *Elephas* and species *maximus*. It is helpful to the reader to give the common (popular, or vernacular) name, if one exists, as well as the Latin name. The Latin name should appear in brackets (parentheses) after the common name, if the equivalence is exact; e.g. "rice (*Oryza sativa*)", but "the crop plant *Oryza sativa*". Avoid capitalizing Latin names that have become part of common English usage when they are used in a non-taxonomic way; e.g. "the iris plant" but "the species *Iris versicolor*". A multiplication sign (×) indicates a hybrid. Common names do not have capital letters except for proper nouns or to avoid ambiguity; e.g. Red deer, Toy poodle, Miniature Yorkshire terrier, Old English sheepdog, Frisian, Arabian, Sussex blue.

Latin words In addition to words of Latin derivation − which form a large part of the English language − English includes many unaltered borrowings from Latin. Some are perfectly acceptable (such as agenda, alga, alias, alibi, apex, aquarium, atrium, axis, to list but a few from the *a* entries in this Dictionary). Apart from presenting possible problems with plurals (*see* plurals; -us), these are useful words which have no simple "English" equivalents. The *a* entries also contain *ab initio, ad hoc, ad infinitum, ad lib* and *ad nauseam*, all of which parade their Latin origins by usually being typeset in italics. These do have more familiar (and to many readers easier to understand) English equivalents, and for this reason their use is not recommended. It was overuse of such words that prompted George Orwell to remark "A mass of Latin words falls upon the facts like soft snow, blurring the outlines and covering up the details". (*See also* **foreign words and phrases**.)

Some areas of science, particularly medicine and biology, legitimately have Latin or Latinized terms as part of their specialized vocabulary (*see*, for example, **Latin classification**).

latter = the second of two (but only two) things mentioned, near the end of a period of time ("the latter part of the week"). Latter should not be misused for **last**, which has to be used in reference to the final one of three or more things mentioned; e.g. "Of the two boys, John and Jim, he resembled the latter; among Ann, Betty and Catherine, he preferred the last." Similar rules apply to *former* and *first*.

laudable (not *laudible*) = worthy of praise; **laudatory** = containing or expressing praise. E.g.:

"The child's drawing was a laudable effort considering her age."
"The chairman made a laudatory speech about his retiring colleague."

launder, meaning to infiltrate stolen (or counterfeit) money into legitimate financial dealings, is a useful new metaphor.

lawful/legal *See* **unlawful**.

laws, scientific *See* **named effects and laws**.

lay (verb) is transitive ("lay something down"), inflexion: *lay – laid – laid* (compare *lie – lay – lain*). Note also *overlay – overlaid – overlaid. See also* **lie**.

lazaretto (pl. lazarettos).

le, as part of a proper name, generally has an initial capital letter; e.g. Louis Le Van, Charles Le Brun. Follow the style of the name's owner.

lead (verb) has the past tense and participle **led** (pronounced "led", as is the heavy metal spelled *lead*). Note that the verb **read** has the past tense and participle **read**, which is pronounced "red".

leading question *See* **question**.

leak = gap through which gas, liquid or secrets escape; **leek** = vegetable that resembles an onion.

lean The preferred past tense and participle is **leaned** (not *leant*).

leap The preferred past tense and participle is **leaped** (not *leapt*).

learn = to assimilate knowledge, to get to know something; **teach** = to impart/pass on knowledge; what A teaches B learns. E.g.:
"I want to learn to drive a car."
"He taught me to drive a car."
Like **lend** and **borrow** (which *see*), the two verbs are sometimes confused. The preferred past tense and participle of **learn** is **learned** (not *learnt*).

lease is granted by a **lessor** to a **lessee**. *See also* **hire**.

leastways/leastwise are, according to the *OED*, dialect or vulgar for *or at least*, which is therefore preferred.

leave (verb) inflects *leave* − *left* − *left*.

Lebanon The derived adjective and noun is *Lebanese*.

lecture, lecturer, lecturership (but lectureship at Oxford University).

led *See* **lead**.

ledger = account book, method of fishing; **ledger-line** = type of fishing line; **leger line** = line to locate notes off the staff in music.

leek *See* **leak**.

leftward can be an adjective (e.g. "a leftward turn") or an adverb (e.g. "move leftward"), although **leftwards** is the preferred form of the adverb. There are no corresponding words derived from *right*. *See also* **-wards**.

legal, legalize, legalization. *See also* **unlawful**.

legend *See* **fable**.

legible *See* **readable**.

legislation = laws or their enactment; **legislature** = law-making body of the State, the courts. E.g.:

"The government introduced legislation making seat belts compulsory for all car passengers."
"The new administration guaranteed the independence of the legislature."
Somebody who makes laws is a **legislator**.

legitimate, legitimize (not *legitimatize*), legitimization. *See also* **unlawful**.

leisure, leisurely (characterized by leisure), leisured (having leisure).

lend inflects *lend – lent – lent. See also* **borrow; loan**.

lengthy should not be used when **long** is intended.

lenient, leniency (not *lenience*).

lens is a singular word (pl. lenses), originally meaning *lentil*. Its adjective *lenticular* is unfamiliar to many readers, with *lens-shaped* the awkward but more readily understandable alternative.

lento (pl. lentos).

less and **fewer** *Less* denotes degree, quantity or extent (of something that is uncountable); *fewer* refers to number (of things that are countable). E.g.:

"Fewer trees, less timber."
"Less interest, fewer readers."
"Fewer sales, less profit."

lesser, like *less*, is a comparative of *little* (the superlative being *least*). *Less* usually denotes quantity or size (*see* **less**), whereas *lesser* generally qualifies significance or value. E.g.:

"Wendy takes less time than John to paint a wall."
"John is the lesser of the two painters."

lest is archaic for **unless** (or *for fear that, in case*), (as in the cliché "lest we forget"); the old term should be avoided.

leuco- (= white) is the preferred form of the prefix (except in *leukaemia*).

levee = a reception, or an elevated river bank (no accent).

level, levelled, levelling, leveller.

lexicon (pl. lexicons, not *lexica*).

liable = answerable for, responsible; it should not be used to mean apt, capable or likely.

liaise, liaison (note spelling).

liar = somebody who does not tell the truth; **lyre** = harp-like musical instrument.

libel, libelled, libelling, libeller, libellous. Libel is defamation by means of a statement made in writing (or, by extension, on radio or television − where programmes are assumed to be scripted), whereas **slander** is defamation by means of the spoken word. Slander is a civil offence, whereas certain kinds of libel can result in criminal charges.

liberal, liberalize, liberalization.

libido (pl. libidos).

libretto (pl. libretti).

licence (noun) = a permit; **license** (verb) = to authorize, grant a licence. The verb produces licensing, licensed, licensable, licensee; the proper term for a shop that sells alcoholic drinks is an *off-licence* (with a hyphen and two *c*s).

lich- (= corpse) is the preferred spelling (not *lych-*) in compounds such as lich-gate, although the *y* form survives in some place-names (such as Lychpit, Hampshire).

lickerish *See* **liquorice.**

lido (pl. lidos).

lie (verb) is intransitive ("lie under or on something"); inflexion: *lie* − *lay* − *lain* (compare *lay* − *laid* − *laid*). The confusion between *lay* and *lie* probably stems from the fact that the present tense of the former is the same as the past tense of the latter ("I lay the book down", present; "He lay on the floor", past). Note also *overlie – overlay – overlain*.

lifebelt, lifeblood, lifeboat, lifebuoy, life cycle, life-guard, life-jacket, lifelike, lifeline, lifelong, life-sized (preferred to life-size), lifespan, lifestyle, lifetime, life-work, life's work.

lifelong = for the span of life (e.g. "he had a lifelong interest in the theatre"); **livelong**, archaic/poetic for enduring, protracted, very long (as in the cliché "for the livelong day"), should be avoided.

ligature = a binding together, tying tightly round (a blood vessel, for instance); in typesetting, a ligature is a joining of two letters, such as æ and fl. **Digraph** = a two-letter combination that represents a single sound, such as *ch*, *ph* and *ae* (as in formulae) and the Old English æ (ash). **Diphthong** = the combination of two vowel sounds to form one sound, as in *gait* and *loud*. **Diaeresis** = the mark ¨ over a vowel, indicating that the vowel is pronounced separately, as in Noël. **Umlaut** = the mark ¨ over a vowel in German which modifies its sound, as in *Mann* and *Männer* (pronounced "man" and "menner"). Ligatures should be avoided and the letters separated (e.g. Caesar, naevus, phoenix, oesophagus), except in quotations of Old English, Icelandic, and so on.
Digraphs should also be avoided wherever possible (as in medieval), except in medical and other scientific terms (archaeology, foetus, oestrogen). Diaeresis should also be avoided (e.g. naive, not naïve).

light (verb) has the preferred past tense and participle **lit** (not *lighted*), although *lighted* is retained as an adjective (e.g. "lighted candle").

light bulb (= electric lamp), light-fingered, light headed, lighthearted, lighthouse, light meter, lightship, lights out, lightweight, lightwood, light-year.

lightening = making less heavy; **lightning** is what precedes thunder.

light-year = the distance light travels in a year (9.46×10^{12} km or 5.88×10^{12} miles); it is thus not a measure of time but one of distance, which should be remembered when it is used figuratively (as in "The Christmas holiday seems light-years away", which is incorrect).

like, likeable, likely, likeness, likelihood, likeliness, likewise. *Like* should not be misused for *as*; e.g. "Do as I do" is the correct form of "Do like I do". Neither should *like* be misused for *such as*; e.g. "Mammals like cats and dogs" is correct only if the mammals referred to are attracted to cats and dogs; *such as* should be used in contexts such as this.

-like Longstanding words ending in *-like* have no hyphen (e.g. childlike, godlike, ladylike, workmanlike) unless the letter before the *l* in *-like* makes a hyphen necessary for readability (e.g. jelly-like protoplasm, mouse-like odour, shell-like ear, vice-like grip). More recent or temporary words ending in *-like* are usually hyphenated.

limbo (pl. limbos).

lime, limy (like lime); **Limey** = American slang for *Englishman*.

limerick is a five-line doggerel verse, with three long lines (*A*) and two short lines (*B*) using the rhyming scheme *AABBA*. Many begin "There once was a young man/lady/woman from..." The following example (a comment on the pronunciation of English words ending in *-ough*) is called "Cough Mixture":

There's a man from the borough of Slough,
Whose cough set him wondering how
He got through the stuff,
But enough was enough -
His trachea's quite clear right now.

linchpin is the preferred spelling (not *lynchpin*); **lynch** = to execute someone without proper trial.

line, linable (= can be lined or aligned), linage (= number of lines), lineage (= ancestry).

lineament = distinguishing mark, feature; **liniment** = embrocation, thin ointment.

lingerie is condemned by some as a genteel synonym of *underwear*, but the term also includes night-clothes and excludes men's clothes; it therefore seems to serve a useful purpose.

linguistics *See* **grammar**.

liquefy, liquefaction. *See also* **liquid**.

liqueur = sweet alcoholic drink; **liquor** = any alcoholic drink.

liquid, liquefy (= turn a gas into a liquid), liquefiable, liquefaction, (= the process of liquefying), liquidize (= turn a watery solid into a liquid or purée), liquidization, liquidate (= to kill, assassinate, wind up a company), liquidator. The word for turning a waterless solid into a liquid is *melt*; for incorporating a solid into a liquid (solvent) is *dissolve*. The potential pitfall among the words derived from *liquid* is failing to distinguish between *liqui-* and *lique-*.

liquorice (not *licorice*) is the strong-tasting plant and its extract; **lickerish** is a rare variant spelling of *lecherous*.

lira (pl. lire).

lissom, a little-used adjective meaning *lithe* (which should be used), is the preferred spelling (not *lissome*).

list *See* **item**.

litchi (Chinese fruit).

literal = relating to the precise meaning (of words); **littoral** = neighbouring the shore; **literate** = able to read and write; **literary** = to do with literature. *See also* **illiterate**.

literally should not be used for emphasis and applied to something that cannot be taken literally. The word is particularly inapt when applied to a metaphor (which by definition should not be taken literally), as in "He took me by surprise and I was literally frozen to the spot".

literato (pl. literati).

literature = the whole corpus of "quality" written works: drama, poetry and prose. The word has been devalued and taken over as part of salesmen's jargon to stand for any printed matter from a single-sheet press release to a thick trade directory (as in "I'll send you some literature about the new machine"), a use to be avoided.

lithe *See* **lissom**.

little-known etc. is hyphenated when adjectival (e.g. "little-known fact", "little-used technique") but unhyphenated when following a verb (e.g. "the artist is little known outside England").

live, liveable, liveable-in.

livelong *See* **lifelong**.

liven up The preferred term is **enliven**.

livid, strictly = blue-grey, the colour of lead; many authorities regard its use to mean *extremely angry* as colloquial. *See also* **hectic**.

llama *See* **lama**.

llano (pl. llanos) = open plains (steppes) in northern South America; **pampas** = open grassland (savanna) in southern South America.

Lloyds (plc) is the name of the British bank; **Lloyd's** is the name of the London-based insurance company.

load has the past tense and participle **loaded**.

loadstone is the preferred spelling (not *lodestone*, although *lodestar* is preferred to *loadstar*).

loaf (noun) (pl. loaves).

loan is a noun, not a verb (the verb is *lend*); a *loan* is granted by somebody who *lends* one money.

loath/loathe *See* **loth**.

local, locality, localize, localization. **Local** = nearby; **locale** = scene of activity.

locate, location. **Location** = definite position, precisely where something can be found; **locality** = general situation or position of a thing or place, approximately where it can be found. **Locate** should not be used merely to mean *find*. *See* **find.**

locomotive and train names should be italicized, with initial capital letters. E.g. locomotives: *King Henry V, Mallard, Rocket*; trains: *Cheltenham Flier, Golden Arrow, Orient Express*.

locum, the common shortening of **locum tenens** (= deputy, especially of a doctor), is a singular word (pl. locums); the full form would require the plural *locum tenentes*. **Locus** (= particular mathematical curve) is also singular (pl. loci).

lodestar is the preferred spelling (not *loadstar*, although *loadstone* is preferred to *lodestone*).

lodge, lodgeable, lodgement, lodging.

logogram = symbol that stands for a whole word or words, often called simply a **logo** in modern advertising and publishing. *See also* **colophon; ideograph; monogram.**

lone *See* **alone; lonely**.

lonely (= isolated, alone) is apparently formed from *alone* through the obsolete word *alonely*; its comparative and superlative are *lonelier* and *loneliest*. **Lonesome** (= solitary) is formed from *lone*, although most British people now regard its secondary meaning of *feeling lonely* as an Americanism. E.g.:
"He was marooned on a lonely island";
"The only tree in sight was a lonesome palm" (British/American);
"He soon became lonesome for his hometown in Kansas" (American).
See also **alone**.

long-ago (adj.), longboat, longbow, long-distance (adj.), long division, long-eared, longhorn, long johns, longhand, long jump, long-legged, long-lived, long-playing, long-range (adj.), longship, long-shore (adj.), longshoreman, long shot, long-sighted(ness), long-standing, long-suffering, long-term (adj.), longways, long-winded.

longitude (not *longtitude*).

long sight, long-sighted, long-sightedness (medical name *hypermetropia*). Far-sighted(ness) is best reserved to mean *good at anticipation*, and not used as a synonym for long-sighted(ness). *See also* **short sight**.

looker-on (pl. lookers-on).

look over = to inspect, read through; **overlook** = to look over the top of, to look down on (from a higher position), to fail to see. (**Oversee** = supervise.)

loose (verb) = to unbind, to undo, to set free; **loosen** = to slacken, to relax. E.g.:

"She loosed the prisoner from his bonds."

"He loosened his tie because he felt too hot."

(**Loose** should not be confused with **lose** = to mislay, to be unable to find.)

lory = Asian parrot; **lorry** = goods road vehicle, a truck.

lose, losable. Lose inflects *lose – lost – lost*.

loth, an alternative spelling of **loath** (the adjective meaning reluctant, unwilling), prevents possible confusion with **loathe** (the verb meaning to detest, despise, hate).

lots of (= many, much, a great deal) should be avoided; **a lot of** is just acceptable.

lotus (pl. lotuses).

lour (a little-used word meaning to *frown*) is the preferred spelling (not *lower*), which also encourages the correct pronunciation (rhyming with *sour*, not "low-er").

love, lovable, love affair, love-bird, love-hate, lovely, love-in-a-mist, love-knot, love-letter, love-lies-bleeding, lovelock, lovelorn, lovers' knot, lovesick, love-song, love story, love token.

low (adj.) = not high, not loud; **lowly** (adj.) = humble, modest. The logical adverb from low is *lowly* (= in a low way), as in "He bowed lowly before her"; the logical adverb from *lowly* is *lowlily*, as in "He bowed lowlily before her". These difficulties can be avoided by using *low* instead of *lowly* (adv.) and *in a lowly manner* (or *humbly*) for *lowlily*. E.g.:

"He bowed low before her";

"He bowed before her in a lowly manner".

(A similar pronunciation problem occurs with godly/godlily, holy/holily, jolly/jollily and ugly/uglily.)

low-down, low-lying.

lower *See* **lour**.

lowly, lowlier, lowliest, lowliness, lowlily (*see* **low**).

lucerne is preferred to **alfalfa** for the fodder crop.

luggage *See* **baggage**.

lumbar = to do with the loins, the lower back (*lumbago* = pain in the loins); **lumber** = disused furniture, useless items, or an Americanism for timber.

lunch = meal eaten about mid-day, a portable snack (e.g. "Take a packed lunch with you"); **luncheon** = formal lunch, usually with invited guests and possibly speakers (e.g. "a literary luncheon"); **brunch** = Americanism for a mid-morning meal that combines breakfast and lunch. *See also* **dinner**.

lunge, lunged, lunging.

lure *See* **allure**.

lustful = full of (sexual) lust; **lusty** = hearty, vigorous. E.g.:
"He studied the girl with a lustful stare."
"She tackled the food with a lusty appetite."

luxuriant = growing profusely or abundantly; **luxurious** = extravagant, rich. **Luxury** should be reserved as a noun, and not used as an adjective to mean *expensive* (as in "a luxury car").

lynch *See* **linchpin**.

lynx (pl. lynxes).

lyre *See* **liar**.

M

-m- or **-mm-** Monosyllabic words ending in *-m* preceded by a single vowel double the *m* before suffixes beginning with a vowel. E.g.:

dim	dimmed, dimmer, dimming
drum	drummed, drummer, drumming
glum	glummer, glummest
hem	hemmable, hemmed, hemming
slam	slammed, slamming

The *-m* remains single if it is preceded by a long or double vowel. E.g.:

bloom	bloomed, bloomer, blooming
form	formable, formed, former, forming
maim	maimed, maiming
roam	roamed, roamer, roaming
cream	creamed, creamer, creamery, creaming

With polysyllabic words, the choice of *-m-* or *-mm-* depends on where the accent falls. If it is on the last syllable, the rule is as for monosyllabic words; e.g. outswimming, overbrimming, undermanned, undimmed (short vowels), performed, uniformed (long vowels). If the last syllable is unaccented, the *-m-* is not doubled; e.g. customized, ransomed, systematic, victimization (exceptions include words ending in *-gram*: diagrammatic, telegrammic).

macadam (even though it was named after John McAdam), or tarmacadam; *Tarmac* is a trade name.

mackintosh (even though its inventor was Charles Macintosh, without a *k*).

macramé is the preferred spelling (not *macrami*).

mad = insane (and is an imprecise term now avoided by both the legal and medical professions). Colloquially *mad* can mean *angry* (e.g. "She makes me mad") or *impractical* (e.g. "A mad scheme"). The former colloquialism should be avoided in formal writing; the latter should be changed for another, more acceptable synonym (such as *illogical* or the more colourful *crackpot* or even *hare-brained*). **Mental** is a pejorative and slang term for describing somebody who is mentally ill (or somebody who is not!).

Madam (pl. Mesdames) is the formal English form of address to a lady or other member of the nobility, abbreviated to **Ma'am** when addressing royalty; *Madame* (italics, pl. *Mesdames*) is the French form of address to a married woman; **madam** (no initial capital letter) = woman in charge of a brothel.

madeira (note *-ei-* spelling).

maestro has the preferred plural maestros (not *maestri*).

magic (adj.) = to do with magic; **magical** = entertaining, apparently caused by magic. E.g.:
"The pantomime fairy waved her magic wand."
"It was a magical moment: the fairy seemed to appear from nowhere."

magisterial = to do with a magistrate, authoritative, dictatorial; **magistral** = to do with a master.

magma (pl. magmata).

magnate = wealthy or powerful man; **magnet** = bar of metal that attracts ferrous metals.

magnet, magnetic, magnetism, magnetize, magnetization. *See also* **magnate**.

magneto (pl. magnetos).

magniloquence is a lofty expression for *a lofty expression*, and often no more than a euphemism for boasting.

maharaja is the preferred spelling (not *maharajah*).

maintain, maintenance (not *maintainance*). *See also* **allege**.

maize is the preferred spelling for the crop called **corn** in America; in English, *corn* is a general name for any cereal crop.

majority, like **major part**, should be avoided when it means merely most. *Majority* should be reserved for contexts in which there is a significant difference betweena majority and a minority (and *major part* should be reserved for a contrast with *minor part*).

majuscule *See* **minuscule**.

make inflects *make – made – made*.

make-believe (noun, not *make-belief*), make believe (verb), makeready (noun), makeshift, make-up (noun), makeweight.

mako (pl. makos).

malapropism *See* **non-standard English**.

Malawi The derived adjective and noun is **Malawian**.

Malay words, derived from languages spoken today in Malaysia, Singapore and parts of Indonesia, were borrowed and then assimilated into English during early colonial times. Today's survivors include:

amok	cassowary	gingham	paddy (rice)
bamboo	catechu	gong	sago
batik	cockatoo	kapok	sarong
cachou	compound	launch (boat)	
caddy (tea)	(enclosure)	orang-utan	

Some share origins with words in the Tamil language (*see* **Indian words**).

mal de mer is an old-fashioned euphemism for seasickness, which should be used.

male describes the sex of an organism; **masculine** describes the characteristics of a male (the "opposites" are *female* and *feminine*). *Male* is a poor synonym for *boy* or *man*.

malfunction *See* **dysfunction**.

Mali The derived adjective and noun is *Malian*.

malign (adj.) = injurious, evil (e.g. "malign influence""); **malignant** = actuated by great hatred, tending to go from bad to worse, cancerous (e.g. "malignant tumour"), Cavalier (i.e. pro-Charles I).

malnutrition has been condemned as officialese for "(virtual) **starvation**". The two words now have subtly different meanings.

Someone with nothing to eat eventually dies of *starvation*; someone given the wrong type of food (such as a child fed only on polished rice) may suffer from *malnutrition* which, admittedly, can also end in death. Similarly **malnourished** = lacking in some essential dietary factor(s); **undernourished** = lacking enough food.

Malta The derived adjective and noun is *Maltese*.

mamba = poisonous African snake; **mambo** = lively Latin-American dance (or its music).

man has no initial capital letter in such expressions as Neanderthal man, Cro-Magnon man; *Man* should be capitalized when it is used as a generic term for the human race. *See also* **mankind**.

manage, managed, managing, manageable, management.

manakin = small Central American bird; **manikin** = little man, puppet, artist's jointed model; **mannequin** = person who models clothes.

mañana (with tilde).

mandrel = spindle, former on which to shape something; **mandrill** = large baboon.

manège = riding-school; **ménage** = household; both of these French forms should be avoided.

mango (pl. mangoes).

mangold is the usual spelling for the root vegetable, not *mangel*, although the full name is more often **mangel-wurzel** (not *mangold-wurzel*).

maniacal = like a maniac or madman; **manic** = exhibiting or provoking mania, a severe mental disorder characterized by euphoria and hyperactivity (often involving violence) out of proportion to the prevailing circumstances; the word should not be used just of any lively or happy mood, nor to describe someone who is merely unresponsible to reasoned argument. Similarly **mania** should not be applied to mere enthusiasm (e.g. "He has a mania for football") or unconventional behaviour. **Maniac** = a psychotic person exhibiting mania as a chief symptom, not just someone who behaves irresponsibly (as in "He drives like a maniac"). With all these words, the adoption of a scientific term for ordinary or figurative use has lost impact through overexposure. *See also* **paranoia; schizophrenic**.

manifesto (pl. manifestos).

mankind (= human race) has the pronoun *it*; **man** or **Man** (generically) has the pronoun *he*. The use of the term **humankind** overcomes sexist objections to *mankind*. *See also* **gender; human**.

mannish is properly applied to a woman who is unwomanly; it is not a synonym of **masculine** (*see* **male**). The corresponding term applied to men is *effeminate*.

manoeuvre, manoeuvred, manoeuvring, manoeuvrable, manoeuvrability.

man-of-war (pl. men-of-war); the poisonous jellyfish is a Portuguese man-o'-war.

manqué (acute accent).

manse *See* **rector**.

manservant (pl. menservants – unusually, both halves of the compound word are pluralized).

manslaughter *See* **homicide**.

mantel = shelf over a fireplace; **mantle** = cloak. E.g.:

"There was an ornate Victorian clock on the marble mantel."
"The thieves escaped under the mantle of darkness."

many takes a plural ("Many books have been sold"); **many a** takes a singular ("Many a book has been sold").

many and **much**. *Many* applies to numbers (of things that can be counted); *much* denotes quantity or extent (of something that cannot be counted). E.g.:

"Much money, many possessions."
"Many voices, much noise."
"Much furniture, many chairs."

manyfold is an adverb, and should not be used as an alternative to the adjective **manifold**. E.g.:

"Because of errors, the time taken was increased manyfold."

"Errors resulted in a manifold increase in the time taken."

Maori (pl. Maoris).

mare (pronounced "mar-ay"), a large flat area or "sea" on the Moon, has the plural **maria**.

marginal = to do with or written in the margin (of a page), or borderline; it should not be used to mean **small**. E.g. "the cost of the extras was marginal" should be ". . . was small"; "marginal improvement" is better put as "slight improvement". **Minimal** = smallest possible; e.g. "We must paint the inside of the factory but with minimal disruption to production."

marijuana is the preferred spelling (not *marihuana*).

marital = to do with marriage ("marital bliss"); **martial** = to do with war or the military ("martial arts", "martial law").

market, marketed, marketing.

marquess is now the usual spelling in England (not *marquis*).

marriage, marriageable.

marshal (not *marshall*), marshalled, marshaller, marshalling; the noun is also *marshal*.

mart is archaic for **market**, which should be used, although it survives in such expressions as "used car mart" (= second-hand car market).

marten = weasel-like animal; **martin** = swallow-like bird.

martial *See* **marital**.

marvel, marvelled, marvelling, marvellous.

mask = covering for the face; **masque** = a masked ball (masquerade), old form of drama involving masked performers.

massif = group of neighbouring mountains; **massive** = bulky, solid, heavy, having a great mass. *Massive* should not be used to mean merely *large* or *huge*. E.g.:

"Stonehenge is build of massive blocks of stone" (correct);
"Stonehenge attracts a massive crowd of people each day" (incorrect).

master-class, master-mind, master of ceremonies, master-key,
masterpiece, master-stroke, master switch, master-work.

masterful = imperious, high-handed; **masterly** = with the skill of a
master. E.g.:
"She admired him for his masterful manner in dealing with other
people."
"She envied him his masterly command of languages."

mate, matey (preferred to *maty*), matily.

maté (tea) (acute accent).

mater *See* **pater**.

material, materially, materialize, materialization. **Material** (noun) =
something from which things can be made, fabric; **material** (adj.) =
to do with matter or a necessary factor in reasoning; **matériel** =
paraphernalia of an army. **Materialize** = to become visible or real
(from something insubstantial), as in "Gradually a human form
materialized out of the mist"; the word should not be used to mean
merely *happen* or *come about*.

matinée (acute accent), despite being French for a morning's worth, is
English for an afternoon performance (of a concert, film, play etc.).

matrass = long-necked flask (obsolete); **mattress** (with two *t*s and two
*s*s) = large, stuffed bag for sleeping on, large mat used in foundations
of roads and buildings.

matrix (pl. matrices).

matt is preferred to *mat* or *matte* for the word meaning dull,
unpolished; **matte** = (impure) product of the first smelting stage in
metal extraction from an ore.

matzo (pl. matzoth).

maudlin (not *maudling*).

maunder = ramble foolishly (in speech); **meander** = wind, wander aimlessly. E.g.:

"The old man maundered about his experiences in the Great War."
"We meandered round the back streets of the town."

Mauritania The derived adjective and noun is *Mauritanian*.

Mauritius The derived adjective and noun is *Mauritian*.

mausoleum = elaborate large tomb; **museum** = building in which old objects are exhibited.

maxilla (pl. maxillae).

maximum (pl. maxima), maximize, maximization. *See also* **increase**.

may *See* **can**.

maybe (adv.) = perhaps (e.g. "Maybe she will come"); **may be** (two words) is a verb used in such constructions as "She may be late", "It may be that she will not come".

mayday (one word) = international distress signal (from French *m'aidez*).

mayonnaise (note spelling).

Mc Proper names beginning with *Mc* should be alphabetized (and indexed) as though they begin with *Mac*.

mead = alcoholic drink made by fermenting honey, or a meadow (archaic); **meed** = reward (even more archaic).

mean (verb) inflects *mean – meant – meant*. For **mean** (noun), *see* **average**.

meander *See* **maunder**.

meaningful, as in "We have a meaningful relationship", is a vogue word to be avoided. *See* **vogue words**.

means (noun), = method or course of action, has its singular and plural spelled the same; **means**, = resources/income, is always plural. E.g.:

"The telephone is a means of communication."

"There were several means of getting to town."
"My means are insufficient to pay for it."

meantime/meanwhile (each one word).

measles is a singular word; "cases of measles" achieves a plural construction.

measure, measurement, measurable.

measurements *See* **quantities and measurements.**

meat-eater (carnivore).

meatus (pl. meatuses).

medal = coin-like disc given to commemorate or reward; **meddle** = to interfere.

media *See* **medium.**

median *See* **average.**

mediate, mediator (= someone who, without authority, tries to bring together conflicting parties to resolve a dispute). *See also* **arbitrate.**

medieval (not *mediaeval*).

mediocre = neither good nor bad, of intermediate quality; the word should not be used to mean definitely *poor* or *bad*.

Mediterranean (one *d*, one *t* and two *r*s).

medium (spiritualist) has the plural *mediums*; a communications medium has the plural *media*. **Media** (pl. mediae) is also a technical term in phonetics and botany.

medium-sized is preferred to **medium-size** as the adjective; e.g. "A medium-sized dog", but "A dog of medium size".

meet (adj.) is archaic for **fitting** or **seemly** (as in "It is meet and right so to do"); either of the modern alternatives should be used.

meet (verb) inflects *meet – met – met*. **Meet** a person or a date, but **meet** *with* disaster, approval and so on. The use of the latter to mean the former is an Americanism. *See also* **metre.**

mega is the prefix for a million times ($\times 10^6$), as in *megawatt* (*see* **units**).

meiosis, in biology, = cell division that leads to the formation of gametes (sex cells); **mitosis** = cell division that forms two identical new (daughter) cells, the normal multiplication process.

mélange = mixture; the French form should be avoided.

mêlée, defined by Chambers as "a fight in which the combatants are mingled together", has no short English synonym and so the French form (with two accents) lives on.

melliferous = yielding honey; **mellifluous** = sweet-sounding (voice).

melody *See* **harmony**.

melt has the past tense and participle **melted**, although **molten** is retained for certain adjectival uses (e.g. *molten* lava, metal or rock but *melted* butter, ice or wax).

memento (pl. mementos).

memorandum (pl. memorandums).

memory, memorable, memorize.

ménage (acute accent) = household; the French term should be avoided.

mendacity = a lie (adj. *mendacious*); **mendicity** = begging (adj. and noun *mendicant*).

meniscus (pl. menisci).

-ment *See* **suffixes**.

mental *See* **mad**.

menu (pl. menus).

merchandise (verb) (not *-ize*).

meretricious = gaudy, insincere, suitable for a whore; **meritorious** = deserving honour, praise or reward.

merino (pl. merinos).

merry-go-round (hyphens).

Mesdames *See* **Madam**.

mesmerize (not -*ise*), mesmerism.

mestizo (pl. mestizos).

metal, metalled, metalling, metallurgy, metallurgist, metallize. **Metal** = usually shiny, dense, conducting elementary substance, or a mixture of such substances (an alloy); **mettle** = human spirit or courage (as in the cliché "put on one's mettle"). The latter is an aberrant, but accepted, spelling of the former.

metamorphosis (pl. metamorphosis), metamorphose.

metaphor = the most common figure of speech, involving the transfer of meaning of a word or words (which cannot then be taken literally). E.g.:
"The kettle is boiling" (the *water* boils, not the *kettle*);
"They were given a warm reception" (in which *warm* = enthusiastic);
"They were given a lukewarm reception" (in which *lukewarm* = unenthusiastic).
Many metaphors are used unconsciously, and repeated metaphorical use of a particular word soon becomes one of its figurative uses (such as *warm* and *lukewarm* in the previous examples). New or unfamiliar metaphors should generally be avoided in text intended for translation into another language. "Dead" metaphors, whose imagery belonged to former times (e.g. "at half-cock", "to bite the bullet", "this sceptered isle"), should also be avoided. Another potential pitfall is the mixed metaphor, in which two or more types of inconsistent imagery are juxtaposed, often to ludicrous effect (e.g. "We must grasp the nettle, put our shoulders to the wheel, and leave no stone unturned"). *See also* **cliché; inseparable pairs**.

metastasis (pl. metastases).

mete inflects *mete − meted − meted*. *See also* **meet**.

meter = instrument/apparatus that measures; **metre** = basic unit of length in the SI (metric) system of units, the "rhythm" of poetry or music.

meticulous = overcareful, pernickety, fussy over trifles. It should not be used to mean merely *careful* or *scrupulous*.

métier = skilled ability or accomplishment (similar to *forte*), a calling; the French word should be avoided.

metre *See* **meter.**

metric = to do with metre, the unit of length; **metrical** = to do with metre, the measure/rhythm of poetry (the named examples of which are perversely spelled *-meter*, as in *pentameter* and *hexameter*).

metric units *See* **units.**

mettle *See* **metal.**

mews (noun) has the same spelling in the singular and plural.

micron = unit of length equal to a millionth (10^{-6}) of a metre (abbreviation μ), also called a *micrometre*.

microbe *See* **germ; micro-organism.**

micro-oganism is the general term for any organism that is too small to be seen with the naked eye. Chief of these are *bacteria*, which can be seen with the aid of an optical (light) microscope, and **viruses**, which can be made visible only by using an electron microscope. Also included are other microscopic organisms such as amoebas, rickettsia, various protozoa and minute fungi (moulds). Disease-causing micro-organisms are known as *pathogens* or, in everyday language, *germs*; the term *microbe* is now seldom used.

mid should not be used for **amid**, which is itself archaic for **among** (the preferred term), but better than **amidst**. Mid- is retained as a prefix meaning **middle**, taking a hyphen when attached to a word beginning with a capital letter; e.g. mid-Atlantic, mid-July, mid-Victorian. With most other roots, the hyphen is retained only as an aid to pronunciation; e.g. mid-air, midbrain, midday, mid-leg, midnight, mid-off, mid-on, mid-season, midships (and amidships), midshipman, midstream, midsummer, midway, mid-week, Midwest (of USA), mid-wicket, mid-winter. *See also* **midst.**

middle *See* **centre.**

Middle Ages (with initial capital letters).

Middle East includes eastern Mediterranean and Arab countries (chief of which are Egypt, Israel, Jordan, Lebanon and Syria). Afghanistan and its neighbours are generally excluded.

midst and **in the midst of** are archaic for **among**, which is preferred.

migrant/migrate *See* **emigrant**.

mile, mileage (preferred to *milage*). Mile(s) should not be abbreviated; miles per hour can be abbreviated to mph. 1 mile = 1,760 yards (= 1.6093 km); 1 nautical mile (British) = 2,026.7 yards (= 1.8532 km); 1 nautical mile (international) = 2,025.4 yards (= 1.852 km). *See also* **knot**.

milieu = environment; the French term should be avoided.

militate (against) = to act as a powerful influence; **mitigate** = to lessen the intensity or severity of something. E.g.:
"His untidiness militated against his getting the job."
"His paralysis mitigated the untidiness of his appearance."

millennium (pl. millennia, both with two *l*s and two *n*s) = a thousand (not a million) years.

milli- is the metric prefix for a thousandth ($\times 10^{-3}$), as in *milligram*.

milliard = 1,000 million, increasingly being called a **billion** (which *see*).

million should be spelled out in all numbers, e.g. "3 million cars", "12 million people", "37.5 million miles" and "£7 million". *See also* **billion**.

mimic, mimicked, mimicking.

min is the abbreviation of minute(s).

mina (= Asian bird) is the preferred spelling (not *myna* or *mynah*).

miner = somebody who works in a mine; **minor** = somebody who is under age (less than 18 years old in Britain).

mineralogy (not *-ology*).

minimal *See* **marginal**.

minimum (pl. minima), minimize. *See also* **diminish**.

minority *See* **majority**.

minus shuld be confined to mathematical or scientific expressions, and not used as a synonym of *less* or *without* (e.g. "They all came, minus George" and "The car arrived minus its windscreen" are incorrect).

minuscule (not *miniscule*) = extremely small; its opposite **majuscule**, which should be used only of large handwriting, is rare.

minutiae (sing. minutia) = tiny details; the Latin term should be avoided.

mis- Note that this prefix, meaning wrongly or poorly, has only one *s*. E.g.:

misapply	miscarry	misfit
misbehave	misconduct	mishit, etc.
(exception *missfire*)		

Adding the prefix to a word beginning with *s*, however, forms a word with two *ss*; *see* **mis-say**.

misappropriate *See* **expropriate**.

mischief, mischievous (not *mischievious*).

miserable = very unhappy, wretched, feeling misery; the word should not be used as a general pejorative adjective. E.g.:

"The book had miserable sales" (*miserable* should be poor or disappointing);

"They gave us a miserable amount to eat" (*miserable* should be little or inadequate).

misogamy − hatred of marriage; **misogyny** = hatred of women; **misanthropy** = hatred of mankind.

misremember *See* **disremember**.

misrepair *See* **disrepair**.

missal = book listing (Church) masses; **missile** = weapon that is thrown or projected (the words are homonyms in American English).

mis-say, (mis-said), misshape(n), missort, misspell, misspend, misspent, misstate. The preferred past tense and participle of *misspell* is **misspelled** (not *misspelt*).

mistake, mistakable. The verb **mistake** has the past tense **mistook** and past participle **mistaken.**

mistaken = in error, wrong; **misunderstood** = failed to understand. E.g.:
"I gave her directions but I was mistaken and sent her the wrong way";
"I gave her directions but she misunderstood and went the wrong way".

misuse = use incorrectly; **ill-use** = abuse, treat badly. E.g.:
"He broke the machine by continually misusing the cut-out switch."
"He ill-used his wife, who is suing for divorce."
See also **abuse.**

mitigate *See* **militate.**

mitochondrion (pl. mitochondria).

mitre (verb), mitred, mitring, mitral.

mix, mixable, but note *immiscible* = (and is preferred to) unmixable. **Mix** is a well-known verb (meaning to combine thoroughly, intermingle), with **mix up** meaning to confuse. The usual noun forms are **mixture** (= the product of mixing) and **mix-up** (a confusion). A lesser-known word rapidly gaining currency is the noun **mix,** which often replaces its synonym *mixture* (e.g. "A strange mix of old and new").

mixed metaphor *See* **metaphor.**

mnemonic = memory aid. *See* **pneumatic.**

moat = defensive ditch full of water; **mote** = speck (of dust); **motte** = mound on which a castle (bailey) is built.

mobile, mobilize, mobilization. **Mobile** (adj.) = capable of moving (under its own power); **movable** = capable of being moved (by some external agency). Thus a mobile crane may be used to lift a movable

container. **Immobile** = still, stationary, not moving (although capable of movement); **immovable** = incapable of being moved. E.g.:
"The young animal remained immobile, despite the close approach of the children."
"The girder remained immovable, despite every attempt to lift it."

moccasin (with two *c*s and one *s*).

mode *See* **average**.

model, modelled, modeller, modelling.

moderate, moderator, moderation.

modern, modernize, modernization.

modest should not be misused for **moderate**. *Modest* = bashful, retiring, unassuming, unobtrusive; *moderate* = unextreme, temperate, middling (of size). E.g.:
"He lived in a modest house of moderate size".

modicum is archaic for **small amount**; the Latin term should be avoided.

modifiers, dangling *See* **participles, related and unrelated**.

modish words *See* **vogue words**.

modus operandi (italics) = method of working; the Latin term should be avoided in ordinary writing.

modus vivendi (italics) = a truce before the parties settle their dispute; it does not mean *way of life* (even if the original Latin did), and should be avoided.

Mohamet etc. *See* **Muhammed**.

Mohammedanism The preferred term is **Islam** (which *see*).

moire = watered silk. The characteristic pattern of moire fabric (sometimes seen in printing when a halftone original is reproduced by the halftone process) is **moiré** (with an accent), which is also the spelling of the adjective.

moist, moisten, moisture, moisturize (= moisten, which is preferred).

molten *See* **melt**.

moment *See* **instant**.

momentarily = lasting for a moment, briefly. It should not be used to mean *immediately, in a moment*. E.g.:

"The sound of the car backfiring momentarily distracted her attention." (correct)
"You go on ahead; I will follow momentarily." (incorrect)

momentary = occupying a moment; **momentous** = of great consequence. E.g.:

"The error revealed a momentary lapse in concentration."
"Pressing on proved to be a momentous decision."

momentum (pl. momenta).

money has the plural **moneys** (not *monies*, which would be the plural of *mony*). The preferred style for British currency is £10.75, £1,023.05 or 25p (no full point).

mongolism should be avoided; use instead Down's Syndrome or trisomy 21.

mongoose (pl. mongooses).

monogram = set of initials worked into a design; **monograph** = an article written about a single subject. *See also* **ideograph; logogram**.

mono- or **uni-** *See* **numerical prefixes**.

monster, monstrous.

Moon usually has a capital letter when referring to the Earth's natural satellite, especially in scientific contexts, but no capital in other uses. E.g.:

"The gravitational attraction of the Moon affects tides on Earth."
"Titan is one of the moons of Jupiter."

moose (pl. moose). *See also* **elk**.

moot = debatable; **mute** = dumb, silent. E.g.:

"Whether to use troops to unload ships in the strike-bound docks is a moot question."

"When asked to confess the accused remained mute and immovable."

moped (verb, rhymes with "doped") = past tense and participle of verb *to mope*; **moped** (noun, rhymes with "go-bed") = motorized bicycle.

moral, moralize. Moral = pertaining to correct behaviour; **morale** = state of mind regarding confidence or courage. *See also* **ethics.**

moratorium (pl. moratoriums).

mordant (adj.) = biting, caustic; **mordant** (noun) = substance for fixing dye into cloth; **mordent** = musical ornament.

more is plural ("Are any more people coming?"); **more than one** is singular ("Was more than one person hurt?"); **more than (any other number)** is plural ("More than three people are needed to play this game", "More than twenty of the prisoners were recaptured"). More should not be misused for *other*; e.g. "he listed beer, cider, lager and many more examples" should be ".. many other examples".

more/most *See* **comparative and superlative.**

more or less (no hyphens).

mores (= customs, conventions) is a plural word.

more than is preferred to *over* in references to number; "He wrote more than a hundred articles" not "... over a hundred articles". *See* also **above.**

more than one requires singular verb. E.g.:
"More than one person has signed his name in the book."

morgue The preferred term is **mortuary.**

moribund = on the point of death; it does not mean merely *ailing, declining* or *dormant* (as in "The ship-building industry remained in a moribund state during the early 1980s").

Morocco The derived adjective and noun is *Moroccan.*

mortar *See* **cement.**

mortgage, mortgager (who grants a mortgage), mortgagee (who gets a mortgage), but mortgagor in law.

mortise, mortising. Note the noun is also *mortise* (not *mortice*).

mortuary is preferred to **morgue** for a building in which dead bodies are (temporarily) housed.

Moslem The preferred spelling is **Muslim** (see also **Islam**).

mosquito (pl. mosquitoes).

most is absolute; it should not be confused with **the most** (which is relative). E.g.:

"What I should most like to eat is kippers"
"Which do you like the most − kippers, bloaters or rollmops?"

Note that "Which do you like the more − kippers or bloaters?" would be correct for a choice between two, but is stilted (better as "Which do you prefer − kippers or bloaters?").

mostly = for the most part; it should not be misused for **most**. E.g.:

"The food was mostly good and certainly plentiful" is correct;
"The dishes mostly favoured by the guests were the savoury ones" is incorrect;
"The food was certainly good and most plentiful" is correct.

mote *See* **moat.**

motif = recurring theme; **motive** = something that stimulates behaviour or action; **motivate** = provide with a motive, spur into action; **motivation** = providing with an incentive, the act of motivating.

motivation *See* **incentive; motif; vogue words.**

motive *See* **motif.**

motor, motorboat, motor bus, motor car, motor coach, motorize, motor-launch, motorcycle, motor scooter, motor torpedo boat (MTB), motor vehicle, motorway.

motorbike is colloquial for **motorcycle**, and should be avoided in formal writing.

motorway (= high-speed dual carriageway road restricted to certain vehicles/drivers) has various names outside Britain; e.g. autobahn

(Germany), autopista (Spain), autoroute (France), autostrada (Italy), expressway/freeway (United States). When the foreign names are used in English, they should not be italicized and should be given normal English plurals in *-s* (e.g. autostradas, not *autostrade*).

motte *See* **moat.**

motto (p. mottoes).

mouse, mousy.

mouth is the form of the noun and the verb (not *mouthe*).

move, movable (but moveable in law). *See also* **mobile.**

mow has the past tense and participle **mowed,** although *mown* is retained as an adjective (e.g. "the smell of mown grass").

Mozambique The derived adjective and noun is *Mozambican*.

much *See* **many.**

mucus (noun) − slimy fluid; **mucous** (adj.) = to do with mucus.

muffin *See* **crumpet.**

Muhammed is the preferred spelling for the name of the founder of **Islam** (which *see*).

mulatto (pl. mulattos).

multi- Compounds with *multi-* as a prefix have no hyphen unless the root word begins with *i* (e.g. multi-industrial). The *i* is sometimes omitted when the root word begins with *a* (e.g. multangular). *See also* **numerical prefixes.**

mumps is a singular word; "cases of mumps" achieves a plural construction.

murder *See* **homicide.**

museum *See* **mausoleum.**

musical works Subject titles should be typeset in italics; e.g. Gounod's *Faust*, Wagner's *Die Meistersinger*, Parry's *Judith*. But "New World" Symphony, "Eroica" Symphony, Beethoven's Choral Symphony,

Ninth Symphony should be set in roman face. Opus 4, no. 2 or op. 4, no. 2 should be typeset thus.

Technical names of periods or styles should not have an initial capital letter; e.g. organum, descant, polyphony.

Names of instruments and organ stops should be in roman; e.g. cor anglais, cornet-à-piston, timpani, diapason, vox humana.

The terms leitmotif and motif should also be typeset in roman.

Muslim is the preferred spelling for the followers of **Islam** (which *see*).

must, as a noun meaning a necessity, essential or something that should not be missed (e.g. as in "Keeping to the schedule is a must" or "Do not miss the Turner exhibition at the Tate Gallery − it is a must") seems to be less in vogue than it once was, but nevertheless is probably best avoided in formal writing. **Must** is acceptable as a term for grape juice or new wine.

mutate, mutation, mutable (not *mutatable*).

mutual = shared both ways between two (or possibly more) i.e. involving a two-way exchange; if something is possessed by both parties it is **common** to them. E.g.:

"The opponents' mutual hatred"

"The opponents' common belief in pacifism".

myna/mynah The preferred spelling for the Asian bird is **mina**.

mysterious = difficult to understand, secret, full of mystery; **mystical** = beyond human understanding, symbolic in a spiritual or religious sense, to do with mysticism.

myth *See* **fable**.

N

-n- or -nn- Monosyllabic words ending in *-n* preceded by a single vowel double the *n* before suffixes beginning with a vowel. E.g.:

ban	banned, banning
can	canned, canner, cannery, canning
don	donned, donning
fun	funny, funnier, funniest
gun	gunner, gunnery
man	mannish
thin	thinned, thinner, thinnest, thinning

The *-n* remains single if it is preceded by a long or double vowel. E.g.:

clean	cleaned, cleaner, cleanest, cleaning
dawn	dawned, dawning
join	joiner, joinery
keen	keener, keenest
moan	moaned, moaner, moaning
train	trained, trainee

With polysyllabic words, the choice of *-n-* or *-nn-* depends on where the accent falls. If it is on the last syllable, the rule is as for monosyllabic words; e.g. beginning, japanned, outrunning, trepanning (short vowels); ascertained, detraining, discernible, overturning (long vowels). If the last syllable is unaccented, the *-n-* is not doubled; e.g. awakening, beckoned, frightened, threatened, tobogganed, womanish.

naevus (pl. naevi).

naive, naivety (preferred to *naïve*, *naif*, naïvety, *naïveté*).

name, nameable.

named effects and laws Scientific laws and principles, named effects, biological structures and disorders named after people, and so on should have an initial capital for the person but not the law. E.g.:

Archimedes' principle
Avogadro's hypothesis
Boyle's law

Charles' law (not Charles's law)
Meckel's ganglion
Ménière's syndrome
Mossbauer effect
Newton's law of motion
von Graefe's sign
von Recklinghausen's disease
But the third law of thermodynamics
Newton's second law of motion

See also **personal names**.

names *See* **aircraft names; astronomical terms; capitalization** (proper names, trade names); **car names; Christian names; locomotive and train names; nicknames; personal names; ships' names; space rockets and missiles; trade names** and the preceding entry.

nano- is the metric prefix for a thousand-millionth ($\times 10^{-9}$), as in *nanosecond*.

naphtha, naphthalene (note *-phth-* spelling).

napkin is preferred to **serviette** for the square of cloth or absorbent paper used for wiping the fingers at meals, thus being consistent with the *napkin-ring* that sometimes holds it. *See also* **nappy**.

nappy is now preferred to **napkin** for the baby's garment.

narcissus (pl. narcissi).

nasturtium (pl. nasturtiums).

nationalize, nationalization; note also *denationalize* (= "privatize" in the 1980s) and *renationalize*. **Nationalize** = put a company or undertaking under government ownership and management (such as, at the time of writing, the railways, coal and steel industries in Britain); **naturalize** = make an immigrant a citizen of the adopted country; giving him or her a new nationality.

native(s) Offence can be given by referring to aboriginal or indigenous peoples as natives (say *local people* or some such). *See also* **primitive**.

naturalism = action or system based on natural phenomena; **naturism**

= nature-worship, nudism. A **naturalist** studies natural history; a **naturist** is a nudist.

naturalize, naturalization. *See* **nationalize.**

naught is archaic for **nothing** (as in the cliché "come to naught"), and *nothing* should be used; **nought** = zero; **ought** = should (e.g. "You ought to know better than put *ought* for *nought*"). *See also* **aught.**

nausea = feeling of sickness; **nauseous** = causing one to feel sick; **nauseated** = made to feel sick. A disgusting smell may be nauseous, when the smeller is then nauseated. *See also* **ill/illness.**

nautical mile *See* **knot; mile.**

nautilus has the preferred plural nautiluses (not *nautili*).

naval = to do with the navy; **navel** = depression in the abdomen (where the umbilical cord was attached to the foetus).

navigate, navigator, navigable, navigation.

nearby is an adjective (e.g. "I hailed a nearby taxi"); **near by** is an adverb (e.g. "The taxi passed near by"), although the one-word form of the adverb is gaining ground.

neath is old-fashioned for **beneath,** which is preferred.

nebula (pl. nebulae).

necessary, necessarily (with one *c* and two *ss*). Note that *unnecessary* has two *n*s.

nectar, nectareous (= to do with nectar, preferred to the many alternatives), nectiferous (= producing nectar).

née (acute accent).

need (verb) = require of necessity; **want** = desire (a non-essential thing). E.g.:

"We need air to breathe."

"We want more free time."

ne'er is a poetic abbreviation of **never,** and should be avoided.

ne'er-do-well (note spelling).

negative prefixes Common prefixes meaning *not* include *a-, an-, il-, im-, in-, ir-, non-* and *un-*, to which may be added *dis-* in some of its uses. Originally *il-, im-, in-* and *ir-* were assigned to words of Latin origin, whereas *un-* was reserved for "English" words, a category that includes words that have been made English by a suffix such as *-able* (but not *-ible*), *-ed* and *-ing*. E.g.:

illegal	unlawful	indecisive	undecided
illegible	unreadable	indigestion	undigested
immodest	unashamed	irrational	unreasonable
impractical	unworkable	irresolution	unresolved
inaction	unactionable	irrespective	unrespected

Often two negative forms are equally acceptable (e.g. irreconcilable and unreconcilable), although sometimes they have different meanings. E.g.:

immaterial (= irrelevant)   unmaterial (= having no
                              substance)

immoral (= lacking morals) unmoral (= not concerning
                              morality)

In a similar way, *a-* or *an-* is (or was) regarded as a prefix for words of Greek origin, whereas *non-* is an English prefix. E.g.:

anaemia	nonconformist
anaesthetic	non-resident
analgesic	nonsense
asepsis	non-starter

Again different meanings can result; e.g. asexual (= biologically sexless) and nonsexual (= lacking sexual implications).

The prefix *dis-* can act as a negative prefix (e.g. disabled, disappear, disorientated, dissatisfy), even if the original root no longer exists (e.g. the opposites of disappointed, disgruntled and dishevelled are not "appointed", "gruntled" and "hevelled"). *Dis-* can also form words with a different meaning from the corresponding *un-* version. E.g.:

disarmed (= having had   unarmed (= not carrying
    weapons taken away)   weapons this time)
disinterested (= impartial)   uninterested (= not interested)
dismounted (= climbed down)   unmounted (= not in/on a
                                     mount)

A similar prefix in medical terms is *dys-*, as in dysfunction (compare with malfunction), dyslexia, dystrophy, and so on.
See also **mis-**; **non-**.

neglect, negligible (not *-able*) (= trifling, not worthy of notice), negligence, negligent (not *-ant*) (= careless), neglectful (= negligent, neglecting). E.g.:

"After repeated washing the garment shrank by only a negligible amount."

"The garment has shrunk after being washed only once − you were negligent not to have it dry-cleaned."

"Neglectful of their homework, the children watched television all evening."

negligee (= woman's flimsy dressing-gown) is preferred to *negligé*.

Negrillo (pl. Negrilloes).

Negrito (pl. Negritos).

Negro (pl. Negroes). *See* **black**.

neither is restricted to two things and is followed by *nor* (not *or*). *See* **either**.

nem. con. is the abbreviation of *nemine contradicente* (= no one contradicting); except in the most formal business contexts, the abbreviation should be avoided.

neo-Gothic, neo-Platonism etc. (but neoclassical).

neologism = a new word. There are three main types: *borrowings*, that is words adopted from foreign languages (*see* **foreign words and phrases**); newly coined words, usually made up from existing word elements (e.g. *faction* (= fact + fiction), *gasohol, motel, quadraphonic, resistor, smog*) or by analogy with an existing word (e.g. *grand-parental*); and *nonce-words*, made up (initially) for use on one occasion (such as Lewis Carroll's *chortle, galumph, jabberwocky* and *slithy*) and often then abandoned, such as some of the inventions of advertising agencies (e.g. "Have you Macleaned your teeth today?"). Some authorities also include among neologisms words that have fallen into disuse but are reintroduced with new meanings (e.g. *hospice*) and even current words ascribed new meanings (e.g. *aerobics*). Early in their careers, newly-coined words are sometimes distinguished by quotation marks (e.g. "unisex" haircut). Apart from the ephemeral nonce-words, neologisms serve a useful purpose if they fill a gap in the vocabulary and so enrich the language. Less justifiable are introductions that duplicate – and sometimes displace – perfectly good existing words. Whether they do so depends on usage; as in so many aspects of language development, time is the tester. *See also* **back-formations; vogue words**.

Nepal The derived adjective and noun is *Nepalese* (preferred to *Nepali*).

nerve-racking is the preferred spelling (not *nerve-wracking*).

net (free from deduction) is the preferred spelling of **nett**.

nether is archaic for **lower** (as in the cliché "nether regions"); *lower* should be used.

Netherlands should be used for the country (not *Holland*). The people and language are **Dutch.**

neuron (nerve cell), not *neurone*.

neurotic used properly describes someone suffering from a type of mental disorder classified as a **neurosis** (pl. neuroses). As a synonym for *anxious, obsessive* or plain *nervous* it is grossly overworked (as in "There's no need to get neurotic about it"), and should be avoided in non-medical contexts. *See also* **manic; paranoia**.

neutral, neutralize, neutralization.

névé (acute accents).

never = not ever; e.g. "I never have a good seat at the theatre." It should not be used as an intensified negative when referring to a single occasion; e.g. "I never saw the beginning of last night's play" is incorrect (say "I did not see the beginning..."). E.g.:
"Did you ever steal apples as a child?" "I never did" (correct);
"Did you spill that ink?" "I never did" (incorrect).

never-ending, never-failing, nevermore, nevertheless.

nevertheless (one word).

new-blown, newborn, newcomer, newfangled, new-found, new-laid, New Moon, New World, New Year, New Year's Day.

newborn *See* **baby.**

newfangled (one word) = newly introduced but to no good purpose; it is thus pejorative and should not be used for the neutral **new.**

news is a singular word; "items of news" achieves a plural construction.

news agency (such as AP, which supplies news), newsagent(s) (which sells newspapers), newsboy, news-cast(er), newsletter, newsmonger, newsprint, news-reader, newsreel, news-stand, News Theatre, newsvendor, newsworthy.

next of kin *See* **kin.**

nexus (pl. nexuses).

nice is so overused to mean *agreeable, pleasant* (not its original meaning) that the word is best avoided in this sense. "The skater's execution of the turn displayed a nice sense of timing" is correct usage (**nice** = exact, precise, accurate).

nicknames, unless well known or obvious, are usually identified by inverted commas (e.g. Hal "Scarface" Wilson, "Babyface" Nelson).

nigh = near, nearly or near to; **well-nigh** = nearly, almost. Both (particularly the former) have an archaic ring, and are best avoided.

night-blind(ness), night-cap, night-clothes, night-club, night-dress, nightfall, night-gown, nightjar, night-life, nightlight, night-long, nightmare, nightmarish, night nurse, night-school, nightshade, night-shift, night-shirt, night-spot, night-time, night-watch, nightwatchman.

nimbus (pl. nimbuses).

nitrogen, nitrogenous, nitrogenize.

nitroglycerine (not nitroglycerin), termed glyceryl trinitrate in chemistry and medicine.

no (pl. noes) ("The noes have it").

no. This abbreviation of *numero* (number) should be avoided.

Nobel Prize (initial capital letters), Nobel Prize in chemistry etc. (no initial capital on chemistry); an exception is the Nobel Peace Prize.

noblesse oblige (italics) = imposes obligations (because of rank or position); the French form should be avoided.

nobody (preferred to *no-one*) is singular; e.g. "Nobody under the age of 16 is allowed".

noisome = disgusting, unhealthy (usually referring to a smell); it has nothing to do with *noise*.

no-man's land (note spelling).

nom de plume (italics) = pseudonym, pen-name; the French form was coined in England and should be avoided (the correct French equivalent is *nom de guerre*).

nomenclature, scientific, of plants and animals, *see* **Latin classification**.

nominal = to do with names or nouns, in name only ("a nominal price"); it should not be misused to mean approximate (e.g. "The experiment produced nominal results" is incorrect).

non- Nearly all compounds with the prefix *non-* have a hyphen (exceptions include nonconformist, nondescript, nonentity, nonplus, nonsense). The prefix should not be appended to words that have perfectly good existing negative forms. E.g.:

non-functioning	should be	*malfunctioning*
non-operative	should be	*inoperative*
non-positive	should be	*negative*
non-relevant	should be	*irrelevant*

See also **negative prefixes**.

nonce-word *See* **neologism**.

non compos mentis (italics) = of unsound mind; the Latin form should be avoided.

none is nearly always singular. E.g.:

"None of the workers *has* arrived yet" (none = not one).

"None *has* as much talent as this worker" (none = no-one, no one person).

But compare:

"None *is* so quiet as he who never talks"

and "None *are* so quiet as they who never talk".

none the less (three words) is the preferred spelling, although *nonetheless* (one word), standard in American, is rapidly gaining ground in Britain.

non-flammable/non-inflammable *See* **inflammable**.

nonplus, nonplussed.

non sequitur is a statement, often presented as a consequence or conclusion, that does not logically follow from what precedes it. E.g. "It looked as if it would rain so I wore my red socks." Usually much less obvious than this example, non sequiturs should nevertheless be avoided.

non-standard English should be avoided in formal text, although opinions about what is standard inevitably differ. In terms of "non-acceptable" words for formal writing, there is a group consisting of cant, slang and colloquialisms. **Cant** is a type of jargon, usually the private language of crime and criminals, also called **argot** by some authorities. Many of its words have eventually become **slang** ("words and usages not accepted for dignified use" – Chambers Dictionary), which is the common linguistic coin of everyday speech (*see* **slang**). **Colloquialisms** also include words that are used mainly in informal speech. **Jargon** is the specialized language of science, technology, trade, commerce, and so on (*see* **jargon**).

Other informal expressions, which should be used only in conversation or personal letter-writing, include words such as *can't*, *don't* and *won't*. *Ain't*, described by some as colloquial, is condemned by others as an illiterate or dialect usage. **Dialect**, however, is best regarded as a regional vocabulary, sometimes involving new meanings of existing words and sometimes using words of its own. Thus in Cornwall a tourist is known in the local dialect as an *emmet* (a standard, if archaic, term for an ant), whereas in Devon the seasonal visitors are referred to as *grockles*. Words such as *emmet* (in its original sense) belong to the category known as **archaisms**, which are old-fashioned and should be avoided in modern formal writing (*see* **archaisms**).

There are various other isms in the lexicographer's vocabulary, including bowdlerism, euphemism, genteelism, malapropism and solecism. **Bowdlerism**, by definition an activity indulged in by editors rather than writers, is the (some would say unnecessary) removal from text of words and phrases that might offend a reader's sensibilities. It is close to **euphemism**, which is the use of a mild, and often twee, expression instead of one that might give offence. As a result the vocabulary is burdened with slang and colloquial synonyms such as House of Commons, WC, the smallest room, bathroom (American), cloakroom, convenience, the john, powder room, loo, karsi, lav, lavvy, toilet, thunder-box and even bog for the — to some people apparently unmentionable — lavatory. Indeed most euphemisms relate to bodily functions or sex. Again this sort of usage is similar to **genteelism** which, however, avoids what would be regarded as crude expressions such as *bog*.

A **solecism** is technically a breach of syntax, most often a complete misuse of a word, such as "She done it" or "The South American lama has four legs and a long neck". Examples of the latter type are also called **schoolboy howlers**. A solecism involving euphony and often humour is sometimes termed a **malapropism** (Mrs Malaprop, who habitually made this error, was a character in Sheridan's play *The Rivals*); a modern example is "Most people regard the threat of nuclear war as the ultimate deterrent". Vocal gymnastics are also involved in **spoonerisms** (again named after their champion, Rev. William Spooner), in which initial letters or sounds of words are transposed, resulting in other real but incorrect words (e.g. "heaving the louse" for "leaving the house" and "well-boiled icicle" for "well-oiled bicycle"). *See also* **cliché**; **idiom**.

no-one (but *nobody* preferred).

nor *See* **neither**.

norm = pattern, standard, usual state/quantity (generally expressed as "the norm"); **normal** = agreeing with the standard, non-deviant (and various technical meanings in chemistry); **normality** = the state of being normal; **normalcy** = normality. As an alternative word for *normality, normalcy* (called an "ill-formed word" by Chambers Dictionary) would appear to be redundant and is probably best avoided. Other related words include normalize, normalization.

north, northern, northerly, etc. *See* **compass directions**.

North America *See* **America**.

Northern Hemisphere (initial capital letters).

Northern Ireland *See* **Eire**.

North Pole (initial capital letters).

nosebag, noseband, nosebleed, nose-cone, nosedive, nosegay, nose over (verb), nose-piece, nose-ring, nose-wheel, nosy (not nosey).

nostalgia *See* **homesickness**.

nostrum (pl. nostrums).

notable = worthy of notice or attention; **noted** = well-known, celebrated; **noticeable** = perceptible, claiming one's attention; **noteworthy** = worthy of note. E.g.:

"He made a notable contribution to the science of astronomy."
"He is a noted astronomer."
"He has a noticeable stoop, now that he is older."
"He made some noteworthy remarks to the chairman."

nothing is the opposite of *something*; **no thing** can contrast with *no person* (e.g. "Although many persons annoy him, no thing does").

notice, noticing, noticeable.

not only should always be followed, eventually, by **but** (...) **also**.

notorious = well known for misdeeds, infamous; **famous** = favourably well-known. E.g.:

"Al Capone was a notorious gangster."
"Charlie Chaplin was a famous film star."

notwithstanding (one word).

nought *See* **naught.**

nouns and verbs with the same spelling are usually distinguished by different pronunciations, involving differences in stress. In the following examples, which give the noun use first, the stressed syllable is in italics:

"He speaks with a French *ac*cent."
"Most speakers ac*cent* the first syllable."

"Common salt is a *com*pound of sodium and chlorine."
"You must com*pound* the ingredients thoroughly before adding water."

"Put a cold *com*press on the sprain."
"They use a machine to com*press* the waste paper into bales."

"Bystanders, incensed by what they saw, joined in the *con*flict."
"I do not want my account of the incident to con*flict* with yours."

"Next week we begin working on a new *pro*ject."
"The peak of the cap pro*jects* forwards."

"I must do some *re*search into the true facts."
"I must re*search* the facts behind the case."

Among the many other examples are *ally, consort, conflict, contract, converse, convert, convict, decrease, digest, discount, escort, exploit, extract, import, incense, increase, insult, present, produce, progress, project, protest, record, reject, suspect.* All have the stress on the first syllable in the noun, and on the second syllable in the verb.
See also **adjectives and nouns.**

nouns as verbs In the following examples:

"Who authored the book?"
"He will chair the meeting"
"They elbowed their way through the crowd."
"She promised to gift her ring to her mother"
"They will host the party"
"Man the lifeboats"
"She mothers that dog"
"Paper over the cracks"
"You can pocket the change"

"The article rubbished the government's plan."
"I had to train it to London"

elbow, man, mother, paper and *pocket* are recognized verbs, *chair* is accepted by most authorities, but *author, gift, host, rubbish* and *train* (and many similar examples) should be avoided.

nova (pl. novae).

novel refers to kind, **new** refers to time, state or condition. E.g.:

"He uses a novel way of writing his comments."
"He used a new pen".

nowadays (one word).

noxious *See* **obnoxious**.

nuciferous describes a plant that bears nuts; **nucivorous** describes an animal that eats nuts.

nuclear is preferred to **atomic** in expressions such as nuclear energy, nuclear power, nuclear reactor, nuclear submarine, nuclear warhead.

nucleus (pl. nuclei).

number, like some other **collective words** (which *see*), may be singular or plural. It is usually singular when preceded by the definite article (e.g. "The number of errors was surprisingly small"), and plural when preceded by the indefinite article (e.g. "A number of errors were found"). In other constructions, *number* is singular or plural depending on whether it is regarded as a whole or distributively.

numbers *See* **quantities and measurements**.

numbers and counting The following rules provide a guide to style in modern practice.

1. Cardinal numbers consist of the ordinary counting series one, two, three, four, and so on. The style for numbers over twenty is twenty-one, twenty-two, and so on (with a hyphen). At some stage in the series, it is usually necessary to change from numbers spelled in full to ones represented by numerals (e.g. 197 is briefer and more readable than one hundred and ninety-seven). Many editors/publishers make this change after the number ten. Numbers larger than 100 should not be spelled in full except for the "round" numbers. E.g.:

432 987	1,234	23,456	345,678	4,567,890
but a hundred	a thousand		a million	

Note that numbers larger than a thousand are comma'd off in groups of three, from the right; continental usage places full points, not decimal points (for which commas are used), instead of commas. Modern scientific typesetting uses narrow spaces instead of commas. Whole numbers of thousands or millions are best written as a combination of numerals and words. E.g.:

27 thousand   128 million   (not thousands, millions).

Numerals should also be used to avoid a string of hyphenated words. E.g.:

"a 36-hour interval", not "A thirty-six-hour interval".

Beware of *billion*, which originally in Britain meant a million million but which in North America and increasingly in Britain means 1,000 million (formerly the British *milliard*). For this reason, the American "7 billion" should be written as "7,000 million". For a precise quantity – that is, a number followed by a unit – numerals should always be used. E.g.:

7km   3 miles   120 bhp   1,200 mph   35°C.

Numerals should also be used for times of day, days of the month, years and dates. E.g.:

3 p.m.   3 o'clock   15.00 hours   29 February 1988 (not 29th).

If style or position at the beginning of a sentence demands that a quantity be spelled out, the units should also be spelled in full. E.g.:

six metres   twenty horsepower   a thousand megawatts.

If there is a list of figures (in running text), use spelled-out numbers or numerals depending on the majority. E.g.:

Two, four and seven...
26, 55, 72 and 273...
Three, eight and thirteen...
8, 9, 48, 49 and 438...

In text prepared for translation or co-edition publication, quantities often have to be stated in two systems of units. The usual style is:

320 km (200 miles)   37°C (98.6°F)   1,000 ha (2,470 acres)

or, of course,

200 miles (320 km)   98.6°F (37°C)   2,470 acres (1,000 ha)

Abbreviations of units may be typeset spaced (6 m), close-spaced (6 m) or close-up (6m), depending on the style required by the publisher. Roman numerals should be avoided, apart from World War I, World War II, rulers (Henry VIII, Elizabeth II), and books of the Bible (I Kings, II Kings).

2. Ordinal numbers, used for enumerating, are the series first, second, third, fourth, and so on (the *-th* ending is used from *fourth* upwards). In ordinary running text these should be spelled in full, although the abbreviations 1st, 2nd, 3rd, 4th, and so on may be used to save space in tabular matter. The style for numbers over 20 is twenty-first (21st), twenty-second (22nd), and so on (with hyphens). When used adjectivally, they all take a hyphen (e.g. "in the seventeenth century" but "a seventeenth-century building").

3. Dates See **time**.

4. Money See **money**.

See also **abbreviations; contractions; mathematical material; numerical prefixes; roman numerals**.

numerical prefixes generally have two possible forms, one derived from Greek and one from Latin.

prefix	Greek	Latin
half	hemi- (hemisphere)	semi- (semicircle)
one	mono- (monogram)	uni- (unique)
two	di- (dioxide)	bi- (biennial)
three	tri- (tripod)	ter- (tercentennial)
four	tetra- (tetrarch)	quadri- (quadrilateral)
five	penta (pentangle)	quinque- (quinquereme)
six	hexa- (hexagonal)	sex- (sextant)
seven	hepta- (heptane)	sept- (September)
eight	oct(a)- (octagon)	oct(o)- (October)
nine		non- (nonet)
ten	deca- (decathlon)	decem- (December)
many	poly- (polygon)	multi- (multiplex)
all	pan- (panacea)	omni- (omnipotent)

Purists object to a mismatch of a Greek prefix and a Latin stem (and vice versa), but the adoption of metric prefixes has made this inevitable. Examples of other hybrids from science and technology include bichromate, bicycle, bimetallic, divalent, monorail, multipolar, quadriplegia, tetracyclic, tetravalent, trisect, trivalent and unicycle. *See also* **numbers and counting**.

nuncio (pl. nuncios).

O

O *See* **Oh.**

-o For plurals of words ending in *-o*, *see* **Italian words; plurals.**

oaf (pl. oafs).

oasis (pl. oases).

obese, obesity (not *obeseness*). *See also* **corpulent.**

object, objector, objection.

objectionable (not *objectional*) = disagreeable, unacceptable, open to objection; **objective** (adj.) = from a disinterested impersonal point of view (opposite of *subjective*). E.g.:
"The magistrate condemned the vandal for his objectionable behaviour."
"Because the incident involved my own family, I found it difficult to be objective in reporting the facts to the police."

obeisance (note *-ei-* spelling).

objet d'art (italics, pl. *objets d'art*) = small (usually practical) object of artistic merit.

oblivious = forgetful; it does not mean *unaware*. E.g.:
"They became good friends, but she was oblivious of where they met." (correct)
"He was so engrossed in his work that he was oblivious of the noise of the explosion." (incorrect)

obnoxious = very unpleasant; **noxious** = poisonous. E.g.:
"The rubbish dump gave off an obnoxious smell."
"The area had to be evacuated because of a leakage of noxious gas from the chemical works."

observe, observable, observance (= keeping customs, laws or regulations), observation (= noticing or seeing something, or a comment), observant, observatory. E.g.:

"They believe in strict observance of the sanctity of marriage."
"Astronomy has been called the science of observation."
"He resented your observation about the team's poor performance."

obsolete, obsolescent. *See* **ancient**.

obstacle *See* **impediment**.

obtrude *See* **intrude**.

obverse *See* **inverse**.

obviate = to get rid of, make unnecessary, neutralize; it should not be used to mean *lessen* or *reduce*. E.g.:
"Checking the typescript should obviate the need for a second proof-reading stage" (correct);
"More careful typing should obviate the number of corrections at later stages" (incorrect).

occupy, occupier (who occupies e.g. a house permanently), occupant (who occupies e.g. a telephone box temporarily), occupation (= the act of occupying, employment); occupancy (= the state of an occupant). E.g.:
"The painting of the outside of the flat is the responsibility of the occupier."
"I have kept this seat warm for the next occupant."
"My occupation of the flat dates from my birthday three years ago."
"My greatest wish is occupancy of a seat on Concorde."

occur, occurred, occurring, occurrence (with two *c*s and two *r*s).

octagon, octahedral (not *octo*-), but octogenarian, octopod, octopus (pl. octopuses).

octopus (pl. octopuses).

ocular, oculist, binocular(s) (with one *c*). **Oculist** = a medically qualified specialist who treats disorders of the eye, an ophthalmologist; **optician** = someone who sells spectacles, contact lenses and optical instruments; **ophthalmic optician** or **optometrist** = someone who tests eyesight and prescribes spectacles etc.

-odd, as in 30-odd, needs a hyphen to avoid ambiguity with odd =

strange (e.g. "The 30-odd members of the staff" and "The 30 odd members of staff"); the construction should be avoided.

odious = detestable, hateful; **odorous** = having a (pleasant) smell. E.g.:
"I was shocked by his odious table manners."
"I prefer the odorous flowers of snowdrops to the showy ones of daffodils."

oddity = somebody or something out of the ordinary; **oddment** = piece left over, or one remaining from a set. E.g.:
"While I was walking in the woods I came across an oddity – a white bluebell."
"My mother made a bedspread from oddments of material left over from dressmaking."

odour, odourless, odorous (and malodorous), odoriferous, odorize, odorizer (and deodorize etc.). *See also* **odious.**

-oe- This vowel sound, in words from Greek or Latin, should be written (and printed) as separate letters, not as the ligature œ (e.g. amoeba, foetus, oedema, Oedipus, oestrogen). In a few words, the vowel has been reduced to a single *e* (e.g. ecology, ecumenic, fetid). *See also* **-ae-; homoeopathy.**

oedema (preferred to the old-fashioned term *dropsy*).

oesophagus (pl. oesophagi), oesophageal.

oestrus, oestrogen.

off-and-on, off-beat, off-centre, off-chance, offcut, offend, offhand, offhanded(ly), off-licence, offload, off-peak, offprint, offset, offshoot, off shore (noun), offshore (adj.), offside, offspring, off-stage, offstreet, off-white.

offence, offensive.

offer, offered, offering, offertory.

official (adj.) = with the force of recognized authority; **official** (noun) = someone holding office/position of authority; **officious** = too ready to offer unwanted advice, bossy (pejorative). E.g.:

"Only applications on official forms will be considered."
"He continued to meddle in our affairs and we soon tired of his officious manner."

officialese is another name for **bureaucratic English**.

officious *See* **official.**

often Ambiguity should be avoided when using **often** to mean in many instances, usually or commonly; e.g. "Border Collies often have white tails" is better put as "Most Border Collies have white tails".

oftener/oftenest should be avoided; **more often/most often** are preferred.

oft-times is archaic and precious for **frequently**, which should be used.

Oh is usually followed by a comma ("Oh, now look what you have done!"); the form **O** is used only by poets.

oil-burner, oilcake, oilcan, oilcloth, oil-colour, oilfield, oil- fired, oil gauge, oil-meal, oil-painting, oil-palm, oil-seed, oil-shale, oilskin, oilstone, oil-tanker, oil well.

OK or **okay** is more than a century old and one of the most frequently used words in conversational English; but it is still colloquial and should be avoided in normal writing.

olden is archaic for **former** or simply **old** (as in the clichés "olden days", "olden times"), and should be avoided.

older *See* **elder.**

Oman The derived adjective and noun is *Omani.*

omelette is the preferred spelling (not *omelet,* which is an Americanism).

omit, omitted, omitting, omission.

omnibus (pl. omnibuses); the term for the vehicle is almost invariably shortened to **bus** (pl. buses), except in the names of some long-established bus companies.

omni- or **pan-** *See* **numerical prefixes.**

omnipotent = all-powerful; **omniscient** = all-knowing.

on account of = because, which should be used.

on appro This abbreviation of *on approval* should be avoided.

one (pronoun) is impersonal, often used to express the speaker's or writer's views. Once introduced, it should be used consistently, but can sound over-formal and stilted, as in "One goes out of one's way to make the best of one's appearance". The construction is used here to circumvent the "personal" ring of "I go out of my way to make the best of my appearance". Another type of impersonal construction is exemplified by "One often hears it claimed that a high-fibre diet is good for one's health". The formality of this statement can be avoided by a generalization such as "Many people claim that a high-fibre diet is good for the health". On the whole, it is best to avoid the use of *one*. Less formal writing sometimes uses *you/your* or *they/their* as impersonal pronouns; e.g. "You cannot buy fresh fruit nowadays" and "They say it's going to be a bad winter". Purists object to the first device because the text appears to address the reader, and to the second because it raises the question "Who are the *they* referred to?".

one another *See* **each other**.

one of those should take a plural verb when it is the subject of a sentence (because *those* is the operative word). E.g.:

"He wrote one of those books that are seldom read"
(equivalent to "His book is among those that are seldom read", which presents no problem).

one or more is plural — fairly obvious when the phrase is the subject of a sentence, but less obvious when it is the object. E.g.:

"They will not all accept; one or more are bound to decline."
"Among the replies are one or more refusals."

one or two, or a **(something) or two**, is plural. E.g.:

"One or two are coming to dinner."
"A dog or two have barked."

one's is the only personal pronoun that takes an apostrophe (*hers, its, theirs, ours, yours* have none; neither does *whose*). But note **oneself** (not *one's self*).

ongoing, an overworked vogue word nearly always to be found in the company of *situation* (which *see*), should be avoided.

only Careful writers make sure that **only** qualifies only the word intended; "Make sure it qualifies only the word..." not "Make sure it only qualifies...".

onomatopoeia (note spelling).

on stream should be spelled, if it is used at all, as two words, (not *onstream*). It is technical jargon (e.g. "The new machine will come on stream next week") and should be avoided in formal writing.

on the grounds that = **because,** which should be used.

on the part of = **by,** which should be used.

onto and **on to** can be regarded as different. *Onto* means "to a place or position"; compare "He stepped onto the ladder" and "He walked on to the next house". *On to* is obligatory in constructions such as "He went on to thank us." When in doubt, *on to* should be used. *See also* **into.**

open, opened, opening, opener, openable, openness.

operate, operator, operatable (= can be operated), operable (= can be operated on), operation, operative. E.g.:
"The machine will not be operatable until it is mended."
"The patient has an operable tumour on his arm."

ophthalmia, ophthalmic, ophthalmology, ophthalmologist, ophthalmoscope. *See also* **oculist.**

opossum *See* **possum.**

opposite (noun) takes *of* (e.g. "*Yes* is the opposite of *no*"); **opposite** (adj.) takes *to* (e.g. "*Yes* is opposite to *no*"). *See also* **apposite; inverse.**

oppress, oppressor.

optimistic (believing that good will prevail) and **pessimistic** (always expecting the worst) reflect general attitudes and should not therefore be used as synonyms of *hopeful* and *unhopeful* when applied to a single occurrence. E.g. in "She was optimistic that the train would arrive on time", *hopeful* would be better; in "He was pessimistic that he would complete the task that day", *unhopeful* would be better.

optimum (adjectival) describes "the product of conflicting forces" (Gowers). The optimum rate at which a piece of text can be edited is not the fastest possible, but the rate that achieves the best compromise between the editor's conflicting desires for accuracy, quality, speed and sanity. So *optimum* should not be used as a grandiose synonym of *best*. **Optimal** may be preferred as an adjective (*optimum* is strictly a noun), but its correct use remains as described here. The pseudo-verb *optimize* should be avoided. The plural of *optimum* is *optima*. For *minimize*, see **diminish**.

option is an overworked alternative for **choice**. *See* **vogue words**.

optometrist *See* **ocular**.

opus (preferred plural opuses, not *opera*).

-or-, as a suffix with the approximate meaning "doer", forms the agent noun from a verb – that is, a noun that stands for the person or thing that performs an action. E.g.:

act	actor	invent	inventor
carburet	carburettor	operate	operator
contribute	contributor	protect	protector
create	creator	sail	sailor
exhibit	exhibitor	survey	surveyor

There are also many *-or* agent nouns with no associated English verb; e.g. censor, doctor, mentor, motor, tailor. All the *-or* nouns are, however, greatly outnumbered by those ending in *-er*, and some have both versions. Among these doublets, the *-or* form is generally used of inanimate objects, with the *-er* form reserved for human agents. E.g.:

conveyer (person)	conveyor (machine)
distributer	distributor (in a car)
resister	resistor (electrical)
senser	sensor (electronic)

or the *-or* form is the one usually favoured in legal usage. E.g.:

bailer (usual)	bailor (law)
deviser	devisor

relater	relator
releaser	releasor
voucher	vouchor

A different group of nouns in *-or* represent a state or condition. E.g.:

error	squalor
horror	torpor
torpor	tremor

There is a much larger group ending in *-our*. E.g.:

ardour	favour	humour	valour
clamour	flavour	odour	vapour
colour	glamour	rigour	
dolour	honour	tumour	

The *-our* words can present spelling difficulties in their derived words, in which the *u* of *-our* is sometimes omitted. E.g.:

clamorous	glamorous	humorous	tumorous
coloration	honorary	odorize	valorous
dolorous	honorific	rigorous	vaporize

oral = pertaining to the mouth; **verbal** = pertaining to words. (Gowers cites *oral contraceptive* and *verbal diarrhoea* as reminders of which is which.) *See also* **aural**.

orang-utan (not any of the other spellings).

oratorio (pl. oratorios).

ordain = to order, decree, arrange, establish, admit (to holy orders); **ordination** = act of ordaining (to the ministry); **ordinance** = a rule, regulation, (temporary) law; **ordnance** = artillery, military stores. The original military surveyors gave their name to the Ordnance Survey (not *Ordinance* Survey).

ordinal numbers should be spelled in full in ordinary text (e.g. first, second, ninth, sixteenth, twenty-second, eighty-fourth). *See also* **numbers and counting**.

ore = metal-bearing mineral; **öre** = Swedish money; **øre** = Danish or Norwegian money. *See also* **krona**.

organdie = kind of dress fabric; **organza** = another kind of dress fabric.

organize, organization.

orient (verb, preferred to orientate), orientation, orienteering.

oriental *See* **eastern.**

ornamental describes something that decorates (something else); **ornate** describes something that is (highly) decorated.

orotund = having a full sound, pompous; **rotund** = plump, stout, rounded.

oscillate = to vibrate, fluctuate (regularly); **osculate** = to kiss.

ostensible = shown or professed outwardly; **ostensive** = indicating by direct demonstration, demonstrating. The words are interchangeable, particularly in adverbial form (*ostensibly, ostensively*). **Ostentatious** = showy, over-elaborate.

ostracize, ostracism.

other *See* **another.**

otherwise = *or else* should not be preceded by *or*; e.g. in "The boy will have to study hard, or otherwise he will fail the examination", delete *or*.

-ough This word ending sometimes causes difficulties in pronunciation and consequent ones in spelling. There are at least five possible pronunciations, which just have to be learned.

borough, thorough	rhyme with *"durra"*
bough	rhymes with *cow*
cough	rhymes with *toff*
dough	rhymes with *snow*
enough	rhymes with *duff*
through	rhymes with *shoe*

slough can be pronounced *slow* or *"sluff"*, depending on meaning (and the place-name Slough rhymes with *cow*).

For the author's comment, *see* **limerick.**

ought *See* **aught; naught; owe.**

our *See* **-or.**

ours (no apostrophe; *see* **one's**).

out- as a prefix does not usually take a hyphen except in such
expressions as out-and-out, out-of-date, out-of-pocket, and
out-of-touch, when they are used adjectivally.

outback, outbid, outboard, outbreak, outbuilding, outburst, outcast,
outclass, outcome, outcrop, outcry, outdated, outdo, outdoor(s),
outfield, outfit, outflank, outflow, outgo(ing), outgrow, outgrowth,
outhouse, outlandish, outlast, outlaw, outlay, outlet, outline, outlive,
outlook, outmanoeuvre, outmatch, outmoded, outmost, outnumber,
out-of-date (adj.), out-of-doors (adj.), out of doors (adv.),
out-patient, outpost, outpour(ing), output, outrage, outrider,
outrigger, outright, outrun, outrush, outset, outshine, outside,
outsize(s), outskirts, outspoken, outstanding, outstay, outstrip, out-
talk, outthrust, out-turn, outward(s), outward-bound, outweigh,
outwit, outwork, outworn.

outdoor is an adjective (e.g. "outdoor sports"); **outdoors** is an adverb
(e.g. "cricket is played outdoors"). *Indoor* and *indoors* are similar.

outline = a sketch, skeletal (preliminary) plan; **summary** = a short
restatement, a summing up. One cannot, therefore, produce a
summary of something that does not already exist in greater detail.

outré (italics) = extravagant, eccentric; the French term should be
avoided.

outstanding = excellent/conspicuous, or not yet resolved/known.
Care should be taken to avoid ambiguity from these different
meanings; e.g. in "There was one outstanding reply to the
questionnaire", *outstanding* could describe a reply conspicuous by its
nature or one that has yet to be received.

outward can be an adjective (e.g. "an outward movement") or an
adverb (e.g. "it moved outward"), although **outwards** is the preferred
form of the adverb. *See also* **-wards.**

over should be reserved to relate to position ("over the house") and should not be used to mean **more than**, relating to specific quantities ("more than four houses" not "over four houses"). *See also* **above; all over; more than**.

over- Most words with the prefix over- are spelled as one word. Exceptions include over-active, over-anxious, over-careful, over-confident(-ence), over-determined, over-large, over-react, over-sensitive, over-shoe(s), over-trading, over-train, over-use, over-weighted (but overweight). Note the double *r* in such words as overreach, override, overrule, overrun.

overflow (verb) has the past tense and participle **overflowed**, not *overflown* – which is the past participle of **overfly** (past tense *overflew*). *See also* **flyover**.

overfly *See* **flyover; overflow**.

overkill is a vogue word (e.g. "The employment of ten painters for one small room is an example of overkill"), and should be avoided. *See* **vogue words**.

overlay and **overlie** are analogous in inflexion to **lay** and **lie** (which *see*).

overly, an adverb from *over*, is described in the *Concise OED* – in the sixteenth meaning of *over* – as chiefly American and Scottish (as in "I was not overly surprised when he lost his temper"). As a synonym for *too* it cannot even claim brevity, and lovers of polysyllables would probably substitute *excessively*.

overused words *See* **vogue words**.

overthrow *See* **throw**.

overview should be avoided in the sense *review* or *survey*.

ovolo (pl. ovoli).

ovum (pl. ova).

owe has the past tense and participle **owed**. The obsolete past tense **ought** (= should) has become an auxiliary verb in its own right; the obsolete past participle **own** (= belonging to oneself) has become an adjective.

owing to *See* **due to**.

owing to the fact that = **because**, which is preferred.

own *See* **owe**.

own-ends *See* **endpapers**.

ox *See* **cattle**.

oxygen, oxide, oxidation, oxidize.

P

p, the abbreviation of new penny or new pence, should be typeset close up to the numeral; e.g. 50p. The abbreviation is omitted for amounts of more than one pound; e.g. £1.75. *See also* **money**.

p- The initial *p* is silent in some English words (derived from Greek), usually those beginning with *pn-*, *pt-* or *ps-*. E.g.:

pneumatic	pseudonym	psychic	Ptolemy
pneumonia	psittacosis	psychology	ptomaine
psalm	psoriasis	ptarmigan	ptosis
psaltery	psyche	pteridophyte	
psephology	psychiatry	pterodactyl	

-p or **-pp-** Monosyllabic words ending in *-p* preceded by a single vowel usually double the *p* before the suffixes *-able*, *-ant*, *-ed*, *-er*, *-ing*, *-ish* and *-y* (which begin with, or effectively are, a vowel). E.g.:

flip	flippant
fop, up	foppish, uppish
whip	whippable, whipped, whipper, whipping, whippy

The *p* remains single if preceded by a long or double vowel, e.g.:

reap	reapable, reaped, reaper, reaping
sheep	sheepish
sleep	sleeper, sleeping, sleepy

With polysyllabic words taking these suffixes, the choice of *-p-* or *-pp-* depends on where the accent falls. If it is on the last syllable, the rule is as for monosyllabic words; e.g. entrapping, equipping, unshipping. If the last syllable is unaccented, the *p* is not normally doubled; e.g. chirruping, enveloping, galloping, gossiping, hiccuping, scalloping, walloping. (Exceptions include handicapping, kidnapping, sideslipping, worshipping.) Neither is the *p* doubled, in monosyllabic or polysyllabic words, before the suffixes *-ful* or *-ment*; c.g. development, entrapment, equipment, worshipful. *See also* **suffixes**.

pace, pacey, pacier.

pace (italics) = with due respect to (someone who disagrees); this Latin term should be avoided.

package, packaged, packaging. **Package** (noun) = packet = small parcel; nowadays small items are *packaged*, not *packeted*; large items and suitcases are *packed*.

page, paging, paginate, pagination. *See also* **leaf**.

pagoda (pl. pagodas).

pail = bucket; **pale** (noun) = vertical piece of wood in a fence; **pale** (adj.) = lacking in colour.

pairs Some single objects consisting of two similar parts are known as pairs; e.g. bellows, binoculars, callipers, forceps, glasses (spectacles), jeans, knickers, pants, pyjamas, scissors, secateurs, shears, shorts, tights, tongs, trousers, tweezers. They are, however, plural words (e.g. "my glasses are broken", "these trousers are too tight") and to be represented unambiguously as a single item need to be prefixed by *pair of* (e.g. "she bought a new pair of jeans" because "she bought some new jeans" could mean one pair or more than one pair).

palaeo- (not *paleo-*).

palatal = pertaining to the palate (of the mouth); **palatial** = pertaining to/resembling a palace. E.g.:
"A hare lip is often associated with a palatal defect."
"Lord Askew lives in a palatial house in Scotland."

palate = roof of the mouth; **palette** = artist's tablet for mixing colours on; **pallet** = straw bed, or wooden platform for carrying and moving goods (on a fork-lift truck); **pallatte** = a piece of head armour; **palet** = palea (botany), part of a flower; **pailette** = a spangle, metal foil used in enamel painting.

pale, palely. *See also* **pail**.

pall = dark and gloomy (covering), a cloth spread over a coffin; **pawl** = pivoted catch that engages the teeth of a ratchet.

palpate = to examine with the hands, by touch (noun *palpation*); **palpitate** = to beat rapidly (noun *palpitation*).

pampas *See* **llano**.

pamphlet *See* **booklet**.

pan-, as a prefix meaning all or whole, added to an existing word usually has a hyphen; e.g. Pan-African Games, Pan-American Highway.

Panama The derived adjective and noun is *Panamanian*.

pancake See **crumpet**.

panda = bear-like animal; **pander** (to) = to gratify for base or evil purposes; **pamper** = to spoil, over-indulge (somebody).

pandemic See **endemic**.

pandit The preferred spelling is **pundit** (except as a formal Indian title).

panel, panelled, panelling.

panic, panicked, panicking, panicky.

panties/pants See **knickers**.

pantograph (not *pantagraph*).

papaya is preferred to **pawpaw** for the tropical tree and its fruit.

papier-mâché (with accents).

paraffin (with one *r* and two *f*s). See **kerosene**

parallel, paralleled, paralleling, parallelogram, parallax.

paralysis, paralyse, paralytic.

parameter, a technical term in mathematics (usually meaning a variable quantity assigned a constant value in the case being considered), should be left to the mathematicians and not used as a vogue word for *aspect, consideration, factor* or just any *quantity*. Neither should it be confused with **perimeter**, also a mathematical term, meaning the distance round a closed two-dimensional figure but acceptably used of any other sort of *boundary* (which even then is a more familiar, and thus preferred, word).

paranoia = serious mental disorder involving delusions of persecution; the word (and its adjective **paranoiac**) should not be used of someone of a merely suspicious or mistrusting nature. See *also* **manic**.

parasite, parasitize, parasitism, parasitic.

parcel, parcelled, parcelling.

parenthesis (pl. parentheses). *See* **bracket; punctuation**.

par excellence (italics) = without equal, pre-eminent; the French form should be avoided.

parlous is an archaic form of **perilous** (as in the cliché "parlous state", which is often misused to mean *impecunious* or *hard-up*); *dangerous* or *perilous* should be used.

parricide = murder of one's mother or father (or another near relative); **patricide** = murder of one's father.

part = a fraction, constituent; **portion** = a share, specified component quantity. E.g.:
"She has taken over part of my job" (i.e. some of it);
"She has taken over my portion of the job" (i.e. all of it).
See also **proportion**.

part *from* = separate, leave; **part** *with* = give up. E.g.:
"She was reluctant to part from her friend so soon."
"He was reluctant to part with the money so quickly."

partial = relating to only a part (of something), or favouring one side in a contest/dispute (e.g. "a partial gastrectomy", "a partial point of view"); **partial** *to* = having a preference for (e.g. "She is partial to strawberries"); **partially** = in a biased manner, unfairly (opposite of *impartially*) (e.g. "We thought that the judge summed up partially"); **partly** = in part, incompletely (opposite of *completely*) (e.g. "The judge had only partly summed up before lunch") − there is great difference between a judge's *partially* summing up and *partly* summing up. As the Fowlers said: "... never write *partially* without considering first the claims of *partly*."

participles, related and unrelated Present or past participles should be located in a sentence in such a way that they relate to the correct subject (usually a noun). Failure to do this is a common error − the so-called dangling participle. E.g.:

"Looking over the fence, two horses were grazing" is incorrect unless it was extremely tall grass, so that the horses could bite it off and look over the fence at the same time. The participle phrase is misrelated to "two horses" and the sentence should be restructured:
"Looking over the fence, I saw two horses grazing" is correct.

A misrelated past (or perfect) participle is much more obvious. E.g.:

"Angered by the heckler, his voice shouted in reply" is incorrect. His voice was not angered, he was, so re-cast as:
"Angered by the heckler, he shouted in reply."

An unrelated participle "hangs" and does not relate to any real subject. E.g.:

"Ignoring errors involving participles, it is probably prepositions that cause the most trouble."
Here a spurious "it" dummies for the missing subject of the participle clause. The sentence can be salvaged only by re-writing:
"Except for participles, prepositions probably cause most errors."

particular should not be used with no particular reason (as in this sentence, from which it should be omitted).

partly See **partial**.

passable = can be passed; **passible** = sensitive, exposed to suffering. E.g.:

"Jim is only an amateur decorator, but he made a very passable job of repainting the village hall."
"After the blizzard, it was nearly two weeks before the side-roads again became passable."
"Her acting was so good that most of the members of the audience were passible with her emotions."

passé (acute accent) = jaded, past his or its best; strictly, the French feminine form **passée** should be used to refer to women, although both words are best avoided.

passed is the past tense and participle of the verb *to pass*; **past** is the adjective derived from it. E.g.:

"Did you see the car we passed?"
"I have had this car for the past four years."

passer-by (pl. passers-by).

passim (italics) = everywhere, throughout, from this point onward; a concise term for readers who know what it means.

past *See* **passed.**

paste, pasty (resembling paste), pastry, pasty (a pastry), pasta (spaghetti etc.). *See also* **flan.**

pastel = chalky crayon; **pastille** = medicated sweet, incense pellet. *Pastil* should be avoided for either.

pasteurize, pasteurization.

pastiche = something (such as a painting or piece of music) made up from pieces of other works; **postiche** = superfluous addition(s) to an existing work, a forgery (originally a false hair-piece).

pastoral = relating to shepherds or pastors; **pastural** = (characteristic) of pasture; **pastorale** = pastoral piece of music.

pasty *See* **flan.**

pate = the top of the head; **pâté** (with accents) = meat-paste.

pater, the Latin for father, is (like **mater** = mother) schoolboy slang, belonging to a former era.

pathetic should be reserved to describe objects, actions or situations that evoke *pathos* (pity, grief, sorrow), and not be used pejoratively or merely as a synonym for **mediocre** (which *see*).

pathogen *See* **germ.**

pathos *See* **bathos.**

patio (pl. patios).

patois (pl. patois). *See also* **accent.**

patricide *See* **parricide.**

patrol, patrolled, patrolling.

patron = someone who commissions a work of art or who contributes (financially) to the arts, a protector (as in patron saint), a proprietor.

The word should not be used to mean **customer** (which *see*). Other forms are patronage, patronize (= to act as patron or customer, or to regard with condescension), patronizing.

pave, pavement, pavior (who paves).

pay (verb) inflects *pay – paid – paid*.

pay-claim, pay-day, payload, paymaster, pay-off (noun), pay-out (noun), pay-packet, pay phone, payroll.

peace, peaceable (note *-eable*, = disinclined to cause trouble), **peaceful** (= tranquil, lacking violence). Close meanings that can be distinguished; e.g.:
"The members of the club may be slightly upset but at least their protests are peaceable."
"The older members of the committee persuaded the younger ones not to resort to violence but to organize a peaceful demonstration."

peal = a ringing (chime) of bells; **peel** = the skin or rind of a fruit. The verbs are: *peal* = to ring bells; *peel* = to skin fruit. The noun **peeler** = skinner of fruit, or a nineteenth-century name for a policeman (after Sir Robert Peel).

pease *See* **capers**.

peccadillo (pl. peccadillos). Like Piccadilly (London), this word has two *c*s, two *l*s and only one *d*.

pedal, pedalled, pedalling, pedaller (who pedals a bicycle).

peddle, peddled, peddling, pedlar (who peddles goods; *peddler* is an Americanism).

peel *See* **peal**.

peer (noun) = nobleman; **peer** (verb) = look at hard or closely; **pier** = long jetty, or bridge support.

pejorative often, because of its usual pronunciation, attracts the misspelling *perjorative*.

pen-and-ink, pen-feather, pen-friend, penholder, penknife, penman(ship), pen-name, pen-pal.

penal, penalty, penalize, penology.

pencil, pencilled, pencilling.

pendant (noun) = something that hangs; **pendent** (adj.) = hanging.

pendulum (pl. pendulums).

penetrate, penetrable (not *penetratable*).

peninsula (noun) = narrow neck of land; **peninsular** (adj.) describes it.

penny, as a unit of currency, has the plural **pence** (one penny, two pence, abbreviated to *1p, 2p*) but the plural **pennies** when it is a coin ("a pile of pennies"). *See also* **money**.

penta- or **quinque-** *See* **numerical prefixes**.

peony is the preferred spelling (not *paeony*).

people may be singular or plural. The singular *people* (= a nation or race) has the plural **peoples**; the plural *people* (= human beings) has the singular **person**. E.g.:
"As a group the British are insular, but so are many other island peoples."
"He is a strange person, but so are many people."
See also **folk; person**.

per *See* **a/an**.

per capita = "according to heads" (i.e. of each person) in a group or population (e.g. "a nation's per capita national debt ascribes an equal fraction of the debt to each member of the population"). It does not strictly mean *per head* (which would be *per caput*, singular), and is best avoided except in statistical data.

perceive, perceiver (note *-ei-* spelling). **Perceptible** (preferred to *perceivable*) = able to be perceived, observable; **perceptive** = capable of perceiving, quick to notice, intelligent; **percipient** = perceptive. E.g.:
"The replica was so like the original there was no perceptible difference."

"She was so perceptive that she noticed a difference between the replica and the original."

per cent (two words, no full point), not percent, per cent. or %, although the symbol may be used to save space in tables and captions. Note that **percentage** is spelled as one word. It should not be used to mean *a number* or *some*, as in "Drinking was a contributory factor in a percentage of cases."

perchance is archaic for **perhaps** (= maybe), either of which should be used.

percolate, percolator (not *perculator* or *percolater*).

père (grave accent) = senior, which should not be used unless it refers to a Frenchman.

peremptory = allowing no refusal; **perfunctory** = hasty, superficial. E.g.:
"The manager did not discuss the change in policy with the staff but merely issued a peremptory order defining what was to be done."
"I have given the script a perfunctory look through but have not yet read it in detail."

perfect, perfectible (not *-able*).

perfecter = a Catharist; **perfector** = a printing press (which prints on both sides of the sheet at the same time).

perfidious *See* **insidious**.

perfunctory *See* **peremptory**.

perimeter *See* **parameter**.

period (= full stop) *See* **punctuation**.

permanent *See* **temporal**.

permissible describes an allowed action or event, something that is unprohibited; **permissive** describes an attitude that allows things to be done or take place, even if they are not generally acceptable (as in "permissive society"). E.g.:
"Allowing dogs to run free off the lead is permissible in this park."

"John and Gill are too permissive with their daughter — they allow her to do anything she wants."

permit (verb) = actively give (formal) permission; **allow** = tolerate, sanction, let happen. Adjectives are *permissible, allowable*. E.g.:

"The authorities permit nude bathing on this beach."
"The authorities have allowed contractors to dump rubbish on the beach."

perpetrate = commit something outrageous; **perpetuate** = preserve, prolong (for ever). A man's actions may perpetrate a crime against society, and perpetuate a feeling of hostility towards himself.

perquisite *See* **pre-**.

per se (italics) = in itself (or him/herself or themselves); the Latin form should be avoided.

persecute = to hound, harass, punish (usually for moral, political or religious views); **prosecute** = to bring legal proceedings (against), follow up, pursue. Thus a transvestite, Marxist or Jew may be *persecuted* (at certain times and in certain places), whereas a thief or a formal complaint against an official body may be *prosecuted*.

Persian *See* **Iran**.

persist, persistence, persistent. *See also* **consistent**.

person = any human being, child or adult (neutral connotation); **personage** = somebody of importance (with slightly pompous overtones); **personality** = somebody famous (with popular overtones). The usual plural of *person* is *people*, although *persons* may be used in formal and legal contexts; it is also the usual American plural. *See also* **gender; people**.

personable = of pleasing/pleasant appearance; **personal** = private; **personnel** = staff (strictly a singular word, but often now used as a plural). E.g.:

"The new office boy is a very personable young man."
"Managers should not make personal remarks about staff."
"The new office boy increased the number of personnel to 18."

personal names can enter the language and become words in their own right (known as eponyms). When used as scientific units (particularly common in physics) they have no initial capital letter and form plurals as if they were ordinary English words. The many examples acknowledge the scientist's contributions:

ampere (amp)	André-Marie *Ampère*
angstrom	Anders *Angström*
baud	Jean-Maurice *Baud*ot
becquerel	Antonie-Henri *Becquerel*
bel	Alexander Graham *Bell*
biot	Jean-Baptiste *Biot*
coulomb	Charles de *Coulomb*
curie	Marie *Curie*
debye unit	Peter *Debye*
farad	Michael *Farad*ay
gauss (pl. gauss)	Karl *Gauss*
gilbert	William *Gilbert*
henry (pl. henries)	Joseph *Henry*
hertz (pl. hertz)	Heinrich *Hertz*
joule	James *Joule*
kelvin	Lord *Kelvin*, William Thomson
lambert	Johann *Lambert*
maxwell	James Clerk *Maxwell*
mho	Georg *Ohm*, backwards
newton	Isaac *Newton*
oersted	Hans Christian *Oersted*
ohm	Georg *Ohm*
pascal	Blaise *Pascal*
poise	J.M. *Poise*uille
röntgen	Konrad *Röntgen*
sabin	Wallace *Sabine*
siemens (pl. siemens)	William *Siemens*
stokes (pl. stokes)	George *Stokes*
svedberg	Theodor *Svedberg*
tesla	Nikola *Tesla*
torr	Evangelista *Torricelli*
volt	Alessandro *Volta*
watt	James *Watt*
weber	Wilhelm *Weber*

Personal names given to other things generally retain their initial capital letter until the word is totally assimilated into the language (e.g. cardigan, wellingtons). *See also* **Christian names; eponym; named effects and laws; trade names.**

personal pronouns *See* **pronoun.**

persona non grata (italics) = an unacceptable person (originally in a diplomatic function). The Latin term should be avoided in ordinary writing, as should the rarer *persona grata* (= an acceptable person).

personnel is a plural noun (e.g. "the personnel are very skilled").

perspective = method (in drawing, painting, etc.) of representing three-dimensional objects in two dimensions, or (figuratively) viewpoint; **prospective** = likely to be or come about. E.g.:

"The painting was child-like in its simplicity, and lacked any shading or perspective."
"I would like you to meet our prospective Conservative candidate."

perspicuous describes an explanation that exhibits *perspicuity*, and so is clear, easy to understand, even obvious; **perspicacious** describes someone who exhibits *perspicacity*, or clear-sightedness. E.g.:

"I was able to follow the complex argument because of the perspicuous nature of its presentation."
"I was able to follow the complex argument because of the perspicacious nature of its presenter."
Perspicuous should not be confused with *conspicuous*.

persuade, persuadable, persuasible, persuasive, persuasion.
Persuadable/persuasible both = open to persuasion; **persuasive** = able to persuade (someone else). E.g.:

"The customer proved to be persuasible and finally agreed to the salesman's changes."
"The salesman was persuasive and obtained the customer's agreement to the terms of sale."

Peru The derived adjective and noun is *Peruvian*.

peruse = read thoroughly (not to read carelessly or incompletely); **pursue** (not *persue*) = chase, follow. *See also* **scan.**

perverse = obstinate, deliberately unreasonable or inappropriate;
perverted = corrupted, turned wrong or evil; **pervert** = somebody
who is perverted. E.g.:

"Her perverse attitude makes her disagree with everybody just to be
awkward."

"Only somebody who is perverted could have tortured his victim in
such a way."

"Only a pervert could have committed such a crime."

petal, petalled.

petit (French for *small*) occurs in some English expressions; e.g. petit
four (small biscuit), petit mal (type of epilepsy), petit pain (bread),
petit point (embroidery), petits pois (peas). Care should be taken with
plurals (e.g. petits fours).

petrol is preferred in English text to the American *gasoline* (preferred
to gasolene), known colloquially as *gas*. **Petroleum** is the mineral, and
includes crude oil and natural gas. **Petrel** is a sea-bird. *See also*
kerosene.

pH (lower case *p*, capital *H*) is used in chemistry to express the acidity
(or alkalinity) of a solution. (It is the negative logarithm of the
hydrogen ion concentration.) A pH of 7 is neutral; a pH of less than 7
is acidic; a pH of more than 7 is alkaline.

phalanx = wedge-shaped formation of troops (pl. phalanxes), or a
bone in a finger or toe (pl. phalanges).

phantasy The preferred spelling is **fantasy** (which *see*).

pharmacopoeia, pharmacopoeial.

pharynx (pl. pharynges).

phenomenon (pl. phenomena, often misused as a singular) gives the
adjective *phenomenal*, which means to do with a phenomenon or
apprehension by the senses. The use of the word to mean *remarkable*
is therefore strictly incorrect and certainly overdone (as in "Her
contribution made a phenomenal difference to the week's output").

phial is the preferred spelling (not *vial*).

Philippines (with one *l* and three *p*s). The derived adjective and noun is *Filipino*.

philtre *See* **filter.**

phlegm, phlegmatic (the *g* is silent in the first word but pronounced in the second).

phobia (pl. phobias) = mental disorder (classified as a neurosis) involving morbid fear (of something); the adjective is **phobic**. The many examples range from *acrophobia* (= fear of heights) to *xenophobia* (= fear of strangers). None of the words should be used for mere *dislike* (as in "He has a phobia about going out in the rain").

phone (not *'phone*) should be avoided as an abbreviation of telephone in formal writing.

phoney (if it must be used) is the preferred spelling of **phony.**

photo (pl. photos) should be avoided as an abbreviation of photograph in formal writing.

-phth- This element is often misspelled in such words as diphtheria, diphthong, ophthalmia, naphthalene, phthisis, etc. (especially if mispronounced "diptheria", etc.).

phylum (pl. phyla).

physic = archaic term for medicine; **physics** = science that deals with the properties of matter and energy; **physique** = bodily type.

physician = doctor; **physicist** = somebody who studies or practises physics. *See also* **doctor.**

piano (pl. pianos).

picaresque = to do with a **picaroon** (= vagabond, someone who lives by his wits). The latter word is obsolete, and the former should (very strictly) be reserved to describe episodic seventeenth-century fiction (novels) that featured rogues (picaros). The words are included because of possible confusion with **picturesque** (= quaint, picture-like); their only common feature is their foreign origin.

piccolo (pl. piccolos).

picket, picketer, picketed, picketing. *See also* **pique**.

picnic, picnicked, picnicking, picnicker.

pico- is the metric prefix for a million-millionth ($\times 10^{-12}$), as in *picofarad* (*see* **units**).

pidgin = type of language (formed of two others); **pigeon** = bird.

piebald = black and white; **skewbald** = brown (or another colour, but not black) and white.

pièce de résistance (italics, grave and acute accents, pl. *pièces de résistance*) = the best item; the French form should be avoided.

pier *See* **peer**.

pigeon *See* **pidgin**.

pigmy The preferred spelling is **pygmy**.

pikelet *See* **crumpet**.

pilaster (with one *l*) = flat buttress on a wall; **pillar** = free-standing support, column.

pilau (rice) is the preferred spelling, not *pillau, pilaw, pilaf* or *pilaff*.

pilot, piloted, piloting.

pimento (pl. pimentos).

pincushion, pin-head, pin-hole, pin-money, pin-point, pinprick, pinstripe, pin-table, pintail (duck), pin-up (noun), pin-wheel.

pincers = tool for gripping nail-heads, etc.; **pinchers** = people who pinch; **pinschers** = kinds of dog. *Pincers* is a plural word; "a pair of pincers" achieves a singular construction.

Pinyin is an official method of transcribing Chinese characters to represent their sounds to Westerners (e.g. *Beijing* is the Pinyin form of *Peking*, *Mao Zedong* is Pinyin for *Mao Tse-tung*).

pique = resentment (noun), to annoy (verb) – piqued, piquing; **piqué** = thick cotton fabric; **piquet** = card-game; **picket** = pointed stave, guard.

pirouette, pirouetted, pirouetting.

pistachio (pl. pistachios).

pistil = part of a flower; **pistol** = handgun; **pistole** = old Spanish coin.

pity, pitied, pitying, piteous, pitiable, pitiful. **Piteous** = stimulating pity; **pitiable** = deserving pity, contemptible; **pitiful** = feeling pity, despicable. The words, of similar meaning, tend to be used in a pejorative way, as in the second and third examples that follow. E.g.:

"He commented on the piteous state of the old beggar."
"She laughed at my pitiable attempts to draw a face."
"Pressure of work is a pitiful excuse for lateness of delivery."

pivot, pivotal, pivoted, pivoting. *See also* **vogue words**.

pixie (= fairy) is the preferred spelling (not *pixy*).

pizza *See* **flan**.

pl. is the abbreviation of plural.

placable = easy to appease or pacify, mild; **placeable** = can be placed or positioned; **placatory** = conciliatory (of actions or things, not people).

placebo (pl. placebos).

placid (= calm) may explain why **flaccid** (= limp) attracts the misspelling *flacid* and mispronunciation "flassid" (instead of "flaksid").

plague, plagued, plaguing, plaguy (preferred to *plaguey*), plaguily, plaguesome.

plaid = woollen (often tartan) cloth; **plait** = braided strands (of hair, rope or straw).

plain *See* **plane**.

plaintiff = person who brings a legal action (against the *defendant*); **plaintive** = mournful, sad-sounding. Both derive from the archaic word **plaint** = a lamentation, complaint.

planchet = blank metal disc from which a coin is struck; **planchette** = pencil on wheels used at séances.

plane = a flat surface (and a carpenter's tool, a tree); **plain** = a flat area of land (and unattractive, uncomplicated). **Plane** is also an accepted short form of *aeroplane* (which *see*).

planetarium (pl. planetariums).

plantain = low-growing weed, or tropical "tree" that bears banana-like fruit (two different plants with the same name).

plastic = synthetic polymer that can be cast or moulded; the former use of *plastics* as an adjectival form (e.g. "a plastics container"), to distinguish it from the older adjective *plastic* = mouldable, should be avoided (e.g. "plastic bag", "plastic doll", "plastic flowers", "plastic tubing" are current usage − a fact possibly unwelcome by a plastic surgeon). Note also the adjective *plasticky*.

plate, platy (= plate-like, formally *laminar*).

plateau (pl. plateaux).

plateful (pl. platefuls).

platypus (pl. platypuses).

plausible (not -*able*).

play-acting, play-actor, playback (noun), playbill, playgoer, playground, playhouse, playmate, play-off (noun), play-pen, plaything, playtime, playwright.

plead has the preferred past tense and participle **pleaded** (not *pled*).

pleasant (= giving pleasure), pleasurable (= able to give pleasure), pleasantness (= quality of being pleasant), pleasantry (= remark that causes pleasure).

plebeian (note -*ei*- spelling).

plectrum (pl. plectra).

plenty, plentiful, plenteous (= plentiful), plenitude (not *plentitude*, − plenty).

pleonasm = use of more words than necessary, and should be avoided (except for effect). *See also* **tautology**.

plexus (pl. plexuses).

pliers (= tool for gripping) is a singular word; "a pair of pliers" achieves a singular construction. *See also* **pincers**.

plimsoll is the preferred spelling of **plimsole** (= a light, canvas shoe); **Plimsoll line** = marking on a ship's hull near the waterline, which indicates the freeboard (maximum permitted loading) allowed.

plum, plummy (= like or having plums).

plumb, plumbic (= like lead). In *plumb, plumber, plumbing* and *plumb-line* the *b* is silent; it is pronounced in *plumbago, plumbic, plumbism* and most other words derived from the Latin word for lead.

plunge, plunging.

plurals Words taken from foreign languages, particularly French, Greek and Latin, generally take the "foreign" plural.

Examples:		
	amanuensis	amanuenses
	bureau	bureaux
	codex	codices
	corpus	corpora
	genus	genera
	graffito	graffiti
	meninx	meninges
	mitochondrion	mitochondria
	omentum	omenta
	phenomenon	phenomena
	plateau	plateaux
	polypus	polypi
	protozoon	protozoa
	radius	radii
	sarcoma	sarcomata
	septum	septa
	spermatozoon	spermatozoa
	stoma	stomata
	stratum	strata

Increasingly, however, some such words are taking an "English" plural:

alibi	alibis
aquarium	aquariums (not aquaria)
cornea	corneas (not corneae)
medium	mediums (but media used in "the news media")
pharynx	pharynxes (not pharynges)
referendum	referendums (not referenda)
ultimatum	ultimatums (not ultimata)

Note also:

mongoose	mongooses (mongeese is incorrect)
octopus	octopuses (octopi is incorrect)
platypus	platypuses

Two forms of plurals are sometimes retained for different usages (the more "scientific" usage usually retains the classic plural):

antenna	antennas (radio)
	antennae (zoology)
appendix	appendixes (of books)
	appendices (of intestines)
genius	geniuses (clever people)
	genii (spirits)
index	indexes (of books)
	indices (powers or exponents in maths)
lemma	lemmas (themes)
	lemmata (seed husks)

Occasionally the adopted word is already (strictly) plural although used in a singular sense and an *s* is added to re-pluralize it:

fauna	faunas
flora	floras

The word *data* is also generally regarded as a singular word, particularly in computer terminology (e.g. "data is obtained"); it then has no plural.

Some words ending in -*s* are singular and do not have plurals. They include (mostly games or medical):

billiards	draughts	mumps	rackets (game)
bowls (games)	herpes	news	rickets
darts	innings	ninepins	shingles
dominoes (game)	measles	quoits	skittles

Country names ending in *-s* are also singular:

| Bahamas | Philippines | Wales |
| Netherlands | United States | West Indies |

Another group of words end in *-s* and are plural but have no singular (mostly "pairs" consisting of a single thing):

binoculars	jeans	pyjamas	spectacles
callipers	knickers	scissors	tights
compasses	pants	secateurs	tongs
forceps	pincers	shears	trousers
glasses	pliers	shorts	tweezers

Some words have the same form in both singular and plural (e.g. deer, sheep, and the names of various kinds of food fish such as cod, mackerel, plaice, and so on).

One should be careful to pluralize the correct element in compound words.

Examples:	aide-de-camp	aides-de-camp
	court martial	courts martial
	man-o'-war	men-o'-war
	mother-in-law	mothers-in-law
NOTE:	manservant	menservants (pluralize both elements)
	spoonful (etc.)	spoonfuls (not spoonsful)

Proper names are pluralized in the normal way by adding *s* or *es*.

Examples:	Toms, Dicks, and Harrys
	a collection of Herculeses
	the Joneses
	four Hail Marys
	there were two Beatrixes

NOTE: henrys (plural of henry, the unit of inductance)

Letters, numerals and abbreviations without full points form the plural by adding *s*.

Examples: There are eight *E*s in this sentence.
              There are two twos in 22.
              The early 1980s resembled the mid-1930s.
              Seven MPs included four VCs, but only two had
              A-levels.

NOTE: the plural of MS (manuscript) is MSS; that of St (saint)
              is SS.

Abbreviations with full points should be pluralized by adding *'s*.

Examples: He engaged two Q.C.'s.
              All applicants' c.v.'s were considered.

NOTE the following exceptions:
                   p. pp. (pages)
                   f. ff. (folios)
                   v. vv. (verses)
                   w. ww. (words)
                   sp. spp. (species)

Abbreviations and contractions of units and measurements should *not* be pluralized.

Examples:

1 in	3 in	1 ft	4 ft
1 ml	18 ml	1 cwt	7 cwt
1 sec	30 sec	1 hr	24 hr

See also **abbreviations; contractions**.

Of the 134 words ending in *o* in the following list, 96 form the plural by adding *s*, 29 take *es* to form the plural, and others form a plural ending in *i* — so there is no obvious general rule.

adagio	adagios	bravado	bravados
albino	albinos	bravo	bravos
alto	altos	bronco	broncos
archipelago	archipelagos	buffalo	buffaloes
armadillo	armadillos	calico	calicos
arpeggio	arpeggios	cameo	cameos
bamboo	bamboos	canto	cantos
banjo	banjos	cargo	cargoes
bolero	boleros	casino	casinos

cello	cellos	imago	imagines
cockatoo	cockatoos	imbroglio	imbroglios
comedo	comedoes	impresario	impresarios
commando	commandos	incognito	incognitos
concerto	concertos	innuendo	innuendos
contralto	conraltos	intaglio	intaglios
credo	credos	Jingo	Jingoes
crescendo	crescendos	kilo	kilos
curio	curios	lasso	lassos
dado	dados	lazaretto	lazarettos
dago	dagoes	libido	libidos
desperado	desperadoes	libretto	librettos
dingo	dingoes	lido	lidos
dodo	dodos	limbo	limbos
domino	dominoes	literato	literarti
dynamo	dynamos	llano	llanos
echo	echoes	maestro	maestros
embargo	embargoes	magneto	magnetoes
embryo	embryos	mango	mangoes
Eskimo	Eskimos	manifesto	manifestos
falsetto	falsettos	matzo	matzoth
farrago	farragoes	memento	mementos
fiasco	fiascos	merino	merinos
flamenco	flamencoes	mestizo	mestizos
flamingo	flamingoes	mosquito	mosquitoes
folio	folios	motto	mottoes
fresco	frescoes	mulatto	mulattos
gabbro	gabbros	negrillo	negrilloes
gaucho	gauchos	negrito	negritoes
gecko	geckos	negro	negroes
ghetto	ghettos	no	noes
gigolo	gigolos	nuncio	nuncios
graffito	graffiti	oratorio	oratorios
grotto	grottoes	ovolo	ovoli
halo	haloes	patio	patios
hero	heroes	peccadillo	peccadillos
hidalgo	hidalgos	photo	photos
igloo	igloos	piano	pianos

piccolo	piccolos	solo	solos
pimento	pimentos	soprano	sopranos
pistachio	pistachios	stiletto	stilettos
placebo	placebos	studio	studios
poncho	ponchos	taboo	taboos
portfolio	portfolios	tango	tangos
portico	porticos	tattoo	tattoos
potato	potatoes	tiro	tiros
potto	pottos	tobacco	tobaccos
proviso	provisos	tomato	tomatoes
quarto	quartos	tornado	tornadoes
radio	radios	torpedo	torpedoes
ratio	ratios	torso	torsos
salvo	salvos	trio	trios
scenario	scenarios	two	twos
scherzo	scherzi	veto	vetoes
seraglio	seraglios	virago	viragoes
shako	shakos	virtuoso	virtuosi
shampoo	shampoos	volcano	volcanoes
silo	silos	zero	zeros

Plurals of words ending in *f* also defy logic, although sometimes the form of the plural distinguishes a noun from a verb. The following are the preferred forms:

belief	beliefs (*believes* being a verb form)
brief	briefs
calf	calves
chief	chiefs
delf	delfs (*delves* being a verb form)
dwarf	dwarfs
elf	elves
gulf	gulfs
half	halves
handkerchief	handkerchiefs
hoof	hoofs
leaf	leaves
loaf	loaves (verb form is *loafs* = idles)
oaf	oafs

proof	proofs (*proves* being a verb form)
relief	reliefs (*relieves* being a verb form)
roof	roofs
scarf	scarves (verb from is *scarfs* = joins)
self	selves
serf	serfs
sheaf	sheaves
shelf	shelves
spoof	spoofs
thief	thieves
turf	turfs
wharf	wharfs
wolf	wolves
woof	woofs

Other unusual plurals are knife/knives, still life/still lifes (painting) and wife/wives.

NOTE: fez and quiz double the *z* in the plural (fezzes, quizzes).

plus should be reserved for actual or implied mathematical expressions, and not used merely as a synonym for *and*. E.g.:
"The cost is £7,200 plus interest at 32 per cent" is correct (if expensive);
"The cost includes the car plus all accessories" is incorrect.

pneumatic refers to air or air pressure (e.g. pneumatic drill);
pneumonic refers to the lungs (e.g. pneumonia); **mnemonic** is a memory aid (e.g. "Run off you girls, boys in view" is a mnemonic for the letters ROYGBIV, the initial letters of the colours of the rainbow — see also **acronym**).

pocket, pocketed, pocketing.

podium (pl. podia).

poetess Most women who write poetry prefer to be called a *poet*. See also **gender**.

points of the compass *See* **compass directions**.

poison = substance that injures the health of a living organism (or, by extension, injures anything else, such as the mind or an industrial catalyst); **toxin** = poison released (in the body) by a micro-organism such as a bacterium; **venom** = poison secreted by an animal. The corresponding adjectives are *poisonous, toxic* and *venomous*; the first two are synonyms in general use, the last is often employed figuratively. **Antitoxin** and **antivenin** are medical terms for antidotes to specific kinds of poisoning.

poky = confined, cramped (not *pokey*).

pole, polarize, polarization.

police car, police constable, police-court, police-dog, police inspector, policeman, police officer, police sergeant, police state, police station, policewoman.

policy = general course of action or conduct, or an insurance contract; **polity** = form of government, the State.

poliomyelitis is the preferred term for the virus disease (not *infantile paralysis*).

politburo (not *-bureau*).

politic = prudent, judicious, cunning, crafty, expedient; **political** = pertaining to politics. E.g.:
"His comment about company security was a politic criticism of the management."
"The councillor's comment about national security was a political, rather than personal, response."
The corresponding adverbs are *politicly* and *politically*.

poltergeist (note *-ei-* spelling).

polypus has the preferred plural polypuses (not *polypi*), although the simpler word **polyp** (pl. polyps) is now more common.

Polythene is a trade-name for the plastic polyethylene.

pomander *See* **pot-pourri**.

pommel = a knob on a sword-hilt or saddle; **pummel** = to hit repeatedly.

pom-pom = rapid-firing, self-loading (anti-aircraft) gun; **pompon** = spherical tuft or flower so shaped (as are some types of dahlias).

poncho (pl. ponchos).

pony *See* **horse**.

popular, popularity, popularize.

popular names (of plants and animals) *See* **Latin classification**.

pore (verb) = study closely, gaze attentively at (usually with *over*);
pour = make or allow liquid to flow in a stream (usually with *out* or
away), rain heavily. E.g.:

"The student pored over her books all evening."
"Please pour out some more wine."
"I would pour that home-made wine down the sink."

portentous = ominous, foreboding an unusually calamitous event;

pretentious = florid, showy, pompous.

portfolio (pl. portfolios).

portico (pl. porticos).

portion *See* **part; proportion; quota**.

portmanteau (pl. portmanteaus, not *portmanteaux*).

portrait format *See* **format**.

Portugal The derived adjective and noun is *Portuguese* (with two *u*s).

Portuguese words − themselves often based on Latin − have
contributed to English, sometimes from former Portuguese colonies in
Africa and Asia. They include:

albatross	cobra	marmalade	port (wine)
albino	dodo	pagoda	tank
caste	mandarin	palaver	

See also **Spanish words**.

position (noun) = location, precise place; **position** (verb) = to place,
to locate precisely (but this use should be avoided). As a vogue word
(which *see*), *position* passes for *circumstance* or the equivalent vogue
word *situation* (e.g. "If I were in your position" = "If I were you").

positive should not be used as an emphatic synonym of *sure* or *certain*;
it should be reserved for contexts in which it contrasts with *negative*

(which need only be implied). E.g. in "Are you positive she said she would come?" substitute *certain* for *positive*. "His positive approach to the project encouraged the others" is correct usage (although *positive approach to* is probably better put as *enthusiasm for*).

positively = in a positive (as opposed to negative) manner; it should not be used as an intensifier. E.g. in "The talk was positively boring" delete *positively* (or substitute *extremely* or *very*). "He reacted positively and granted my request" is correct, if slightly tautological, usage.

possess, possessor (not *-er*), possession (all with four ss). **Possessed** *of* = have; **possessed** *by* = in the grip of. E.g.:
"She is possessed of an analytical mind."
"He is possessed by extreme jealousy."

possessive pronouns See **pronoun**.

possessives See **gerund; punctuation** (apostrophe).

possible and **probable** (like *possibly* and *probably*) should not be confused, but sometimes are. **Possible** = capable of existence or occurrence; **probable** = likely to occur. Thus, theoretically, nearly all things are possible, but perhaps only a few are probable. Similarly, it is often argued that nothing is impossible, but even the most optimistic have to agree that some things are highly improbable.

possibility that...may/might is a tautological construction, as in "There is a possibility that the train may be late". Correct versions include "... a possibility that the train will be late" and the simpler "The train may be late". *Might* would be wrong in all the examples.

possum is colloquial (in Britain and the United States) for **opossum**, which should be used.

post-bag, post-box, postcard, post-classical, post code, post-date(d), post-free, postgraduate, post-haste, posthorn, posthouse, Post-Impressionist, postman, postmark, postmaster, postmistress, post mortem (pl. post mortems), postnatal, post office, post-paid, postscript, post-war, postwoman. When the prefix *post-* means after or behind, there is generally a hyphen (except in post mortem, postscript).

poste restante = accommodation address, a place where letters are left until called for; *accommodation address* should be used.

posterior is a euphemism for **backside, behind** or **buttocks**, any of which is preferred; **derrière** is twee and colloquial, **bum** is vulgar and slang.

posthumous (note spelling).

postiche *See* **pastiche**.

postscript, an afterthought added below the signature of a letter, is preceded by the abbreviation PS (*post scriptum*). Further postscripts are denoted by PPS, PPPS, and so on.

potato (pl. potatoes).

poteen is the preferred spelling for the illicit Irish whiskey (not *potheen*).

potent = powerful, strongly influential; **potential** = latent, possible but not necessarily real.

pot-pourri = mixture, medley; the French term should be avoided. A pot-pourri of herbs or petals is known as a **pomander**.

potto (pl. pottos).

pouf (= a soft, stuffed ottoman or footstool) is the preferred spelling (not *pouff, pouffe* or *pouffé*).

pour *See* **pore**.

practicable = able to be done/achieved (in practice); **practical** = concerned with or adapted to actual practice, efficient (in action), practised. E.g.:
"The use of half-sized photocopies was not practicable (= was impracticable) because our machine's maximum reduction is only 60 per cent."
"The use of photocopies instead of bromides was a practical way of reducing costs."
Practical should not be misused for *virtual*. E.g.:
"Obtaining consistently good photocopies from our machine is a practical impossibility" (*practical* should be *virtual*). Similarly,

practically should not be misused for *virtually* or *nearly* or *almost*; as A.P. Herbert says *practically* often means *not practically* (e.g. you cannot get somewhere "practically on time" or be "practically awake" or "practically first in a queue").

practical/practically *See* previous entry.

practice is the noun; **practise** is the verb (although Americans economize and have only *practice* for both).

pray = to address (a prayer) to a deity; **prey** = an animal that is hunted (by a predator). The "target" of a human hunter is usually called the **quarry**. *See also* **predate**.

pre-, as a prefix meaning *before*, usually takes a hyphen only before elements beginning with *e* or another vowel (e.g. pre-arrange, pre-election, pre-engage(ment), pre-establish, pre-exist(ence), pre-ignition, pre-ordain). Exceptions include pre-Cambrian, pre-cancerous, pre-Christian, pre-cook, pre-date, pre-glacial, pre-heat, pre-med(ication), pre-menstrual, pre-Raphaelite, pre-select(or), pre-shrink, pre-stress(ed), pre-tax, pre-war. **Pre-** is usually superfluous in such compounds as precondition, preplanned, prerequisite, in which the idea of "beforeness" is carried in the main part of the word (most conditions, plans and requisites have to be considered before the event). Thus a "necessary precondition" is merely a *condition*, "detailed preplanning" is merely *planning* and an "essential prerequisite" is usually only a *requisite*. **Prerequisite**, if it must be used, should not be confused with **perquisite** (often shortened to *perk*) = extra payment, more often in kind than in cash, for a task.

precede = go before (in time or place); **proceed** – go forward, go on (with). The related nouns are *precedence* (which see), *procedure* (= method of going forward) and *progress* (going forward).

precedence = superiority (in order); **precedent** = previous example that establishes a ruling; e.g. "Giving precedence to the Managing Editor (on his birthday) should not establish a precedent."

precentor = cathedral musician-in-chief; **preceptor** = teacher.

pre-Christian, pre-Classical, pre-Columbian, etc.

precipitous(ly) = very steep(ly); **precipitate(ly)** = very hurried(ly). As Eric Partridge says, the only way of leaving a room precipitously is to jump out of the window.

precondition See **pre-**.

précis (acute accent), a textual abstract, can be used as a verb; if they must be so used, the past tense and participle is *précised* ("pray-seed") and the present participle is **précising** ("pray-seeing").

predate = to date before the actual writing, to antedate. As a verb meaning to prey upon (as a back-formation from predator) the word has not found favour, and should be avoided. Acceptable derived words include *predatory* (preferred to predaceous, predacious or predative) and *predation* (preferred to predacity).

predicate (verb) = to affirm, assert; it forms **predicable, predication**. Predict = foretell; it forms *predictable, prediction.*

predilection (not *predilection*) seldom means more than **preference** (not *prefrence*), and should be avoided.

predominant See **dominating**.

preface = an introduction to a book, about the book, written by the author(s) or general editor; **foreword** = an introductory piece written by someone other than the author (indeed it may be about the author and not about the book itself). In a book containing both a preface and a foreword, the former usually precedes the latter; both should follow the **contents** (if any).

prefer, preferred, preferring, preferable, preference. The first four forms take *to*; *preference* takes *for*. **Preferable**, already comparative, should not be qualified by *more* or *most*.

prefix See **ante-; ex-; negative prefixes; non-; numerical prefixes; pre-**. See *also* **suffixes**.

prehensible = can be grasped; **prehensile** = can grasp.

prejudgement (note spelling).

prejudice, correctly pronounced, does not attract the misspelling *predudice*. **Prejudice** *against* or *in favour of* = bias; **prejudice** *to* = disadvantage, detriment.

premature *See* **immature**.

premier = first (in importance, order or time); **première** = first performance (of a film, play, etc.).

premise (verb) = to state first, to prefix; **premise** (noun) = a proposition (something stated first for later discussion); **premises** = buildings (it has no singular); **premiss** = premise (noun).

premium (pl. premiums).

preoccupy and **preoccupation** take *with* (not *by*).

preplan *See* **pre-**.

preposition = word that links a noun or pronoun to another part of the sentence; **proposal** = an offer (of marriage); **proposition** = terms of an enterprise (business proposition), something propounded, a promise.
Pedants abhor a preposition at the end of a sentence; to paraphrase Winston Churchill, it is something up with which they will not put. The absurdity of this last clause is proof that avoidance of prepositional sentence-endings usually requires a complete recasting of the sentence; alternatively, let them stand − what is wrong with "it is something they will not put up with?" Most of the enlightened authorities now allow this construction. Prepositions and adverbs connected phrasally with verbs are usually called phrasal verbs; in this way *go* can be modified into *go away, go down, go in, go into, go off* and *go up*, all of which convey meanings different from plain *go*.

prerequisite *See* **pre-**.

pre-school child *See* **baby**.

prescribe = appoint, order, advise; **proscribe** = ban, prohibit, condemn.

present-day is overworked for *present* or *contemporary* (or *today's*).

presently = soon (e.g. "She will be here presently"). The word is also often used to mean *at present* (e.g. "She is presently in the other room"), which purists continue to resist.

preserve *See* **reserve**.

press agent, press-button (but push-button preferred), press conference, press-cutting, press-fastener, press gang (noun), press-gang (verb), pressman, press-stud, presswork.

pressure, pressurize (= raise to high pressure), pressurized (= under additional/high pressure). Thus the contents of an aerosol can be pressurized, although the word should not be extended figuratively to people (who may, however, be pressed, pressured or under pressure).

prestigious (not prestigous) = having prestige, esteemed, or high standing; **prodigious** (not prodigous) = unusually large, monstrous. An author's task in compiling a reference book can be prodigious; after publication, he or she may hope that the book becomes prestigious.

presume, presumable, presumptive, presumption, presumptuous. For **presumably**, *see* **supposedly**. *See also* **assume**.

presumptuous is usually spelled correctly by people who do not mispronounce it *presumtious*.

pretend, pretence, pretension, pretentious, pretentiousness. **Pretence** = the act of pretending; **pretension(s)** = claim, aspiration, pretext; **pretentiousness** = claiming (too) much. Note that the spelling *pretention* does not exist. E.g.:
"She made a pretence of leaving the house so that she could creep back and eavesdrop on their conversation."
"His superior attitude was based on pretensions to noble birth."

pretension *See* **pretend**.

prevaricate = evade, mislead; **procrastinate** = postpone, put off. E.g.:
"When asked a direct question he prevaricated and turned the conversation to the weather."
"When asked to mow the lawn he procrastinated and said he would do it at the weekend."

prevent, preventive (preferred to preventative). **Prevent** someone *from* doing something, or prevent someone's doing something are the correct forms. E.g.:

"She prevented him from going" is correct;
"She prevented him going" is incorrect;
"She prevented his going" is correct.

previous to should not be used as a preposition; e.g. Previous to the new typist's coming..." should be "Before the new typist came...". *See also* **prior**.

pre-war (with hyphen).

price, pricey.

priceless *See* **valuable**.

prima facie (italics) = at first sight; except in legal contexts, the Latin form should be avoided.

primeval is the preferred spelling (not *primaeval*).

primitive People should not be described as primitive, which is regarded as derogatory in this context.

principal = main, chief; **principle** = an origin, source, theoretical basis. Reminder: *Principal — Head* or *chief* (of a college).

prior as an adjective is correct (as in "a prior arrangement"), but **prior to** as a preposition is not ("prior to receiving your letter" should be "before receiving...").

prise = to force apart/open; **prize** = a reward (in a competition).

pristine = old and unspoiled, persisting and untouched. It should not be used to mean merely *fresh* or *new*.

privilege (note spelling).

probable *See* **possible**; **probe**.

probe, probeable (with an *e*, to prevent confusion with *probable*).

proboscis (pl. proboscises).

proceed, procedure, procedural, proceeding(s) (noun), proceeds (noun). **Proceed** = go forward, continue; **progress** (verb) = go forward, make something carry on; **process** (verb) = prosecute, put something through a prescribed procedure or process. E.g.:

"The guard signalled the driver to proceed."
"The manager must progress the job at each stage."
"The clerk processes the forms as they come in."

proceed should not be used as a pompous synonym for *go, walk, drive* etc. or to add weight to a simple statement, devices sometimes (at least in popular fiction) part of a policeman's vocabulary. E.g.:

"As I was proceeding down the High Street, I apprehended the accused."
"When I apprehended the accused, he proceeded to run away."
See also **precede**.

process, processor.

procrastinate *See* **prevaricate**.

procure = to win, gain, obtain by effort of contrivance (obtain for immoral purposes); **secure** = to make safe, obtain for certain. Both are stronger forms of the neutral *obtain* and the slovenly *get*.

prodigious *See* **prestigious**.

prodigy = very talented (young) person; **progeny** = children, offspring; **protégé** = protected (young) person. E.g.:

"Mozart was a child prodigy and gave public performances when he was only six years old."
"During the breeding season, most birds spend the daylight hours collecting food for their progeny."
"Smith was a protégé of Lord Millford, who paid for all his schooling."

produce, producer, producible; **product,** productive, productivity (preferred to productiveness).

Prof. is the abbreviation of Professor, when used as a title, but should be avoided in narrative text.

profess, professor (abbreviation of the title is Prof.).

proffer, proffered, proffering (not *proferred, proferring*).

proficient *See* **efficient**.

profit, profited, profiting.

profuse = excessively liberal, extravagant, lavish; **prolific** = abundant, fertile, fruitful. E.g:

"The winner embarrassed the adjudicators with her profuse thanks."
"Judging by the amount of apple blossom on the trees this year, we shall have a prolific crop of fruit."

progeny *See* **prodigy.**

prognosis (pl. prognoses). *See* **diagnosis.**

programme (but computer program), programmer, programmed, programming.

progress *See* **proceed**.

project (noun and verb), projector.

proliferate = to increase rapidly (and greatly), not merely to increase.

prolific should describe the creator, not the creation. E.g.:

"She was prolific in her output of articles" (correct);
"Her output of articles was prolific" (incorrect).
See also **profuse.**

proletariat (note spelling).

promise, promissory.

promote, promoter.

prone = lying face downwards; **prostrate** = lying face downwards (in a faint); **recumbent** = lying down; **supine** = lying face upwards.
Prone (to), in the sense having a proclivity or tendency (to), is becoming overworked and is often misused for *susceptible* (to) e.g.
"People of the district are prone to sleeping sickness" is incorrect (even though they probably do finish up face downwards!), although
"... are prone to contracting sleeping sickness" is just about acceptable.

pronoun is a word that stands for a noun, and there are various kinds. Most *personal pronouns* have two forms, nominative (when they are the subject of a sentence) or accusative (when they are the object):

I	me
you	you
he, she, it	him, her, it
we	us
they	them

(*you* and *it* do not change).
Possessive pronouns include:

my	mine
your	yours
his, her,	
its	his, hers, its
our	ours
their	theirs
one's	

(*his* and *its* do not change).
The addition of *-self* forms *reflexive pronouns*:

myself
yourself
himself, herself, itself
oneself
ourselves
yourselves
themselves

Others include *interrogative pronouns* (who?, whom?, whose?, which?, what?), *relative pronouns* (who, whom, whose, which, that) and their extensions (whoever, whomever, whichever, whatever), and *demonstrative pronouns* (this, that, these, those).
See also **which** and **that**; **who, whom, whose** and **who's**.

pronounce, pronouncing, pronounceable, pronouncement, pronunciation.

proof (verb) has the past participle **proofed**. *See also* **prove**.

propaganda is singular (and has no plural).

propel, propelled, propeller, propelling. **Propellant** is the noun (= something that propels); **propellent** is the adjective (= relating to that which propels). E.g.:

"Nitrogen is used as a propellent gas in some aerosols; others have fluons as propellants."

proper names *See* **capitalization**.

prophecy is the noun; **prophesy** is the verb.

proportion = a stated relation (in terms of magnitude) between one thing and another, ratio, due relation; e.g. "He mixed tonic with gin in the proportion of three to one." It should not be misused for *portion, part* or *number*; e.g. "The greater proportion of children have bad handwriting" is incorrect, at least in the use of *proportion* – it should be written "Most (= a large number of) children have...". A *proportion* of usually means merely *some*.

proposal *See* **preposition**.

proposition *See* **preposition**.

proprietary (not proprietory) = of a proprietor or property, patented, trade-marked; **proprietry** does not exist; **propriety** = decency, rightness, conformity with convention (opposite *impropriety*).

pro rata = in proportion; the Latin form should be avoided.

proscribe *See* **prescribe**.

prosecute *See* **persecute**.

prospect, prospector.

prospectus (pl. prospectuses).

prostate = gland surrounding the urethra in men; **prostrate** = lying face downwards (*see also* **prone**).

prosthesis (pl. prostheses), prosthetic.

pro tem is an abbreviation of *pro tempore* (= temporarily); the Latin term should be avoided.

protagonist = a principal character (actor) in a story or incident. It does not mean *champion, advocate* or *supporter* of something; i.e. it is not the opposite of **antagonist** – it is from *protos* = first (fore-), not *pro* = in favour of (for).

protect, protector, protection.

protégé (pl. **protégés**) (two acute accents). *See also* **prodigy.**

protein (note *-ei-* spelling).

protest (verb) needs a preposition – which is *against*, not *at* – when it means to express disapproval; *protest* without a preposition means solemnly affirm (e.g. to protest one's innocence).

protozoon (pl. **protozoa**).

protract, protractor.

protrude *See* **intrude.**

prove (verb) has the past participle **proved**, although **proven** is often used in law. An adjectival form is also *proven*. E.g.:
"He proved his assertion."
"He was a proven friend."
Note also *provable* (with no *e*). *See also* **proof.**

provided that should introduce a stipulation (and in this use is preferred to **providing**); e.g. "I said I would write the article provided that he edited it." *Provided that* should not be used for *if*; e.g. "I will go away on Monday provided that it does not rain" should be "... if it does not rain".

provident = thrifty, frugal (providing for the future); **providential** = unexpectedly lucky (the result of divine providence). E.g.:
"Through the provident use of fuel, we were able to cook every day for a week."
"Through the providential discovery of the key, we were able to unlock the door."

proviso (pl. **provisos**) = stipulation; the Latin form should be avoided.

provocative *See* **evocative.**

prowess = daring, bravery (not merely *mastery* or *skill*).

prudent = displaying prudence, cautious, discreet; **prudential** = taking prudence into account. E.g.:

"Faced with the problem he took the prudent course, but later regretted not taking the riskier alternative."

"Prudential decisions are not always the best decisions."

pry = enquire, peer (into), be nosey; it does not mean **prise** (open).

psyche, psychic, pyschiatry, psychoanalysis, psychoanalyse, psychology, psychedelic (illogical, but preferred to *psychodelic*).

public, publicly (not *publically*).

publicize = to make an effort to get something widely known (often using a medium such as advertising); the result is **publicity**. **Publish** = to issue in printed form; the result is **publication**. Most publications benefit from publicity.

pudendum (pl. pudenda).

puerile, puerilely. *See also* **juvenile**.

pun is a (humorous) play on words, a device that depends for its effect on a double meaning (often involving homonyms, which *see*), such as the classic:

Q: "When is a door not a door?"
A: "When it's ajar."

Used very occasionally, puns can be effective in informal (and journalistic) writing; used to excess, they soon elicit groans. They should be avoided in formal text, and not even allowed to happen accidentally (e.g. "the swallow is a swift bird", "large noses ran in his family", "a lone idea about borrowing money"). *See also* **journalese**.

punctilious (with one *l*) = scrupulously observant of details; **punctual** = scrupulously observant of an appointment time; people who are the former are always the latter.

punctuation Authorities continue to argue about punctuation. Today common sense and readability (not, as in former times, read-out-ability) should be the guide. As a general rule, punctuation should be kept to a minimum.

1. *Full point* A full point (also called a full stop or period) marks the end of a sentence which has been defined as the complete expression of a thought. So this is a sentence. And so is this. And this.

A full point is also used to terminate an abbreviation, such as "etc.", "a.m.", "fig." (*see* **abbreviations**).

Do not put a full point after an exclamation mark or a question mark (which *see* later).

For decimal point, *see* **fractions**.

2. *Comma* Commas are for sense, not decoration.

Unless the clauses in a compound sentence are short and of similar form, a comma should be used before the conjunction, especially if there is a change of subject. E.g. "Most of the editors who work in reference book publishing are more than 80 years old, whereas most of the designers are under 20." The sentence "Editors work and designers play" needs no comma. Two or more adjectives which independently modify the same noun should be separated by commas: "a long, muddy river", "a small, round table", "a huge, hairy, green monster". If "and" could be substituted for the comma (and the sentence still make sense), then a comma should probably be used. But if the combination of the second adjective and the noun are modified (jointly) by the first adjective, no comma is necessary: "a long white dress", "a small red ball".

Parenthetic nouns and phrases should be enclosed between commas: "The chief editor, John Jones, refused to accept the article", or "*My Life in Publishing*, a best-seller for ten years, was John Jones' first book". Pairs of dashes or parentheses (brackets) can be used as an alternative to commas in this type of sentence. But no commas are required in such constructions as "The editor John Jones refused to accept...", or "The best-seller *My Life in Publishing* was John Jones' first book", in which the identifying noun is used in a restrictive sense. Clauses or phrases relating to a previously stated subject should be enclosed between commas: "The editor is admired, and even respected, by his colleagues".

Comma off items in a list, but not preceding "and" or "or": "Her favourite names were John, James and George", "She could not stand John, James or George". But if one or more items in a list contain "and", use a comma before the final "and": "The books included *The Animal World, Men and Machines*, and *Physics Today*". If one or more items in a list include a comma, use semicolons to separate the items: "The books included *Animals, Vertebrate and Invertebrate*; *Unicellular Organisms*; and *Man, Matter and Energy*".

Normal style for large numerals is to comma off in threes to the left of the (implied) decimal point: "2,300 people", "£1,473,000", "the conversion factor is 1,560.764", "12,125.8432" (note no commas after the decimal point). Modern scientific setting often employs a thin space instead of a comma in large numerals. Do not use a comma in dates, for which the style is "13 November 1937" (not 13th).

Use a comma after "that is" and "for example": "All three women were present – that is, Jane, June and Joan." "Many names begin with J: for example, Jane, June and Joan."

3. *Semicolon* A semicolon is a stronger stop than a comma, but not as strong as a full point. Preserve the relation between two related sentences by using a semicolon (but no conjunction): "Modern punctuation is complicated; modern grammar is non-existent." The inclusion of a conjunction would reduce the semicolon to a comma: "Modern punctuation is complicated, but modern grammar is non-existent." If the sentences are not related, a full point should be used: "Modern punctuation is complicated. Modern motor cars are expensive."

Use semicolons to separate items in a list when individual items contain commas or are lengthy (see previous examples under *Comma*).

4. *Colon* A colon is no longer used as a stop or pause in a sentence (for which the comma and semicolon serve). A colon should be used to introduce a list or an example:"He had three main interests: wine, women and song." To test if such a colon is correctly used, try replacing it with the word, "namely"; do not follow such a colon with a dash. A colon may also be used to emphasize the contrast yet relationship between two related sentences (as in the first use of a semicolon described previously).

5. *Parentheses* (brackets). Use parentheses to enclose a definition or equivalent, as in the heading to this paragraph. Use them also to enclose an abbreviation following the term(s) abbreviated: "The World Health Organization (WHO)", "The British Broadcasting Corporation (BBC)". Use parentheses to give equivalents in a second system of units: "The road was 80 km (50 miles) long". Use them also to enclose dates: "Jones, John (1912–1985), was a well-known editor." "During World War II (1939–1945), John Jones served in the army." "At the end of World War II (1945), John Jones returned to publishing."

Use parentheses round letters or numerals in lists and captions: "There are three types of material: (1) animal, (2) vegetable and (3) mineral."
"They can be specified in terms of (a) mineral content or (b) water content."
"The exterior view (A) shows the skin texture, whereas the cross-section (B) reveals the internal anatomy."
Apart from these technical uses, parentheses enclose an afterthought or an aside which is not crucial to a sentence (and can be omitted without altering the meaning), as in this sentence. Pairs of commas set off similar phrases or clauses, but set them off less completely. Pairs of dashes set them off more completely, if less formally. Compare:
"He rode the bicycle, a green one, as fast as he could."
"He rode the bicycle (it was a green one) as fast as he could."
"He rode the bicycle — which was bright green — as fast as he could."
(See also later examples under *Dashes*.)
Only parentheses can be used to set off a whole sentence: "He rode the bicycle as fast as he could. (It was a green bicycle with red handles.)"
See also **brackets**.

6. *Dashes* Use a dash before "that is":
"Many great apes are bipedal — that is, they can walk upright on their hind limbs."
Use a dash before a summarizing final clause:
"Wine, women and song — these were his main interests."
Use dashes to enclose an afterthought or aside which bears little relation to the rest of the sentence:
"He rode the bicycle — which was bright green — as fast as he could."
Use dashes also around parenthetic expressions which would normally be set off with commas but which themselves contain commas:
"He rode the bicycle — an ancient, rusty, green one — as fast as he could."
(See also previous examples under *Parentheses*.)

7. *Quotation marks* Double or single quotation marks may be used; editors should find and follow the publisher's style. If no guidance is given, use double quotation marks (") and use single quotes (') for quotations within quotations:

He declared: "I have to agree with Henry Ford, 'History is bunk'".
Any punctuation marks belonging to the quoted text should be
enclosed within the quotation marks; punctuation marks belonging to
the sentence as a whole are kept outside. Interpolations in quotations
should be set in brackets (i.e. square brackets, not parentheses):
He said:"The man [John Jones] is a scoundrel."
Omissions in quotations should be indicated by ellipses (...):
He said: "The man is a rascal...and a scoundrel."
Use quotation marks round words or phrases that are being ascribed
new or unfamiliar meanings:

   Notes in the mid-range are regarded as "safe".
   Known to chemists as a "condensation" reaction, it...

(If overused, this device becomes tedious. Italicization is often a better
alternative in constructions such as the second one: Known to chemists
as a *condensation* reaction, it...).
See also **inverted commas**.

8. *Apostrophe* An apostrophe is used to show possession (form the
genitive case), normally by adding *'s*; e.g. John Brown's body, the
dog's claws, NATO's ability, sheep's clothing, actress's dress.
Exceptions are the pronouns *hers, its, theirs, ours* and *yours*, although
one's does have an apostrophe. Possessives of plurals ending in *s* are
formed by adding merely the apostrophe; e.g. victims' bodies, the two
dogs' dinners, the Joneses' children, the actresses' dresses. Some
modern usage omits the apostrophe from phrases containing
possessive plurals; e.g. in two weeks time, four days holiday.
Most singular, monosyllabic proper names ending in *s* take an
additional *'s* to form the possessive; e.g. Jones's car, St James's
gospel, Strauss's waltzes. The additional *s* is usually omitted with di-
and polysyllabic names; e.g. Williams' book, Adams' design. It is also
omitted with Greek and French names (in which such an *s* would not
be pronounced); e.g. Archimedes' principle, Charles' law. Possessives
of proper names applied to products tend to drop the apostrophe; e.g.
Chambers Dictionary, Clarks shoes, Smiths crisps.
Usage favours also the omission of an unpronounced *s* in other
possessive forms; e.g. conscience' sake, appearance' sake,
convenience' sake, goodness' sake, old times' sake (plurals
consciences' sake, appearances' sake).

An apostrophe should be used in forming plurals where it is necessary to avoid confusion; e.g. *p's* and *q's*, *do's* and *don'ts*, *set-to's*. Plurals of "ordinary" abbreviations do not need an apostrophe; e.g. BAs, MBEs, MPs, UFOs.

An apostrophe is used to indicate that a letter or letters have been omitted; e.g. *it's* (= it is), *don't* (= do not), although these abbreviated forms should be avoided in formal writing. No apostrophe is needed in the following:

bus, cello, flu, fridge, phone, plane, teens.

See also **'s.**

9. *Question mark* Do not normally use any other punctuation (except quotation marks) immediately after a question mark. For example, compare the punctuation in this sentence: He wondered briefly whether to go, but decided not to. And this one containing a question: He asked himself "Should I go?" but quickly answered "No", where the expected comma after the question mark is omitted. The question mark has some special uses, as in chess notation where it indicates a poor or risky move.

10. *Exclamation mark* Do not use exclamation marks except in quotations or in names or titles that have an exclamation mark as part of the names; e.g. *Hello, Dolly!*, Westward Ho! Do not use a full point immediately after an exclamation mark.

11. *Hyphen See* **compound words; word breaks.**

pundit is the preferred spelling (not *pandit*).

pupa (pl. pupae).

pupil = someone who attends school; **student** = someone who attends university or other institution/course of higher education. Because the ages (and standards) at which young people − even old people − make such attendance, *student* is the preferred blanket term for all but the youngest of them.

purchase, purchasable, purchaser.

purée (acute accent).

purloin is usually a euphemism for **pilfer** or **steal** (and of these two, the former is often a euphemism for the latter); *purloin* should be avoided.

purposely = intentionally, on purpose; **purposefully** = determinedly, with specific purpose. E.g.:

"He wrote small purposely, to save paper."

"She canvassed purposefully on behalf of the candidate."

purvey, purveyor.

pursue (not persue), pursuer, pursuing, pursuit. *See also* **peruse.**

put inflects *put – put – put*. **Put** = place in position; **putt** = strike the ball at golf.

Q

quadraphony (not *quadriphony, quadrophony*).

quadri- or **tetra-** *See* **numerical prefixes**.

qualifying adverbs, such as *almost, possibly, probably, rather* and *somewhat*, should be used sparingly or they lose their effectiveness. Many editors employ them – indeed some are encouraged to do so – to introduce a slight doubt into what would otherwise be a definite statement with no exceptions. E.g.:

"The common cold is the most prevalent disease" may be edited to "The common cold is probably the most prevalent disease" (just in case it is not), which is better than alternative ways of hedging such as "Many experts believe that the common cold is. . ."
Almost, rather and *somewhat* should not be used to qualify an incomparable adjective, such as *perfect* or *unique*. For example it is nonsense to talk of a "rather unique machine"; either the machine is the only one of its kind (= unique) or it is not. *Possibly unique* (implying considerable doubt) and *probably unique* (implying only little doubt) are acceptable constructions. *See also* **absolute words.**

quandary is the correct spelling (not *quandry*, despite the usual pronunciation).

quantitative = relating to quantity or number; **qualitative** = relating to quality or composition.

quantity (correctly applied to something that is uncountable) should not be misused for **number** (applied to something that can be counted). E.g. "a quantity of sand" but "a number of bricks".

quantum (pl. quanta).

quarrel, quarrelled, quarrelling, quarreller, quarrelsome.

quarry = a (wide) hole in the ground from which sand, gravel, stone or minerals are excavated; or the "prey" of a hunter (two distinct words with the same spelling).

quatercentenary (not *quartercentenary*), quaternary.

queer = strange, odd, quaint; the modern slang usage meaning *homosexual* (adj. and noun) makes *queer* a word to use with care, at least for the time being.

query (verb) should not be used to mean *ask* (e.g. "I queried her about her childhood" is incorrect); the verb can, however, be used to mean *raise doubts about* (as in "The surveyor queried the dimensions of the house"). **Query** (noun), in typography, is an alternative name for **question mark**.

question is part of two idioms that are commonly misused. To *beg the question* = to prove an assertion by means of another (different) assertion. (Fowler's example is that "democracy must be the best form of government because the majority are always right"); it does not mean to avoid giving a straight answer. A *leading question* is one phrased in such a way as to help elicit the required answer, and for this reason is not allowed in a court of law (e.g. "Would you say that the confusion of the accused was consistent with drunkenness?"); it does not mean a searching question or one that strikes at the nub of a problem.

question mark *See* **punctuation.**

questionnaire (note spelling).

queue, queued, queuing. *See also* **cue.**

quiche *See* **flan.**

quick is an adjective meaning speedy; **quickly** is an adverb meaning speedily. E.g.:
"He wanted to make a quick escape."
"He wanted to escape quickly."
The colloquial use of *quick* as an adverb should be avoided (as in "She had to run quick to catch the bus"). The archaic use of *quick* to mean "alive" persists only in the cliché "the quick and the dead" and in compounds such as *quicklime* and *quicksilver*.

quiescent = inactive, motionless; **quiet** = free from or not emitting sound or noise.

quieten, quieting (= quietening).

quire = (nominally) 25 sheets of paper, 1/20 of a *ream*; **choir** = group of singers; **coir** = coconut fibre.

quit has the preferred past tense **quitted** and past participle *quit*.

quite = completely, entirely; it should not be used to mean **moderately** or **somewhat**. E.g.:

"The job is quite finished" (correct);
"The job is quite interesting" (avoid).

qui vive (italics) = **alert**; the French term should be avoided.

quiz (pl. quizzes), quizzed, quizzing, quizzer, quizmaster.

quoin is the preferred spelling of **coign** for a corner-stone and the only one for the wedge that locks type in a forme (both words are old versions of *coin*, whose pronunciation they still share).

quorum (pl. quorums, not *quora*).

quota = an allocation, predetermined share or portion (*see* **portion**); e.g. "She did not drink her quota of wine" is incorrect unless it was a two-glasses-of-wine-per-person-and-no-more-and-no-less kind of a party. *Quota* is a singular word (pl. quotas); it is not the plural of **quotum** – a little-used synonym of quota.

quotation marks *See* **punctuation**.

quotations should be transcribed accurately, keeping the original spelling and punctuation. In quoting poetry, reproduce also the type layout/line breaks if possible. *See also* **ellipsis; punctuation** (quotation marks); **sic**.

quoth is archaic for **said**, and should be avoided.

R

-r- or **-rr-** Monosyllabic words ending in *-r* preceded by a single vowel double the *r* before *y* or a prefix beginning with a vowel. E.g.:

blur	blurred, blurring, blurry
stir	stirrable, stirred, stirrer, stirring

The *r* remains single if preceded by a long or double vowel. E.g.:

bear	bearable, bearing
leer	leered, leering
moor	moored, mooring
wear	wearable, wearing

With polysyllabic words, the choice of *-r-* or *-rr-* depends on where the accent falls. If it is on the last syllable, the rule is as for monosyllabic words; e.g.;

conferring	deterring	occurring
debarring	disinterring	preferring
demurring		

(exceptions include inferable, preferable, referable, severable, transferable, in which the accent changes, and registrable, in which the spelling changes). If the last syllable is unaccented the *r* is not doubled; e.g.:

capering	motoring	suffering
entering	offering	tittering

Neither is the *r* doubled, in monosyllabic or polysyllabic words, before suffixes that begin with a consonant; e.g.:

bothersome	deferment	internment
dapperly	fearful	tearfully

rabbet (verb = to make a groove or joint in woodwork), rabbeted, rabbeting.

rabbi (pl. rabbis).

rabbit (verb = to catch rabbits), rabbited, rabbiting, rabbiter.

race should be used with care. The inhabitants/citizens of a country are rarely of one race (e.g. the Germans are a *nation* or *people*, most of them belonging to the Caucasian *race*). In ordinary contexts, to refer to blacks or Asians as a race is pejorative and regarded as **racism** (preferred form to *racialism*). It is also incorrect to refer to members of a particular religious faith as a race (e.g. there is no Jewish race or Muslim race). The *human race* is a correct term to distinguish people from other animals. *See* **racism**.

racism should be assiduously avoided in all writing (and editing). Among the most controversial terms in this context are the names used by one group of people to describe members of another group. Some are neutral (unintended) and acceptable, some dubious, some derogatory (intended) and unacceptable, and some downright offensive. Terms in the last two categories are generally regarded as racist. Sensitive writers do not use them, and editors should be aware of the pitfalls in dealing with texts from writers who do. Three broad groups can be compiled; terms in the "dubious" category should be used only with care.
Neutral/acceptable Black/black, Chicano, Coloured (South Africa only), gaucho, gentile, mestizo, mulatto.
Dubious Aussie, Brit, Eurasian, infidel, Jock, Kiwi, Murphy, Negro, Negress, Negrillo, Negrito, paddy, pommy, Springbok, Taffy, Tyke.
Racist Abo, Anglo-Indian, Argie, Bosch, Chinaman, Chink, colonial, coloured, coon, Croakie, dago, darky, diddy, Frog, gippy, gook, goy, greaser, gringo, Guinea, gypo, Hun, half-breed, half-caste, honky, Iti, Ivan, Jap, Jerry, Jim Crow, Kaffir, Kanook, Kike, Kraut, Limey, munt, Newfie, nigger, nig-nog, Nip, Octaroon, Paki, polak, quadroon, sambo, Sassenach, Scand, spade, spik, Swartz, tink, wetback, wog, wop, Yank, Yid.

rack *See* **wrack**.

racket is the correct spelling of all meanings (not *racquet*).

radical = basic, fundamental, root or stem of a word, an active unit in a chemical compound; **radicle** = embryonic root of a seed.

radio (pl. radios), radioed, radioing, radioactive, radioactivity, radio-carbon (etc.), radiography, radio-isotope, radiology, radiotherapy.

radius (pl. radii).

---

rainbow, rain-cloud, raincoat, raindrop, rainfall, rain-gauge, rainforest, rainhat, rainproof, rainstorm, rain-water.

raise is transitive (e.g. "Raise your arms"); **rise** is intransitive (e.g. "I saw the balloon rise in the sky"); **raze** = to lay level with the ground (e.g. "The building was razed by the fire"); **arise** = to occur, come into existence ("The meeting should finish early, as long as nothing unexpected arises"). Raise can also = bring up (young), rear; some authorities insist that animals are *raised*, whereas human children are *reared*. **Raisable** = can be raised; **risible** = laughable, silly. Of all the words discussed, only **rise** can be used as a noun (an employee applies for a *rise*; *raise* is an Americanism in this context).

raison d'être (italics) = reason/purpose of existence; the French form should be avoided.

rajah is the preferred spelling (not *raja*).

râle (= abnormal chest sound).

rancour, rancorous.

rapped is the past tense and participle of the verb to *rap*; **rapt** is an adjective from *rapture*; **wrapped** is the past tense and participle of the verb to *wrap*. E.g. knuckles may be *rapped*, an audience may be *rapt*, and a parcel may be *wrapped*.

rarefy, rarefaction.

rarely ever = rarely (which is preferred). **Rarely or ever** is nonsense and incorrect for **rarely or never** (or *rarely if ever*). One of these last two is intended in "Layout artists can rarely or ever draw straight lines." *See also* **seldom ever**.

rarity *See* **scarcity**.

rat-catcher, rat-flea, rat-poison, ratrace, ratsbane, rat's-tail, rat-tail, rat-trap.

ratchet, ratcheted, ratcheting.

rate, rateable, rating.

ratio (pl. ratios).

rational = sane, judicious, logical, showing/accepting reason (opposite of *irrational*); **rationale** = basic principle, theoretical explanation; **rationalize** = to make rational. E.g.:

"His bigotry closed his mind to rational argument."

"He gave tiredness as the rationale for his poor performance."

"He rationalized his poor performance by claiming to be tired."

ravage = destroy, lay waste, ruin; **ravish** = carry off by force, rape, or (different meaning) enrapture. E.g.:

"Villages were ravaged by the invading forces."

"Local women were ravished by the invaders."

"The invaders were ravished by the beauty of the local women."

Possible ambiguity between the two meanings of *ravish* probably make it a word to avoid.

raze *See* **erase; raise**.

razzmatazz is an Americanism which some American dictionaries no longer include. The consensus of those that do indicates the spelling given, although British dictionaries offer also the alternatives *razmataz* and *razzamatazz*. The word is used less frequently than it once was, and if it must be used the preferred spelling is the American one.

re should not be used in formal writing to mean **about** or **concerning**.

re-, as a prefix meaning again, takes a hyphen when the root word begins with an *e* or when the resulting compound word could be mispronounced or confused with another word. E.g.:

re-cede (= give back)	recede (= shrink)
re-collect (= collect again)	recollect (= remember)
re-cover (= cover again)	recover (= get better)
re-count (= count again)	recount (= narrate)
re-dress (= dress again)	redress (= compensate)
re-do, re-done	
re-echo	
re-edit	
re-elect	
re-enter	
re-establish	
re-examine	

re-export	
re-fuse (= fuse again)	refuse (= decline offer)
re-heat	
re-lay (= lay again)	relay (= pass on)
re-route	
re-serve (= serve again)	reserve (= keep for later)
resign (= sign again)	resign (= relinquish)
re-soluble (= dissolvable again)	resoluble (= capable of resolution)
re-sort (= sort again)	resort (= turn for help)
re-strain (= strain again)	restrain (= hold back)
re-turn (= turn again)	return (= to give/go back)

The use of *again* with any of the *re-* words in the first column is a tautology that should be avoided (*see* **tautology**).

read has the past tense and participle **read** (pronounced "red"). Thus it is not possible, out of context, to determine the tense of the simple sentence "I read books". *See also* **lead**.

readable = interesting to read; **legible** = written or printed clearly, can be read without difficulty.

reafforest(ation) is preferred to **reforest(ation)**.

realistic = resembling something real (as in "a realistic painting of a cat"). It should not be over-used to stand for *big*, *large*, *reasonable* or *sensible* (as in "a realistic price").

reality = the state of being real, actual; **realty** = real property, real estate. In the United States, a *realtor* is an estate agent.

realize, realizable, realizer, realization.

really, like *actually* and *definitely*, is overworked as an intensifier. Good writers make sure *really* is really needed — this sentence does not need the second one.

realty *See* **reality**.

ream (verb) = to enlarge a hole or bore; **ream** (noun) = (nominally) 500 sheets of paper (= 20 quires), although in printing reams of 480 and 516 sheets are also used.

reason (why) should be followed by *is that*; e.g. "The reason editors make mistakes is that they..." *Why*, however, is superfluous and should be omitted. *See also* **cause**.

rebel, rebelled, rebelling.

rebuff = reject (an offer of help), repulse; **rebuke** = censure, reprove; **rebut** = disprove an allegation by answering in kind; **refute** = prove beyond all doubt that an allegation is wrong. E.g.:

"She felt hurt because he rebuffed her offer to assist him."
"He rebuked her for making the error, even though she offered to correct it."
"She rebutted his accusation by pointing out that he had made similar errors."
"She refuted his allegation of carelessness by showing him that the previous version was free from errors when she passed it on."

rebuke *See* **rebuff**.

rebus (pl. rebuses).

rebut, rebutted, rebutting, rebuttal. *See also* **rebuff**.

recall = deliberately to remember; **recollect** = suddenly to remember, or succeed in remembering. E.g.:

"You must try to recall her name."
"Now that I see her photograph, I recollect her name is Maria."

receipt = paper acknowledging that money has been paid; **recipe** = list of ingredients and method for cooking/preparing a dish. The former word is no longer used for the latter.

receive, receiver (all meanings), receivable (describes somebody or something that can be received), receptive (describes somebody who is willing or readily able to receive new ideas), recipient (somebody who receives), receptacle (something which receives, a container).

received English, or received pronunciation (RP), was originally a term coined by Alexander Ellis and embodied in Daniel Jones's description of the socially acceptable non-regional English accent associated with public schools, Cambridge and Oxford Universities, the educated speech of the Home Counties.

recherché (acute accent).

reckless = without heed of the consequences, rash; **ruthless** = without compassion/mercy, unscrupulous. E.g.:

"The driver was reckless in his disregard of the speed limit."
"The employer was ruthless in her disregard for people's feelings."

recognize, recognizable, recognizance, recognition.

reconcile, reconcilable, reconciler, reconciliation.

reconnaissance (with two *n*s and two *s*s).

reconnoitre, reconnoitred, reconnoitring.

record player *See* **gramophone**.

recourse = turning to someone or something for help; **resource** = a reserve (which can be drawn on, especially when in difficulty); **resort** = expedient, something that can provide help. *Resource* and *resort* overlap in meaning; they should not be misused for *recourse*. E.g.:

"They were reassured that they always had recourse to the military in times of trouble."
"They were offered the resources of the military in times of trouble."
"They could turn to the military as a last resort in times of trouble."

rectify *See* **justify**.

recto = right-hand page of a book; **verso** = left-hand page.

rector = parson who formerly received the living (tithes) of a parish; **vicar** = parson who earns a stipend/salary (the living being held by others). Their respective dwellings are a *rectory* and a *vicarage*. A *manse* is the residence of a minister (particularly of the Church of Scotland).

rectum (pl. rectums).

recur (not *reoccur*), recurred, recurring, recurrence, recurrent.

red admiral, red-belly, red biddy, red-blooded, redbreast, red-breasted, redbrick (adj.), red cabbage, redcap, red carpet, redcurrant, redeye, red face, red-faced, red hair, red-haired, red-handed, redhead, red-headed, red-heat, red herring, red-hot (adj.), red lead, red-letter day, red-light (adj.), redpoll, red-shank(s), redskin, red tape, red-water fever, red wine, redwing.

Red Indian The preferred term is (**North**) **American Indian**.

redolent (= odorous, smelling) requires *of*.

reduce, reducer, reducible (not reductible), reductant. *See also* **deplete**.

redundancy in language *See* tautology; verbiage.

refer, referred, referring, referable, referrer, reference, referral, referee. **Refer** does not need the preposition *back* (write "refer to" not "refer back to").

reference marks *See* footnotes.

referendum (pl. referendums, not *referenda*).

reflect, reflectible (= able to be reflected, as light is), reflective (= able to reflect, as a mirror is, hence *reflection*), reflector; **reflexive** = of a reflex or reflex action, a grammatical term.

reflexive pronouns *See* pronouns.

reforest(ation) The preferred form is **reafforest(ation)**.

refract, refractor, refractable (preferred to refrangible).

refraction *See* diffraction.

refrigerate, refrigerator, refrigeration. The informal abbreviation for refrigerator is **fridge** (with a *d*).

refute *See* deny; rebuff.

regalia is a plural word (and has no singular).

regenerate, regenerator, regeneration.

regime (no accent) = administration, government; **regimen** = a course of treatment (such as a diet).

register, registrable (not registerable), registrar, registry (but, strictly, Register Office).

regret, regretted, regretting, regrettable (describing something that

causes regret), **regretful** (describing the state of having regret). *See also*
regretfully.

regretfully (= with regret) should not be used for **regrettably** (= to be
regretted). *Regretfully* has become a vogue word, used (incorrectly) to
give an apologetic tone to a statement (e.g. "Regretfully the item you
require is out of stock", in which *regrettably* is intended and "I am
sorry but . . ." would be better). *See also* **hopefully; thankfully**.

regulate, regulator (all meanings). **Regulate** = control, hold within
prescribed limits; **relegate** = move to a lower position; **delegate** =
hand over to somebody else to deal with. E.g.:
"The function of the hormone insulin is to regulate the level of
glucose in the bloodstream."
"After a poor season, Arsenal were relegated to the second division."
"The manager's chief fault is her unwillingness to delegate some tasks
to her assistant."

rein = leather strap to control a horse; **reign** = period of a monarch's
rule. There are also verbs with the same spellings. (Note the *-ei-*
spelling of both words.)

relapse, relapsable.

relate, relater (who relates), but relator in law (who informs
authority).

relations *with* someone, not relations *to*. *See also* **family relationships;
relative**.

relative (noun) is preferred to **relation** when referring to a member of a
family (e.g. "We are going to stay with my wife's relatives").

relative pronouns *See* **pronoun**.

release, releaser (who releases), but relcasor in law (who grants a
release).

relegate *See* **regulate**.

relevant, relevance (and irrelevant, irrelevance). *See also* **material**.

relic = object of historical interest, souvenir; **relict** = widow.

relocate is a vogue word for **move**, which is preferred.

reluctant = unwilling to act; **reticent** = unwilling to talk, reserved. E.g.:

"When asked to attend the conference, he was reluctant to go."
"During the heated debate, she was too reticent to state her view."

remainder *See* **balance**.

remediable = able to be remedied; **remedial** = meant as a remedy. E.g.:

"The car suffered slight damage but is remediable."
"She will need remedial treatment after they remove the plaster from her broken leg."

remedy, remedied, remedying.

reminisce, reminiscent, reminiscence.

remit, remitted, remitting, remittal (= referring a legal case to another court), remittance (= payment of money), remission (= shortening of a prison sentence), remissible, remitter (who gives), remittee (who receives).

remonstrate *See* **demonstrate**.

remove, removable.

remunerate = to pay recompense; **renumerate** = to count again; **enumerate** = to count (the number of). E.g.:

"I shall remunerate you for doing the job."
"To avoid further mistakes, I shall renumerate the things to be done."
"Before you start, I shall enumerate the things to be done."

renaissance is preferred to **renascence** in all uses (and has an initial capital letter when it refers to the artistic revival).

rend, an archaic verb for to **tear,** inflects *rend* − *rent* − *rent*.

render, rendible (but *translatable* preferred, unless of fat).

rendezvous (pl. rendezvous); the verb form is he (or she) rendezvouses.

renounce, renounceable, renunciation (preferred to renouncement).

rent *See* **hire; rend.**

reoccur The preferred form is **recur** (which *see*).

reorganize, reorganization.

repair, repairable (= can be repaired), reparable (of a loss that can be made good), reparation.

repast is precious for **meal**, which is preferred.

repeat, repetition, repetitive (= involving repetition), repetitious (= annoyingly repetitive). E.g.:
"The text was fairly well written but inclined to be repetitive in places."
"The repetitious sound of the dripping tap kept me awake."

repel, repelled, repelling, repeller, repellent (adj. and noun, preferred to repellant), repulsive. **Repel** = drive back (opposing forces), refuse (an offer), or offend the senses, cause repugnance; something that drives back is *repellent*, something that causes repugnance is *repulsive*. **Repulse** also = drive back or rebuff, but does not form the adjective *repulsive* (which is reserved for the meaning defined previously). E.g.:
"She repelled his amorous advances."
"He accepted her repellent response."
"She found his behaviour repulsive."
"The garrison repulsed the enemy attack."

replace, replaceable. Replace something *by* something else (not *with* or *for*); A is replaced by B, not B with or for A. **Substitute** something *for* something else, not *with* or *by*; A is substituted for B, not with or by B. Thus *replace* = take the place of; *substitute* = put in the place of. E.g.:
"Please replace Wendy by Maria on the team" and
"Please substitute Maria for Wendy on the team" convey the same meaning.

reply = an answer; **retort** = a sharp reply, retaliation; **riposte** = sharp witty reply, repartee.

reprehend, reprehensive, reprehensible (not *-able*). See also **apprehend.**

represent, representable (also re-present, re-presentable), representation, representative (adj. and noun); *represetive* does not exist.

repress, represser, repressible, repression.

reprieve (note *-ie-* spelling).

reproduce, reproducible, reproducer, reproduction.

reproof (verb) = to proof again; **reprove** = to rebuke; **reproof** (noun) is common to both.

repulse *See* **repel**.

repute, reputable, reputation.

require, requirement, requisition, requisite. *Requirement(s)* = a need or condition; *requisition* = a written order for something that is needed; *requisite* (noun) = something that is needed; *requisite* (adj.) = required. E.g.:
"A science degree is a requirement for the post."
"He made a requisition for a new desk."
"Driving experience is a requisite for the job of milkman."
"He lacked the requisite experience."
See also **pre-**.

reredos (pl. reredoses).

research in *or* into a subject (not *on*).

reserve, reserver (but reservor in law), reservist, reservable (= can be reserved); also re-serve (= serve again), re-servable (= can be served again). **Reserve** = place set aside for a special purpose, often the protection of wild animals, also known as a *sanctuary* (as in *game reserve*, *bird sanctuary*); **preserve** = place set aside for animals that are hunted/killed for sport. *Reservation* for *reserve* in this sense is an Americanism.
See also **preserve**.

resin = natural gum from plants or an artificial substitute used in paints and plastics. The natural resin used on violinists' bows, boxers and ballet dancers' shoes, and gymnasts' hands is known as **rosin**.

resist, resister (= someone who resists), resistor (= that resists electric current), resistance (no longer used for *resistor* in electronics), resistant, resistible.

resolve, resolvable (and re-solve, re-solvable).

resort *See* **recourse.**

resource *See* **recourse.**

respect, respector, respectable (= worthy of respect), respectful (= showing respect), respective (= pertaining to, appropriate), respectively (= in the order previously listed/stated). E.g.:
"He would not accept the cleaner's job because he did not regard it as sufficiently respectable."
"It is rare to find modern teenagers who are respectful to their parents."
"The soldiers were dismissed and told to go to their respective posts."
"Anne and Jane prefer tea and coffee respectively."

respirate, respirator, respiration.

respond, responsive, responsible. **Responsible** = accountable (for) (e.g. "She was responsible for approving designers' layouts"), or cause of (e.g. "A broken suspension was responsible for the crash"). Care is needed to avoid the first meaning being mistaken for the second (e.g. "The office manager is responsible for holes in the carpet"). *See also* **irresponsible.**

restaurateur (not *restauranteur*).

restive = intractable, unco-operative; **restless** = unsettled, uneasy, never still. E.g.:
"I was worried because the sounds from the jungle had made my horse restive."
"The speaker was late in arriving and the audience had become restless."

restore, restorer, restorable, restoration.

restrain *See* **constrain.**

resume, resumable, resumption.

résumé (with two accents).

resuscitate, resuscitation, resuscitator.

reticent See **reluctant**.

reticulum (pl. reticula).

retina (pl. retinas).

retire = withdraw deliberately (in an organized fashion), or cease working for good; **retreat** = withdraw in haste (and disarray). E.g.:
"The sergeant decided that his platoon should retire behind the protection of a low stone wall."
"The chairman decided to retire on his fiftieth birthday."
"The continuous shelling forced the enemy to retreat for nearly three miles."

retort See **reply**.

retrace, retraceable.

retract, retractor, retractable (= retractile), retraction.

retrieve, retrievable, retriever, retrieval.

retrospective = looking back, in restrospect; **retroactive** = acting backwards (in time).

retroussé (acute accent).

rev, revved, revving.

revel, revelled, revelling, reveller.

revenge See **avenge**.

reverend = deserving reverence; **reverent** = showing reverence. *Reverend* (abbreviated to **Rev.** or **Revd**) is a form of address for a priest or minister.

reverse, reversible (not *-able*), reversal. **Reversal,** = a turning back or the other way round, should not be confused with *reversion* = a return to previous state or condition. The former is from *reverse*, the latter from *revert*. E.g.:

"In the second game our team won 2−1, a reversal of the score in the first game."

"The patient's behaviour seemed like a reversion to childhood."
See also **inverse, revert**.

revert, revertible, reversion. *See also* **reverse**.

review = survey, formal inspection, critical opinion on a book, film or play; **revue** = entertainment (usually on stage), generally with humorous sketches and songs. *See also* **overview**.

revise, revisable, revision.

revive, revival, reviver (who revives = brings back to life), but revivor in law.

revoke, revocable, revocation.

revolt, revolution(ary), revolutionize.

reward *See* **award**.

rhesus factor abbreviates to Rh-factor; also Rh-positive, Rh-negative (abbreviated further to Rh+, Rh- if necessary).

rhetorical question is one that is used for effect and does not require (or expect) an answer. It nevertheless still requires a question mark. E.g.:

"Why should ex-public schoolboys get all the best jobs?"

rhinoceros (pl. rhinoceroses).

rhombus (pl. rhombuses).

rhyme is the preferred spelling (not **rime**, except when *rime* = frost).

rhyming slang *See* **slang**.

riches is usually regarded as a plural word (e.g. "Riches are a common goal of ambitious people").

rick (verb) is the preferred spelling (not *wrick*), for the verb meaning to twist or sprain.

rickettsia (pl. rickettsiae) is a type of disease-causing micro-organism.

ricochet, ricocheted ("riko-shayed"), ricocheting ("riko-shaying").

rid, ridding, riddance. The preferred inflexion of the verb is *rid – rid – rid*. *See also* **ride**.

riddle *See* **puzzle**.

ride, riding, ridable. The inflexion of the verb is *ride – rode – ridden*. *See also* **rid**.

rider *See* **corollary**.

right and **rightly** can both be adverbs, but the former always follows the verb whereas the latter usually precedes it. E.g.:

"She answered right."
"He rightly refused to answer."

right-angle, right-angled, right-handed(ness), right-minded, right-of-way (pl. rights-of-way), right-whale, right-wing(er).

rigor (= unresponsiveness, stiffness, chill), rigor mortis; **rigour** (= strictness, over-exactness), rigorous, rigorousness.
Rigorous = strict, with rigour; **vigorous** = forceful, strong, with vigour. E.g.:

"The boss insists on rigorous attention to detail."
"He takes vigorous exercise each day."

rill = a stream; **rille** = a valley on the Moon.

rime The preferred spelling is **rhyme** (for the poetic device), although *rime* is correct for a type of frost.

ring (verb = to sound a bell) has the past tense **rang** (not *rung*), and past participle **rung**. **Ring** (verb = to encircle, put a ring round something) has the past tense and participle **ringed**.

riot, rioted, rioting.

riposte *See* **reply**.

rise has the past tense **rose** and past participle **risen**. *See also* **arise**; **raise**.

risible *See* **raise**.

risky = hazardous, potentially dangerous; **risqué** (with an accent) = bordering on impropriety.

risotto (pl. risottos).

ritual, ritualize, ritualization.

rival, rivalled, rivalling.

rivet, riveted, riveting (not *rivetted, rivetting*).

road-bed, roadblock, road-hog, road-map, roadside, road-works, roadworthy, roadworthiness.

rodeo (pl. rodeos).

role (no circumflex) = part in a play, function in an event/process; **roll** (noun) = register, list of names, anything of cylindrical shape.

Roman Catholic *See* **Catholic.**

roman numerals should be avoided except as part of a monarch's name (e.g. Charles II, Henry VIII), book of the Bible (e.g. I Kings, II Kings), in the terms World War I and World War II, and in certain technical conventions (such as the numbering of the cranial nerves and valence in chemistry). Lower-case roman numerals are sometimes used for folios (page numbers) on the preliminary matter in books (i.e. i, ii, iii, iv, etc.). The "modern" roman numerals are:

I = 1, V = 5, X = 10, L = 50, C = 100, D = 500, M = 1,000.

Romania, Romanian (not *Rumania, Rumanian*).

rondo (pl. rondos).

röntgen (preferred to *roentgen*).

roof (pl. roofs).

rosary = string of (55 or 165) beads for "telling" devotions; **rosery** = rose garden.

rosé (wine)

rosin *See* **resin.**

rostrum (pl. rostrums).

rota (pl. rotas).

rotate, rotor (= rotating part of machinery), rotary (= having a circular motion), rotatable (= capable of rotary movement), rotator (= a muscle that rotates a joint), rotatory (= causing, or in, rotation), rotational (= acting in rotation), rotative (= turning like a wheel, produced or caused by rotation). *Rotatory* has largely replaced *rotary*, and can be used for *rotative*.

rotisserie (not *rôtisserie*).

rotund *See* **orotund**.

roué (acute accent).

rough-and-ready, rough-and-tumble, roughcast, rough house, roughneck, rough-rider, roughshod, rough-spoken.

round *See* **around**.

round about should be avoided to mean approximately, near (e.g. "She is round about two metres tall", "He lives round about here"). In the first example, *round about* means merely *about*; in the second, it means *near*. **Roundabout** (one word) is a large traffic island at a junction or intersection of roads, or a merry-go-round.

rouse *See* **arouse**.

rout (verb) = to put to flight; **route** (verb) = to direct along a particular path.

roux = mixture of flour and fat; **rue** = to be sorry, regret.

rudimentary = to do with an early stage of development (a rudiment); vestigial = to do with a surviving trace of something that has almost disappeared (a vestige). E.g.:

"At the age of only three weeks a human foetus has a rudimentary heart."
"The coccyx in the human skeleton can be regarded as a vestigial tail."

rue, rueful, rueing.

rumen (= cow's stomach), ruminate, ruminant (= animal that chews the cud), ruminator (= person who chews things over).

run (verb) has the past tense **ran** and past participle **run**.

runabout, runaway, run-down, runner-up (pl. runners-up), runoff (noun), run-of-the-mill, run-on (noun).

rural = pertaining to the country(side) (opposite of *urban*); **rustic** = pertaining to countryfolk, unsophisticated, roughly made. E.g.:

"Some foxes abandon a rural environment and live on the outskirts of cities."

"His origins were obvious from his rustic manner of speech."

Russia should be used for the nation before November 1917; references after that date should be to the **Soviet Union** (abbreviate to USSR if necessary in tables etc.). The corresponding adjectives are *Russian* and *Soviet*.

Russian words assimilated into English sometimes present spelling difficulties; here are some examples:

balalaika	dacha	samoyed	troika
bortsch	knout	steppe	tundra
borzoi	samovar	taiga	vodka

More recently, words such as *glasnost* and *perestroika* have been in the news, although it remains to be seen whether they become an accepted part of the language.

ruthless *See* **reckless**.

S

**$**, the dollar sign, should be avoided when there are only occasional references to currency (when dollar(s) should be spelled out). In either case, unless the context makes it clear, write US dollar ($) or Australian dollars etc., at least at first mention. For large amounts, note the style of 300 million dollars, $300 million.

's forms the possessive (genitive case) of nouns – e.g. cat's, (singular) Jones's, (plural Joneses') women's – see **gerund; punctuation** (apostrophe); the possessive of only one pronoun (*one's*, which *see*); a short form of *is* – e.g. it's (= it is), there's (there is); a short form of *us* – e.g. let's (= let us); an abbreviation of *God's* – e.g. the exclamations 'sdeath (= God's death), 'strewth (= God's truth). The exclamations and abbreviated forms such as *it's, there's* and *let's* should be avoided in formal writing.

-s- or **-ss-** Words ending in -*s* may double the *s* before a suffix beginning with a vowel (e.g. *gassed, nonplussed*) or they may not (e.g. *biased, chorused, gaseous, focused*), although some people prefer the spellings *biassed, focussed*. There is no general rule, and the spellings have to be learned. *See also* **bus.**

Sabbath (initial capital letter); it is not necessarily synonymous with *Sunday.*

saccharin = artificial substitute for sugar; **saccharine** = sugary.

sacred = holy; **sacrosanct** = inviolate, secure from infringement or abuse.

sacrilege, sacrilegious (note spelling, which does not parallel *religious*).

safety-belt, safety-catch, safety curtain, safety film, safety glass, safety lamp, safety-match, safety net, safety-pin, safety razor, safety-valve.

saga (pl. sagas).

sailer = a sailing vessel (e.g. "that yacht is a good sailer"); **sailor** = member of a ship's crew (not necessarily on a sailing ship), a seaman, someone in the Navy.

Saint has the abbreviation **St** in personal and place-names (St John, St Albans, St Helens). The French female **Sainte** has the abbreviation **Ste; San** abbreviates to **S; Santa** abbreviates to **Sta;** none has a full point. The abbreviation of *Saints* is **S.S.** Names beginning with *St* are alphabetized as if *Saint* were spelled in full (*see* **alphabetization**).

sake (noun) usually has no plural (e.g. "for our sake", "for the animal's sake") and constructions such as *for all their sakes* should be avoided (say "for the sake of them all") − note also the idioms *for goodness' sake, for conscience' sake;* **sake** (preferred to *saki*) = Japanese rice wine; **saki** = South American monkey.

salami = Italian (etc.) sausage; **salmi** = game stew.

salary *See* **wage**.

sale, saleable.

salon = elegant business establishment ("beauty salon"); **saloon** = large (public) room ("billiards saloon").

salt-cake, salt-cellar, salt-glaze, salt lake, salt-marsh, salt-mine, salt-pan, saltpetre, saltspoon, salt water (noun), salt-water (adj.) (but seawater, noun and adj.).

salubrious = beneficial to one's health, healthful; **salutary** = beneficial to one's morals; **salutatory** = welcoming. E.g.:
"I always enjoy the salubrious atmosphere at the spa."
"The punishment he received after being caught stealing taught him a salutary lesson."
"The chairman introduced the speaker and made some salutatory remarks."

salvage (noun) = property rescued from hazard; **selvage** (not *selvedge*) = reinforced edge of a length of cloth.

salve (verb) = to save property from hazard, gives the words *salvage* and *salvor* (= one who salvages); **salver** = a tray. The word for to save a person (people) from hazard is **rescue**.

salvo (pl. salvos).

same denotes (exact) identity; **similar** implies (mere) likeness. The reply "No, similar" to the question "Same again?" is, however, that of a thirstless pedant.

sanatorium (pl. sanatoriums).

sanatory = healing, of healing; **sanitary** = concerned with the promotion of health, concerned with drainage and sewerage. E.g.:
"The Romans dressed wounds with willow bark because of its sanatory properties."
"Those blocked drains are a job for a sanitary engineer."
The similarity in meanings has resulted in their respective nouns, **sanatorium** and **sanitarium**, being interchangeable, although the second is usually regarded as an Americanism.

sanction (verb) = to give approval to, authorize; **sanction** (noun) = something that makes an oath binding, penalty for non-obedience of a law. The verb does not mean "to impose sanctions" and the noun does not mean "ban" or "embargo", although the politicians' "impose economic sanctions" threatens to change the distinctions.

sanctum (pl. sanctums).

sandal, sandalled.

sandbag, sandbank, sandbar, sand-blast(ing), sand-castle, sand-dune, sandfly, sand-glass, sandman, sandpaper, sandpiper, sand-pit, sandstone, sandstorm, sand-trap, sand-yacht.

Sanskrit *See* **Indian words**.

sapid = palatable, with an agreeable flavour; its opposite is *insipid* (which *see*).

sarcasm *See* **irony**.

sarcoma (pl. sarcomata).

sari (pl. saris).

Satan (initial capital letter).

satire (= exposure of vice or folly, through ridicule), satirize, satirist; **satyr** = a woodland god; **satyriasis** = the male equivalent of nymphomania.

Saudi Arabia The derived adjective and noun (for the people) is *Saudi*.

sauté, sautéd, sautéing.

savanna (not *savannah*). *See also* **llano**.

save is archaic (and affected) for **except** or **bar** (as in "all save one"); *except* should be used.

savory = a herb; **savoury** = appetizing, non-sweet dish.

saw (verb = to cut with a saw) has the past tense **sawed** and preferred past participle **sawn** (not *sawed*). **Saw** (noun) = a saying. *See also* **see**.

say inflects *say* – *said* – *said*.

scale, scaler (who or which scales), scalable; **scalar** = a real number in mathematics.

scallop, scalloped, scalloping (not *scollop*, even though it reflects the pronunciation).

scan = to examine closely, scrutinize (it does not mean to glance at casually or hurriedly). *See also* **peruse**.

scandal, scandalize.

Scandinavian languages As well as the many words derived from Old Norse, English contains several borrowings from Denmark, Finland, Iceland, Norway and Sweden, such as:

fjeld (Norwegian)	ombudsman (Swedish)
fjord (Norwegian)	rug (Swedish)
geyser (Icelandic)	sauna (Finnish)
lemming (Norwegian)	ski (Norwegian)
mink (Danish)	smorgasbord (Swedish)

scarcely *See* **barely**.

scarcity = a temporary lack of a necessity; **scarify** = to scratch, lacerate, cause to become scarred; **rarity** = a long-term or permanent lack of something. E.g.:

"There is a scarcity of fresh vegetables in winter."
"Foxes are a rarity in London."
"Fresh fruit is scarce in winter."
"Foxes are rare in London."

scare (verb) is transitive. *Scared of* should not be misused for *afraid of* or *frightened by*; e.g. correct usage is "Some children are afraid of the dark and frightened by spiders; the dark and spiders scare some children."

scarf (pl. scarves).

scenario (pl. scenarios) is a vogue word to be avoided. *See* **vogue words**.

sceptic (= someone who disbelieves or holds profound doubts) is the preferred spelling of **skeptic; septic** = pertaining to sepsis or putrefaction.

scherzo (pl. scherzi).

schizophrenic describes someone with a severe psychotic disorder who has lost contact with reality (schizophrenia). The word should not be used of mere **ambivalence** or to describe frustration caused by a **dilemma**. *See also* **maniacal; paranoia**.

school-book, schoolboy, schoolchild, schoolfellow, school-friend, schoolgirl, school bus, school-days, school-leaver, schoolmaster, schoolmistress, schoolroom, schoolteacher.

schoolboy howlers *See* **non-standard English**.

scientific laws *See* **named effects and laws**.

scissors is a plural word; "a pair of scissors" achieves a singular construction.

scone *See* **crumpet**.

Scotland is inhabited mainly by Scots, many of whom speak with a Scottish accent; it is not unknown for them to drink Scotch (whisky, without an *e*). Neither the people nor their language should be referred to as Scotch. The term *Scotch* is also retained for Scotch pancakes and Scotch eggs. Note: in a general biographical work, especially if it is for international consumption, the nationality of someone born in Scotland (or Wales or Ireland) after the respective Act of Union should be given as *British* – Wales after 1543, Scotland 1707 and Ireland 1800.

scrimmage = a (spontaneous) tussle; **scrummage** = a set formation at rugby football.

script (typeface) *See* **cursive**.

scrutinize (not -*ise*).

scull = a short, light oar or the boat employing it; **skull** = the bones of the head.

sea-bed, sea-bird, seaboard, sea-borne, sea breeze, seafarer, seafaring, seafood, sea-going, seagull, sea-horse, sea-level, seaplane, seaport, seascape, sea serpent, sea shell, sea-shore, seasick(ness), seaside, sea-urchin, seawater (noun and adj.), seaway, seaweed, seaworthy, seaworthiness.

séance (with accent).

sear = to scorch; **seer** = a prophet; **sere** = a catch in a gun-lock.

seasonable = appropriate to a given season (as log fires are in winter); **seasonal** = characteristic of a given season (as hay fever is in summer).

seasons (spring, summer, autumn, winter) do not normally have an initial capital letter.

secateurs (not *sécateurs*) is a plural word; "a pair of secateurs" achieves a singular construction.

Second World War The preferred form is **World War II**.

second-best, second childhood, second-class (adj.), second-cousin, second-floor (adj.), second-hand (adj.), second-in-command, second name, second-nature, second-rate (adj.), seconds-hand (on a watch), second-sight, second wind.

secret = hidden, unrevealed, confidential; **secrete** = to hide, to produce a substance. The former gives the adjective *secretive*; the latter the adjective *secretory*. E.g.:

"Biologists have tried to discover the secret of hormone production in the human body."

"He secreted the results of his researches into hormones."

"The pancreas secretes the hormone insulin."

seduce, seducible (not *seductable*), seducer (not *seductor*), seduction (preferred to seducement).

see/see also See **cross-references**.

see has the past tense **saw** and past participle **seen**. See also **saw**.

seek inflects *seek* − *sought* − *sought*. Unlike **look**, seek does not need *for* (e.g. "Seek a way out", "look for treasure").

seesaw (no hyphen).

seize = grasp, take hold of (possibly using force); **siege** = using forces to surround a building or town (and note *-ei-* spellings). E.g.:
"He seized his assailant by the throat."
"They lifted the siege when the enemy troops surrendered."

seldom ever = seldom (which is preferred). **Seldom or ever** is nonsense and incorrect for **seldom or never** (or *seldom if ever*); one of these last two is intended in "Editors seldom or ever have legible handwriting". See also **rarely ever**.

sell inflects *sell* − *sold* − *sold*.

selvage See **salvage**.

semantics See **grammar**.

semi- Most compound words with this prefix have a hyphen; exceptions include semibreve, semicircle, semicolon, semifinal, semiquaver. See also **numerical prefixes**.

semicolon See **punctuation**.

semi-monthly/semi-weekly See **biannual**.

Semitic = concerning the Semites or the Arabic, Aramaic, or Hebrew languages; **Hebrew** = an (early) Israelite or their language or its modern version as spoken in Israel; **Hebraic** = concerning the Hebrews or their language; **Jewish** = concerning Jews; **Israeli** = concerning modern Israel. **Anti-Semitic** is commonly used to mean **anti-Jewish**. See also **Hebrew words**.

send inflects *send* − *sent* − *sent*.

Senegal The derived adjective and noun is *Senegalese*.

senhor (italics) = Portuguese for Mr; ***senhora*** = Portuguese for Mrs; ***senhorita*** = Portuguese for Miss. *See also* ***señor***; ***signor***.

señor (italics) = Spanish for Mr (pl. *señores*); ***señora*** = Spanish for Mrs; ***señorita*** = Spanish for Miss. *See also* ***senhor***; ***signor***.

sensible = showing or using common sense; **sensitive** = easily affected or stimulated. E.g.:

"You can rely on Bill to take sensible action in an emergency."
"I grazed my hand last week and the area is still sensitive."

sensual = lewd, voluptuous, concerning sexual gratification; **sensuous** = emotionally concerned with or received by the senses, alive to the pleasures of sensation; **sensory** = biologically concerned with the senses or sensation; **sensitive** = easily stimulated, responsive. E.g.:

"After a day's hard work, a hot bath gives me almost sensual satisfaction."
"After a day's hard work, listening to Mozart gives me sensuous pleasure."
"The skin contains various kinds of sensory receptors."
"A psychiatrist has to be sensitive to his patients' moods."

sentence, in grammar, is difficult to define. One definition makes a sentence "a complete expression of a thought". In writing or printing, a sentence begins with a capital letter and ends with a full stop (point, or period). Thus this is a sentence. And so is this. And this. In normal writing, however, it is usual for a sentence to include a verb, the most common simple sentence structure being subject + verb + object (as in "The boy kicked the ball"). Sentences without verbs attract criticism, and should therefore be avoided in formal writing.

sentential = to do with a (grammatical) sentence; **sententious** = in an affectedly pithy, brief or formal way (usually of writing), or moralistic in tone (usually of speech). The latter word is sometimes misused to mean *unconvincing*, *specious* or simply *wordy*.

sentiment = emotion, feeling, opinion; **sentimentality** = exaggerated feeling, false emotion.

separate, separator, separable (not separatable), separation.

septic *See* **sceptic**.

septum (pl. septa).

sérac (acute accent).

seraglio (pl. seraglios).

seraph (pl. seraphs, preferred to seraphim) = highest-ranking angel;
serif (preferred to seriph or ceriph) = short cross-line at the end of a
stroke of a letter, as in this capital **I**. A typeface lacking this feature is
called a *sanserif* face.

serf (pl. serfs) = slave; **surf** = breaking waves.

sergeant is the preferred spelling of **serjeant**, except in historical titles
such as *serjeant-at-arms*.

serial *See* **cereal**.

series (pl. series).

serif *See* **seraph**.

serious = earnest, of importance, life-threatening, not light-hearted;
serous = to do with or resembling serum (the watery component of
blood). E.g.:
"The child had only a slight temperature, but the doctor regarded the
illness as serious enough for hospital treatment."
"The wound remained wet because of leakage of serous fluid."

serrated = shaped like a saw's teeth; **serried** = arranged in close
ranks. E.g.:
"A nettle's leaves have serrated edges."
"The field was planted with serried rows of cabbages."

serum (pl. serums).

service, serviceable.

serviette The preferred term is **napkin**.

sesqui- Little-used prefix meaning one-and-a-half (as in sesquioxide,
sesquiplane). *See* **numerical prefixes**.

session *See* **cession**.

set (noun), = block of stone or wood used for paving and (formerly) surfacing roads, is the preferred spelling (not *sett*); **sett** = badger's burrow.

seta (pl. setae).

set-back, set-off, set piece, set-screw, set square, set-to, set-up.

settee *See* **couch**.

settle, settler (who settles), but settlor (who makes a settlement in law).

sew has the past tense **sewed** and past participle **sewn**. *See also* **sow**.

sewage is the stuff in the pipes; **sewerage** is the system of pipes that carry sewage.

sexism *See* **gender; mankind**.

Seychelles The derived adjective and noun is *Seychellois*.

s.g. is the abbreviation of specific gravity.

shake has the past tense **shook** and past participle **shaken**.

Shakespearian is the preferred spelling (not *Shakspearian* or *Shakespearean*).

shako (pl. shakos).

shall and **will** *Shall* is the normal, "neutral" way of forming the first person future tense (I shall go, we shall go), and *will* forms the normal second and third persons (you, he, she, it or they will go); used in this way they express what Eric Partridge calls "mere futurity". For emphasis, the roles are reversed. E.g.:

"I will get there" = "I am determined to get there";
"He shall not suffer" = "He must not suffer";
"Thou shalt not kill" is a command (well, Commandment);
"We will finish on time" – or else.

shammy is an accepted spelling which reflects the pronunciation of the alternative spelling **chamois** when it is applied to a type of soft leather.

shampoo (pl. shampoos), shampooed, shampooing.

shape, shapable.

shard (a piece of broken pottery) is preferred to **sherd**.

share, shareable.

shave has the preferred past tense and participle **shaved,** although *shaven* is retained as an adjective (e.g. "a shaven chin").

she/her should not be used in reference to ships or countries (use *it* or *its*).

sheaf (pl. sheaves).

shear has the preferred past tense and participle **sheared,** although *shorn* is retained as an adjective (e.g. "a shorn sheep").

shears (noun) is a plural word. "A pair of shears" achieves a singular construction.

sheath (noun) = a holder (e.g. of a dagger), scabbard, part that encloses; **sheathe** (verb) = to place in a sheath, to enclose.

sheep-dip, sheepdog, sheep-farmer, sheep-pen, sheepshank, sheep tick, sheep's-head, sheep-shearer, sheepskin.

sheikh is the preferred spelling (not *sheik, shaik* or *shaikh*).

shelf (pl. shelves).

shellac, shellacked, shellacking.

sherif (preferred to shereef) = Muslim leader; **sheriff** = British Crown's representative in a county, American law officer (of a county).

shew/shewn These archaic spellings should not be used; use *show/shown*. The old form persists in *shewbread*.

Shiah = Muslim sect whose members are known as **Shiites** (sometimes represented as *Shi'ites*).

shine, shiny. *Shine* inflects *shine – shone – shone*.

shingles (the virus disease) is a singular word; "cases of shingles" achieves a plural construction.

ship *See* **boat.**

shipbuilder, shipbuilding, shipmate, ship-owner, shipshape, shipwreck, shipwright, shipyard.

ships' names should be typeset in italic with an initial capital letter; e.g. *Queen Mary*, HMS *Beagle*, SS *Mauritania*. A ship should be referred to as *it*, not *her*. See also **HMS**.

"shock horror" See **horror**.

shoe (verb) inflects *shoe – shod – shod* (not *shoed*). Other verb forms include shoes, shoed, shoeing.

shoot (verb) inflects *shoot – shot – shot*. For **shoot** (noun), *see* **chute**.

shop assistant, shop-boy, shop-fitter, shop-front, shop-girl, shopkeeper, shop-lifter, shop steward, shop-walker.

short See **brief**.

shortened words, invented for convenience (or, some might say, adopted through laziness), often begin life as slang but through usage may force their way into the standard vocabulary. The following forms are thus acceptable:

amp (ampere)	cox (coxswain)	pram (perambulator)
bra (brassière)	curio (curiosity)	pub (public house)
bus (omnibus)	lase (laser)	vet (veterinary surgeon)
cab (cabriolet)	plane (aeroplane)	
cello (violoncello)	polio (poliomyelitis)	

The following list of shortened words have not yet gained standard status, and should be avoided in formal writing:

ad (advertisement)	flu (influenza)
artic (articulated lorry)	fridge (refrigerator)
bike (bicycle)	gym (gymnasium)
bookie (bookmaker)	hanky (handkerchief)
brolly (umbrella)	hi-fi (high fidelity)
deb (debutante)	homo (homosexual)
demo (demonstration)	intro (introduction)
disco (discothèque)	lino (linoleum)
comfy (comfortable)	marge (margarine)
exam (examination)	memo (memorandum)

meths (methylated spirit)
mike (microphone)
motorbike (motorcycle)
nighty (nightdress)
nympho (nymphomaniac)
panto (pantomime)
para (paragraph)
phone (telephone)
photo (photograph)
pop (popular)
pro (professional, prostitute)
psycho (psychopath)
recap (recapitulate)
recce (reconnaissance)
semi (semidetached house)
spec (speculation)
sub (submarine, subscription, substitute)
super (superintendent)
telly (television)
temp (temporary employee)
turps (turpentine)

No doubt survivors from the second list will eventually find a place in the first; some, such as *fridge, memo* and *phone*, are well on the way there already.

shorts See **knickers.**

short sight, short-sighted, short-sightedness (medical name *myopia*). *See also* **long sight.**

should is the normal past tense of *shall*, as *would* is of *will*. Thus as auxiliaries indicating tense they follow the same rules as do *shall* and *will* (which see). E.g.:

"I thought that if I kept going, I should get there soon."
"I hoped that you would come too."
"He said that he would let me know."
Transposing *should* and *would* conveys emphasis (but tangles with the subjunctive). E.g.:

"I knew that if I kept going I would get there on time."
"I thought that you should come, too."
"He admitted that he should let me know."

shovel, shovelled, shovelling, shoveller, shovelful (pl. shovelfuls).

show (verb) has the past tense **showed** and preferred past participle **shown**. Do not use *shew/shewed/shewn*.

show business, show-case, show-down, showgirl, showground, show house, showjump(ing), show-off (noun), showman, show-piece, show-place, showroom.

shred (verb) has the past tense and participle **shredded** (not *shred*).

shrewd now almost always means of good judgement, often demonstrating foresight (noun *shrewdness*). For this reason its former meanings relating to the mouse-like *shrew* (i.e. bad-tempered, biting) are best avoided.

shrink has the past tense **shrank** and past participle **shrunk**, although *shrunken* is retained as an adjective (e.g. "a shrunken head").

shut inflects *shut – shut – shut*. It describes the physical action of doing something; **close** (verb) is the general opposite of *open*. E.g.:
"The dog will escape, so please shut the gate at once."
"Please close the cupboard door when you have finished."

shy (= to throw), shied, shying; **shy** (= bashful), shyer, shyest, shyly, shyness.

sic (italics) (= thus, Latin) usually indicates that an odd-looking word is being quoted exactly. E.g.:
"The editor wrote to the author criticizing his grammer (*sic*)." It is also used to indicate ironic comments.

sick/sickness See **ill/illness**.

side-arm(s), side-bet, sideboard, sideburns, side-car, side-dish, side-door, side-drum, side-effect, sidelight, sideline, sidelong, side-road, side-saddle, side-show, side-slip, side-step, side-street, side-table, side-track, side valve, sideways.

side-head *See* **subheadings**.

sidle, sideling (not *sidling*).

siege *See* **seize**.

sign, signatory.

signal, signalled, signalling, signaller.

signor (italics) – Italian for Mr (pl. *signori*); *signora* = Italian for Mrs; *signorina* = Italian for Miss. *See also* **senhor**; **senor**.

silhouette (note spelling).

silica, silicate, siliceous.

silicon is a metalloid chemical element (Si), used to make semiconductors (silicon chips), and is the main component of silica (sand) and quartz; **silicone** is a type of silicon-containing plastic, valued for its lubricating, heat-resisting or water-proofing properties.

silo (pl. silos).

similar See **analogous**; **same**.

simplistic, used to mean *oversimplified*, is a vogue word to be avoided. See **vogue words**.

simply, used to mean **merely**, can lead to ambiguity, as in "He was simply careless". The different uses are compared in:
"He worked simply" (= in an uncomplicated way)
and "He simply worked" (= only worked, and did not recite poetry at the same time).

simulate = pretend, copy, imitate, appear to be; **assimilate** − absorb, take in, become like. E.g.:
"Some textured plastics simulate the appearance of leather."
"Many children assimilate the mannerisms of their parents."
See also **dissimulate**.

since, in the sense *because*, needs care with tenses; e.g. "What an improvement since we have used the new machine" should be
". . . since we used the new machine".

sine qua non (italics) = an essential condition; except in legal contexts, the Latin phrase should be avoided.

sing has the past tense **sang** and past participle **sung**.

Singapore The derived adjective and noun is *Singaporean*.

singe, singed, singeing.

Sinhalese is the preferred spelling, for the majority population and language in Sri Lanka (not *Singhalese*).

sink has the past tense **sank** and past participle **sunk**, although *sunken* is retained as an adjective (e.g. "sunken eyes").

sinus (pl. sinuses).

siren is the preferred spelling of **syren**.

sirocco is the preferred spelling (not *scirocco*).

-sis Nouns ending in *-sis* (e.g. genesis, hypothesis, synthesis, thesis) form the plural *-ses* (e.g. geneses, hypotheses, syntheses, theses).

sister-in-law *See* **in-laws**.

sit inflects *sit − sat − sat*.

site *See* **cite**.

situate should be avoided as an adjective meaning **situated**.

situation is a versatile if imprecise word which can mean location, place, condition or even circumstances surrounding a fact or event. Perhaps because of this imprecision it is often associated with another, precise, word but contributes nothing and serves only to fog what is already there. If the other word is also a vogue word, whole vogue phrases can be created. The many examples include "crisis situation", "ongoing situation" (or "ongoing crisis situation"), "feedback situation" (or "ongoing crisis feedback situation"), and so on. *See* **vogue words**.

size, sizable (= able to be sized; it does not mean *fairly large*).

-sized is preferred to **-size** in such expressions as life-sized model, medium-sized house.

skein (note *-ei-* spelling).

skewbald *See* **piebald**.

ski (pl. skis), ski'd (past tense of verb, not *skied* = past tense of to sky), skiing, skier (who skis; someone who skys a ball is a *skyer*).

skilful and **skilled** both = having/showing skill, but the latter should be reserved to describe labour, crafts and technical skills (a skilful editor but a skilled plumber). Note that *skilful* has only two *l*s.

skittles (the game) is a singular word; "games of skittles" achieves a plural construction.

skull *See* **scull**.

skulduggery (note spelling).

slacks *See* **knickers**.

slander *See* **libel**.

slang includes words and expressions that are still a long way from becoming formally accepted into standard English. Slang terms are usually invented to reinforce group identity to the exclusion of outsiders and may become **colloquialisms** (which *see*) before, perhaps, emerging as members of the formal vocabulary. Specialized slang includes argot, cant and jargon, each of which comprises expressions that are (sometimes deliberately) understandable only to the initiated (*see* **jargon; non-standard English**).

slatternly *See* **slovenly**.

slay has the past tense **slew** and past participle **slain**. Like the verb *slaughter* (except when used to describe killing animals for meat), it has an archaic ring to it and should not be used merely as an alternative for *kill*.

sledge = platform on runners for moving goods or people, usually over ice or snow (a *toboggan*); **sleigh** = passenger-carrying sledge pulled by animals (note -*ei*- spelling); **sled** is a technical word or an Americanism for *sledge*.

sleep (verb) inflects *sleep – slept – slept*.

sleight = cunning, dexterity (as in *sleight of hand*; note -*ei*- spelling); **slight** (noun) = disrespectful affront or disregard, insulting indifference; **slight** (adj.) = flimsy, lacking significance, small (e.g. "a slight increase in weight").

slide (verb) inflects *slide – slid – slid* (not *slidden*).

slight *See* **sleight**.

sling (verb = to throw) has the past tense and participle **slung**. When **sling** = to put on or into a sling, the past tense and participle is **slinged**.

slink has the past tense and participle **slunk**.

slivovitz is the preferred spelling (not *slivovic, slivovica, slivowitz*).

slough *See* **-ough.**

slovenly = untidy, dirty; **slatternly** = unclean, untidy, loose (morals). The former can be applied to anyone; the latter should be reserved for women and girls.

sly, slyer, slyest, slyly.

smell (verb) The preferred past tense and participle is **smelled** (not *smelt*).

smidgen (not *smidgeon*).

smite (archaic for to *strike*) has the past tense **smote** and past participle **smitten. Smitten** is the most commonly used of the three, as in "smitten with plague" or colloquially just "smitten" (with love).

smoke, smokable, smoky.

smooth (verb) forms the third person singular **smooths** (not *smoothes*).

snoek is preferred to **snook** for the edible fish (usually barracouta).

snorkel (preferred to schnorkel), snorkelled, snorkelling (not *snorkling*).

snowball, snow-berry, snow-blind(ness), snow-drift, snowdrop, snowfall, snowflake, snow-goggles, snow leopard, snowman, snow-plough, snowscape, snowshoe.

so, much overworked for *therefore,* needs care to avoid ambiguity; e.g. "It was her first commission, and she was so painstaking" could mean either "she was therefore painstaking" or "she was extremely painstaking".

soar = float on air, fly high; **sore** = painful

sobriquet = **nickname,** which is preferred.

so-called has a hyphen before a noun (e.g. "so-called assistant") but no hyphen after a verb (e.g. "is so called because...").

sociable = naturally inclined to be with others, company-seeking, affable; **social** = consisting of or relating to groups of (friendly) people, to communities, to society. E.g.:

"He is not a sociable person and prefers to keep himself to himself."
"The government has a social responsibility for protecting underprivileged people from exploitation."

socialize (not *-ise*).

-soever is used as an affix to add vagueness to *how, what, where, who* (howsoever, whatsoever, wheresoever, whosoever).

sofa *See* couch.

soirée (acute accent).

solemn, solemnize.

solicitor *See* **barrister**.

solid-state (adj.), solid state (noun); e.g. "solid-state physics" and "poisonous even in the solid state".

solo (pl. solos).

solve, solvable (= can be solved); **soluble** = can be dissolved/solved.

Somalia The derived adjective and noun is *Somali*.

sombrero (pl. sombreros).

some should not be misused for part; e.g. "He wasted some of the time day-dreaming" should be ". . . part of the time day-dreaming".

somebody, something and **sometime** should be distinguished from **some body, some thing** and **some time** (although the first pair are seldom confused). E.g.:

"Somebody must be responsible for the error."
"The wine would benefit from some body."
"Something is wrong with the table."
"It was not an animal; some thing did that damage."
"It must have happened sometime in the night."
"Take some time and make sure you get it right."

some day should always be spelled as two words (*someday* is an Americanism).

somersault (note spelling).

sonar (no initial capital letter).

songbird, songbook, song-cycle, song-hit, songthrush, songwriter.

soprano (pl. sopranos).

sore *See* **soar.**

sort of *See* **type of.**

sortie, sortied, sortieing.

so that = *with the result that;* it should not be used to mean *in order that.* E.g.:
"She worked late so that the work was completed" is correct usage;
"She worked late so that she could complete the work" is poor usage;
"She worked late so that her boss was impressed" is ambiguous −
with the result that, or in order that, the boss was impressed?

sotto voce (italics) = as an aside, under one's breath; the Italian expression should be avoided.

soufflé (acute accent).

soupçon = a pinch, suspicion (of), minute quantity; the French word should be avoided.

South Africa has English and Afrikaans as its official languages. Afrikaans, based originally on Dutch, has contributed several words to the standard English vocabulary. *See* **Dutch words.**

south, southern, southerly, etc. *See* **compass directions.**

Southern Hemisphere (initial capital letters).

South Pole (initial capital letters).

Soviet = to do with the Soviet Union − i.e., the USSR post-1917; **Russian** = to do with Russia or the Russian Empire pre-1917.

Soviet Union *See* **Soviet; Russia.**

sow (verb) has the past tense **sowed** and past participle **sown.** *See also* **sew.**

space rockets and **missiles** Capitalize the name and use Arabic numerals; e.g. Atlas, Exocet, Saturn 5, Titan 3. Space programmes are similar; e.g. Gemini 3, Apollo 13. Note also terms such as ABM (anti-ballistic missile), ICBM (intercontinental ballistic missile) and SAM (surface-to-air missile).

spacious = roomy, having plenty of space; **specious** = plausible yet deceptive, insubstantial. E.g.:

"He had a spacious office, large enough for three people."
"His argument was specious and based on a false assumption."

spaghetti, and most of the names of the other types of pasta, is a plural word in its original Italian but is normally regarded as singular (and has no plural) in English.

Spanish words have contributed to English over the centuries, sometimes taking the long route via South, Central or North America. They include:

aficionado	cask	lasso	plaza
alligator	cigar	macho	ranch
anchovy	cochineal	marijuana	rodeo
armada	cockroach	mascara	savanna
armadillo	desperado	merino	sherry
bonanza	El Dorado	mosquito	siesta
booby	embargo	mulatto	sombrero
bravado	fiesta	mustang	stampede
cafeteria	flotilla	negro	toreador
canyon	grandee	patio	tornado
cargo	guerrilla	peccadillo	vanilla

For plurals of words ending in -*o*, *see* **plurals**. *See also* **Portuguese words**.

spate = flood, torrent; it should not be used to mean merely more than usual, slight excess (as in "The spate of thefts increased the crime rate by two per cent").

spatula (pl. spatulas).

speak has the past tense **spoke** and past participle **spoken**.

special, specialize, speciality (general and cooking), specialty (legal and medical). E.g.:

"Yorkshire pudding is my mother's speciality."
"Orthopaedics is Doctor Brown's specialty."

specially = specifically, for a certain purpose; **especially** = particularly, outstanding. E.g.:

"The article was specially written for this book."
"It is a good book, especially the article written by him. It is especially good."

specie = coined money; it has no plural. **Species** = member of an interbreedable group of plants or animals (one category down from genus, one up from variety or race; *see* **Latin classification**). *Species* is the singular and plural form; the corresponding abbreviations are *sp.* and *spp.*

spectacles (= glasses) is a plural word. "A pair of spectacles" achieves a singular construction.

spectral = like a ghost (from *spectre*), or to do with a spectrum.

spectrum (pl. spectra).

speculate, speculator, speculation, speculative.

speed (verb) inflects *speed – sped – sped*; **speed up** inflects *speed up – speeded up – speeded up*..

spell (verb) has the preferred past tense and participle **spelled** (not *spelt*).

spelling Much of this Dictionary is to do with spelling, and for specific queries see the word concerned. For some general spelling rules (and their exceptions), *see* **Americanisms**; **-b- or -bb-**; **-l- or -ll-**; **negative prefixes**; **-m- or -mm-**; **-n- or -nn-**; **numerical prefixes**; **-ough**; **plurals**; **-p- or -pp-**; **-r- or -rr-**; **-s- or -ss-**; **suffixes**; **-t- or -tt-**; **verbs**.

spend inflects *spend – spent – spent*.

sperm has the preferred plural **sperm** (not *sperms*). It is derived from *spermatozoon* (pl. spermatozoa).

spice, spicy.

spike, spiky.

spill (verb) has the preferred past tense and participle **spilled**, although *spilt* is retained as an adjective (e.g. "spilt milk").

spin (verb) inflects *spin – spun – spun*.

spin-dry, spin-drier (not *spin-dryer*).

spiral, spiralled, spiralling.

spiritual = pertaining to the spirit, mind or soul; **spiritous** = alcoholic. E.g.:
"I have long been friends with Amanda, but our relationship has been only spiritual."
"The plastic surface should be cleaned with spiritous liquid."
See also **temporal.**

spirt/spurt/squirt all mean to spout, shoot out in a sudden jet or stream. The first two are merely spelling variations, with *spurt* being more common.

spit (verb) has the past tense **spat** and preferred past participle **spit** (not *spat*).

split infinitive This construction is to be avoided, but that may not always be possible without creating an awkward or stilted sentence. For instance, "He used to continually interrupt" is better than "He used continually to interrupt" and more direct than "He used to interrupt continually". In a sentence such as "He expects to more than double his output" the infinitive cannot be unsplit without changing the sense ("He expects to double more than his output?"). From this it can be concluded that to unnecessarily split an infinitive is not good style. As Douglas Adams said (*The Hitch Hiker's Guide to the Galaxy*): "... all dared...to boldly split infinitives that no man had split before".

spoil (verb) has the preferred past tense and participle **spoiled**, although *spoilt* is retained as an adjective meaning *marred* or *damaged*.

sponge, spongeable, spongy.

spoonful (pl. spoonfuls).

spouse is archaic for **husband** or **wife**, although it is convenient when the sex cannot be indicated and is common in legal texts.

spread inflects *spread* – *spread* – *spread*.

spring (verb) has the past tense **sprang** and past participle **sprung**.

spring (as a season, no initial capital letter), springbok, springtide (= springtime), spring tide (= tide of greatest height).

sprint *See* **spurt**.

spry, spryer, spryest, spryness, spryly.

spurt *See* **spirt**. **Spurt** has the additional meaning of a sudden increase in speed ("He put on a fine finishing spurt"), and should not be confused with **sprint**, which is run in its entirety at full speed.

squalor (not -*our*).

square brackets *See* **brackets**.

squirt *See* **spirt**.

stabilize, stabilizer.

stable = firm, steady, established, constant; **static** = unmoving, stationary, unchanging. The meanings overlap, but the words are not interchangeable in usages such as:
"A tall building must have a stable foundation."
"The weather was too poor for flying, so the crowd could see only a static display of aircraft."

stadium (pl. stadiums, not *stadia*).

staff has the usual plural **staffs**, but *staves* in music (which has given rise to the new singular *stave*).

stage-coach, stagecraft, stage door, stage fright, stage-manage(r).

staid = solemn, humourless; **stayed** = supported/propped up, remained.

stalactite = calcium carbonate (limestone) formation that hangs from the ceiling of a cave; **stalagmite** = similar formation that grows up from the floor of a cave. Both are formed extremely slowly by the evaporation of dripping water containing dissolved minerals.

stallion *See* **horse.**

stamen (pl. stamens, not *stamina*).

stanch = to stem (stop the flow); **staunch** = true, loyal. E.g.:
"Use a pad of cloth to stanch the bleeding."
"James has always been a staunch friend of mine."

stand (verb) inflects *stand − stood − stood*.

standard, standardize, standardization.

standard English *See* **English; non-standard English.**

stanza (pl. stanzas).

star, starred, starring, starry (compare **stare**, stared, staring, stary).

start (verb) should not be used for **begin** when referring to inanimate objects; e.g. "He starts work on Monday" but "The article begins on page 24".

state, stater (= one who states, old Greek coin), stator (= stationary part of a machine).

states of the USA *See* **US states.**

static *See* **stable.**

stationary = static, unmoving; **stationery** = writing materials.

statue = sculpture; **stature** = person's height; **statute** = law.

status quo = the previous position, and has come to mean also *the present position* (e.g. "return to the status quo", "maintain the status quo"); it is therefore tautologous and incorrect to write "return to the former status quo" or "maintain the present status quo". The Latin form should, however, be avoided.

staunch *See* **stanch.**

stave (verb) has the preferred past tense and participle **staved**, although *stove* is still used for broken in barrels or ships' hulls (e.g. "The rocks stove in the ship's hull").
See also **staff.**

Ste is the abbreviation of the French (female) Sainte.

steal has the past tense **stole** and past participle **stolen.**

steamboat, steam-driven, steam engine, steam-hammer, steam iron, steamroller, steamship (but Steam Ship, abbreviated to SS, in a ship's name), steamtight, steam train, steam turbine.

steer *See* **cattle.**

stencil, stencilled, stenciller, stencilling.

step- = prefix added to a family relationship which acknowledges the remarriage of a parent. **Stepchild** (stepdaughter or stepson) = spouse's child by a former marriage; **step-parent** (stepfather or stepmother) = one's parent's second or subsequent spouse after remarriage; **stepbrother/stepsister** = child of one's step-parent; *See also* **family relationships; half-brother.**

steppes *See* **llano.**

stere is preferred to **stère** for the little-used metric unit equal to a cubic metre.

sterile = incapable of reproduction, germ-free; **sterilized** = made incapable of reproduction (although formerly able), made germ-free (although formerly contaminated). Other forms are sterilize, sterilizer, sterilization. E.g.:
"Mules, the hybrid offspring of a horse and a donkey, are usually sterile."
"Geldings are young male horses that have been sterilized."

stet = instruction (on a typescript or proof) to a typesetter to ignore a previous instruction for amendment (*stet* = Latin "let it stand"). The word is written at the end of the line in the margin, and the letters or words concerned underlined with a broken line.

stick (verb) inflects *stick − stuck − stuck*.

stigma = brand, part of a flower (pl. stigmas), one of Christ's wounds (pl. stigmata) or their miraculous reappearance in someone else.

stile = vertical member forming the edge of a door, a step over a fence; **style** = a pen, custom, manner. The latter gives rise to *stylize*. *See also* **stylish**.

stiletto (pl. stilettos), stilettoed, stilettoing.

still life (pl. still lifes).

stimulant = a substance (such as a drug) that produces or increases activity; **stimulus** (pl. stimuli) = something that arouses a nerve or sense organ; **stimulation** = excitement, arousal. E.g.:
"The only way I could stay awake was by taking stimulants."
"To make the muscle contract, the researchers employed an electric current as a stimulus."

sting (verb) inflects *sting – stung – stung*.

stink (verb) has the past tense **stank** and past participle **stunk**.

stoep = South African veranda; **stoop** = container for holy water (and an Americanism for a front porch).

Stone Age (initial capital letters).

stopcock, stop-gap, stop-go, stop-off (noun), stop-over (noun), stop-press, stop valve, stop-watch.

store, storable.

storey/story *See* **floor**.

straight = unbent, direct; **strait** = narrow, close (hence strait-jacket, strait-laced).

straightaway/straightforward (each one word).

strain *See* **sprain**.

strata is plural (singular *stratum*).

strategy = overall plan (of attack); **tactics** = (minute-by-minute) deployment of forces. E.g.:

"The marketing director has decided on the strategy for our new advertising campaign."

"As the campaign develops, our tactics will be to move salesmen into the areas with the best response."

streamline(d) (one word).

strew has the preferred past tense and participle **strewed**, although *strewn* is retained as an adjective (e.g. "a floor strewn with petals").

stria (pl. striae), striated, striation.

stride has the past tense **strode** and past participle **stridden**.

strike (verb) has the preferred past tense and participle **struck**, although *stricken* is retained as an adjective (e.g. "a stricken ship").

string (verb) has the preferred past tense and participle **strung**, although *stringed* is retained as an adjective (e.g. "stringed instruments").

stripe, stripy.

strive has the past tense **strove** and past participle **striven**.

student *See* **pupil**.

studio (pl. studios).

stupefy, stupefaction.

stupor (not *-our*), stupid, stupidity, stupidness, stupefy.

sty = pig house (pl. sties); **stye** = pimple at the base of an eyelash (pl. styes).

style *See* **stile**.

stylish = smart, fashionable; **stylized** = unnatural, conformist. *See also* **stile**.

stylus (pl. styluses, of record players).

sub- Most words with this prefix are now spelled as one word (without a hyphen); e.g. subatomic, subclass, subheading, and so on.

Exceptions include sub-basement, sub-branch (and others with two *b*s), sub-edit(or), sub-lieutenant, sub-plot.

subconscious = only partly aware, not firmly part of the consciousness (of the mind); **unconscious** = in a faint, completely unaware, carried out with conscious thought. The psychological meanings (stated last in each case) can also be used as nouns.

Subliminal = below the threshold of consciousness; it has recently come into prominence in the term *subliminal advertising*, a proscribed technique of introducing advertisements as single frames interlaced in a film or video programme (which pass too rapidly to register on the consciousness).

subject to = liable to, exposed or open to, particularly something disadvantageous; **addicted to** = given to a harmful practice or habit, often leading to physical or psychological dependence.

submerge, submersible (noun and adj.).

submit, submitted, submitting.

subnormal *See* **abnormal.**

subpoena (pl. subpoenas), subpoenaed, subpoenaing.

subsequent to = after, which is preferred.

subsidence = sinking (of land); **subsidy** = grant (of money). E.g.:
"Subsidence has caused a crack in a wall of my house."
"I will get a subsidy from the council to repair my house."

subsidiary (note spelling).

substantial = having substance/solidity, of real value, existing; it should not be used to mean merely **large.**

substitute *See* **replace.**

substratum (pl. substrata).

subtle (adj.), subtleness (noun), subtlety (noun), subtly (adv.).
Subtle = finely discriminated, delicate, cunning; **supple** = lithe, pliant. E.g.:
"He failed to notice the subtle implications of her statement."
"He admired the dancer's supple contortions."

such as introduces a previously defined example; **such that** introduces a consequence. E.g.:

"An initial letter *p* is silent in some words, such as psalm and ptarmigan."

"The position of the window is such that it overlooks the main entrance."

See also **like**.

suchlike (one word).

sudden, suddenly, suddenness. The expression *all of a sudden* (= suddenly) should be avoided.

sue, sued, suing.

suede (no accent).

suffer *from* a disorder, not **suffer** *with*.

sufficient, like **adequate**, seldom means other than plain **enough**.

suffixes A common difficulty with suffixes concerns the spelling of the resulting word, particularly the change (if any) to the termination of the root word when the suffix is added. Here are some rules.

1. *-able* or *-ible* A special case with no simple rules. *See* **-able** and **-ible**.

2. *-c* Many words ending in *-c* change the *c* to *ck* when a suffix is added. *See* **-c** to **-ck-**.

3. *-ed* and *-ing* Monosyllabic words ending in a consonant preceded by a single vowel double the consonant on adding *-ed* or *-ing*. E.g. (in terminal consonant order):

bag	bagged	bagging
bar	barred	barring
con	conned	conning
fob	fobbed	fobbing
hem	hemmed	hemming
knit	knitted	knitting
pad	padded	padding
quiz	quizzed	quizzing
slap	slapped	slapping
trek	trekked	trekking

Exceptions include *bus − bused − busing* and words ending in *w*, *x* or *y*:

fix	fixed	fixing
sew	sewed	sewing
stay	stayed	staying

Other monosyllabic forms, with a long vowel sound, do not normally double the consonant:

bait	baited	baiting
boil	boiled	boiling
dent	dented	denting
foul	fouled	fouling
heal	healed	healing
jail	jailed	jailing
lamb	lambed	lambing
moan	moaned	moaning
mount	mounted	mounting
rant	ranted	ranting
seed	seeded	seeding
siege	sieged	sieging
sort	sorted	sorting
spurt	spurted	spurting
vamp	vamped	vamping

Polysyllabic words with a stress on the last syllable follow the double consonant rule:

allot	allotted	allotting
occur	occurred	occurring
prefer	preferred	preferring
preplan	preplanned	preplanning
refer	referred	referring
remit	remitted	remitting

Exceptions are words ending in *w*, *x* or *y*:

allow	allowed	allowing
annoy	annoyed	annoying
relax	relaxed	relaxing

The last consonant is generally not doubled, however, if the final syllable is unaccented (unless the consonant is an *l*):

ballot	balloted	balloting
bias	biased	biasing
focus	focused	focusing
market	marketed	marketing
proffer	proffered	proffering
profit	profited	profiting
rivet	riveted	riveting

but

channel	channelled	channelling
enrol	enrolled	enrolling
level	levelled	levelling
travel	travelled	travelling

(exceptions include *appeal, parallel* and *repeal*).

4. *-er* and *-est* With monosyllabic words, these two suffixes follow the same rules as for *-ed* and *-ing*. E.g.:

hot	hotter	hottest – double
		consonant
low	lower	lowest}
lax	laxer	laxest} no doubling
coy	coyer	coyest}
damp	damper	dampest}

Polysyllabic adjectives generally form the comparative and superlative using *more* and *most* (not *-er* and *-est*). *See* **comparatives and superlatives**.

5. *-ic* and *-ics* Certain adjectives ending in *-ic* become nouns on the addition of an *s*. E.g.:

acoustic	acoustics
athletic	athletics
ceramic	ceramics
economic	economics
geriatric	geriatrics
mathematic	mathematics
narcotic	narcotics
politic	politics
semantic	semantics

Many of the nouns are regarded as singular (e.g. "acoustics is a branch of physics", "semantics is the study of the meanings of words" but "cosmetics are becoming increasingly expensive").

6. *-ize*, *-ise* and *-yse* See **-ize** or **-ise**.

7. *-ment* Words ending in *-dge* retain the *e* when the suffix *-ment* is added. E.g.:

abridge	abridgement
acknowledge	acknowledgement
estrange	estrangement
judge	judgement (but judgment in law)
lodge	lodgement
prejudge	prejudgement

8. *-s*, *-es*, *-ies* and *-ves* Most English words, including those ending in *-e*, *-ee* or *-y* preceded by a vowel, form plurals by adding *s*. E.g.:

comb	combs
dome	domes
employee	employees
key	keys
monkey	monkeys
ploy	ploys

Words ending in *-s* or *-x* form the plural by adding *-es*:

loss	losses
box	boxes

(exception *ox*, plural *oxen*).

Words ending in *-y* preceded by a consonant change the *-y* to *-ies* to form the plural:

try	tries
lorry	lorries
pony	ponies

Words ending in *-f* form the plural by adding *-s* or by changing the *-f* to *-ves*. For a list of examples, *see* **plurals**.
For plurals of foreign words and words ending *-o*, *see* **plurals**.
See also **-ee**; **-ize** or **-ise**; **-ly**; **-or**; **-y**.

sugar beet, sugar-bowl, sugar-cane.

suggest, suggestible (= open to suggestion, persuadable), suggestive (= hinting at indecency). E.g.:

"You can easily persuade Bill that the milk is turning sour − he is highly suggestible."

"Bill embarrassed us all by telling suggestive jokes."

suit = a set of armour, clothes or cards, or a court action; **suite** = a set of furniture, related pieces of music, or adjacent rooms.

summary *See* **outline**.

summons (law), summonsed (= issued with a summons).

sumo *See* **judo**.

sumptuous is usually spelled correctly if it is not mispronounced "sumptious".

Sun (the star of our Solar System) has an initial capital letter, as have the words Solar System, when referred to as an astronomical object. In other meanings and in compounds − of which there are many − sun has no capital; e.g. sunbathe, sun-baked, sunbeam, sun-bonnet, sunburn(ed), sundew, sundial, sundown(er), sun-dress, sunflower, sun-glasses, sun-god, sun-hat, sunlight, sunrise, sunroof, sunset, sunshade, sunshine, sunspot, sunstroke, sun-tan, sun-trap, sun-up, sun-worship.

super- Most words with this prefix are spelled as one word (without a hyphen). An exception is *super-ego*.

supercilious (note spelling).

superficial = concerning only the surface, shallow; **superfluous** = extra to requirement, more than enough, redundant. E.g.:

"Despite his experience, his knowledge of the basic principles is only superficial."

"We are moving to smaller premises, so please throw away any superfluous stock."

superintend, superintendent, superintendency.

superior to (not superior *than*).

superlatives *See* **comparatives and superlatives**.

supersede (not *supercede*) = to take the place of; **surpass** = to do better, do better than; the two words are not synonyms.

supervise, supervisor, supervision.

supine *See* **prone**.

supper *See* **dinner**.

supple, supplely (to prevent confusion with the unrelated word *supply*).

supplement (noun) = an addition to something previously thought to be complete; **complement** (noun) = an integral part, that which completes the whole; both words also have special meanings in mathematics. **To supplement** = to augment or add something to; **to complement** = to complete by adding an essential part, to supply what is (obviously) wanting. *Supplementary* and *complementary* are the corresponding adjectives. **Compliment** = an expression of praise, regard or flattery.

supposedly should not be misused for **presumably**; e.g. in "Fred was supposedly to blame", *presumably* is presumably intended.

suppress, suppressor.

supra-, a prefix meaning above, does not take a hyphen except in *supra-axillary, supra-orbital*.

surf *See* **serf**.

surfeit (note -*ei*- spelling).

surgeon *See* **doctor**.

surmise (not -*ize*).

surplus (pl. surpluses).

surprise = to take off guard or unawares; **astonish** is stronger; **astound** is even stronger; **amaze** is strongest. The corresponding nouns are *surprise, astonishment, astoundment* and *amazement*. One of the stronger words should not be used when mere *surprise* is intended.

surrender, surrenderer (-*er*, even in law).

surveillance (note *-ei-* spelling).

swap The preferred spelling is **swop**.

swat = to hit (a fly); **swot** = to study hard.

Swaziland The derived adjective and noun is *Swazi*.

swear has the past tense **swore** and past participle **sworn**. *See also* **curse**.

sweep (verb) inflects *sweep − swept − swept*.

swell (verb) has the past tense and participle **swelled**, which can mean *increased*; **swollen** is used adjectivally to mean *increased to a harmful extent* (e.g. "a swollen ankle").

swim (verb) has the past tense **swam** and past participle **swum**.

swing (verb) inflects *swing − swung − swung*.

swinging = oscillating; **swingeing** = chastising.

syllable, syllabication (not *syllabification*).

syllabus (pl. syllabuses).

symbol, symbolize. *See also* **cymbal**.

sympathy Have sympathy *for*; be in sympathy *with*; sympathize *with*; be sympathetic (or unsympathetic) *to*. *See also* **empathy**.

syncope = omission in pronunciation of the sound(s) of letters in the middle of a word. Thus the nautical terms *boatswain* and *coxswain* (originally *cockswain*) are pronounced *bosun* and *coxun*. This phenomenon has allowed *bosun* to become an accepted alternative spelling (but not, so far, *coxun*). Note also *forecastle* (pronounced *foke-sel*).

synonyms = two or more words of the same meaning. They are uncommon in a rich vocabulary such as that of English (Fowler refers to *gorse* and *furze* as "that very great rarity, a pair of exact synonyms", a fact that resulted in at least one dictionary defining each only in terms of the other). Usually the terms *synonym* and *synonymous* refer to words that are almost the same in meaning, often more dependent on context than consideration of words in isolation. Thus the words *usually* and *often* are sufficiently synonymous to be transposed in the previous sentence without significantly changing its meaning.

T

-t- or **-tt-** Monosyllabic words ending in -*t* preceded by a single vowel double the *t* before *y* or a suffix beginning with a vowel. E.g.:

pot	pottable, potted, potter, potting, potty
skit	skitter, skitting, skittish

The *t* remains single if preceded by a long or double vowel. E.g.:

heat	heatable, heated, heating
sprout	sprouted, sprouting

With polysyllabic words, the choice of -*t*- or -*tt*- depends on where the accent falls. If it is on the last syllable, the rule is as for monosyllabic words. E.g.:

abutting	formatting	permitting	remitting
allotting	omitting	pirouetting	submitting
besotting	outfitting	rebutting	
committing	outwitting	regretting	

If the last syllable is unaccented, the -*t*- is not doubled. E.g.:

balloting	defeating	mistreating	riveting
benefiting	exhibiting	picketing	valeting
buffeting	fidgeting	piloting	
combating	interpreting	rabbiting	
crediting	marketing	rioting	

Neither is the *t* doubled, in monosyllabic or polysyllabic words, before suffixes that begin with a consonant. E.g.:

fitful
commitment
creditworthy

table-cloth, table-knife, tableland, table-linen, table-maid, table-mat, tablespoon, tablespoonful(s), table tennis, table-top, table-ware, table wine.

tableau (pl. tableaux).

table d'hôte *See* **à la carte.**

taboo (pl. taboos), tabooed, tabooing (preferred to **tabu**). *Taboo* words are those that are considered inappropriate for use in polite company.

tabulate, tabulator.

tachograph = instrument in the cab of a lorry or coach for recording on a card the speed of a vehicle and the time for which it is driven; **tachometer** = rev(olutions) counter, instrument for indicating speed of rotation; **tachygraph** = Medieval shorthand; **tachymeter** = instrument for locating points in surveying.

tactics is plural; it has no singular. *See* **strategy.**

taenia = tapeworm or ribbonworm; **tinea** = ringworm (caused by a fungus).

tail-back, tail-board, tail-end(er), tail-gate, tail-lamp, tail-light, tail-off (noun), tailpiece, tailpipe, tailplane, tailstock.

take has the past tense **took** and past participle **taken.**

take into consideration = **consider,** which is preferred.

take umbrage is an archaism and cliché for **take offence,** which should be used.

talisman (pl. talismans, not *talismen*).

tamarin = small South American monkey; **tamarind** = tropical tree with edible pods.

tame, tameable.

Tamil *See* **Indian words.**

tampon = cotton-wool plug (for a wound or body orifice); **tampion** = plug for the muzzle of a gun; **tompon** = tampion; **tompion** = kind of early watch.

tam-tam = orchestral gong; **tom-tom** = American Indian or African drum.

tangible (not -*able*).

tango (pl. tangos).

tantalize, tantalization.

tarantella = lively dance (originating in Italy), thought to mimic the effect of being bitten by a **tarantula** spider.

tariff (note spelling).

tarry (verb) = linger, wait; **tarry** (adj.) = covered with or resembling tar.

tarsus (pl. tarsi).

tart *See* **flan**.

tartan = traditional Scottish design woven into cloth, used to make kilts and plaids (*see* **plaid**). **The tartan** is synonymous with *Highland dress*.

tasteful = in good taste; **tasty** = having a good flavour. E.g.:
"The walls were adorned with a tasteful collection of prints."
"My favourite snack is a bread roll and a tasty piece of cheese."

tattoo (pl. tattoos), tattooed, tattooing, tattooer, tattooist.

taut = tight; **taught** = past tense and participle of the verb **to teach**.

tautology is unnecessary repetition. Common phrases that are usually tautologous (and therefore should be avoided) include:

added bonus	close down/up	drink down/up
adequate enough	close/through	each and every
all alone	scrutiny	earlier on
all-time/new record	collaborate/	early beginnings
as and when	co-operate together	eat up
assemble/attach	collect/combine/	end product/result
together	connect together	end up
blend together	completely/totally	equally as
burn down/up	destroyed	false illusion
but nevertheless	completely/totally	file away
check out/up	surrounded	final completion/
circle round	continue on	outcome
climb up	cut back	finally/ultimately end
close proximity	divide off/up	in

finish up

first/initially conceived/

first prototype

follow after

free gift

free and gratis

from hence (forth)/thence

future prospects

gather together

general consensus

grateful thanks

head up

hurry up

if and when

in between

indirect allusion

inside of

join/link together

just exactly

later on

lend out

lose out

mental telepathy

meet/merge/mix together twice (etc.) over

minute detail

more especially

more inferior/ superior

more preferable

mutual co-operation

nearly dead (although *near death* is acceptable)

joint partnership

new innovation

newly created

opening gambit

original source

over again

pair of twins

past history

pay off

plan ahead/on

polish up

puzzling mystery

raze to the ground

reason why

reduce down

refer back

reiterate again

renew/repeat again

repeat again

rest up

return/revert back

rise up

root cause

round ball

seldom ever

self-confessed

send on

settle up

sit down

solitary isolation

still remain

trigger off

true facts

try out

ultimate conclusion

unexpected surprise

unite together

unless and until

usual habit

watch out for

whether or not

In many pairs, the second word (often a preposition) can be omitted.

taxi (verb), taxied, taxiing. **Taxi** (noun) has the plural *taxis*.

tea-bag, tea-break, tea-caddy, teacake, tea-chest, tea-cloth, tea-cosy, teacup, teacupful(s), tea-garden, tea-house, tea-leaf (tea-leaves), tea-party, teapot, tea-room, tea-rose, tea service, tea-shop, teaspoon, teaspoonful(s), tea-table, tea-time, tea-towel, tea-tray, tea-trolley, tea-urn.

teacake *See* **crumpet**.

teach inflects *teach* – *taught* – *taught*. *See also* **learn**.

tear (verb) has the past tense **tore** and past participle **torn**.

technical expressions Many "ordinary" words have been taken over by science, technology and crafts and given a special meaning; e.g. *transparency*, the state of being transparent, is used for a positive photographic image on (colour) film, also called a *slide* or *diapositive*. But the traffic has been two-way, and some technical expressions have been adopted into the general vocabulary with non-technical meanings; e.g. *catalyst*, in chemistry a substance that (in small quantities) accelerates a reaction without taking part in it, is used figuratively for something or someone who initiates an act, particularly one that was previously bogged down. Such exchanges can enrich the vocabulary without the need to invent new words (*see* **neologisms**). Care should be exercised, however, in using borrowed technical expressions, particularly if they are employed merely for novelty, emphasis or exaggeration (such as the misuse of the psychological terms manic, paranoiac and schizophrenic and various others included in this Dictionary).

technics is obsolete for **technology** (= the study and practice of applied science), as **technic** is for **technical** (= to do with applied science or engineering). Someone with technical skills is a **technician**, who applies various **techniques** in his work; *technique* also describes the skills/methods of an artist or musician. A *technician* often works in a narrower field than an **engineer; a mechanic** generally deals only with mechanisms (e.g. computer engineer, dental technician, car mechanic), although the terms are interchangeable.

teenage, teenaged, teenager (*see also* **baby**).

teeth is the noun; **teethe** is the verb.

teetotal, teetotaller, teetotalism.

televise, television ("No good will come of this device. The word is half Green and half Latin" – C.P. Scott).

tell inflects *tell* – *told* – *told*.

temerity = audacity, rashness; **timidity** = faint-heartedness, lacking in courage. E.g.:

"Only Jane has the temerity to talk to the boss like that."
"June cannot overcome her timidity and complain to the boss."

temperance *See* **abstain**.

templet is the preferred spelling (not *template*).

tempo (pl. tempos).

temporal, = to do with the time or relating to a lifespan (opposite of *spiritual, eternal*), gives the adverb **temporally**; **temporary**, = of short duration, fleeting, transient (opposite of *permanent*), gives the adverb **temporarily**. The spellings of the adverbs are sometimes confused. A derived verb is **temporize** = to play for time, hedge, negotiate (compare with *extemporize* = to play/speak without preparation). **Temporal** also means to do with the temple(s) (at the side of the head). *See also* **transient**.

tendency *to* (not tendency *for*).

tensimeter – instrument for measuring vapour pressure; **tensometer** = instrument for measuring elasticity (by stretching).

tepid = luke-warm, half-hearted; **torpid** = sluggish, lethargic, inactive.

tera- is the metric prefix for a million million times ($\times 10^{12}$). (*See* **units**).

terminate, terminator, terminable (not *terminatable*, = able to be ended), terminal (= coming to or causing an end), termination. *See also* **terminus**.

terminus (pl. termini), terminate, terminator, termination. Also note **terminal** (noun) used of an airline terminus (airport).

ter- or tri- *See* **numerical prefixes**.

terrible should be reserved in formal writing for things or circumstances that invoke *terror* and not used of something that is merely **unpleasant** or **disagreeable**. Similarly **terribly** should not be used as a meaningless intensifier (as in "She was terribly pleased").

terrific should be reserved in formal writing for things or circumstances that *terrify* and not used to mean *enjoyable* or *very good*.

terrorize, terrorist.

test-bed, test case, test drive, test flight, test match, test pilot, test-tube (baby).

tetchy (note spelling).

tête-à-tête = private (conversation); the French term should be avoided.

textual = pertaining to text; **textural** = pertaining to texture.

Thailand The derived adjective and noun is *Thai*.

than Apart from *other, otherwise, else* and *elsewhere*, the only words that can be followed by *than* are comparatives (e.g. older, younger, better than). So beware of using *than* as a preposition in such constructions as "He is richer than her" which, strictly, should be "... richer than she (is)".
Do not misuse *than* for *as*; e.g. "Twice as many errors had been made than in the other article" is incorrect – it should read "... had been made as in the other article".

thankfully = in a thankful way. It should not be used to mean *let us be thankful* (that). E.g.:
"He took the drink thankfully" is correct;
"Thankfully, there is more time" is incorrect.
This misuse is currently in vogue (*see also* **hopefully, regretfully**) but is not (yet) acceptable in good writing – it may, however, go the way of that other common "sentence adverb" **importantly**, which has more or less gained acceptance:"More importantly, the mayor will be there".

that and which *See* **which**.

theca (pl. thecae).

theirs (no apostrophe). *See* **one's**.

their, there and they're have only pronunciation in common (*see* **homonyms**). **Their** is a possessive pronoun meaning *of them* (e.g.

"They paid for their tickets"). **There** usually indicates position, and is thus an adverb (e.g. "I used to go there"), although it can also be a pronoun (e.g. "There is a bad smell in this room"). **They're** is a contraction of *they are* (e.g. "They're over there!"), and should be avoided in formal writing.

thence is archaic for **from there**, which should be used.

thenceforth is archaic for **from that time on(ward)** which, although longer, is preferred. *See also* **thereafter**.

theory, theorize.

thereafter = after a particular (designated) time (e.g. "He made his views known and thereafter said no more"). It has an archaic ring and can usually be replaced by *from that time* or *from then*. Similarly **thereof** = *of that* and **theretofore** = *up to that time* (or **before**). *See also* **thenceforth**.

there are many is correct (not *there is many*).

thesis (pl. theses).

thief (pl. thieves).

think inflects *think – thought – thought*.

this/these Usually these demonstrative pronouns should not be used as the subject of a sentence; they should be made into adjectives modifying a noun. E.g.:
"This is a sign of vague writing" should read "this error is a sign of..."

thither is archaic for **to there** (as in the cliché "hither and thither"), and should be avoided.

tholus (pl. tholi).

thorax (pl. thoraxes), thoracic.

though *See* **although**.

thrash = to flog, beat soundly (transitive), move about violently (intransitive); it also means to **thresh** (corn), but *thresh* should be used for this meaning (and threshing machine etc.). **Thrash out** = to discuss/debate exhaustively.

threshold (not *threshhold*).

thrive has the preferred past tense and participle **thrived** (not *throve, thriven*) although *thriven* (= developed, succeeded) is sometimes used as an adjective.

throe = spasm, violent pang (usually in the plural − e.g. "throes of starvation"); not to be confused with **throws**.

thrombus (pl. thrombuses, not *thrombi*).

throughout *See* **all over**.

throw (verb) has the past tense **threw** and past participle **thrown** (paralleled by its compounds *overthrow* and *underthrow*). *See also* **throe**.

thymus (pl. thymuses).

tibia (pl. tibias).

tic = muscular twitch; **tick** = sound of a clock, blood-sucking insect, strong fabric, or mark signifying *correct*.

tie, tying, tied.

tilde = mark over Spanish *n*, as in cañon, mañana, Señor, vicuña.

till should not be used for **until**.

timber = wood; **timbre** = quality of a sound.

time (dates, months, days) The preferred style is: 13 November 1989; November 1989; 13 November; 56 BC; AD 56; the eighteenth century (not 18th century, unless unavoidable in captions); an eighteenth-century house; 1980s or the eighties (not 1980's, 80's or 'eighties).
The form 5/11/89 (or 5.11.89) should be avoided, which in Britain means 5 November but which in the United States means 11 May. The international system is 1989−11−05 (for 5 November). In ranges of years, both years should preferably be given in full: 1400-1419 (not 1400−19), 1988−1989 (not 1988−9).

Names of months should be given in full text, but may be abbreviated to save space in tables thus:

Jan Feb Apr Aug Sept Oct Nov Dec

(March, May, June and July in full).

Names of days should be given in full in text, but may also be abbreviated thus in tables:

Sun Mon Tues Weds Thur Fri Sat

Time should be given thus:

8 a.m. (not 8.00am); 8.30 p.m.; half past three; nine o'clock; 10hr 14 min; 14.00 or 14.00hr ("14 hundred hours"); 18.20 or 18.20hr.

Biographical dates: birth and death dates should be given, unless identified as otherwise; e.g. Queen Victoria (1819–1901) but Queen Victoria (reigned 1837–1901). Use the terms flourished, died and born in text but *fl.*, *d.* and *b.* with life dates in captions, annotations and time charts. If a date is not known with precision, use *c.* (*circa*), not "?". If both birth and death dates are obscure then the style is (*c.*1250-c.1300) not (*c.*1250–1300). If the subject is still alive the preferred style is (1949-   ), not (*b.*1949). Two character spaces should be left after the dash, unless the subject was born in the nineteenth century, when four spaces should be left after the dash. (In this way, both spaces will accept the death date in a subsequent revision without the need to re-set more than one line.)

time, timeable. Some of the compounds are time-and-motion, time bomb, time-consuming, time exposure, time-fuse, time-honoured, time-lag, time-lapse (adj.), time-limit, timepiece, time-saving, time-scale, time sharing, time-sheet, time-signal, time-signature, time-switch, timetable, time-worn (adj.), time zone.

times See × (multiplication sign).

timid/timorous See **apprehensive**.

timidity See **temerity**.

timpano = orchestral kettledrum (pl. timpani); **tympanum** = the ear-drum, semicircular panel over a door (pl. tympana).

ting (= to ring), tinged, tinging; **tinge** (= to tint/colour), tinged, tinging. The spellings of the past tenses and present participles of each verb are the same.

tiny, tinier, tiniest.

tiptoe, tiptoed, tiptoeing.

tire is the verb; **tyre** is the preferred spelling of the noun (as in bicycle tyre). *See* **tyre**.

tiro (pl. tiros) (not *tyro*).

titillate = to arouse pleasure in; **titivate** = to smarten up, tidy oneself.

title(d) (= name(d)). The preferred verb is **entitle(d)**.

titles and ranks *See* **capitalization; honours.**

to and fro is the adverb (e.g. "the piston moved to and fro"); **to-and-fro** is the adjective (e.g. "to-and-fro motion"); **toing and froing**.

tobacco (pl. tobaccos), tobacconist.

toboggan, tobogganed, tobogganing. *See also* **sledge.**

to boot is archaic for **moreover** or **in addition**, either of which is preferred.

tocsin = an alarm; **toxin** = a poison (of biological origin).

today, tomorrow and **tonight** are the preferred spellings (not *to-day, to-morrow* and *to-night*).

. . . to death Expressions such as *burned to death, choked to death, drowned to death, hanged to death, shot to death, starved to death, strangled to death* and *suffocated to death* should be selected carefully. The addition ". . . to death" is redundant after *drowned, hanged, strangled* and *suffocated* because drowning, hanging, strangling and suffocation ultimately cause death. The addition can be justified in the other expressions because burning, choking, shooting and starvation, while possibly causing severe injury or ill-health, do not necessarily lead to death.

toe (verb), toed, toeing.

toga (pl. togas).

Togo The derived adjective and noun is *Togolese*.

tolerance = ability to endure/tolerate (and various technical meanings); **toleration** = act of enduring/tolerating. E.g.:

"My mother has enough tolerance to look after the children all day."
"Many difficulties between parents and teenage children stem from a lack of toleration on both sides."

tolerant *of* is correct (not tolerant *to*).

tolerate, tolerable (not *toleratable*).

tomato (pl. tomatoes).

tom-tom *See* **tam-tam**.

ton, in Britain, is 2,240 pounds weight; **ton** in the United States, is 2,000 pounds (= a short ton); **tonne** is 1,000 kilograms (= 2,204.62 pounds). The term *metric ton* should not be used for **tonne**. **Tun** is a large barrel or cask.

Tonga The derived adjective and noun is *Tongan*.

tongs, like scissors and trousers, is a plural noun; "a pair of tongs" achieves a singular construction.

tonsil, tonsillar, tonsillitis.

top brass, topcoat, top dog, top drawer (noun), top-drawer (adj.), topdress (verb), top-dressing, topgallant, top-hat, top-heavy, top-knot, topless, top-level (adj.), top-line, topmast, topmost, topsail, top-secret (adj.), topside, topsoil, top table.

tophus (pl. tophi).

toponym = a word formed from a place-name. Many examples are words for cloth or clothing; e.g.:

balaclava (Balaclava, Crimea)	jodhpurs (Jodphur, India)
calico (Calicut, India)	limerick (Limerick, Ireland)
cashmere (Kashmir, India)	limousine (Limousine, France)
damask (Damascus, Syria)	magenta (Magenta, Italy)
denim (de Nîmes, France)	manilla (Manila, Philippines)
duffel (Duffel, Belgium)	marathon (Marathon, Greece)
fez (Fez, Morocco)	muslin (Mosul, Iraq)
homburg (Homburg, Germany)	panama (Panama, C. America)

rugby (Rugby, England)
spa (Spa, Belgium)

spartan (Sparta, Greece)
tarantula (Taranto, Italy)

torment, tormentor.

tornado (pl. tornadoes).

torpedo (pl. torpedoes).

torpor (not *-our*), torpid, torpidity, torpidness.

torsion (but note *contortion, distortion*).

torso (pl. torsos).

tortuous = twisting and turning, not straightforward; **torturous** = cruel, causing pain. E.g.:
"The so-called short cut involved a tortuous journey along narrow country lanes."
"We were glad to leave the factory building and escape the torturous noise of the machinery."

torus (pl. tori).

total, totalled, totalling.

touché (italics, acute accent).

toupee (not italics, no accent).

tour de force (italics) = feat of skill or strength; the French form should be avoided.

tournedos (pl. tournedos).

tourniquet (note spelling).

towards is preferred to **toward**.

to whit is an archaism for **namely**, which should be used.

toxin *See* **poison; tocsin.**

trace, traceable.

trachea (pl. tracheae).

trade, tradeable.

trade-in (noun), trade mark, trade name, tradesman, trades-people, tradeswoman, trade union (pl. trade unions, but TUC = Trades Union Congress), trade unionism, trade wind.

trade names or proprietary names (and trade marks) still in current use should be spelled with an initial capital letter. Long-standing ones that have entered the language (i.e. have become generic names) are usually spelled as ordinary words with no initial capital. For example, each of the following was once a trade name:

aspirin	carborundum	gramophone	polythene
autogiro	caterpillar (track)	gunk (slang)	nylon
bakelite	celluloid	linoleum	rayon
barathea	duralumin	melamine	
brilliantine	escalator	mimeograph	

Some trade names that are, in everyday language, acquiring generic status are listed here, but they are still registered trade names and should be capitalized when they appear in print.

*Araldite	Land-Rover	*†Pullman
†Ascot	Leica	Pyrex
Aspro	Letraset	*Rexine
Bendix	*Levis	*Roneo
*Benzedrine	Librium	*Scotch tape
*†Biro	Linotron	*Sellotape
†Boeing	*Linotype	*Spam
*Calor gas	*Lysol	Sweetex
Celanese	*†Martini	Tampax
*Cellophane	*Monotype	*Tannoy
CinemaScope	*Muzak	Tarmac
Coalite	*Nembutal	*Technicolor
*Coke (drink)	*Neoprene	Teflon
†Cow gum	*Novocaine	*Terylene
Dacron	*Ouija	*Thermos
Durex	Ozalid	*†Triplex
Ektachrome	Pentothal	*Valium
Elastoplast	*†Perrier	*Vaseline
*Formica	*Perspex	*Velcro
Freon	*Photostat	*Wimpy
*†Hoover	*Plasticine	*Xerox

*Jeep	Polaroid	*†Yale lock
*Klaxon	Pomagne	Y-Front(s)
*Kodak	*Primus	*Yo-Yo

Names marked * are listed in the *Concise OED* (although not all with an initial capital). Most trade names are based on a set of initials or are invented words (*see* **acronym; neologism**); the ones marked † are unaltered personal names or place-names. *See also* **drug names**.

traffic, trafficked, trafficking, trafficker.

tragedy See **misfortune**.

train names *See* **locomotive and train names**.

traipse is the preferred spelling (not *trapes*).

trammel, trammelled, trammelling.

tranquil, tranquillity, tranquillize, tranquillizer (the single *l* spelling is an Americanism).

transatlantic (not *trans-Atlantic* or *Transatlantic*).

transcend, transcendent, transendence.

transcendent = surpassing, supremely excellent; **transcendental** = idealistic, visionary, beyond human experience.

transfer, transferred, transferring, transferrer (transferror in law), transferee, transference, transferable.

tranship, transhipment are preferred to the more logical **transship**, transshipment.

transient = of short existence, passing, fleeting (*see also* **temporary**); **transitional** = in a state of change or passage, intermediate (with the implication of short-lived); **transitory** = lasting for a very short time, rapidly vanishing.

translate, translator, translatable.

translucent describes the optical property of a material that, while allowing the passage of light, diffuses it; **transparent** describes a material that allows the unimpeded passage of light. The associated nouns are *translucence* (preferred to translucency) and *transparency* (preferred to transparence), also used for a colour positive photograph (a "slide").

transmit, transmitter, transmissable (preferred to transmittable).

transonic (not *transsonic*).

transpire = to become known, to come to light, to leak (of information). It should not be used to mean simply to **happen**. E.g.:
"After the evidence had been accepted it transpired that there had been collusion between the witness and the accused" is correct; "Let us wait for next week's delivery and see what transpires" is incorrect.
Transpiration = respiration-like exchange of gases in plants.

transport = method of moving people or goods; **transportation** = punishment that involved moving people to another continent. The latter has not yet superseded the former in English (as it has in American).

transsexual (not *transexual*).

transverse (adj.) = across (e.g. "the car has a transverse engine"); **traverse** (verb) = cross (e.g. "the power line traverses the gorge").

trapes The preferred spelling is **traipse**.

trapezium (pl. trapeziums).

trauma (pl. traumas, not *traumata*).

travel, travelled, travelling.

treachery is betrayal of trust, committed by a **treacher; treason** is a crime (against the state), committed by a **traitor**, who is often also blamed for treachery.

tread (verb) has the past tense **trod** and preferred past participle **trodden** (not *trod*).

trek, trekked, trekking.

tremendous/tremendously should be reserved for things that are *overpowering* or *fearful*, and not used to mean *excellent* or *very large* (as in "I heard a tremendous record yesterday", "We collected a tremendous amount of money").

tremor (not -*our*).

triceps *See* **biceps.**

trillion = 1 million million in the United States (a number formerly known as a *billion* in Britain); originally a trillion = 1 million million million in Britain, but is increasingly being used in the American sense. Therefore, to prevent possible ambiguity, use "million million" and "million million million". Scientific texts may use 10^{12} and 10^{18}. *See also* **billion.**

trio (pl. trios).

triumph, triumphal (= pertaining to triumph), triumphant (= conquering, pertaining to a winner). E.g.:
"A triumphal parade celebrated the victors' return."
"The champion was once again triumphant in the final of the tournament."

trivia is a plural word; it has no singular.

troop = group of soldiers; **troupe** = group of performers; **trooper** = soldier; **trouper** = professional performer.

trousers is a plural word. "A pair of trousers" achieves a singular construction. *See also* **knickers.**

trust, trustee, trusting (= having trust in), trustful (= lacking suspicion), trustworthy (= reliable, worthy of trust). **Trusty** is archaic for **trustworthy,** particularly when applied to a person; it survives in various clichés (such as "my trusty steed/companion" for a horse/dog).

tsar is the preferred spelling of **tzar** and **czar.**

tsetse (one word).

tsunami (note spelling).

tuba (pl. tubas) = deepest-pitched orchestral brass instrument; **tuber** = swollen, underground part of a plant (such as a dahlia or potato).

tumour, tumorous.

tune, tuneable. *See also* **attune.**

tunnel, tunnelled, tunnelling.

turbid = cloudy, muddy, unclear; **turgid** = swollen. Good writing is neither turbid nor turgid.

turf (pl. turfs) = grass sods for making a lawn; **turves** = blocks of peat.

Turkish *See* **Arabic words**.

turnabout, turnbuckle, turncoat, turn-down (adj.), turnkey, turn-out (adj.), turnover, turnpike, turn-round (noun), turnstile, turnstone, turntable, turn-up (noun).

twain is archaic for **two** (as in the expression "never the twain shall meet"); *two* should be used.

tweezers is a plural word; although *tweezer* is given as the singular in the *OED*, few people would say "Please pass me the tweezer". The preferred singular construction is "a pair of tweezers".

'twixt should not be used for **between**.

tympanum (pl. tympana). *See* **timpano**.

type of (like *kind of, sort of*) usually takes a singular noun. E.g.:

"It was the type of dog that . . ."
"He is the kind of person who . . ."
"This is the sort of example . . ."

The expressions *types/kinds/sorts of* should have a plural noun. E.g.:

"There were many types of dogs on show"
"They remind me of the kinds of people who . . ."
"This Dictionary contains all sorts of examples".

tyrant, tyranny, tyrannize, tyrannical.

tyre is the usual English spelling for the air-filled rubber case round the wheel of a bicycle, car etc. (*tire* being an Americanism in this sense), although the *OED* and others give *tire* as the preferred spelling for a metal band shrunk onto the rim of a wooden wheel. The *y* spelling avoids possible ambiguity between the verbs *retyre* (to put on a new tyre) and *retire* (to withdraw or go to bed).

tzar The preferred spelling is **tsar**.

U

U-boat, U-turn (capital U and a hyphen).

Uganda The derived adjective and noun is *Ugandan*.

ugli = grapefruit-like fruit (pl. uglis).

ugly, uglier, ugliest, ugliness, uglily.

ukulele (note spelling).

Ulster See **Eire**.

ult. is a business abbreviation of ultimate, = last month, which should not be used (say "your letter of the 22nd of last month", not "of the 22nd ult.").

ultimatum (pl. ultimatums, not *ultimata*).

ultra- Most compounds with this prefix are spelled as one word. Exceptions include ultra-high, ultra-rapid, ultra-tropical.

umlaut = German accent mark, as in röntgen, Müller. It can be avoided (if, for instance, a typeface does not include the characters) by adding an *e* to the *o* or *u* (e.g. roentgen, Mueller). *See also* **accents and diacritical marks**.

un- *See* **negative prefixes**.

unable, inability. *See also* **incapable**.

unadvisable *See* **inadvisable**.

unanimous (unanimity) = of one mind; **single-minded** (single-mindedness) = of one view to the exclusion of all others. It takes two or more people to be unanimous; one person may be single-minded.

unarmed *See* **disarmed**.

unaware is the adjective; **unawares** is the adverb. E.g.:
"She was unaware of his presence in the room."
"He jumped out and took her unawares."

unbalance(d) *See* **balance**.

unbeknown is archaic for **unknown** (as in the cliché "unbeknown to him"); *unknown* should be used.

unbiased (not *unbiassed*).

unchangeable (note *-eable*).

uncircumcised (not *-ized*).

uncle = brother of one's parent and, by extension, husband of one's aunt. *See also* **family relationships**.

unconscious *See* **subconscious**.

uncooperative (no hyphen).

uncoordinated (no hyphen).

uncorrected *See* **incorrect**.

unction, unctuous = greasy, oily (not *unctious*); **unguent** = ointment.

under *See* **beneath; above**.

under- Most compounds with this prefix are spelled as one word. Exceptions include under-secretary, under-sexed, under-sized, under way (as a vessel on the move, not *underway* or *under weigh*).

underhand = sly, secret, "sneaky"; **underhanded** = undermanned.

underlay (verb) and **underlie** are analogous in inflexion to **lay** and **lie** (which *see*).

underline is a poor synonym of **emphasize**.

underpants *See* **knickers**.

underpass *See* **flyover**.

understand inflects *understand – understood – understood*.

undertake has the past tense **undertook** and past participle **undertaken**.

under the circumstances, although not incorrect when properly used, is often misused for **in the circumstances**. The latter is correct in reference to mere situation, the former in reference to the performance of an action affected by the circumstances; e.g. "In the circumstances the meeting could not take place" and "He had a broken wrist and, under the circumstances, could not type." When in doubt, use *in the circumstances.*

underthrow *See* **throw.**

underwrite has the past tense **underwrote** and past participle **underwritten.**

undeveloped countries, or underdeveloped countries, are better referred to as developing countries.

undiscriminating *See* **indiscriminate.**

undo has the past tense **undid** and past participle **undone.**

uneatable *See* **edible.**

unequal takes *to,* not *for.* E.g.:
"The candidate was unequal to the task. "

unequivocal (not *unequivocable*), unequivocally (not *unequivocably*).

unexceptionable *See* **exceptionable.**

unexplainable The preferred term is **inexplicable.**

unfertilized = not fertilized; **infertile** = incapable of being fertilized or of fertilizing; e.g. "the fertile female moth remained unfertilized because all the males were infertile" (although *sterile* would be better here than *infertile; see* **sterile**).

unfrequented is preferred to **infrequented,** but **infrequent** is preferred to **unfrequent.**

unilateral, bilateral and **multilateral** are better put as one-sided, two-sided and many-sided, unless being used as technical terms in diplomacy or physiology.

unintelligible (not *-able*) = impossible to understand (lacking intelligibility); unintelligent = ignorant, stupid (lacking intelligence).

uninterested *See* **disinterested.**

unionized = having a trade union; **un-ionized** = not ionized.

unique = only one of its kind, and so should not be qualified by words such as *rather*. *See* **qualifying adverbs**.

United Kingdom *See* **Great Britain**.

United States is the preferred name, although USA (not U.S.A.) may be used in tables, etc. to save space. *See also* **America; Americanisms; American spelling**.

unlawful = against the law of the land, or against religious or moral law; **illegal** = against the law of the land; **illegitimate** = not recognized by the law, born outside marriage (bastard).

unless should not be misused for **except**; e.g. in "Ball pen may be used unless you are marking up bromide proofs", *unless* should be *except* (when).

unmanageable (note *-eable*).

unmeasurable *See* **immeasurable**.

unmistakable (note *-able*, not *-eable*).

unnameable (note *-eable*).

unnecessary (note spelling).

unobservant *See* **oblivious**.

unparalleled (note spelling).

unpractical *See* **impractical**.

unravel, unravelled, unravelling.

unreadable = too obscure or dull to read (with comparative ease); **illegible** = indecipherable. E.g.:
"The article was so badly written that it was unreadable by anyone but an expert in the subject."
"The letter was so badly written that it was illegible to everyone but the writer."

unrelated participles *See* **participles**.

unreligious *See* **irreligious.**

unresponsible = not in the position of responsibility; **irresponsible** = undependable, feckless, lacking a responsible attitude; **unresponsive** = failing to respond (not *irresponsive*).

unridable (= cannot be ridden).

unrivalled (with two *l*s).

unsaleable (note *-eable*).

unsatisfied *See* **dissatisfied.**

unscalable (note *-able,* not *-eable*).

unserviceable (note *-eable*).

unshakeable (note *-eable*).

unskilful (with only two *l*s).

until such time as = **until,** which should be used.

untraceable (note *-eable*).

unused *See* **disused.**

unwanted = not required/needed; **unwonted** = unusual, unaccustomed. E.g.:

"Have you any unwanted items for the jumble sale?"
"She awoke with the unwonted symptoms of a hangover."

unwieldy (not *unwieldly*).

up-and-coming, up-and-down, upbeat, upbraid, upbring(ing), up-country, update, up-draught, up-end, upflow, upflung, upgrade, upheaval, upheave, upheld, uphold, upkeep, upland, uplifted, up-line, up-market, upraise, uprising, uproar, uproot, upset, upshot, upside-down, upstage, upstairs, upstart, upstream, upstroke, upsurge, uptake, upthrust, up to date (noun), up-to-date (adj.), uptown, up-train, uptrend, upturn, upward (adj.), upwards (adv.), upwind.

uphold inflects *uphold* – *upheld* – *upheld*. *See also* **hold up.**

upward can be an adjective (e.g. "an upward movement") or an adverb (e.g. "move it upward"), although **upwards** is the preferred form of the adverb. *See also* **-wards**.

urban = to do with a city; **urbanize**, urbanization; **urbane** = courteous, civil, blandly polite. E.g.:

"A surprising number of wild animals live entirely on urban land."
"An urbane manner is a good asset to a television presenter."

Urdu (not *Hindustani*) is the preferred term for the official language of Pakistan. *See also* **Indian words**.

-us There is an increasing tendency for words that end in *-us*, even if they are derived from Latin, to form the plural as *-uses*; e.g.:

apparatuses	ignoramuses	polypuses
buses	octopuses	prospectuses
calluses	platypuses	rebuses
hiatuses	plexuses	viruses

Genius (very clever person) has the plural *geniuses*, although *genius* (spirit) has the plural *genii*. Other words that form the plural in *-i* include:

bacillus	bacilli	radius	radii
gladiolus	gladioli	terminus	termini
narcissus	narcissi		

Another small group of words form the plural in *-a*:

corpus	corpra	opus	opera
genus	genera		

See also plurals.

usage = mode of use, habitual practice or custom. It should not be used merely to mean *use* (noun). E.g.:

"Increasing usage of the photocopier contributed to extra costs" is incorrect;
"Rough usage of the photocopier contributed to its breakdown" is correct.

use, usable.

used is the past tense and participle of the verb **use** (= employ); e.g. "The editor used the wrong word." As an adjective, its principal modern meaning is *second-hand* (e.g. "a used car"). In both senses, the *s* in *used* is generally pronounced like a *z* ("you-z'd"). **Used to** = did habitually at one time, or accustomed to; e.g. "The editor used to make mistakes", "I became used to his mistakes". In these senses, *used* is generally pronounced with a sibilant *s* (to rhyme with *juiced*). It is bad style to employ both meanings in the same sentence; e.g. "The editor used to use a pencil", "I got used to him using a pencil" (say "The editor used to write in pencil", "I have become accustomed to his using a pencil"). Note also **ill-used** = mistreated.

USSR (not U.S.S.R.) is the abbreviation of the Union of Soviet Socialist Republics, for which the preferred name is Soviet Union; USSR may, however, be used in tables etc. to save space. *See also* **Russia**.

US states The names of American states should be spelled in full in formal writing, although the context may allow abbreviations after place-names (e.g. Chicago, Ill.) and in tables and captions.

uttermost The defunct Old English *ut* (= out) had the comparative *utter* and the superlative *utmost*. *Uttermost* is therefore an absurdity and should be avoided. In current usage, **utter** = extreme, complete (e.g. utter darkness, utter stranger); **utmost** = greatest or highest degree, number or amount; most extreme (e.g. with the utmost care).

V

vacant *See* **empty**.

vacation = time when universities, colleges and law courts are closed. Its use to mean **holiday** is an Americanism.

vaccine, vaccinate, vaccinator, vaccination (with two *c*s, from *Vaccinia*, cowpox).

vacillate (with one *c* and two *l*s).

vacuum (pl. vacuums), although *in vacua* is sometimes used in science.

vagary (not *vagiary*), = a diversion of caprice, is a noun (pl. vagaries).

vagina (pl. vaginas, not *vaginae*).

vagueness *See* **ambiguity**.

vain = conceited, self-complacent, over-proud of oneself; **vane** = blade (of a propeller or windmill sail); **vein** = vessel that carries blood to the heart. The noun associated with *vain* is *vanity* (preferred to *vainness*).

valance = pelmet or curtain; **valence** = chemical bond(ing).

vale = valley; **veil** = covering for the head.

valet, valeted, valeting.

valour, valorous.

valuable − having intrinsic value; **valued** describes something regarded as having value; **invaluable** = priceless, valuable to a high degree (the opposite of *invaluable* is *valueless*; of *priceless* is *worthless*). E.g.:
"Lady Brown donated a valuable necklace to the church fund."
"Certain kinds of sea shells are valued for their magical properties."
"The vicar thanked the volunteers for their invaluable help."

van and **von**, as part of a proper name, do not usually have a capital *v* (except at the beginning of a sentence). Follow the style of the name's owner.

Vandyke beard, Vandyke brown (although the painter's name was Van Dyke).

vane *See* **vain.**

vapour, vaporize, vaporization, vaporizer, vaporous.

variegated (note spelling).

various *See* **different.**

varix (pl. varices), varicose.

vas deferens (pl. vasa deferentia). The alternative term *sperm duct* avoids the Latin plural.

vasectomy, vasectomize.

vegan (= a strict vegetarian who eats no animal products) appears to have passed into the language and no longer needs an initial capital letter.

veil (note *-ei-* spelling). *See also* **vale.**

vein, venous (= pertaining to veins), venose (= having prominent veins).

veld is the preferred spelling (not *veldt*).

vena cava (pl. venae cavae).

venal = able to be bought over, corruptly mercenary; **venial** = pardonable, trivially wrong.

vend, vendible, vendor (who sells), vendee (who buys), vending machine.

vengeance *See* **avenge.**

venial *See* **venal.**

venom/venomous *See* **poison.**

ventilate, ventilator, ventilation.

venture *See* **adventure**.

venue = meeting place, not merely any place.

veracious = truthful; **voracious** = greedy, with an insatiable appetite. E.g.:

"He was veracious to the point of hurting people's feelings."
"Even three portions did not satisfy his voracious appetite."

veracity should be avoided as a pretentious synonym of **truth** or **truthfulness**.

veranda (pl. verandas) is the preferred spelling of **verandah**.

verbal *See* **oral**.

verbalize, verbalization.

verbal noun *See* **gerund**.

verbatim = literally, word for word; the Latin term should be avoided.

verbiage = use of too many words in writing; **verbosity** = use of too many words in speaking.

verbs Most English verbs inflect − that is, form the past tense and participle − by adding *-d* or *-ed* to the inifinitive (or by changing *-y* to *-ied*); they are known as weak verbs. E.g.:

tame (present)	tamed (past)	tamed (participle)
bang	banged	banged
worry	worried	worried

Verbs that do not follow this pattern are termed irregular (the most notorious being *to be*). One group of irregular verbs, which could be considered to be all too regular, have the same form for the present (infinitive), past and past participle. They include:

beset	hit	rid	split
bet	lit	set	spread
burst	hurt	shed	thrust
cast	let	shred	upset
cost	put	shut	
cut	read	slit	

With *read*, the pronunciation changes for the past tense and participle, although the spelling remains the same.

Another group of verbs have irregular past tenses and participles although, as with regular verbs, they take the same form (e.g. *bleed – bled – bled*, *fight – fought – fought* and *stand – stood – stood*). A third category includes verbs – the thoroughly irregular ones – whose past tense and participle differ (e.g. *break – broke – broken*, *ring – rang – rung* and *wear – wore – worn*).

Some older forms of past participles are no longer used as such but have been retained as adjectives; e.g. the verb *to melt* is now regular (*melt – melted – melted*) but its old participle *molten* is retained as an adjective (e.g. molten iron). The inflexions of common irregular verbs of the second and third types described here – known as strong verbs – are given in this Dictionary under each verb, with an additional note about any adjectival use of defunct or alternative participles.
See also **nouns and verbs.**

verify *See* **corroborate.**

vermilion (not *vermillion*).

vermin is a singular word; it has no plural.

vernacular name (in biology) = common name. *See* **Latin classification.**

verruca *See* **farruca.**

verso = left-hand page of a book; **recto** = right-hand page of a book.

vertex = uppermost point, apex; **vortex** = whirl, as in a tornado or a whirlpool. When the words are used scientifically, their plurals are *vertices* and *vortices*; when used figuratively, they can be pluralized to *vertexes* and *vortexes*.

very Overuse of *very* (and other intensifiers) should be avoided, and it should not be misused for **much** to modify a past participle; e.g. "It is very improved" should be "...much improved".

vestigial *See* **rudimentary.**

veterinary (note spelling).

veto (pl. vetoes).

via = by the way of, and refers to the direction of a journey or voyage, not the means of travel; e.g. "He went via the train" is incorrect; "He travelled to Paris via London" is correct.

viable describes the ability of a plant or animal to continue its existence; it should be reserved for that meaning. Thus "viable alternative" = "workable alternative" (or, even better, "choice"); "more economically viable" = "cheaper"; "viable solution" = "practicable solution". Often **viability** means little more than **feasibility** (see **vogue words**).

vial = small bottle (more commonly spelled **phial**); **viol** = old musical instrument.

vibrate, vibrator, vibration.

vicar See **rector.**

vice versa (not italics, no hyphen).

vicious = wicked, spiteful (full of vice); **viscous** = thick, sticky (of a liquid), syrupy. The associated nouns are *viciousness* and *viscosity*.

victimize, victimization.

victuals, victualler, victualling. **Victuals** is archaic (and imprecise) for **food**, which is preferred.

vicuña (with a tilde).

vide (italics) = see, consult (instruction in text); the Latin term should be avoided — use *see* or *see also* instead.

vie, vied, vying.

vigour, vigorous.

vile, vilely.

villain = a person who is evil; **villein** = a serf.

villus (pl. villi).

vintage, originally applied only to wine, is now acceptable to describe anything old (e.g. a vintage car).

viol *See* **vial**.

violate, violable (not *violatable*), violator.

virago (pl. viragoes).

virtual/virtually *See* **almost; practicable**.

virtuoso (pl. virtuosi).

virus (pl. viruses).

visage is precious and archaic for **face**, which is preferred.

vis-à-vis (italics) = face-to-face, with reference to, regarding; the French form should be avoided (*about* is often a good substitute).

viscera is plural (singular viscus).

viscous *See* **vicious**.

visible = can be seen; **visual** = to do with sight. E.g.:
"A child with measles is infectious even before the rash becomes visible."
"The laser lights made an impressive visual display."

visit, visitor. A **visit** involves paying a call on somebody; a *visitation* is a formal visit by somebody in authority.

vista (pl. vistas).

visualize, visualizer, visualization.

vitamin Style is vitamin A, vitamin D, etc. with a lower case *v* and capital A, D etc. In vitamin B_6 the 6 is set as a small inferior numeral.

viz is an abbreviation of *videlicet*, Latin for **namely**, which is preferred.

vocalize, vocalization.

vogue words suddenly come into fashion, enjoy a short but gay life of overuse and misuse, and then usually fade away. Some writers and speakers adopt them to demonstrate that they are "with it", but such words can be habit-forming and seriously damage the health of the language. Many are imprecise, many usurp perfectly good and precise alternatives, and a few persist and become established. Several are listed (and condemned) in this Dictionary; for an example, *see* **situation**.

The following words seem to be particularly popular (at this moment in time):

aspect	dynamic	low profile	problem
aspirations	environment	marginal	relocate
ball game	escalation	meaningful	scenario
basically	feedback	motivation	shortfall
bottom line	framework	ongoing	simplistic
charisma	grass roots	option	spearhead
confrontation	grey area	overkill	syndrome
cut-off (noun)	hopefully	parameter	thankfully
dialogue	in-depth	pivotal position	traumatic
dimension	interface	pragmatic	viability

One of the entertaining features of Bruce Fraser's many contributions to Gowers' *Complete Plain Words* is the "buzz-phrase generator". Most lists of vogue words can fulfil a similar function: from the preceding list, choose any three words and generate an impressive (if gobbledygook) phrase, such as:

"Grass-roots aspect of the dialogue",
"A ball-game figure for the key parameters of the present option",
"A simplistic scenario which nevertheless represents meaningful grass-roots motivation".

Now hopefully it is your turn to find a viable in-depth framework which will motivate my readers into adopting a pragmatic approach to prevent the escalation of this aspect of the buzz-word syndrome, and so develop a meaningful environment for an ongoing solution to the dialogue problem.

Or perhaps you can find a way to stop people from using vogue words.

volcano (pl. volcanoes).

volte-face = an about turn; the French form should be avoided.

W

wadi (= dry river bed) has the plural wadis.

wage (noun) usually used as the plural **wages** = payment to a non-professional employee; professional employees earn a **salary**.

wage-earner (with hyphen).

wagon (not *waggon*), wagoner, wagonette, wagon-lit (pl. wagon-lits).

waist = narrow part of the body; **waste** = unused material, rubbish.

wait *See* **await**.

waive = forgo, relinquish, disperse with; **wave** = move (the hand) backwards and forwards, flutter. The corresponding nouns are *waiver* and *waver*.

wake/waken *See* **awake**.

wallaba = South American timber tree; **wallaby** = Australian marsupial, a small type of kangaroo; **wallaroo** = large type of kangaroo.

wallop, walloped, walloping.

wane *See* **wax**.

want of = lack of (e.g. "for want of a nail the structure collapsed") is archaic and should be avoided; the noun **want** is best reserved to mean **poverty** (see **need**).

wapiti (pl. wapitis). *See also* **elk**.

war-cloud, war crime, war-cry, war damage, war-dance, war-drum, warfare, war-game, war-gaming, war-god, warhead, war-horse, warlord, warmonger, war-paint, war-path, warship, wartime, war-worn.

-wards is the preferred ending (not *-ward*) on such adverbs as *afterwards, backwards, forwards, heavenwards, inwards, outwards, skywards, towards, upwards*, etc. The preferred adjectival forms are *backward, forward*, etc. (e.g. "move backwards" but "a backward movement").

warn = to give notice of impending danger or unpleasantness; it should not be used for giving notice of merely neutral or pleasant happenings. E.g.:

"I have to warn you that no bonus will be paid."

"I have to advise you that a large bonus will be paid."

Correct usage is to warn *against* danger, not *of* it.

warrant, warranter (but warrantor in law), warrantee (who warrants), warranty (which warrants).

waste, wastable, wasteful, waste paper (noun), waste-paper (adj.), waste-pipe, waste product. **Waste** = useless expenditure or consumption, squandering, and the (non-) products thereof; **wastage** = loss by use, decay, evaporation, leakage, etc. The latter should not be used merely in an attempt to dignify the former. *See also* **waist**.

watchcase, watch committee, watch-dog, watchful, watchglass, watchmaker, watchman, watch-spring, watch-tower, watchword.

water-bath, water-bed, water-beetle, water-bottle, water-borne, water-butt, water closet, water-colour, watercourse, watercress, water diviner, waterfall, waterfowl, waterfront, water gas, water-glass, water hen, water-hole, water-jacket, water-level, water-lily, water-line, waterlog(ged), water-main, waterman, watermark, water-melon, water-mill, water-pipe, water-polo, waterproof, water-pump, watershed, waterside, water softener, waterspout, water supply, water-table, watertight, water-tower, waterway, water-wheel, water-wings, waterworks.

wave *See* **waive**.

waveband, waveguide, wavelength, wave number.

wax, meaning to **grow** or **increase**, is an archaism that should be reserved for describing the Moon in the first half of the lunar month (after which it attracts the partner archaism **wane**).

way-out (= unusual, unconventional, excellent) is at best colloquial and at worst slang; it should be avoided.

-ways is usually not hyphenated as a suffix (e.g. broadways, edgeways, endways, lengthways). *See also* **leastways/leastwise; -wise**.

weal (= a raised area on the skin left by a whip or a skin disorder) is the preferred spelling (not **wheal** or **wale**). **Wale** = a ridge on fabric, a horizontal timber; **wheal** = a Cornish (tin) mine.

wear (verb) has the past tense **wore** and past participle **worn**.

weather = local climate; **wether** = castrated sheep; **whether** = conjunction that introduces the first of two alternatives (the second of which is preceded by *or*).

weave (cloth) has the past tense **wove** and past participle **woven; weave** (in and out of obstructions) has the past tense and participle **weaved**.

wed, although the origin of the word *wedding* and its compounds, should not be used as a verb meaning *to marry* (which is preferred).

weep inflects *weep – wept – wept*.

weigh = to measure the weight (mass) of something. The nautical expression "to weigh anchor" means "to raise the anchor"; this probably accounts for the misuse of *weigh* for *way* in the expression "get under way" (= "start moving").

weir (= dam; note *-ei-* spelling).

weird (note *-ei-* spelling).

welch *See* **welsh**.

well- as a prefix takes a hyphen in adjectival forms; e.g. well-meaning, well-intended, well-known (as in "a well-known author" but "the author is well known"). Note the hyphen in the nouns well-being, well-doer, well-wisher, and the absence of a hyphen in wellnigh.

wellnigh = **near** or **nearly**, which are preferred.

welsh (= to fail to pay a debt) is the preferred spelling (not **welch**).

Welsh *See* **Celtic words; Scotland**.

wench is archaic for **girl**, and should be avoided.

wend is archaic for to turn, direct one's steps (as in the cliché "wend one's way"), and should be avoided. Its past tense, *went*, has been taken over by the verb *to go*.

werewolf is the preferred spelling (not *werwolf*).

west, western, westerly, etc. *See* **compass directions**. Note the West, Western countries, Western world (with a capital *W*).

Western Hemisphere (initial capital letters).

West Indian words that have been assimilated into English include some from local Carib languages and others that early immigrants took there from Africa. For examples, *see* **Americanisms**.

wet (= make very moist) has the preferred past tense and participle **wet** (not *wetted*); **whet** = (sharpen) has the past tense and participle **whetted**.

wharf (preferred plural *wharfs*).

what, as a subject, can be regarded as singular or plural, depending on the number of the "object". E.g. "What he wants is help" and "What he needs are helpers" are both correct; in the first sentence *what* stands for *that which*, and in the second sentence it stands for *those which*.

whatever and **whatsoever** are each one word (not *what ever*).

whatnot = piece of furniture with shelves; **what not** = other things. E.g.:
"The aspidistra was in a pot on the whatnot."
"The room was full of aspidistras, antimacassars and what not."

when, misused for whereas, leads to ambiguity; e.g. "When editors shuffle words, designers manipulate colours" — meaning? It is best to reserve *when* for its temporal sense. *See also* **while**.

whence is archaic for **from where**, which should be used.

whereas implies contrast; **while** means "contemporaneous(ly) with". The latter is often misused for the former (or for merely *and*). E.g.:
"He prefers Mozart while I prefer Bach" should be "... whereas I prefer Bach".

"Jim played the violin while Pat played the cello" is correct only if they both played at once; compare:
"Nero fiddled while Rome burned".

whet *See* **wet.**

which and **that** The word *that* should be used to introduce a definitive or restrictive clause, which cannot be omitted from the sentence without greatly altering its meaning; e.g. "I always buy the books that he recommends". (Not books generally but only those defined by the *that* clause.) The word *which* should be used to introduce a non-restrictive clause, which gives extra information (and the rest of the sentence can stand without the *which* clause). *Which* can be preceded by a comma, *that* cannot: "I always buy his books, which are well written". (The clause does not limit "his books" but gives a reason – because they are well written – or adds new information – and they are well written.) The distinction between *which* and *that* is increasingly being blurred – and ignored. *See also* **pronouns; who, whom, whose** and **who's.**

of which *See* **who, whom, whose** and **who's.**

while should be used consistently in preference to **whilst.**

while = at the same time as; it should not be misused for *whereas* or *although* or even plain *and*. E.g.:
"Fred bought the first drink while Jack bought the second" and is intended;
"Fred bought the crisps while Jack had to pay for all the drinks" whereas is intended;
"Fred finished his beer while the others played cards" while is intended.

whinge, whinged, whingeing.

whir (the sound of a whirling object, to make such a sound) is the preferred spelling (not **whirr**); other forms of the verb are whirred and whirring.

whisky is the drink from Scotland; that from Ireland, Canada or the United States is spelled **whiskey.**

white, whiten, whitish, whitening (= making white; a pigment), whiting (= a fish, powdered chalk).

white admiral, white arsenic, whitebait, whitebeam, white-beard, whitecap, white-collar (adj.), white elephant, white-faced (adj.), whitefish, white flag, white gold, whitehead, white-headed (adj.), white heat, white-horse, white-hot (adj.), White House, white lead, white lie, white light, white man, white metal, white noise, white-out, white paper, white pudding, white slave(r), white spirit, whitethorn, whitethroat, white vitriol, whitewash, white-water, white whale, white wine.

whither is archaic for (to) **where**, which should be used.

whizz (to make the sound characteristic of a missile flying through the air) is the preferred spelling (not *whiz*).

who, whom, whose and **who's** *Who* is the nominative (subjective) case, *whom* is accusative (objective) and *whose* is genitive (possessive). *Who* and *whom* are reserved for persons (i.e., *that* should not be used for people: e.g. "men who", not "men that"). But *whose* can be used for *of which* and avoids stilted constructions; e.g. compare "The machine, the complex components of which are made of plastic, manufactures biscuits" and "The machine, whose complex components are made of plastic, manufactures biscuits". (And compare both with "The machine, which has plastic complex components, makes biscuits".) The case of the pronoun is determined by its role in a clause or sentence. Consider the following examples:

"The person who erred is my friend" (*who* is nominative, the subject of "erred").

"The person whom you criticized is my friend" (*whom*, accusative, is the object of "criticized").

"He criticized whoever made errors" (*whoever*, nominative, is the subject of "made").

"He criticized whomever he chose" (*whomever*, accusative, is the object of "chose").

"He criticized the person whose work contained errors" (*whose*, possessive, refers to "person": ". . . the person, the work of whom . . .").

"Whom do men say that I am?" is incorrect (a rare example of an error in the Bible).

Who's is a contraction of *who is*, and should be avoided.

See also **one's**; **pronouns**.

whoever and **whosoever** are each one word (not *who ever*).

whole, **wholly**.

widgeon is the preferred spelling for a type of duck (not *wigeon*).

widow = jargon term for a single word on a line of text.

wife (pl. wives).

wildebeest (preferred to **gnu**) is spelled the same in the singular and plural.

wile (verb), archaic for to trick, coax or beguile, should be avoided, although the plural noun *wiles* (= cunning) persists; **wily** = full of cunning, crafty; **while** (verb), usually with *away*, means to pass without boredom (e.g. "I read a magazine to while away the time").

wilful (with only two *l*s).

will and **shall** (See **shall** and **will**).

will-o'-the-wisp (note spelling).

win inflects *win* − *won* − *won*.

wind (verb) inflects *wind* − *wound* − *wound*.

winter, **wintry**.

-wise should usually be hyphenated as a suffix (e.g. end-wise, cross-wise), except in clockwise, likewise and stepwise. Constructions such as work-wise, time-wise should be avoided. *See also* **leastways/leastwise**; **-ways**.

wisent See **bison**.

wistaria (not *wisteria*, despite the common pronunciation).

with and **by** The former should be used of the instrument and the latter of the agent. E.g.:

"He was flattered with a kiss."
"She was flattered by an admirer."

withal (not *withall*) is archaic for **beside** or **nevertheless**, either of which is preferred.

withhold, withheld (with two *h*s).

within *See* **in**.

with regard to, like *with relation to* or *with respect to*, seldom means more than **about**, which is preferred.

wivern is the preferred spelling (not *wyvern*).

wolf (pl. wolves).

wolverine is the preferred spelling of the American weasel (not *wolverene*).

womanize (not *-ise*).

wonderful = evoking wonder; it should not be used as a vague superlative (as in "We had a wonderful time on holiday").

wondrous (preferred to wonderous) is archaic for **wonderful** (which *see*), and should be avoided.

wont is an archaism for custom or habit (as in the cliché "as was his wont") and can be carelessly read as *won't* (= will not); *custom* or *habit* should be used.

won't should not be used for **will not** in formal writing.

woo, woos, wooed, wooing, wooer.

wood-alcohol, wood-anemone, wood-ant, wood-ash, woodbine, woodblock, wood-borer, -boring, wood-carver, -carving, woodcock, woodcraft, woodcut, wood-cutter, -cutting, wood engraving, wood-flour, wood-grouse, wood-hyacinth, woodland, wood-lark, wood-louse (wood-lice), woodman, wood-naphtha, wood-nymph, woodpecker, wood-pigeon, wood-pulp, woodruff, wood-screw, woodshed, woodsman, wood-warbler, woodwind, woodwork, wood-worm.

wooded = covered in trees (e.g. "The wooded slopes of the mountain"); **wooden** = made of wood, lacking life or animation (e.g. "The carpenter used a wooden mallet", "The addict's face retained a wooden expression"); **woody** = to do with a wood (of trees), having the appearance/properties of wood (e.g. "We rested in a cool woody glade", "Each large carrot had woody fibres along its centre").

wool, woolly (= resembling wool, fluffy, unclear), woollen (made of or pertaining to wool), woolliness.

word breaks There are two main rules that govern where, in a single word, a hyphen may be inserted so that the word may be split over two lines of text. The rules are cited below, but note also that there are some words that simply cannot be broken, and different rules may apply to foreign words.

The rules are:

1. Insert the hyphen where the word breaks naturally into two or more elements:

hum-bug	mari-time	thim-ble

This is a simple matter in compound nouns:

cup-board	fat-head	pot-hole

And is just as simple after prefixes and before suffixes:

anti-macassar	care-less	con-tempt
establish-ment	fellow-ship	hand-some
inter-vention	loveli-ness	per-vade
peri-helion	pot-hole	pre-clude
retro-grade	skil-ful	sub-vert
trans-gression	vibra-tion	widow-hood

If possible, avoid two-letter elements, although this may be difficult in tightly set justified copy:

de-fer	ex-cept	re-tain

Beware also of elements that may vary in combination:

palaeo-arctic	but	palae-ontology
ortho-paedic	but	orth-optic

But there are some exceptions in which breaking the word into component elements is not correct; the guiding principle is readability.

2. Insert the hyphen so that each element of the broken word can be pronounced correctly at sight (often between a double consonant):

> travel-ling
> exceed-ingly
> horri-ble, terri-ble (not: hor-, ter-)
> batt-ling (not: bat-tling or battl-ing)
> miss-ile (not: mis-sile, as in mis-guided)
> fu-ture (not: fut-ure, but avoid two-letter elements)
> tet-rarch, oli-garch (but mon-arch, matri-arch)
> oper-ation (not: ope-ration or opera-tion)

For reasons of pronunciation, particularly of stress, there are occasions when the hyphen cannot be inserted following the rule (1) above, although it may still be possible to break:

> consul-tation (not: con-sultation, although con-sultant)
> persever-ance (not: per-severance or perse-verance)
> perti-nent (not: per-tinent)
> predi-cate (not: pre-dicate, although pre-dicatively)
> tran-sition or transi-tion (not: trans-ition)

For reasons of stress, there are some words that should not be broken:

> period
> detail
> prefect
> perfect (adjective; although the verb can be split, per-fect)
> epitome

Other words cannot be split because the fragments would consist of unpronounceable elements:

angry	guidance	hungry
mission	panache	session

or create misleading elements:

leg-end	mans-laughter	read-just
reap-pear	the-rapist	

3. In typewritten copy mark *obligatory* hyphens that happen to come at the end of a line thus: =

> (e.g. . . . and they co =
> operated in marking the copy.)

work (verb) has the past tense and participled **worked**, although the form *wrought* is used adjectivally (to describe metals).

workaday, work-bag, workbench, workbox, workday, work-force, workhouse, workman, workmanlike, workmanship, workmaster, work-mate, work-out, work-people, workpiece, workroom, worksheet, workshop, work-table, work-to-rule (noun).

work at = make an intensive or prolonged effort, is a modern cliché (e.g. "The only way he will pass his final examination is to work at it"); it is best avoided.

world-weary, worldwide.

World War I and **World War II** are the preferred forms (not The Great War, First World War, Second World War).

worship, worshipped, worshipping, worshipper.

worthwhile is the adjectival form, but use **worth while** following a verb. E.g.:
"A worthwhile task creates job satisfaction."
"Fair wages make working worth while."

would-be (hyphen) = aspiring.

wrack = type of seaweed; all other meanings should use the spelling **rack** (= ruin; stress; support, grating or shelf; toothed bar; torture machine).

wrapped *See* **rapped.**

wreath (noun) = a bunch or circlet of flowers; **wreathe** (verb) to encircle, to garland (as with flowers); **wrath** = violent anger; **wraith** = ghost.

wrick The preferred spelling is **rick** (for the verb meaning to twist or sprain).

wring inflects *wring* − *wrung* − *wrung.*

write has the past tense **wrote** and past participle **written.**

XYZ

× (multiplication sign) should not be used for **times** in expressions such as "shown magnified 500 times" (i.e. not "×500"), nor for **by** in "a room 8 metres by 6 metres" (i.e. not "8×6 metres").

-x- or -ct- *See* **-ection**.

X-chromosome (capital X, hyphen).

Xerox is the trade name of a type of photocopying machine and should have an initial capital letter. Increasingly it is being used as a generic verb (e.g. "I have xeroxed the typescript"); *photocopy* is a better alternative (e.g. "I have photocopied the typescript").

Xmas should be avoided as an abbreviation of Christmas.

X-rays (capital X, hyphen), **X-ray** (adj.).

-y Nouns ending in *-e* generally drop the *-e* when forming adjectives ending in **-y** (e.g. bony, cagy, crazy, icy, racy, spongy). Exceptions include bluey, dicey, gluey and holey.

Yank (= an American) has acquired derogatory overtones, as has **Yankee** (= New Englander), except in historical references.

Y-chromosome (capital Y, hyphen).

yearling *See* **horse**.

Yiddish *See* **Hebrew words**.

yodel, yodelled, yodelling, yodeller.

yoga – Hindu philosophical meditation; **yogi** (pl. yogis) = somebody who practices yoga.

yoghurt is the preferred spelling of the fermented milk food.

yoke = combined collar that allows two draught animals to pull together, or similar arrangement that allows a person to carry two panniers or buckets; **yolk** = yellow centre of an egg.

yonder is archaic and poetic for **(that) over there**, which is preferred.

you can be used as an impersonal pronoun, much less formal than *one* (e.g. "You have to be mad to work here", "The sights you see these days"). It should be avoided in formal writing, if only because it can appear to address the reader directly. *See also* **one**.

yours has no apostrophe (*see* **one's**).

yucca is preferred to **yuca** as the spelling of the Central American agave plant.

-yse/-yze *See* **-ize** or **-ise**.

Yugoslavia (not Jugoslavia). The derived adjective and noun is *Yugoslav* (not Yugoslavian).

Zaire The derived adjective and noun is *Zairian*.

Zambia The derived adjective and noun is *Zambian*.

zero (noun, pl. zeros). Forms of the verb include zeroes, zeroed and zeroing.

zig-zag, zig-zagged, zig-zagging.

zoo (pl. zoos).